HIGH ISLAND

High Island

An Irish Monastery in the Atlantic

JENNY WHITE MARSHALL and
GRELLAN D. ROURKE

TOWN HOUSE & COUNTRY HOUSE, DUBLIN

High Island

First published in 2000 by
Town House and Country House
Trinity House, Charleston Road, Ranelagh, Dublin 6

ISBN: 186059-121-3

© Jenny White Marshall, Grellan D. Rourke 2000

All rights reserved. No part of this publication may be copied,
reproduced, stored in a retrieval system, broadcast or transmitted in any form or by
any means, electronic, mechanical, photocopying, recording or otherwise
without prior permission in writing from the publishers.

A CIP catalogue record for this book is available
from the British Library

Design and Layout: Identikit Design Consultants, Dublin
Cover design: Identikit Design Consultants, Dublin
Photographs: as credited
Illustrations: as credited
Printed by Milanostampa

Extracts from Richard Murphy's poetry
by kind permission of the author and The Gallery Press
from Collected Poems, 2000.

*For our partners,
Philip E. Diamond and J. Kevin Blackwood,
who have been most patient and
understanding throughout.*

Contents

Introduction		ix
Chapter One	High Island	1
Chapter Two	The Island and the Monastery	7
Chapter Three	Pilgrim's Path to the Monastery	23
Chapter Four	The Monastic Enclosure Wall	45
Chapter Five	The Church in the Monastery	69
Chapter Six	The Church Enclosure Wall: Burials	99
Chapter Seven	The Cells	127
Chapter Eight	The Cemetery and Cross Stones	139
Chapter Nine	The Monastic Enclosure Wall	173
Chapter Ten	The Early Medieval Monastic Watermill *by Colin Rynne*	185
Chapter Eleven	High Island Over the Centuries	215
Appendix One		229
Appendix Two		233
Bibliography		245
Index		257

Sponsorship

The authors gratefully acknowledge financial support from:

The American Ireland Fund

Dúchas The Heritage Service

The Heritage Council

Philip E. Diamond

Janpieter and Chris Scheerder

Introduction

Our work on High Island has taken place sporadically over the last two decades and our interest in the site changed and intensified as we worked with many people who generously contributed advice and help. Walter Horn, that great indefatigable explorer of Ireland's Atlantic islands, first introduced us to High Island. One of our earliest experiences was on a visit with him in 1982 when our inexperienced boatman put us off in rough seas at the dangerous south-western landing from where we had to scramble up an uncertain steep ledge. Through this mischance we discovered that this access place had actually been a monastic landing.

By the time more serious study had begun we had made contact with a local boatman, Feichin Mulkerrin, whose knowledge of the island and whose experience of the surrounding sea were of enormous assistance. Always ready to help, he has been most generous over the years in assisting us and keeping a watchful eye whenever we stayed on the island for prolonged periods of study and survey. Moreover, he and his friends have dragged, lifted and hauled innumerable tons of equipment and other indispensable supplies onto the island. Feichin is now the owner of the island and it is in safe hands.

Richard Murphy, former owner of the island, has always promoted archaeological interest in the monastery. He generously gave us access to the island and use of the small cabin he had remade at the end of one of the miners' cottages. This single spartan cell became our base of operations during the periods we remained on the island. Our contact with Richard led to firm friendship and we are most grateful to him and his publisher, The Gallery Press, for permission to use his fine High Island poems that complement the text of this book.

In 1987 we began a detailed survey of the monastery with the help of Kevin Blackwood, Pauric Coffey and Katrin Kleyser. By 1990 John O'Brien, architectural surveyor with Dúchas, had joined us and in subsequent surveying and recording expeditions he became a valued and integral part of the survey, willingly working under extreme weather conditions. His dedication, flexibility and energy provided us with great support; he was the ideal colleague to have alongside us when working on a remote island.

As the work progressed we called upon others. We are thankful to geologist Michael O'Sullivan who visited the island on a number of occasions to help with stone identification and to locate island quarry sources. We invited Colin Rynne to assess the water-mill system. When he found evidence of an extensive mill operation it was an exciting time generating much fresh discussion. His contribution became so important we asked him to write a chapter to deal specifically with the mill system, putting it into an overall context. It was a great pleasure to work closely with Colin and this collaboration confirmed the need for an interdisciplinary approach to our study.

Paul McMahon, Senior Conservation Architect with Dúchas, has responsibility for this site and was for many years graciously supportive of our work. It was enormously significant when he endorsed our recommendation to initiate an excavation programme in order to better understand the relationships of the structures, and to begin conservation work to the monastic buildings that had suffered great damage during the 1980s. Excavation started in

1995 under the co-directorship of Marshall and Scally, and Dúchas took over the funding the following year. The initial excavators, Georgina Scally, Helen Kehoe, Franc Myles, Donal O'Flaherty and Christine Wagner worked hard in extremely uncomfortable conditions in ten-day sessions. Subsequently, friends like Claire Cotter and Daire O'Rourke came along to help. The continuing excavation since 1996 has been under the direction of Georgina Scally to whom we are grateful for agreement to use material including the seasons through 1997 in which Marshall had continued to work.

Late in our study we invited Karen Molloy, Janice Fuller and John Conaghan of the Palaeoenvironmental Research Unit, Department of Botany, University College Galway to undertake pollen core studies. The excellent preliminary results have been incorporated into the book and their report is published as Appendix II. This work confirms our view that the island was inhabited prior to the establishment of a monastic community. Additional studies to provide further insight into the changing environmental conditions and economic strategies of the monks will continue and be reported in later publications.

We also wish to thank others who helped us: Peter Harbison, Gerry McCormac, Finbar McCormick, Proinseas Ní Chatháin and Sara Pavia of Carrig Conservation. They furnished us with references to relevant art historical and bibliographical sources, and radiocarbon and mortar analyses. Patricia Johnson has made elegant and meticulous drawings to illustrate the first group of recorded cross and cross-inscribed stones; we are fortunate to have them in this publication. We are also most grateful to Alberta Horn who generously gave us the use of Walters Horn's study and home in Point Richmond, California; this provided the perfect ambience of peace and tranquility for working on the drawings.

Ours has been an inter-disciplinary approach, gathering together a range of perspectives in order to put them into a broad early medieval context. A fundamental principle has been to communicate this information in a readable and visual format to make this work accessible to as many people as possible. Illustration has been an important and integral component in bringing this remote place to life. Many of the illustrations are photographs taken by Con Brogan, Senior Photographer with Dúchas. In addition to the photographs used in the book and on the cover Con provided us with important aerial study photographs. His attention to detail and willingness to devote much personal time and energy are reflected in the high quality of his work. We are also grateful to both John Scarry and Tony Roche of the Photographic Dept. of Dúchas for their help.

The making of this book has taken us on a journey of discovery. We hope that it will provide inspiration for continued study and exploration of this special island.

Jenny White Marshall and Grellan D. Rourke

Chapter One

High Island

Except a man shall say in his heart
I alone and God are in this world
he shall not find peace.

Anonymous saying of an Egyptian Desert Father.

In the fifth century Theodoret wrote in awe of men in Egypt who 'desirous of living a life like that of angels, have sequestered themselves from the tumult of cities to dwell in deserts...'[1] These Egyptians were monks, followers of St Antony, whose passion for salvation drove him to extreme measures. Instead of traditional Christian service and fellowship within a community, Antony rejected all contact with the world and retreated into desert wilderness to lead a severely ascetic life of solitude and prayer. Antony had created a new, heroic ideal for Christians, that of the monk. The word monk (*monos*) means solitary, he who turns away from humankind in order to perfect his individual salvation, he who fights alone to overcome his sins. In Egypt ordinary Christians and Church leaders alike, inflamed by the challenge of Antony's example, flocked to the desert and soon 'There were monasteries in the mountains, and the desert was made a city of monks'.[2] Athanasius, Patriarch of Alexandria, gave powerful early publicity to Antony by recording his story in the *Life of Antony*, written, he stated, so that Christian brothers in foreign parts might hear about Antony and follow his example.

The news about Antony spread quickly so that by the late fourth century there were two Latin translations of Athanasius's work circulating in Europe.[3] In Milan, St Augustine, undecided and temporising about becoming a Christian, heard about Antony and the desert monks and declared himself 'amazed ... because the deeds were so great...' As he listened to these stories, Augustine had an emotional moment of self-realisation and decision and cried out: 'But while he was speaking, Thou, Lord, didst turn me back to myself, taking me from behind my back, where I had placed myself while I refused my self-scrutiny, and Thou didst set me face to face with myself...' (*The Confessions of St Augustine*, Book VIII, ed. Williams 1953, 23).

Christians everywhere viewed the monk as the focus of spiritual power, the man closest to God, whose prayers could best intercede with heaven. Augustine himself perfectly summed up this attitude when he stated that monks were the embodiment of the Sermon on the Mount and their prayers and sacrificial example offered the greatest service to the Church.[4] For the next eight hundred years, men who wished to practise the ideal religious life, to lead the life of angels, looked back to Antony and the early Egyptian Fathers (Fig. 1).

Centuries after Antony, on the outer edge of the Christian world, men in Ireland enthusiastically adopted monasticism and attempted to follow Antony's example of stark isolation. Withdrawal from the world meant separation from kin and homeland, a separation that the Irish found painful and hazardous. The kin group in rural Ireland during the fifth to the twelfth centuries, the early medieval period, was the source of social status and legal rights in the absence of State and Church institutions. The importance of the family is revealed in the medieval story of the judgment of Húa Suanaig upon murderers: 'the persons who committed the murders ... to be without return to their sept [kin] until the conflagration of Doomsday'.[5] In similar fashion the rules of St Columbanus, written over the years before his death in 615, prescribed ten years in exile for a cleric who commits murder. At the end of ten years the cleric might return home, but 'if he has not made satisfaction to his [the victim's] relatives, let him never be restored to his native land, but like Cain let him be a wanderer and fugitive upon the earth'.[6]

Figure 1

St Antony and St Paul breaking bread together in the desert on the north side of Muiredach's Cross at Monasterboice. Photo Peter Harbison.

The Irish honoured voluntary exile, therefore, as a form of martyrdom and spoke of it as *Peregrinatio pro amore Dei*, pilgrimage or exile for the love of God.[7] *Peregrinatio* became a heroic quest that drove Irish monks to seek out remote places in Ireland as well as venturing into foreign lands. In the sixth to ninth centuries great numbers of Irish monks ventured into Anglo-Saxon England, Merovingian France and Lombardian Italy, to establish monasteries that grew into brilliant centres of scholarship and art, which profoundly influenced and enriched medieval European culture. The pilgrimage of Irish monks into foreign lands had a strong missionary element as well, one most likely inherited from the example and words of Ireland's beloved saint, Patrick. In the fifth century Patrick wrote an angry protest to the war leader Coroticus, who had enslaved a group of Irish Christians, in which he identified himself in the following manner:

> *I, Patrick, a sinner, yes, and unlearned, established in Ireland, put on record that I am bishop. I am strongly convinced that what I am I have received from God. And so I live among barbarian peoples, a stranger and an exile for the love of God.*[8]

In the late sixth century the Irish monk, Columbanus, founder of the continental monasteries of Annegray, Luxeuil and Bobbio, wrote a letter to the Bishops of France that directly echoes the sentiments of the missionary Bishop Patrick but also transforms the stranger into the pilgrim:

> *...it is for the sake of Christ the Saviour, our common Lord and God, that I have entered these lands a pilgrim...*[9]

But other Irish monks desiring pilgrimage in the spirit of St Antony turned to the sea. The origins of these seafaring voyages are lost, but we know that island monasticism was well established by the late sixth century, when St Columba left Ireland to found the famous monastery of Iona, off the coast of Argyll, Scotland. In the *Life of St Columba*, written in the seventh century by St Adomnán, Columba felt compelled to speak to King Brude about the safety of some of his monks who were sailing around the Orkneys: 'Some of our brethren have lately set sail, and are anxious to discover a desert in the pathless sea...'[10]

Thousands of Irish monks passionately dedicated to Antonian monasticism sailed off from the western coast of Ireland into the turbulent north Atlantic, looking for their own 'desert in the pathless sea'. Scarcely an island off the coasts of Ireland and Britain, in the Orkneys and Shetlands, and further, into the Faeroes, even perhaps as far as Greenland, was left untouched by Irish monks. It is among the stone ruins left on the Atlantic islands by small colonies of Irish monks that we find the boldest parallels to early Egyptian monasticism in Europe.

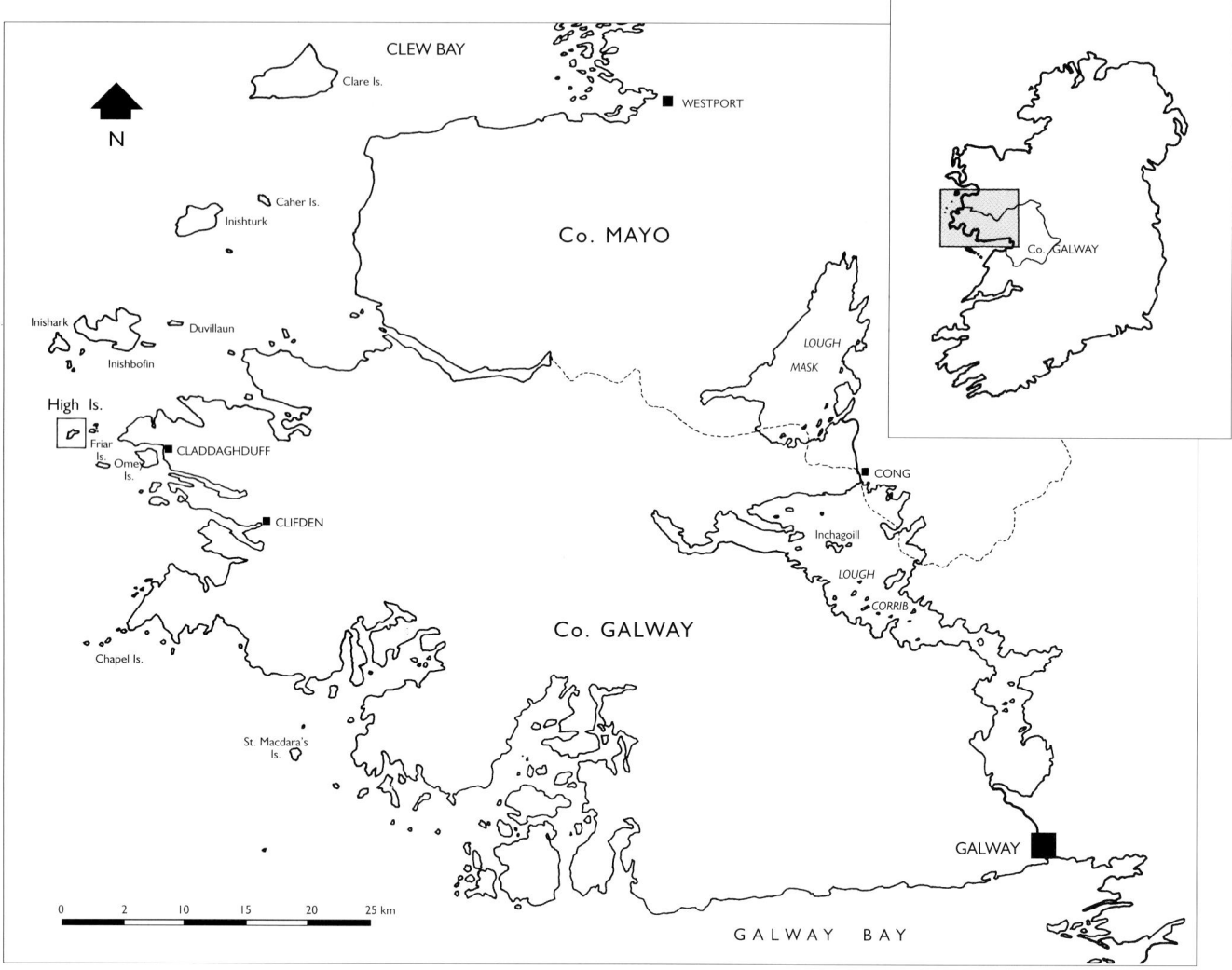

Figure 2

Location map of High Island, Co. Galway, by G.D. Rourke, showing neighbouring monastic islands of Inishbofin and Omey.

The islands off the Galway coast are particularly renowned for their role in the early foundation and establishment of Irish monasticism. Legend relates that some time about the beginning of the sixth century, St Enda sought the seclusion of Inishmore, largest of the Aran Islands, for the foundation of one of the first monasteries in Ireland. Enda's disciples became themselves distinguished founders of great monasteries, such as St Ciarán of Clonmacnoise and St Jarlath of Tuam. So numerous were the number of saints associated with Enda and Inishmore that the twelfth-century *Life of St Ailbe* asserted that: 'No-one but God alone knows the number of saints buried there'.[11] Historical documentation of monastic foundations on the islands off Galway begins with the account by the Anglo-Saxon monk, the Venerable Bede, in his *Historiam Ecclesiasticam Gentis Anglorum*, of the Synod of Whitby in 664. When the Synod decided in favour of the Roman method of calculation for the date of Easter over the Irish method, Colman, the Irish Bishop of Lindisfarne and chief abbot of the Columban monasteries in Northumbria, resigned and left Britain to settle on the island of Inishbofin. Bede's account relates that Colman left Lindisfarne accompanied by 'all the Scots [Irish] he had collected at Lindisfarne, together with about thirty English whom he had likewise trained in the monastic life...'[12] Little survives now of St Enda's foundation on Inishmore, and nothing is visible on Inishbofin of Abbot Colman's seventh-century retreat from Lindisfarne.

The most extensive remains today of an early medieval monastic community on Galway islands are located on Ardoileán or High Island, lying just 6.5km south of Inishbofin and some 3km off the northern Connemara coast (Fig. 2).[13]

The drystone remains of the Early Christian monastery here, although in ruinous condition, have been virtually untouched by later generations. No towns or farms have been built over it or scattered its stones and, its earlier fame forgotten, the curiosity of most visitors has been easily discouraged by the difficulty of landing on the island. High Island is rivalled, consequently, by few other Irish monastic sites in quantity and variety of material remains from the period, and presents an amazingly complete image of the life of these daring seafaring monks who, like Antony, sought salvation in retreat from the world.

High Island is not well known compared to the Aran Islands, but local tradition, nevertheless, places it among the most illustrious of monastic islands. The beloved seventh-century saint, Féchín, 'a man of a bright, summery life, an abbot and an anchorite, fair-worded Féchín of Fore...' is credited with founding a monastery here in the seventh century.[14]

Paradoxically, as well as reclusive island monasticism, there is, at least during one period of the monastery, evidence of more than a small eremitic colony. The material remains of a horizontal watermill, and the construction of ponds, a hillside water reservoir and the mill-races necessary for it, are strong indications of the presence of a community that would have equalled in size a substantial mainland foundation. They vividly testify to early Irish expertise in the modification and use of the landscape for a sizeable community. This exciting evidence alone, a clearly visible medieval landscape perhaps unparalleled anywhere else in Europe, presents compelling environmental and technological perspectives into the culture of the age.

Notes

[1] P.G., ed. Migne, 80–84.

[2] *Life of Antony*, ed. Gregg 1980, 42–43.

[3] According to Jerome in *De. Vir. Ill.*, ed. Herding 1879, 63. The Greek text and the Latin translation done by Evagrius are found in *Patrologia Latina*, ed. Migne 1857, 26: cols. 835–976; the other anonymous Latin version is in Garitte 1939.

4   Augustine, *De Moribus Ecclesiae Catholica,* ed. Gallagher and Gallagher, v. 56: 50–53, 1966.

5   '…na doine doronsat na hechtai. …, cen impód doib fri fine co dé brátha brúd.' From the *Lebar Brecc,* ed. O'Longan, 1872–1876, 90, as cited in *Martyrology of Oengus,* ed. Stokes 1905, 466–467; 133.

6   'Si autem non satisfecerit parentibus illius, numquam recipiatur in patriam, sed more Cain vagus et profugus sit super terram.' *Sancti Columban Opera,* ed. G.S.M. Walker [1957] 1970, 172–173, lines 18–19.

7   'This is the white martyrdom to man, when he separates for sake of God from everything he loves, although he suffer fasting or labour thereat.' From *The Cambray Homily* in *Thesaurus Palaeohibernicus*, ed. and trans. Stokes and Strachan [1901] 1975, 2: 246–247.

8   'Patricius, peccator indoctus scilicet Hiberione constitutus, episcopum me esse fateor. Certissime reor a Deo accepi id quod sum. Inter barbaras itaque gentes habito, proselitus et profuga ob amorem Dei.' Patricius, *Epistola* no. 1, ed. and trans. Hood 1978, 35, 55. For discussion of the text, see Dumville 1993, 117–131.

9   '…pro Christo salvatore, communi domino ac Deo nostro, in has terras peregrinus processerim…' *Sancti Columbani Opera*, ed. and trans. Walker [1957] 1970, 16–17.

10 'Aliqui ex nostris nuper emigraverunt, desertum in pelago intransmeabili invenire optantes…' Adomnán, *Vita Columbae*, ed. and trans. Reeves 1874, 71 and 185.

11 Waddell 1994, 106. Quote from the *Life of Ailbe* as translated from the Latin by O'Connell 1994, 137. For *Life of Enda,* see *Acta Sanctorum Hiberniae*, ed. Colgan [1645] 1948, 704–714.

12 For Bede's story of the Synod of Whitby and Bishop Colman, see Bede, *Historia Ecclesiasticam Gentis Anglorum,* ed. Plummer [1896] 1975, 181–189, 213; for an English translation, see Sherley-Price [1955] 1983, 185–195, 213.

13 *The Archaeological Inventory of County Galway,* ed. Gosling 1993, 1: 89–90, notes that they found a total of twenty-six ecclesiastical settlements, with documentary evidence indicating another eight; they were most frequently identified by the presence of an early medieval church or oratory.

14 '…fer betha[d] soillsi samrata, ab 7 angcoire, Fecin finnfocluch Fabair…' *Life of St Féchín of Fore*, ed. and trans. Stokes 1891, 320–321. For the other two Lives of Féchín, see *Acta Sanctorum Hiberniae*, ed. Colgan [1645] 1948, 130–144.

Chapter Two

The Island and the Monastery

A shoulder of rock
Sticks high up out of the sea,
A fisherman's mark
For lobster and blue-shark.

Richard Murphy, *High Island*.

High Island lies a little over 3km west of Aughrus Point on the mainland, and is substantial in size, comprising approximately 32 hectares of rolling grassland in a peaty gley soil. The island is formed of some of the region's oldest rocks, Dalradian rocks possibly over 600 million years old, primarily dark mica schists with quartz veins, and with sizeable boulders of granite erratics, which were scattered on the island's surface during the retreat of the glaciers in the last Ice Age (Fig. 3) (Whittow [1975] 1978, 162; Morris, Long, McConnell and Archer 1995, 9–13).

Glacial ice and the sea have cut great indentations in the island's perimeter, slicing away massive pieces, a few of which remain nearby as satellite islands, and thereby creating the island's irregular, dramatic shape. The island owes its name to the precipitous, jagged cliffs that form its periphery, undulating cliffs ranging in height from 20m to 70m above the sea.

Access onto the island is possible at only three places; even there, landing is difficult, for strong coastal currents running between the nearby islands and the mainland pound the exposed rock. 'From its height, and the overhanging character of its cliffs', George Petrie wrote in 1820, 'it is only accessible in the calmest weather, and even then, the landing, which can be made only by springing onto a shelving portion of the cliff from the boat, is not wholly free from danger...'[15] The two easiest landing places, each a little over half a kilometre away from the monastery, are in the eastern section of the island, near its narrowest point, one on the southern side and one on the northern side (Fig. 4). The location of these two landings, providing access to the island under two different sea conditions, made it possible to build a monastery here. The northern landing offers easier access to the island, but the more southerly one, the one Petrie referred to, is most commonly used today, being particularly good when the wind or seas are coming in from the north or northwest.

There are very few structures at the northeastern end of the island near these two landing places, and most of these appear to have been connected with the activities of nineteenth-century copper miners. The small stone cabin built by the former owner of the island, the poet Richard Murphy, from the ruins of a nineteenth-century miner's cottage (see below, Fig. 15) is the most obvious structure here. From these landings, rolling grassy hills, without trees or shrubs, lead to the western end of the island. The soil, a wet, waterlogged peaty gley, produces wet heaths with exposed rock surfaces, and in rainy periods numerous small pools form in depressed areas.

The monastery is located in a valley at the island's southwestern end, just north of the larger of the two permanent ponds. This site for the monastery was deliberately chosen in spite of being a great distance from the two best landing places to the northeast. No other place on this exposed Atlantic island offers better protection from the weather or easier access to fresh water. Immediately south of the smaller pond is the third landing on the island, on the southwestern side of the island (Fig. 4), along one side of a narrow inlet.

Access to the island here is much more difficult, contingent on the tides, and the climb up the cliffs is arduous, rarely offering secure footing; a climber burdened with supplies would find it perilous. The sheer cliff, moreover, offers no space to beach a *currach*, the leather boat most commonly used in this period by Irish monks, which could not be left at anchor. Its proximity to the monastery, nevertheless, would have made it the most desirable place to deposit people and supplies on calm days, and a sizeable flat rock-surface at the top creates a level surface for stacking supplies.

St Féchín, Pilgrims and Scholars
The founding of the monastery of High Island is attributed to St Féchín of Fore, a native of County Sligo who founded several monasteries, among them the well-known

Figure 3

Aerial photo of High Island, Co. Galway, from the west. Photo Con Brogan. Courtesy Dúchas The Heritage Service.

abbeys of Fore in Westmeath and Cong in Mayo.[16] According to two of the extant *Lives of St Féchín*, he dreamed one night that it was his mission to go and convert the people of the western isles: 'At the angel's command Féchín goes into the west of Connaught to Imaid (Omey), and he blessed it, and built a cloister therein, and brought those tribes under a yoke of belief and piety...'.[17] Omey Island is a tidal island almost 5km southeast of High Island, and today contains the remains of a medieval church adjoined by an ancient cemetery that is probably on the original site of this monastery. Féchín remains one of Connemara's most beloved saints and his name is still common among the men of the area.

The *Annals of Ulster* note that Féchín died of the Yellow Plague: 'Kal. Jan. 8 A.D. 664, the 'falling asleep' of Feichen of Fabhar (i.e., from the same distemper, i.e., the 'Buidhe chonaill')'.[18] Famous for his austere practices and pious life, Féchín is mentioned in two festologies, calendars celebrating the death days of saints, the

HIGH ISLAND

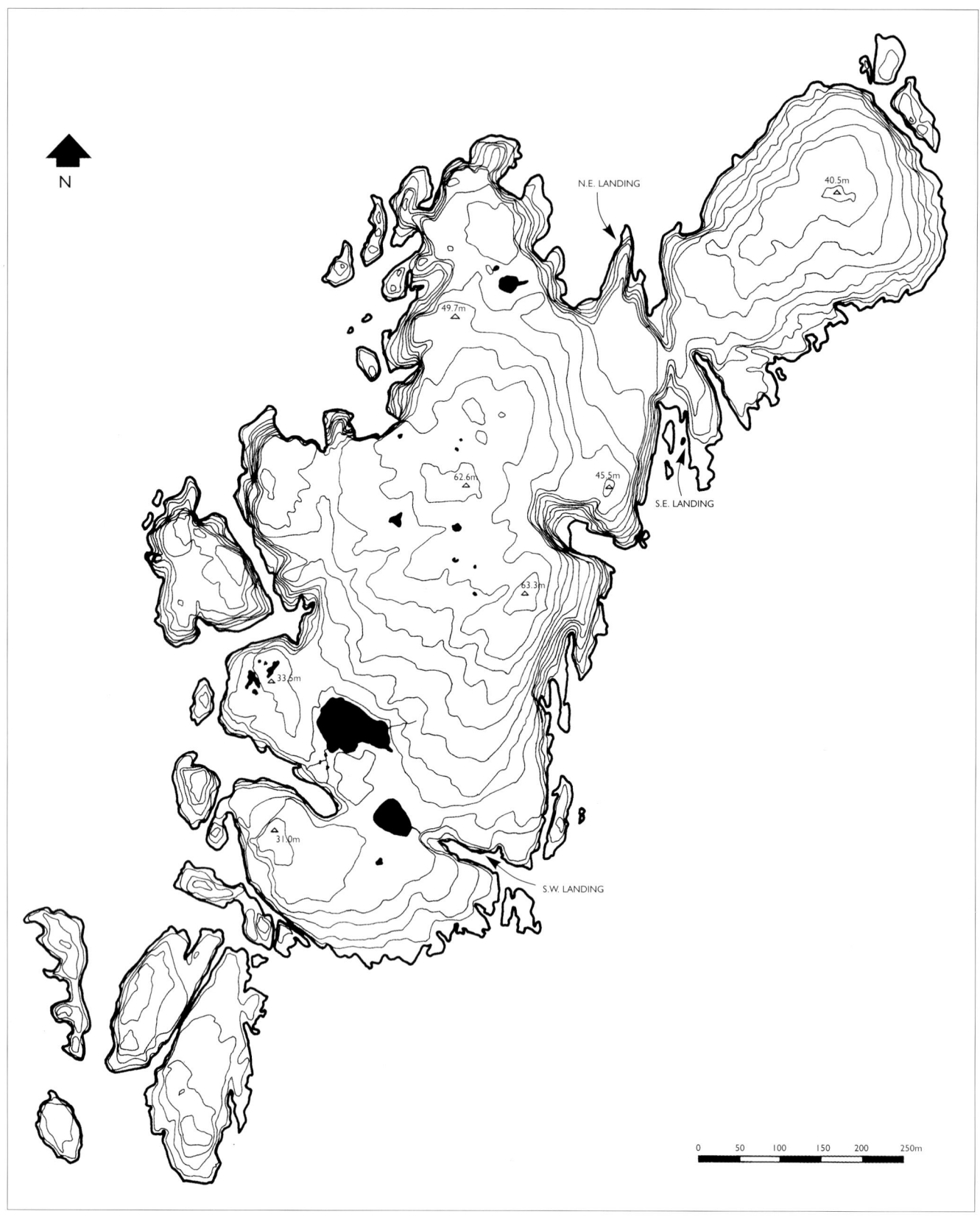

Figure 4

Contour map of High Island, Co. Galway, by G.D. Rourke, showing ponds, elevated points and landing places.

Martyrology of Tallaght and the *Martyrology of Oengus*, written in the late eighth century; both mention St Féchín under January 20.[19]

Féchín inspired a number of hagiographies, most of them recensions based on earlier hagiographies of uncertain date and provenance. Today there are several versions of the *Vita S. Fecini*.[20] Two versions are found in *Acta Sanctorum Hiberniae*, edited by the Irish Franciscan monk John Colgan in 1645. The second *Life* recorded by Colgan was also compiled by him from three Irish Lives and then translated by him into Latin.[21] It is this second manuscript that contains the sole remark connecting St Féchín to High Island, stating that St Féchín founded a monastery on Omey Island and that he afterwards founded another monastery in Ard-Oilean (High Island). One of the three texts Colgan used for his compilation was taken from the *Book of Imaidh*; this text was probably the source for the references to Omey and High Island.[22]

A solitary reference in a document of uncertain date does not constitute sufficient evidence to establish the foundation of the monastery to the seventh century and to Féchín. However, it does seem probable that both Omey Island and High Island belonged to a confederation of monasteries owing allegiance to Féchín, and that High Island, if not founded by the saint himself, was founded by monks from Omey in his name. The date of its foundation remains uncertain.

Most of the small island monasteries on Ireland's western coast are not mentioned at all in the monastic annals. The annals were chronicles written in the large mainland monasteries, and were concerned primarily with recording the actions and deaths of prominent princes and ecclesiastics, and major events such as famine, plague and war. It is not surprising, therefore, that the sole mention of High Island in the monastic annals is that concerning the death of an eleventh-century abbot, Abbot Gormgal. In *The Annals of the Kingdom of the Four Masters* the entry reads: 'The Age of Christ, 1017. The fourth year of Maelseachlainn. Gormgal of Ard-Oilean, *chief anmchara* [roughly, spiritual father] of Ireland.'[23] Gormgal's fame as a spiritual leader must have been widespread for his death to be recorded in such terms of veneration. His celebrity was confirmed by John Colgan, who wrote in the seventeenth-century: 'After St Féchín, St Gormgal, a man of celebrated sanctity ... ennobled it [High Island] very much by his anachoretic habits, and most exact life. The elegant and very pious poem of blessed Corcranus, who flourished at the same time, concerning his praises and relics, is extant in my possession'.[24] Unfortunately, Colgan did not record this poem and it has been lost (for more information on Gormgal possessed by Colgan, see ch. 11). We know, therefore, that the monastery was active and celebrated in the early eleventh century, but no further mention of High Island appears in Church documents. How long the monastery lasted after the death of Gormgal can only be roughly estimated by archaeological evidence.

The next and the only other people recorded as living on the island were nineteenth-century copper miners. The then owner of the island, Colonel Martin of

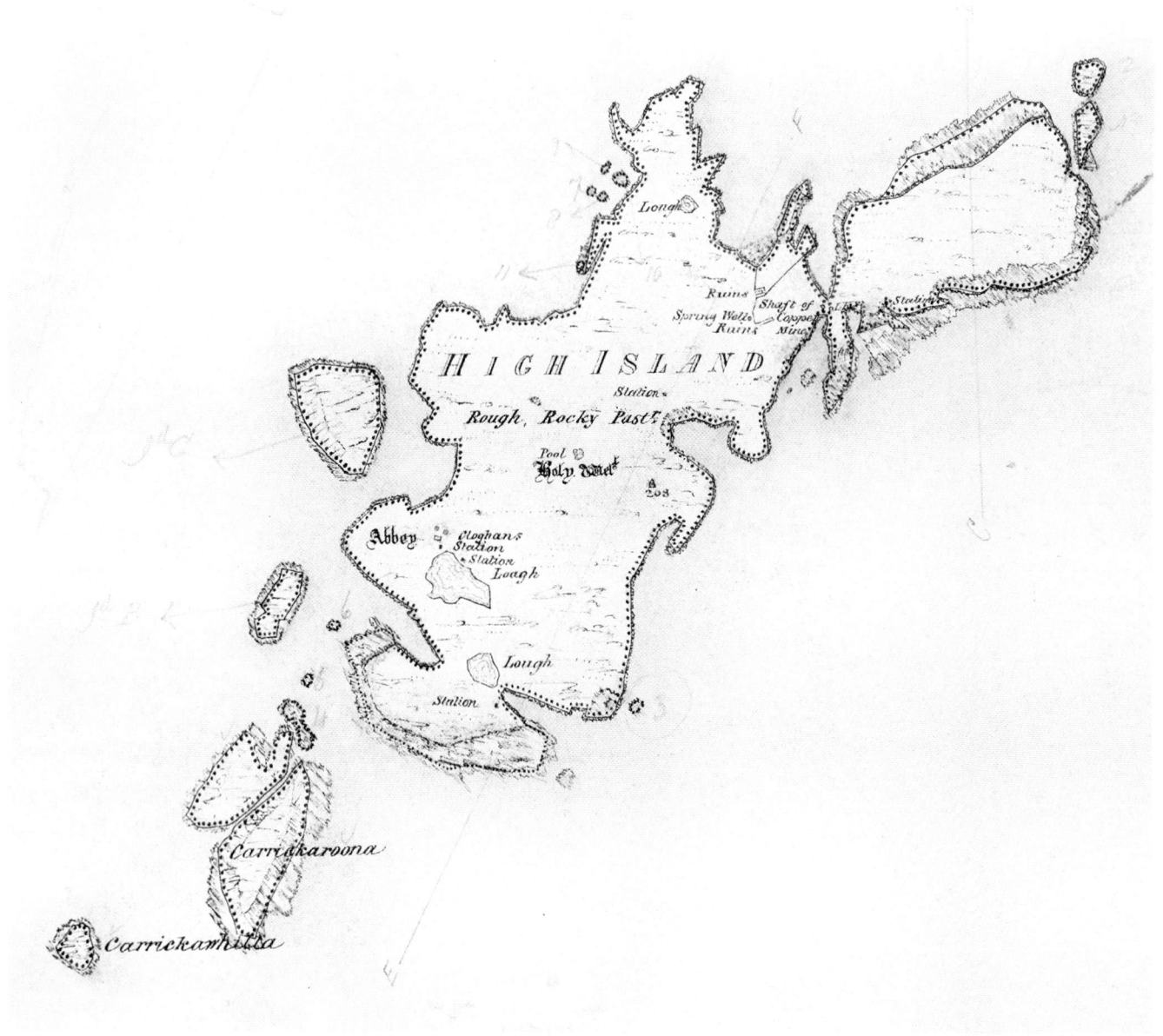

Ballynahinch, the colourful 'King of Connemara', also known as 'Humanity Dick', hoped to repair his desperate financial condition by capitalising on the island's copper. Accordingly, in 1828 he brought in men to dig a shaft and work the mine. The miners worked and lived near the deep mine shaft close to the landing places on the eastern end of the island. *The Exploratory Memoir of the Geological Survey of Ireland, Illustrating the Geological Structure of the District around Clifden, Connemara* (1878), however, indicated that the island's copper vein was not extensive: 'At nine fathoms there was in the lode stuff a good mixture of copper; also at fifteen fathoms; after this no good ground was met with, although the shaft was sunk to twenty-five fathoms'.[25] The logical inference from this report is that the miners did not live on the island for long, although the

Figure 5

Ordnance Survey Fair Plan of 1839. These plans were colour-coded, with red indicating structures. Generally, structures in outline only meant they were in ruins, whereas solidly ink-filled structures indicated those with intact roofs. Courtesy National Archives, Ireland.

solidity of their stone structures indicates an intent to remain. The Ordnance Survey Fair Plan of 1839 shows two buildings close to the copper-mine shaft (Fig. 5). The word *ruins* written next to them also suggests that the copper mining did not last long, perhaps only a season or two.

In 1837 an evaluation by London solicitors made for Thomas Barnwell Martin, son of Colonel Martin, noted that the real value of the island lay in grazing: 'Omey and High Islands are reclaimable and at present produce excellent feed for all kinds of stock'. The island, however, along with most of the Martin property, was put up for sale in 1849 after the death of Thomas Martin and was among a small portion of the estate that sold in 1850.[26] In 1969 the Irish poet Richard Murphy purchased High Island and owned it until 1998, when it was sold again.

Scholarly Studies of the Monastery

No written notice exists about the ownership of the monastery between the eleventh-century, when it was an active monastery during the time of St Gormgal, and its eighteenth-century ownership by the Martin family. Scholars, however, began to show interest in the monastery in the late seventeenth-century. In 1684 Roderic O'Flaherty wrote a brief description in *A Choro-graphical Description of West or Iar Connaught* that implies it was no longer in active use:

> *It is inaccessible but on calm settled weather, and so steep that it is hard after landing in it to climb to the top; where there is a well called Brian Boramy [King of Ireland], and a standing water, on the brook whereof was a mill. There is extant a chappel and a large round wall, as also that kind of stone building called Cloghan. Therein yearly an ayrie of hawkes is found. Here St Fechín founded an abbey, as he did at Imay.*[27]

Serious studies of the monastery began in the nineteenth century, when antiquarian scholars visited High Island and then published descriptions, rough plans, photographs and sketches of the monastery. None of these studies was exhaustive, and most have a number of small errors. The island offers no shelter, consequently most visitors only had time for a rushed day visit in which to select and record details and impressions of a large, complex site. Each report complains about damage, generally unspecified, done to the monastery since the previous visit, damage they attributed variously to copper miners, boys hunting birds, etc. These reports are, nevertheless, valuable today because they provide a record of monastic structures in better condition, as well as structures and features that have since disappeared.

In 1820 George Petrie visited the island and made the earliest study of the architectural remains of High Island for his book, *Ecclesiastical Architecture of Ireland*, which was published in 1845. Although Petrie only made one visit to High Island he regarded the monastery as 'one of the most interesting and best preserved in Ireland, or perhaps in Europe...' Petrie took measurements and made notes which were not transcribed until shortly before publication of his book, thereby increasing the possibility of memory loss and mistakes. Fortunately, Petrie was an astute observer so that most of his measurements were remarkably accurate and his report was the most complete one made in the nineteenth century. His comments about the church and the structures relating to it are particularly interesting since a number of the features described by him vanished shortly afterwards. Petrie was also the only nineteenth-century antiquary to mention a stone pathway running south from the monastery along the large pond, and to suggest that the large pond was not natural but constructed.[28]

In 1824 the Irish Ordnance Survey was established and given the task of delineating townland boundaries in Ireland, the primary taxation and landholding unit, for the purpose of more accurate tax valuation. Not only were these extraordinary maps the world's first large-scale mapping of an entire country, done on the unusually large scale of six inches to the mile, but they also undertook to include a geological survey. In 1826, under the direction of Captain Larcom, the survey, '... this truly imperial idea...', was expanded to include topographical features such as roads, settlements and antiquities.[29] George Petrie was appointed head of the Antiquities and Topographical Department of the Ordnance Survey until its breakup in 1839, and directed the work of the men engaged in field work. The men who met each day in Petrie's home, in that 'little back parlour in Great Charles-street', were among the most illustrious group of Irish scholars ever assembled, and included John O'Donovan, Eugene O'Curry, Patrick O'Keefe and Clarence Mangan, as well as the artists W.F. Wakeman and G.V. Du Noyer.[30]

Petrie's group first collected every accessible writing and ancient manuscript to check on the history and location of antiquities, and the meaning and correct spelling of the original names in Irish, of every place to be visited. The final spelling of names, however, was to continue to be in English. During the summer months the sites were inspected, and local Irish speakers consulted about traditions, legends and names associated with them. Finally they were charged with the writing of a memoir for each parish to accompany the maps.[31]

On 15 June 1839 the inspector for Galway, John O'Donovan, visited High Island, accompanied by the artist W.F. Wakeman. The following day O'Donovan commented in a letter to Captain Larcom that 'we went yesterday to Ard-Oilean or High Island, but found it impossible to get finished there in one day, and it being a desolate island, we were obliged to return to Clifden the same day. Mr. Wakeman goes there tomorrow again...' (Ordnance Survey Letters, Galway 1839, 3:13). O'Donovan wrote a brief report on his visit that concentrated on the enclosure wall and the main

The Island and the Monastery

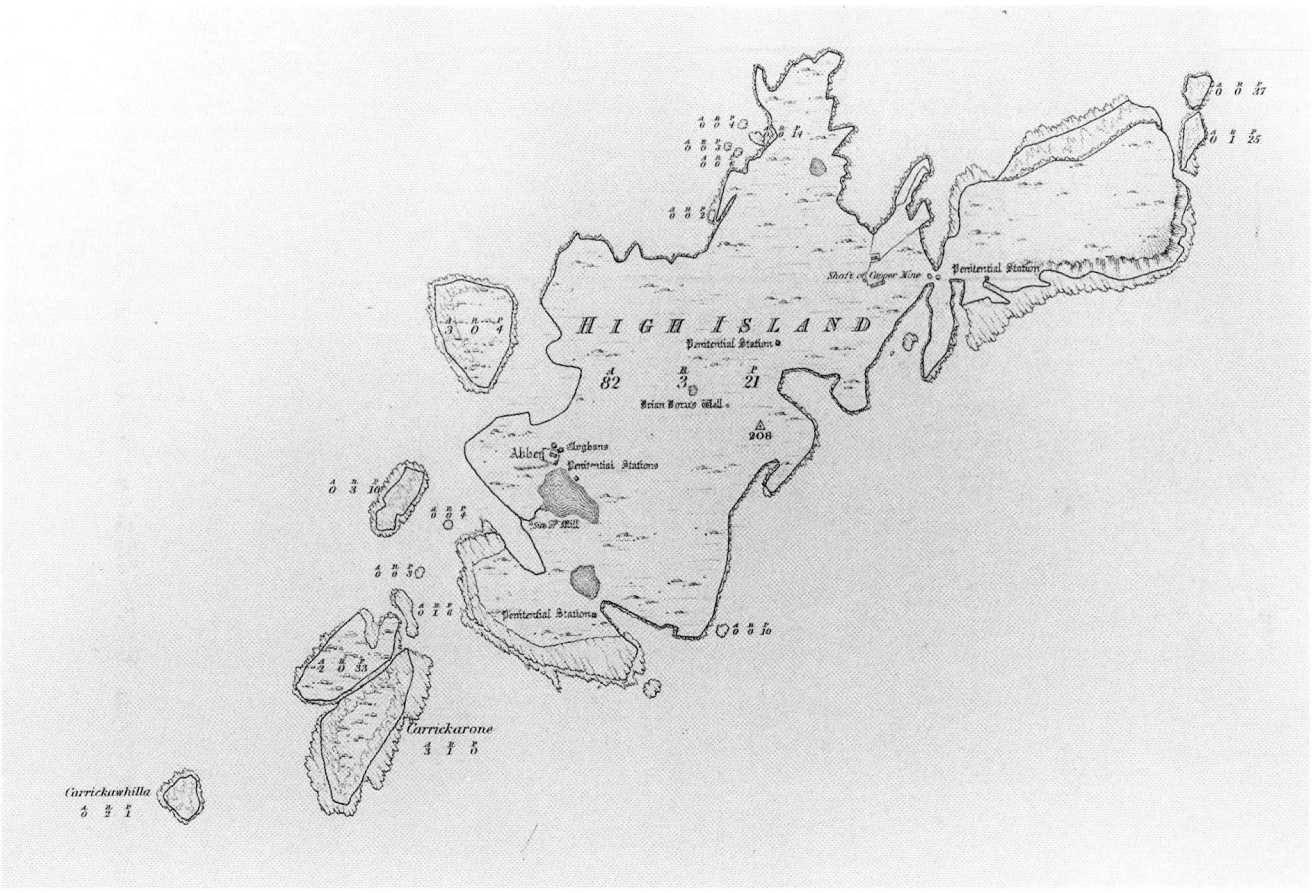

Figure 6
Ordnance Survey Plan of 1841 based on the survey by John O'Donovan. Courtesy Dúchas The Heritage Service.

monastic structures, but made no mention of cross stones, included no plan of the monastery, and his account was less detailed than that of Petrie. He stated that he 'was very much disappointed at finding it [enclosure wall] and the little buildings it encloses in such a state of dilapidation'.[32]

O'Donovan had worked on the Ordnance Survey under Petrie for ten years, since he was twenty years old, and letters between them show that the two men had a warm, close friendship and enthusiastic collaboration (Richardson 1862). It is quite strange, therefore, that O'Donovan makes no mention of Petrie's visit to High Island, and no comparison of the state of the monastery in 1839 to its condition during Petrie's visit, nineteen years earlier. O'Donovan must surely have known about Petrie's earlier visit, but Petrie does not appear to have given him his notes, perhaps because his book was as yet unpublished. It is, therefore, difficult to assess any difference in the condition of the monastery between 1820 and 1839; a period of particular interest, since the copper miners are suspected of doing extensive damage to the monastery around 1828.[33]

In 1839 the Ordnance Survey, based on the work of O'Donovan, made the first topographical map of High Island, plotting the location of the lakes, antiquities, pilgrimage stations, wells, and the copper mining activities (Fig. 5). The map published in 1841 by the Ordnance Survey was based on the Fair Plan of 1839 but differs slightly from it (Fig. 6).[34]

On 26 February 1841 O'Donovan, unhappy with the map as it was proposed, wrote a letter suggesting some additional annotations. Among the changes he proposed were the marking of the site of a monastic mill and the addition of the word penance or penitential to the word 'station', and he also included a small pencil sketch showing a wall of 'great thickness' surrounding the church and connecting three cells (Fig. 7).

His primary report of 1839 did not mention a monastic mill, and, apparently not consulting his original report, he had confused the church enclosure wall with the monastic enclosure wall. His suggestions were not included in the map of 1841.

Of equal importance with O'Donovan's report are Wakeman's sketches of the church (Fig. 8), of one of the beehive cells (Fig. 83a) and of a number of cross stones; Wakeman's drawings are our only evidence for the existence of several of these crosses (see ch. 8).[35] Decades later Wakeman wrote two articles in which he described his visit to High Island with O'Donovan. These articles include an engaging, chatty account of their trip, relating O'Donovan's near disastrous jump from the boat onto the rocks at the landing and a sybaritic description of their provisions: '...a couple of brace of cold roast ducks... With these, some bread, a bottle of potteen, we were prepared for any achievement' (Wakeman 1863, 216). Wakeman also described several tombs behind the church that had not been mentioned before (see ch. 6).[36]

Figure 7

The plan O'Donovan drew of the monastery of High Island in 1841, which differs from his original report in several respects. Ordnance Survey Memoranda, Galway, 1:384–385. Courtesy National Archives, Ireland.

Figure 8

1839 drawing of the west façade of the church on High Island, Co. Galway, made by W.F. Wakeman (Petrie collection of drawings, RIA MS 12T16). During the same visit John O'Donovan also drew a sketch of the west façade and labelled it 'The chapel of St. Féchín from the west and ruins of the wall that went around / surrounded the church. The ground is covered with loose stones blown by storms from the external wall or Caisiol' (Ordnance Survey Letters, Galway 3:82). This is the only mention O'Donovan made of the church enclosure wall. Wakeman drawing courtesy of the Royal Irish Academy.

The Island and the Monastery

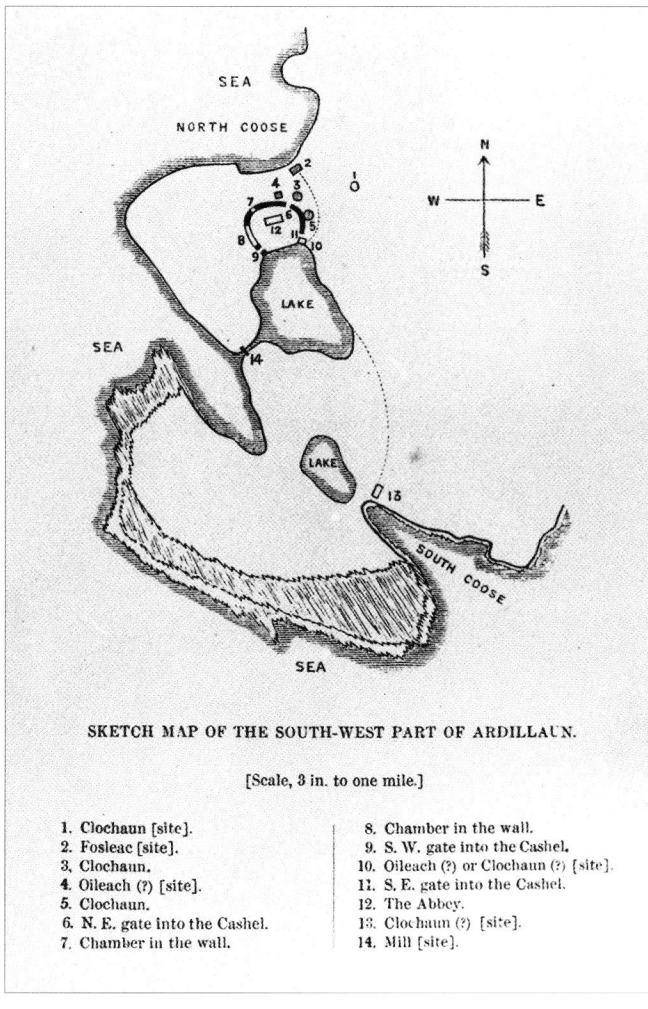

Figure 9
Plan of the monastery on High Island, Co. Galway, made by George Kinahan in 1869 (plate XLV). A fair representation of many features, its largest error was that Kinahan, unaware that there was a separate church enclosure wall, combined sections of this wall with the monastic enclosure wall on the east and thus placed the two cloghans *outside the monastic wall. For the same reason he also inaccurately drew a wall running parallel to the eastern side of the monastic wall. Kinahan, moreover, entirely missed the southern section of the enclosure wall running along the lake. (Kinahan 1869, plate XLV.) Courtesy Royal Irish Academy.*

Thirty years later, in 1869, the geologist George Kinahan visited the island and made the first plan of the monastic site (Fig. 9). He also made the first plans of cells (*cloghans*) A and B, drew plans and a cross-section of other structures, and sketched the cross at the southern landing and the cross at Brian Boru's Well. Kinahan remarked that the monastery had badly deteriorated following the departure of the miners when the Martin family no longer owned the island:

> *Unfortunately, when it passed out of their hands it came into that of an absentee English proprietory, and during the famine and subsequent years (1846 et seq.) many of the most interesting of the carved stones were carried away.*

Kinahan's plan and description of the monastery are erroneous in places because he did not realise that the church had its own separate enclosure wall; apparently, he had not read Petrie's report, which clearly describes the two enclosure walls (compare Fig. 9 with Fig. 29a). His structural dimensions, furthermore, are the least accurate of the antiquaries. He nevertheless provides interesting information about the condition of the structures in 1869, and also explains the reason for the present placement of two of the cross stones.[37]

Kinahan was the first to mention the long wall that runs from an inlet in the north to the monastery and then recommences at the pond south of the monastery and runs the length of the valley to the landing inlet in the south; this wall cuts off the valley containing the monastery and two ponds from the rest of the island.

In 1896 R.A.S. Macalister wrote an article for the Royal Society of Antiquaries of Ireland based on a visit made by members of the Society in 1895. Macalister frankly admits that his article was based on a short stay:

> *As he [the captain] was anxious to reach Aran before dark, he would only allow one hour for the examination of the remains. Though we surreptitiously extended this period, we were unable to exhaust the antiquities of the island, and any account based on our observations must necessarily be imperfect.*

In spite of his short stay on the island, Macalister's article is the first attempt at a systematic comparative study in which the reports of Kinahan and Petrie are contrasted with his own observations in an orderly manner, although occasionally his reliance upon earlier reports caused him to perpetuate their errors.[38] He also published the first photographs taken of the monastery, made by fellow excursionists, including one of the west façade of the church (Fig. 10), and sketched some of the cross stones. Macalister was also the only nineteenth-century antiquary who discussed St Gormgal.

Figure 10
Photo of the church on High Island, Co. Galway, taken by a member of the Royal Society of Antiquaries during an excursion in 1895 and published in 1896 by R.A.S. Macalister. Macalister noted that the west façade of the church appeared much the same as in Wakeman's sketch of 1839, seen above in Fig. 8 (Macalister 1896, 201.) Courtesy Royal Society of Antiquaries of Ireland.

Twentieth-century studies of the island begin with Michael Herity's preliminary report published in 1977, followed later by his more extensive study of the site published in the *Journal of the Royal Society of Antiquaries* in 1990. A lengthy report, Herity's work provided the most detailed survey of the island's material remains to date.[39]

Notes

[15] Petrie 1845, 419. Under exceptionally calm conditions it is possible to land in a number of other areas.

[16] O'Flaherty 1684, ed. Hardiman 1846, 113.

[17] 'Teid Feichin la farcongra in aingil a n-iartur Con[n]acht co hImaidh, 7 do bennaigh hi, > documdaig congbail innte, > docuir na tuatha sin fo cuing creidme > chrabaid,...' (Stokes 1891, 328–329); Phillips Library, Cheltenham, No. 9194, dated 1329.

[18] 'Dormitatio Feicheni Fabair (i. de eodem morbo.1. don buide conaill)', *Annals of Ulster*, ed. Hennessy 1887, 1: 120–21. Also found under the year 664 in *The Annals of the Kingdom of Ireland by the Four Masters,* ed. O'Donovan 1856. For the accuracy of the annalistic records from the late seventh century on, see Hughes 1972.

[19] *Martyrology of Oengus the Culdee*, ed. Stokes [1905] 1984, 48–49.

[20] The only extant complete Life in Irish was translated from Latin in 1329 by Nicholas the Young, the son of the Abbot of Cong. This manuscript, No. 9194 in the Phillips Library, Cheltenham, was edited and translated by Whitley Stokes in 1891, 318–353.

Attached to this life are the incomplete parts of another Life of Féchín, also in Irish, which claims to be the account of Aileran the Wise, a contemporary of Féchín, as does the Latin Life of Magraidin found in *AA. SS. Hib.*, ed. Colgan [1645] 1948, 140 n.12; Kenny [1929] 1968, 459, n.275.

21 Alia Vita seu Supplementum, *Acta Sanctorum Hiberniae*, ed. Colgan [1645], 1948, 133–139.

22 'Fundavit et vir Dei aliud Monasteriumin in vicina insula, quae olim, Inis-iarrhuir hodiè ardoilen appellatur', *AA. SS. Hib.*, ed. Colgan [1645] 1948, 135. On the *Book of Imaidh,* see Stokes 1891, 318.

23 'Gormgal ind Ard ailéim, prim anmcara Ereann.' *The Annals of the Kingdom of the Four Masters*, ed. O'Donovan 1856, 790–791. *The Annals of Ulster*, ed. Hennessy 1887, 540–542 also record the death of Gormgal in 1017: 'Gormgal of Ard-ailen, chief soul-friend of Ireland, rested in Christ; Gormgal in Ard-ailean, prim anmchara Erenn, in Christo quieuit.' Gormgal is also recorded under 1018 in the *Annals of Inisfallen,* ed. Mac Airt [1951] 1977, 188–189: 'Gormgal ind Ardailéoin quieuit; Gormgal of In tArdailén rested', and under 1016 in the *Chronicum Scotorum*, ed. Hennessy, 1866: 'Gormbhall ind Ard ailéin, primh anmchara Ereann, ...décc.'

24 'Post S. Fechinum sua anachoresi, et arctissima vita plurimum nobilitauit S. Gormgalius, vir celebratae sanctitatis, qui de cuius encomijs et reliquijs extat paenes me B. Corrani, qui eodem tempore floruit, elegans et pijssimum poema.' *AA. SS. Hib.*, ed. Colgan [1645] 1948, 141 n.13.

25 *Exploratory Memoir...* Kinahan, Nolan, and Cruise 1878, 162. On the colourful Colonel Martin, see Lynam [1975] 1989.

26 M2429–2433 Public Records Office, National Archives, Dublin. A Petition was made by Henrietta and Richard Beaumont in 1847 claiming ownership of much of the Martin estate due to the delinquency of a mortgage against the land in exchange for £37,475 granted to Thomas Martin by their father, Thomas Wentworth Beaumont. A note added to this petition stated the island was sold on 26 April 1850. At this point a Mrs Bodkin was listed as a tenant of High Island, Friar Island and Cruagh Island for life for a yearly rental of £1 10s and 5d; the Bodkin family are listed in other documents as residents of Omey Island. M3438a, Public Records Office, National Archives, Dublin. See also M3440, Rental of the Estate of T. B. Martin, in which High Island was listed as of August 1849 as part of lot 72. M2429–2433. Particulars, Valuation and Report of the Estates of T. B. Martin by London solicitors Triston and Hardey in 1837 also mention Mrs Bodkin as the tenant: 'Mr Martin's father let the Demesne to the old lady who is the present tenant and pays no rent...' Mrs Bodkin must have been elderly by this time, for Richard Martin granted a lease for High Island to John and Mary Bodkin to run for their lifetimes on 2 August 1794. Book 491, page 448, no. 319813 in the Registry of Deeds, Henrietta Street, Dublin.

[27] O'Flaherty 1684, ed. Hardiman 1846, 115. O'Flaherty was much influenced by John Colgan, even quoting Colgan's confusion of High Island with Innis-hiarthuir, which is Inisheer of the Aran Islands.

[28] Petrie 1845, 128–129, 419–422, 441.

[29] Stokes 1868, 87; Reeves-Smyth 1983, 126–133; *Ordnance Survey in Ireland; An Illustrated Record*, 1991.

[30] Letter written by Wakeman in Stokes, 1868, 96.

[31] Thomas Larcom, administrator since 1828, had broadened the scope of the project to include the memoir which, in addition to historical and orthographic work, was to record details on commerce, geology and natural history. Petrie and O'Donovan had worked to produce the first part of the Memoirs, published in 1837, of the parish of Templemore, Co. Londonderry, called *Memoir of the City and North-western liberties of Londonderry*. Its size, 350 pages for this single parish, and its cost of £1700, was more than three times the original budget for one county. Funding for the project was cancelled as a result; Stokes 1868, 99–104, Richardson 1862; *Ordnance Survey in Ireland* 1991, 24; Seymour 1980, 89–95.

[32] Ordnance Survey Letters, Galway, 1839, Vol 3, 80–87. O'Donovan also included his own rough sketch of the church from the west and Cell B from the east. See also O'Flanagan, 1927a.

[33] Petrie met O'Donovan and Wakeman in Galway in August 1839, where they were working on writing up the Aran Islands, and Petrie noted in a letter to Larcom, dated 20 August, 'I saw his letters and they are admirable, as well for the matter as for the beauty of the illustrations. They already amount to 240 pages. He writes at the rate of twenty pages a day...' Stokes 1868, 130. It is odd he didn't check O'Donovan's work against his own notes, but the volume of work may have overwhelmed them.

[34] Reeves-Smyth (1983, 128–129) notes that there were differences in both content and technique between the Fair Plans and the finally published Ordnance Survey maps, but that they are usually slight; the most common changes are the omission of placenames or alteration of their spelling.

[35] Wakeman's drawings of stones and crosses are in the Royal Irish Academy (m.12T9) and his drawings of the church and the scriptorium are in a Petrie collection of drawings in the Royal Irish Academy (MS. 12T16). Wakeman's sketch of the scriptorium is the model for the engraving published by Petrie in 1845, 128. In an article written in 1891 Wakeman included two drawings of High Island cross stones (Plate one, fig. 49; Plate three, fig. 14) that do not exist today and are not in any of his earlier sketches; it is probable that they were incorrectly labelled.

[36] These articles appeared in *Duffy's Hibernian Magazine* in 1863 and *The Dublin Saturday Magazine* in 1867.

[37] Kinahan 1869, 551–555.

[38] He was unaware of O'Donovan's report until shortly before his article was published, and appended part of O'Donovan's report to his article (Macalister 1896, 197–210). A condensed version of this article was also published in RSAI Guide 1905, 47–53.

[39] Herity 1977, 52–69. There are other descriptive accounts of High Island but they add no new information; Healy 1890, Westropp 1905, Crawford 1907, and Pochin Mould. Higgins (1987) included a number (6) of High Island cross slabs in his corpus of Galway cross slabs, but had not been out to the island at the time, consequently his report is in some areas incomplete or erroneous. *The Archaeological Inventory of County Galway (1993)* describes High Island but it relies primarily on earlier authors, was not written up by the same people who did the field work, and includes some errors ('traces of a window survive in collapsed E gable', p. 96, and p. 170, description of a penitential station on a 'prominent rock outcrop overlooking the oratory to S.' as one of five stations marked on the OS map).

Chapter Three

Pilgrim's Path to the Monastery

Fissile and stark
The crust is flaking off,
Seal-rock, gull-rock
Cove and cliff.

Richard Murphy, *High Island*.

The sea's constant pounding has almost severed the eastern end of the island and has carved small angular coves out of the island's flanks, leaving behind two narrow spits of land, one on the southeastern side of the island and the other, almost directly opposite, on the northern side (Figs. 11 and 12).

Out on these rocky spits are the only two locations where the cliffs slope down to the sea in narrow, stepped rock ledges that most frequently offer secure access onto the island. The landing craft favoured today is a modernised canvas-and-tar version of the medieval leather *currach*, for it remains an easier craft than wooden fishing boats to manoeuvre in the choppy waters along the sides of the cliffs. From the narrow peninsula on the southeastern side, the most frequently used landing area, there is a climb to the top, some 22m above the sea. There, a thin strip of grass-topped rock connects the main body of the island with the cliffs of the landing area. Some 15m east

Figure 11

Aerial photo of the eastern section of High Island, Co. Galway, from the north, showing the two landing places, the most commonly used one on the upper peninsula and the second best one on the lower. The small stone cottage in the centre of the picture marks the location of the miners' cottages of 1828. Photo Con Brogan. Courtesy Dúchas The Heritage Service.

of here are traces of a wall, now level to the ground, running across the width of the island (25m); this wall was probably used to control the movements of sheep or cattle (Fig. 12, no. 3).

The decorated cross stone known as the landing cross stands near the edge of the cliff, another 35m east of this wall (Fig. 12, no. 2; Fig. 13).

The draftsmen of the Ordnance Survey Fair Plan of 1839 annotated their map near this point with the word 'station' (i.e. penitential station)(Fig. 5). We assume that the landing cross was part of this station because W. F. Wakeman described stations on High Island as: 'a cairn-like pile of stones, surmounted by a cross of the same material, of small size... It is supposed that these were penitential stations...' (Wakeman 1863, 218). Today, only the cross, wedged with a few stones, remains. In 1869 Kinahan was the first to mention and to sketch this cross (Fig. 14a), and in 1895 Macalister, who also sketched this cross, noted that it was the only antiquity on the north side of the island (Fig. 14b).

Although it is clear that this cross has stood near here for at least two hundred years, it cannot be determined whether it was placed here by monks or by later pilgrims.[40]

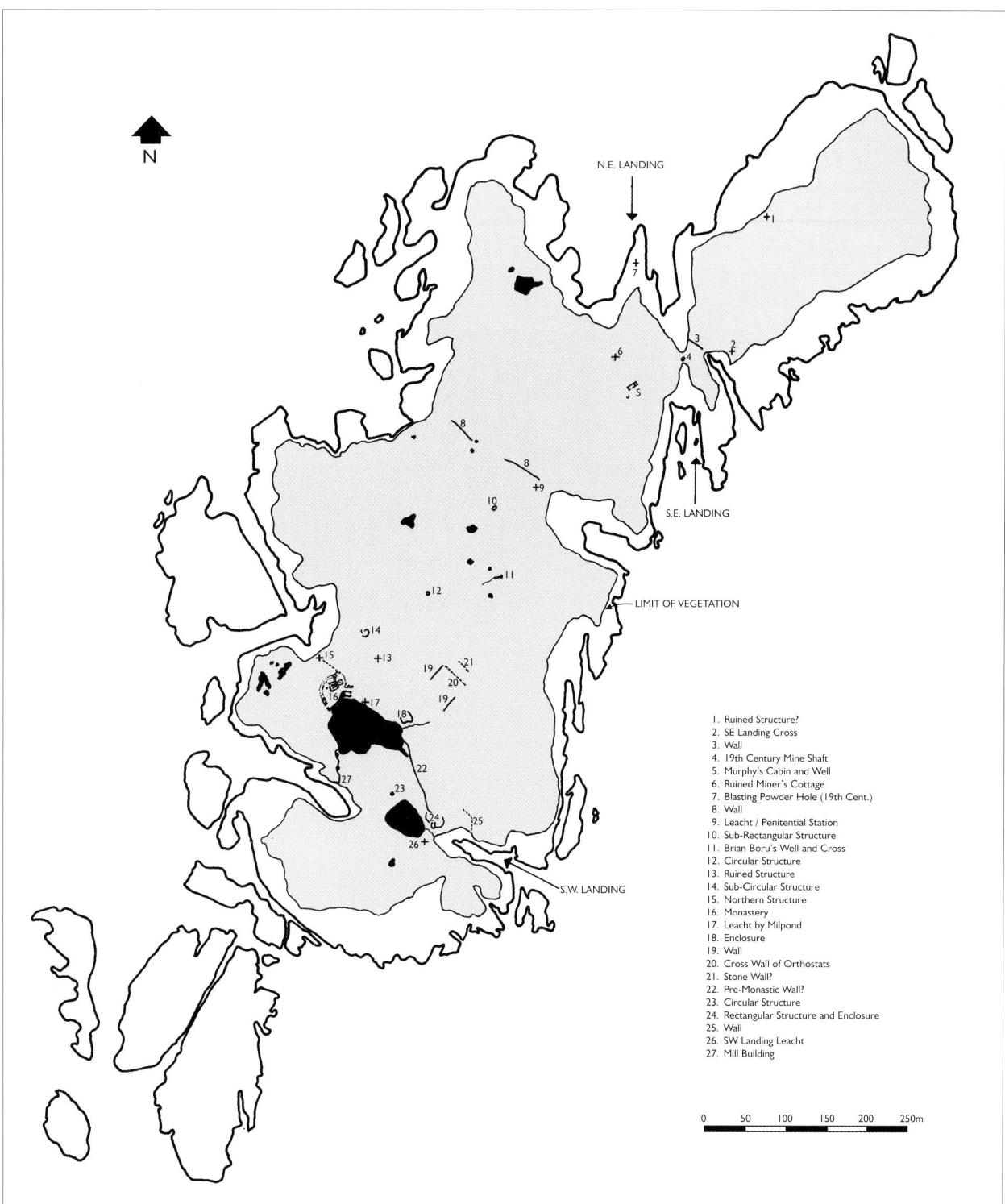

Figure 12

Plan of High Island, Co. Galway, showing all the man-made structures and indicating the limit of vegetation growth on the island. Arrows point to the three landing places. Plan G.D. Rourke.

Turning from the landing cross and heading west back across the remains of the wall, we pass over the narrowest part of the island, a section that is only 11m wide. On the southern edge of the island is the deep round hole that marks the remnants of the copper mine-shaft sunk in 1828. The living area of the miners lies some 50m west of here (Fig. 12, no. 5 and no. 6).

The path to the monastery from the northern landing joins that of the southeastern landing in the area of the miners' cottages. Landing on the northern side is made on the tip of the small jutting peninsula (Figs. 11 and 12). The landing area is considerably broader than that on the southern side and the climb to the top of the cliffs is easier, although the cliffs are slightly higher here. Deeper water makes it simpler for a fishing boat to put in; however, prevailing sea conditions limit its use. While there are no traces of steps or man-made changes in the southeastern landing area, approximately 20m up the cliffs on the northern landing is a little hole drilled in the rock, almost certainly made for a small amount of blasting powder (Fig. 12, no. 7). It appears the miners widened the path in a few places and roughly shaped a few ledges in order to make it easier to bring equipment and animals onto the island.[41] From the top of the cliffs to the area of the miners' cottages, it is approximately 120m, over particularly wet and soggy ground.

The Miners' Cottages

I rose from a desecration of corbelled cells
In holy cashels ringed by the flagellant sea;
Rock taken over by great black-backed gulls
Saluting each other Sieg Heil, claiming the sky.

Richard Murphy, *The Miner's Hut*.

Figure 13
Photo of the cross near the southeastern landing on High Island, Co. Galway. Now quite weathered, this cross-shaped stone is decorated on three faces (see below, Fig. 87). Photo Con Brogan. Courtesy Dúchas The Heritage Service.

Figure 14a
Drawing made by George Kinahan in 1869 of the cross stone at the southeastern landing of High Island, Co. Galway. Kinahan remarked that it was the most 'uninjured cross on the island' (Kinahan 1869, Plate XLIX, Fig.1). Courtesy Royal Irish Academy.

Figure 14b
Drawing made by R.A.S. Macalister in 1895 of the cross stone at the southeastern landing of High Island, Co. Galway. Macalister also drew the small cross inscribed on the side of the cross, but missed the fainter design on the reverse face, stating that the 'seaward side of the stone is plain' (Macalister 1896, 206). Courtesy Royal Society of Antiquaries of Ireland.

In 1971 the owner of the island, Richard Murphy, decided to rebuild part of the larger of the two miners' cottages here for his own use. The original gable-roofed structure, according to Murphy, had three rooms, two bedrooms, one on each side of a central room containing a cobbled hearth. The end room was converted into a small one-room, flat-roofed cabin (4m by 3m) with a high stone wall enclosing a yard (approx. 8m by 4.25m) on the southwest side (Fig. 11; Figs. 15a and 15b).[42]

Traces of other structures built by the miners, a simple well southwest of the house and furrows of raised beds possibly for potatoes extend in the field to the east of the cottage, and a pile of stone debris, the remains of a second, smaller house north of the larger cottage, can still be seen. A stone wall runs behind the two houses and curves around alongside the southern side of the reconstructed cottage (marked on the Fair Plan, Fig. 5). The miners, who clearly wished to live close to the mine and the landings, chose the only sheltered spot on this side of the island, the base of a hill that buffers winds from the west and north. Water running down from the hill supplied the well and was diverted away from the cottages by a ditch running along the exterior of the stone wall. The only other visible evidence of miner activity are the omnipresent rabbits who were probably brought in by the miners and continue to thrive on the grassy tranquillity of the island.

Mining on High Island was probably limited to the summer and early autumn because of the difficulty of landing in other seasons. The presence of the two cottages suggests a standard nineteenth-century mining team of some eight to ten local men in the large cottage, with a mining captain, possibly an experienced miner imported from Cornwall, in the smaller cabin. The presence of only one simple shaft confirms the nineteenth-century geological estimates of a limited amount of copper on the island, and it is likely that mining activities on High Island lasted no more than one or two seasons.[43]

Where did the miners get the stone for their cottages? There is no sign of quarrying on this side of the island,

Figure 15a

Aerial photo taken in 1996 from the south of the stone cabin made from the remains of the larger miners' cottage on High Island, Co. Galway. The raised beds for potatoes show northeast of it, as does the drainage trench that runs behind and along the southern side of the cabin. The remains of the second, smaller cottage show as a pile of stones in the distance north of the cabin. Photo Con Brogan. Courtesy Dúchas The Heritage Service.

Figure 15b

Section and plan of the cabin and courtyard converted from part of the larger nineteenth-century miners' cottage by the former owner of the island. Plan and section by G.D. Rourke.

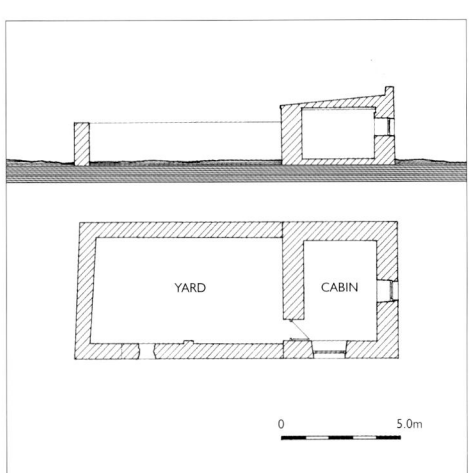

but they might have acquired building stone from a number of sources, such as the rock debris in the coves, nearby field walls or possibly from rock blasted from the mine shaft. The amount of worked stone visible in the cottage walls, however, justifies old accusations that the miners robbed the monastery of stone. The rough style of working the stones indicates early medieval craftsmen rather than the more precise edges made in nineteenth-century stonework, and, moreover, the worked stones are randomly placed, serving no purpose in the cottage construction other than size. One of the clearest examples of monastic working are the jagged tool marks seen along the upper edge of the stone used as a lintel for the eastern window, irregular marks left by an iron chisel. Lintels were not worked in this manner and this stone was shaped and worked for another location. While people could not be expected to carry stones from the monastery over the rolling hills, wheelbarrows, donkeys or mules pulling sleds would have made it possible, although still laborious, to transport stones from the monastery. Evidently, the easy availability of building stone of the desired size in the monastery compensated for the work involved in transporting it.

The way across the island to the monastery heads uphill to the southwest (Fig 12) of the mining settlement. Although there are no traces of a path left on the ground, the steepness of the terrain behind the cottage as well as the location of the first pilgrimage station on the Ordnance Survey Fair Plan are good indications that most pilgrims and visitors to the island followed the gentler slope south of the miners' cottages.

Some 160m past the miners' structures and 25m north of the path is the beginning of a long wall, now consisting of two interrupted segments, that may have once extended to span the width of the island (Fig. 12, no. 8).[44] This may have been another wall used to limit the roaming of sheep and cattle.

The rough remains of a small drystone structure lie shortly beyond this wall (10m) and north of the most comfortable path. This is most likely the remains of the second feature noted as a station on the Ordnance Survey Fair Plan of 1839 (Fig. 5; Fig. 12, no. 9). Today, all that is visible are several tumbled quartz stones in conjunction with a few well-set stones that suggest a *leacht*, the rectangular drystone structures commonly found on early medieval ecclesiastic sites.[45] There is no doubt that pilgrims came to High Island but we know little else; the date when pilgrimages began, the original number of pilgrimage stations and the nature of the pilgrimage there remain unknown. Although the nineteenth-century antiquaries are the first to mention pilgrimage stations, pilgrimage surely predates this period. Primarily preoccupied with the major structures on the island during their hurried visits, antiquaries made only vague and casual remarks about pilgrimage stations.

In 1839, when Wakeman and O'Donovan were there for the Ordnance Survey, Wakeman remarked: 'There is hardly a considerable elevation on the surface of the island which does not display a cairn-like pile of stone...' (Wakeman 1863, 218).

O'Donovan, nevertheless, only marked the Ordnance Survey Plan with five stations (Figs. 5 and 6), and his comments in his report also indicate fewer stations than Wakeman's remarks imply: 'There are several penitential stations on this island but I could not learn their names from the people I met with on the island' (Ordnance Survey Letters, Galway, 3:84). In 1820 Petrie referred to them as 'rude stone altars' and noted several in the ground surrounding the monastery and another 'stone altar surmounted by a cross' down by the smaller lake (Petrie, 1845, 420). These first antiquaries were clearly classifying as pilgrimage stations only those structures that resemble *leachta*. *Leachta* may have been used at various times as reliquary shrines, pilgrimage stations, altars and burial markers.[46]

The number of penitential or pilgrimage stations counted on High Island has varied according to the classification methods of each author. Systematic archaeological study of pilgrimage stations has been very limited and few have been excavated. They are easily set up and dismantled, sometimes hard to recognise and almost impossible to date. It is also possible that the number of stations and their locations on the island varied over the centuries.[47]

Continuing along the route across the island, the subrectangular remains of a drystone structure, shaped almost like an elongated horseshoe, lie some 50m west of the pilgrimage station (Fig. 12, no. 10).[48] The function of a structure in this location is uncertain. From this spot, at 60m above sea level, almost the highest point on the island, is the island's most beautiful view of the Connemara mainland, as well as Croagh Patrick and Achill to the north.

Figure 16a

Drawing of Brian Boru's Well on High Island, Co. Galway, showing the location of the cross stone, the walling of the well, the steps leading down to the well and the drainage ditch running westwards away from the well. Plan shows the level of the bedrock base and the steps on either side. Drawing by G.D. Rourke.

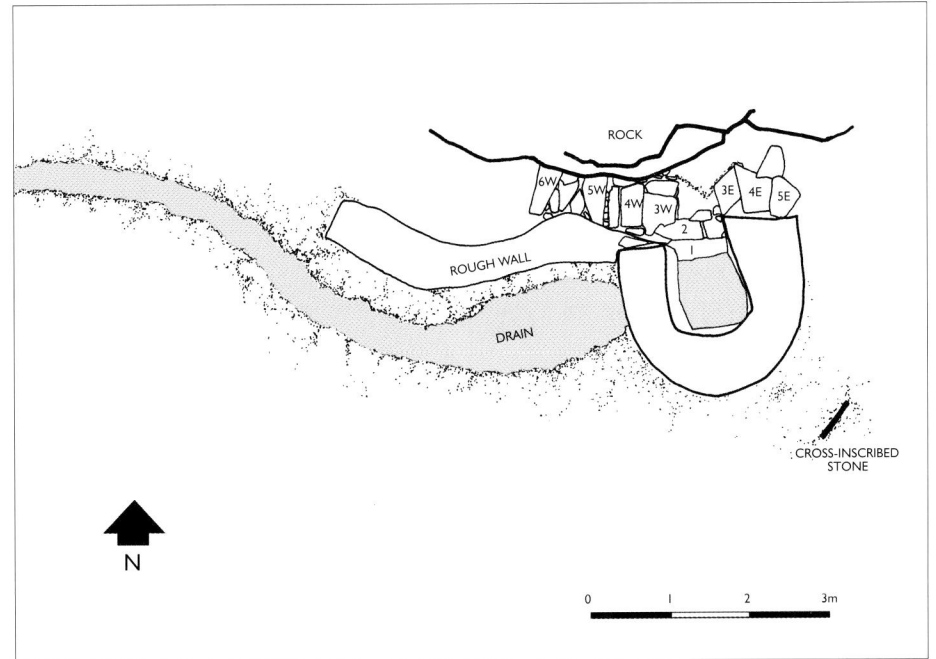

Bedrock base	0.00
Steps: 1	0.59
2	0.66
3E	0.83
3W	0.83
4E	1.03
4W	0.91
5E	1.26
5W	1.02
6W	1.19
Step levels relative to bedrock base of wall	

Brian Boru's Well

How does it rise on top of a hill
And why is it never clear?
By miracle, tradition said:
Instead of springing, the rock shed
A slow continual tainted tear
Since Brian Boru's fall.

It was named by Saint Gormgal,
Hermit, lion, poet, seer
And king's confessor. When it bled
He knew his penitent was dead.
He saw millennial daybreak tear
Unwinding from its spool.

Richard Murphy, *Brian Boru's Well.*

Figure 16b
A view of Brian Boru's Well on High Island, Co. Galway, from above, showing later steps and horseshoe-shaped wall surrounding the well. Drawing Patricia Johnson. Courtesy Dúchas The Heritage Service.

Continuing south, and skirting to the south around a hillock, a pilgrim would arrive at Brian Boru's Well (Figs. 16a and 16b).

From this spot, near the top of a hill in the middle of the island, it is possible to see the monastic valley to the west, although not the monastery itself. There is no apparent reason for the presence of this well here, on an island with two permanent small ponds augmented during rainy periods by additional temporary pools and ponds randomly scattered over the island. The well, moreover, was quite thoughtfully and carefully built, and of far better construction than the simple unlined well of the miners, close to the larger cottage. Brian Boru's Well also predates the mining families by centuries, for in 1684 Roderic O'Flaherty noted that at the top of the island: 'there is a well called Brian Boramy (King of Ireland) his well...' (O'Flaherty, ed. Hardiman 1846, 115). While Gormgal was a contemporary, there is no known historical reason to associate High Island with the great eleventh-century Munster hero and high king, Brian Boru; nevertheless, this association is clearly centuries old. Perhaps, indeed, as Murphy suggests above, Brian Boru made a pilgrimage to the famous anchorite monk, Gormgal, on High Island.

Petrie did not mention the well and O'Donovan commented only that the well was full of stagnant water, surrounded by a 'little enclosure of loose stones and now considered a holy well' (Ordnance Survey Letters, Galway 3:77). The position of the well is marked 'Holy Well' on the Ordnance Survey Fair Plan of 1839 (Fig. 5) but was changed to read Brian Boru's Well on the published Ordnance Survey Plan of 1841 (Fig. 6). Kinahan (1869, 554) remarked that it was a holy well 'said to cure colic and all such complaints' and he drew the cross he found there (Fig. 17a). Macalister described the location of the well in detail, reviewed prior comments on it, and listed the objects found on the well: 'hairpins, fish-hooks, bone buttons, metal button (one only), suspender buckle, fragments of whip-cord, fragment of cloth, key of a Yale lock'. He suggested that the well was considered holy because of its unlikely location 'at the foot of a dry rock, on the top of the island, where no water could either drain into it or spring up from below' (Macalister 1896, 204–205). Should Brian Boru's Well be classified as a pilgrimage station? It is probable that areas where people prayed and left offerings, such as Brian Boru's well and the altar in the church, were used as pilgrimage stations as well as the *leachta*.

The well is located at 57.5m above sea level, just below a large rock outcrop of schist with quartz veining, which was cut back to accommodate it and which also directs water flowing down its surface into the well. Access to the well is on the side by this rock outcrop where two sets of steps lead down (Fig. 16a). The two sets of steps, which lead down to the level, flagged area on the western side of the well, were added by men assisting Richard Murphy in the early 1970s.

The subrectangular well was constructed with a bedrock base and drystone side walls, lined at the base with orthostats, a building style reminiscent of the eastern wall of the church in the monastery (see ch.5). A curved horseshoe-shaped drystone wall (0.6m to 0.73m thick) is a modern addition, also constructed in the early 1970s; the addition is clearly indicated by the awkward junction between the base orthostats and this upper walling.[49]

The well was cleaned out during one of Richard Murphy's short stays on the island in the early 1970s and a trench was dug to carry away overflow water. By August 1992, when the well was cleaned again, a considerable amount of stone and soil had accumulated, as well as a number of recent coins, already badly corroded by the acidic water. The well, when full, has a large capacity (230 litres) and was clearly intended to be a practical, functioning well.

Brian Boru's Well was the location for two of the island's cross stones until recently, when one was removed because of its small size and fragile condition (see p. 142, cross no. 3). The remaining cross stone is decorated on two sides; Kinahan (Fig. 17a) sketched the more elaborately decorated face in 1869.

Kinahan found this cross at the well at the time of his visit in 1869. However, in 1839 Wakeman drew its reverse side on a piece of paper marked 'At the church on High Island' (Fig.17b). The cross must have been

Figure 17a

1869 sketch made by George Kinahan of the main face of the cross stone at Brian Boru's Well, High Island, Co. Galway. Kinahan described it as handsome and symmetrical (Kinahan 1869, 554). Courtesy Royal Irish Academy.

Figure 17b

1839 sketch made by W.F. Wakeman of the reverse face of the cross stone at Brian Boru's Well, High Island, Co. Galway (RIS MS 12T9). R.A.S. Macalister also sketched this side in 1895 and described it as 'a small slab about 2 feet in height, now leaning against the wall of the holy well' (Macalister 1896, 206). Courtesy Royal Irish Academy.

moved from the monastery to the well sometime between 1839 and 1869.

The remains of several structures of unknown function and age lie on the slopes between the well and the monastery, north of the most direct path to the main entrance of the monastery. Some 90m down a gentle slope from the well are the clear remains of a roughly circular structure, approximately 5m in diameter, without visible walling (Fig. 12, no. 12).[50]

Another 100m southwest of this circular structure is the edge of an elevated piece of ground that juts out overlooking the large lake and the monastery (Fig. 12, no. 13). This is the location of Herity's House 1 (1990, 82) which he describes as a tiny circular drystone structure, with dimensions of 1.3m by 1.05m, similar in its situation to a ruined *cloghan* above the west end of Reefert church at Glendalough. We were unable to find evidence for anything as specific as this; all that remains here is a heap of stones without discernible structure.

The Monastery

The monastery was built in the shallow valley formed by grassy hills on the eastern side and extensive exposed rock outcrops rising to the west (Fig. 18).

Two small ponds, naturally occurring catchment pools for water running off the surrounding elevations, lie in the centre of this valley. The monastery borders the northern edge of the larger of two ponds; the smaller one lies to the south.

Although the location of the monastery here has the disadvantage of being distant from the two best landing places, it also had important advantages. The lakes provided an abundance of fresh water, an almost unprecedented luxury for an Irish island monastery, where the supply of fresh water is usually severely limited. Here there was ample water for monks, animals, and even enough for a water mill (see ch. 10). This area is also the most protected location on the island, offering shelter from the worst of gale-force winds and winter storms. The monastery's greatest exposure is to the south, rarely the source of climatic troubles in Ireland. The valley may have also acted as a sun bowl, for it is the warmest spot on the island, promoting the growth of crops and the comfort of its inhabitants. Building material was readily available here, moreover, as the exposed blue-grey schist faces on the west side of the

Figure 18

Aerial photo from the south of the valley in which the monastery on High Island, Co. Galway, is found. This photo shows the monastery with two ponds south of it and the large field wall running to the south from the large pond. Photo Con Brogan. Courtesy Dúchas The Heritage Service.

Pilgrim's Path to the Monastery

Figure 19

Aerial close-up of the monastery at High Island, Co. Galway, from the south. Sod and grass cover most of the collapsed stone of the monastery, so that before excavation began only three structures were recognisable in the northeastern section of the monastic enclosure. Photo Con Brogan. Courtesy Dúchas The Heritage Service.

valley offer closely spaced joint planes from which stone is easily extracted. Signs of rock extraction are quite visible here.[51] This western valley is the best, indeed the only, practical location on High Island for a group of permanent settlers.

Stone debris blurs and conceals the residue of monastic buildings and enclosure wall (Fig. 19). Nevertheless, the most important structures inside the roughly oval monastic enclosure wall are still recognisable: the remains of a rectangular church, itself surrounded by an enclosure wall; the remains of a small roofless cell, Cell A, on the northern side of the church; and another larger cell, Cell B, east of the church, built against the church enclosure wall.

Today there are only two clearly marked entrances into the monastery, both on the south side of the enclosure wall that abuts the lake. On the exterior of the main, southeastern, entrance to the monastery, at the pond's edge, are the foundations of two structures, one a small triangular-shaped chamber, not readily visible in a photograph, and the other a large rectangular building whose perimeter appears to be defined by the lake on two sides. Both of these structures have been reduced to base levels.

33

Figure 20
Photo of the southwestern landing on High Island, Co. Galway, from the west, showing the steep dangerous ascent to the top. Photo Walter Horn, 1982.

Traces of a number of structures and walls are scattered around the monastic valley both to the south and to the north of the monastic enclosure. A monastery needed auxiliary buildings such as animal pens, kilns and barns; these buildings were commonly placed outside the monastic walls, as were the dwellings of monastic tenants.[52] It is unlikely that any of these structures were built by the miners, and most of them probably served the monastery, although it is not certain that they were all monastic. Pre-monastic occupation of a sizeable island only 3km offshore is also a possibility (see ch. 11).[53]

Approach to the Monastery from the Southwest Landing

The third landing lies within a deep narrow inlet at the western end of the island (Fig. 4; Fig. 20). A small rock-shelf on the eastern side of the inlet is the sole landing area here, accessible only near high tide because at low tide the rock-shelf is too high above the boat to reach. The cliffs are low here, only 17m high, but the climb up the crumbling rock-face here is steep and dangerous, with few good hand- or foot-holds until you reach the exposed rock-ledge at the top.[54] The climb may have been easier in monastic times, if there were more hand- or foot-holds that have since eroded, or the landing, only 300m from the monastery, may have been used primarily to unload provisions, with the monks hauling them up by rope. At the top of the cliffs is a sizeable flat stone area that could easily have served as a loading platform for material being both hauled up or lowered down. Doubtless the island monks were agile and skilled climbers, but if the cliffs were as dangerous then as they are now, visitors would have preferred the other landings. The clean fresh-looking rock in this area, however, indicates that this side of the narrow cove, generally, and the flat level space at the top of the cliff in particular, have been eroding back in recent times; it is, therefore, possible that the climb up the cliffs was easier a thousand years ago (personal communication, Michael O'Sullivan, summer 1996).

Clustered down at this end of the monastic valley are a number of ruined structures, most of uncertain date and function. Just north of the top of the landing are faint traces of walling.

Fifty metres further north, not far away from the small pond, is a long rectangular structure, oriented north-south, with an opening in the northern end (Fig. 12, no. 24; Fig. 21; Fig. 22a). This is a good-sized structure, 7m long and roughly 4.5m wide internally, now in poor condition. Only the entrance and the eastern lateral wall are reasonably intact, but on the other sides only the rough outline of walls is perceptible. Traces of a curving wall east of this structure (Fig. 12, no. 25; Fig. 22a) appear to have been part of an enclosure (perhaps a building with a field enclosure).[55]

In 1820 Petrie was the first to mention this structure, which he described as:

> *another stone cell or house, of an oval form, at the south side of the valley in which the monastery is situated. This house is eighteen feet long [5.5m], and nine wide [2.76m], and there is a small walled enclosure joined to it, which was probably a garden. (1845, 421)*

Almost fifty years later, Kinahan arrived at different dimensions for this southern structure, more accurate ones than Petrie's if his width and length dimensions are switched, and saw no walled enclosure, but he did mention an entrance through a wall running the length of the monastic valley (see Fig. 9):

> *The site of a structure about thirteen feet [4m] long by twenty-one feet [6.4m] wide. It was situated alongside the southeast doorway through the outer enclosure wall, and contiguous to the previously mentioned south coose. (1869, 554)*

The southern edge of the smaller of the two ponds in the monastic valley lies nearby, just west of this structure, and from it a stream empties out and runs out over the cliffs

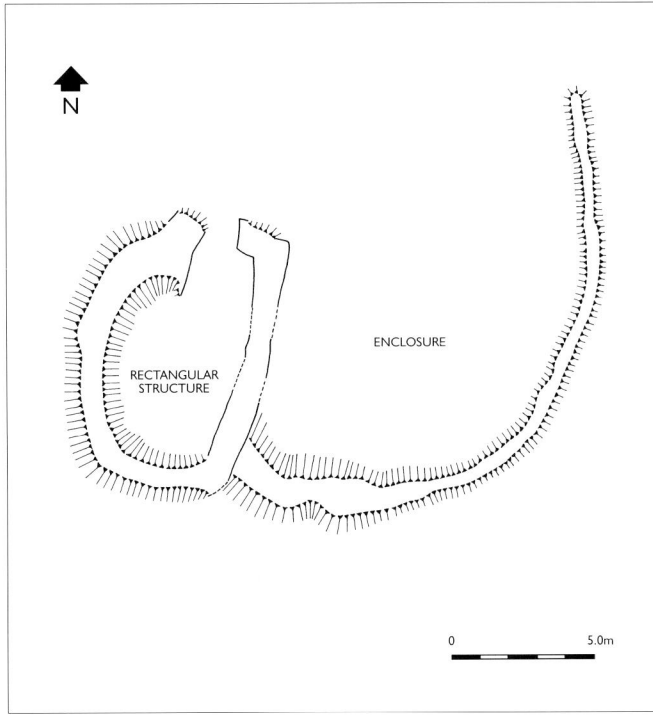

Figure 21

Plan of the rectangular structure and field/garden enclosure walling near the southwestern landing on High Island, Co. Galway. At the entrance the jamb and eastern wall face are still intact. The wall thickness here is 0.8–1.0m wide. The western and southern sides of the structure no longer have wall faces, therefore no dimensions are available. Plan G.D. Rourke.

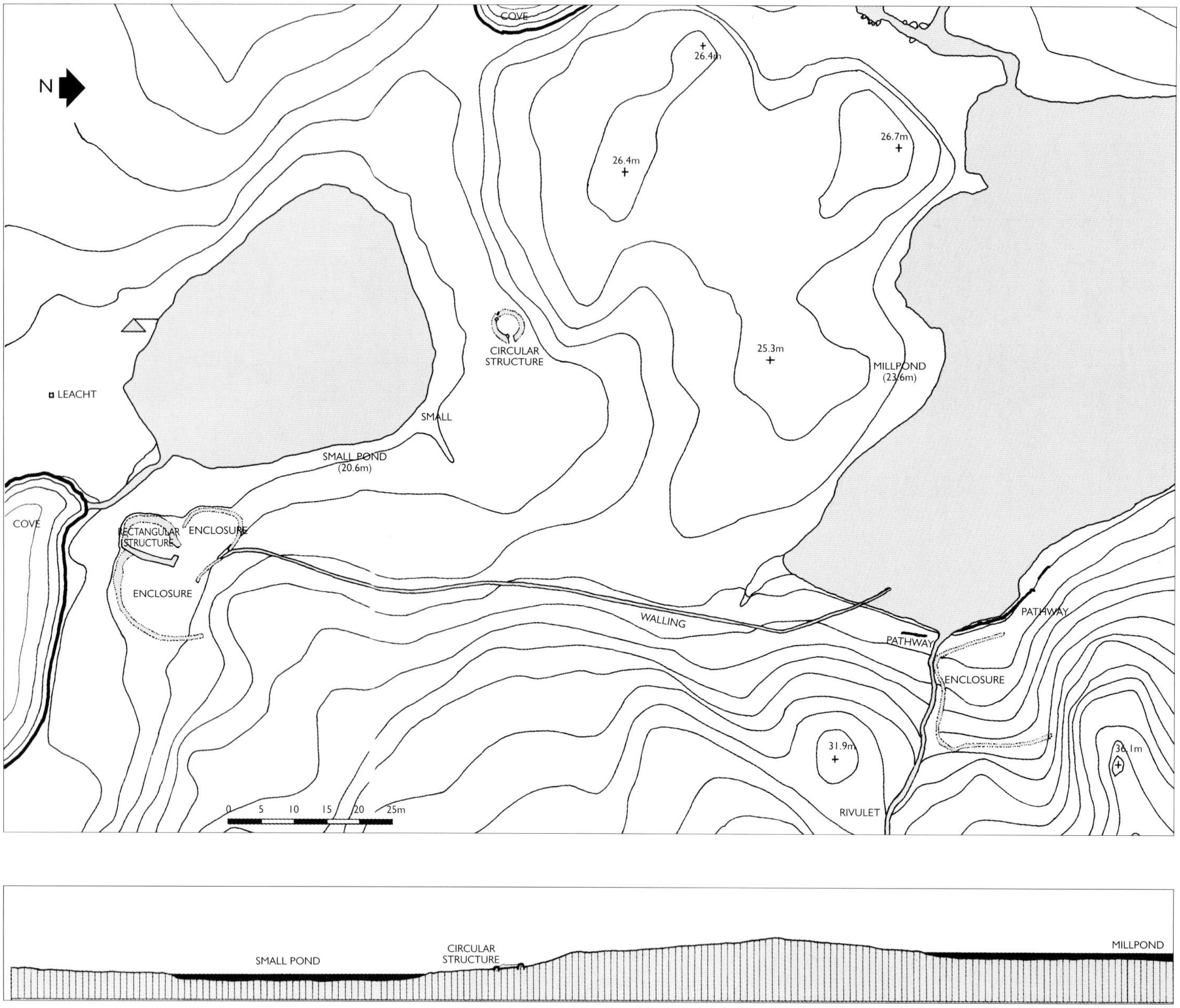

into the southwestern cove. Across this stream are the remains of a rectangular drystone *leacht* (Fig. 12, no. 26; Fig. 22a; Fig. 23).

The *leacht* is about 25m southwest of the rectangular structure, but we believe this was what Petrie (1845, 421) was referring to when he said: 'There is also adjoining to it [the rectangular structure], a stone altar surmounted by a cross, and a small lake...' The Ordnance Survey Fair Plan marked this spot as a station (Fig. 5).[36]

Originally the *leacht* must have been square, with dimensions of 1.5m by 1.5m. Now, however, its damaged and displaced shape is trapezoidal. Six low stones set on edge as kerb stones (orthostats) mark its base, a more solid construction than the

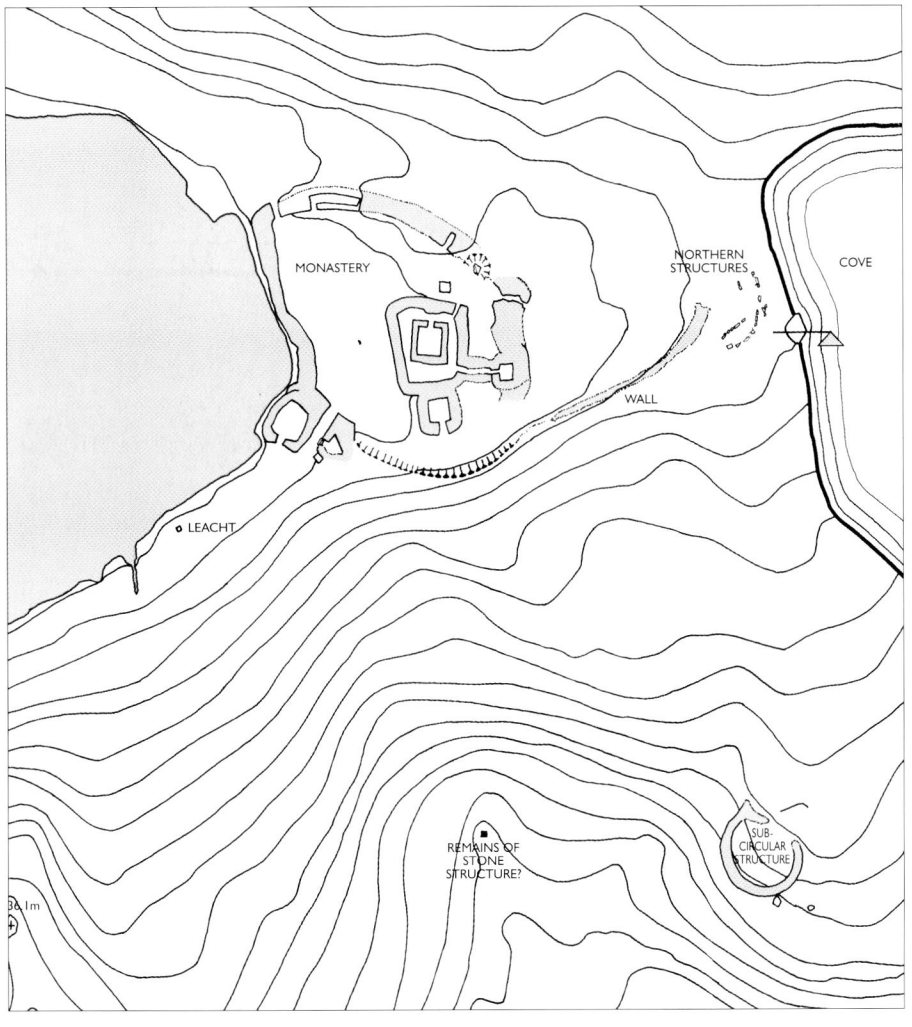

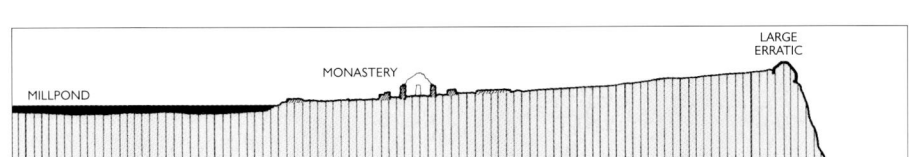

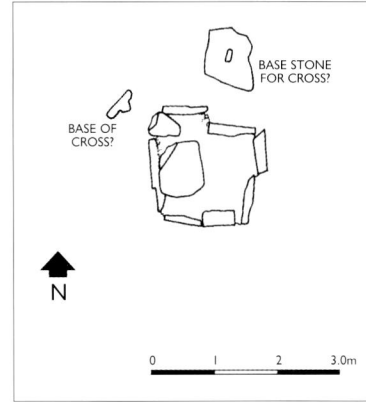

Figure 22a

Plan of the western end of High Island, Co. Galway, showing the structures in the valley from the southwestern landing to the monastery and the structures north of the monastery. Contours at metre intervals. Plan G.D. Rourke.

Figure 23

Plan of leacht *south of the small pond on High Island, Co. Galway. A slotted stone, possibly the stand for a cross, and a tenon stone, possibly the remains of a cross, are also shown. Are the disturbed* leacht *and the two stones all that is left of Petrie's description in 1820 of a stone altar surmounted by a cross? Plan and drawing by G.D. Rourke.*

Figure 22b

A north-south site section through the west end of High Island, Co. Galway. Section by G.D. Rourke.

other 'stations', which were built more simply and quickly by laying stone flat, like most drystone walling. Leaning up against this feature is a stone with a slotted hole, as well as a broken piece of stone. Because the broken stone piece fits neatly into the slotted hole, it is possible that they are the base and the tenon of the cross that Petrie saw in 1820 (see Fig. 23). Because of its different, superior construction, we suspect that this *leacht* was not built as a pilgrimage station, although it may well have been later used as one by pilgrims. Instead, it may have been built to support a landing cross, a cross at the outer perimeter of the monastery, intended to mark the visitor's entry into sacred space.

Pilgrim's Path to the Monastery

Recrossing the stream, the most direct route to the monastery runs along the substantial field wall that leads all the way to the southern end of the large pond (Fig. 12, no. 22; Fig 24). Its very large blocks of stone (up to 0.44m long x 0.26m deep x 0.46m wide) make the wall clearly visible even in aerial photographs. Kinahan, the first to describe it, believed that it was part of a major wall that ran the length of the monastic valley, separating the main monastic structures from the island east of it.

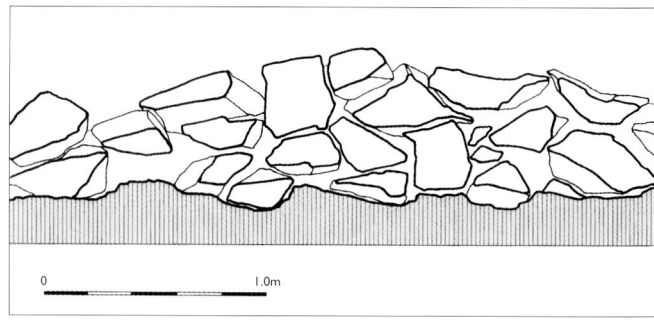

Figure 24

Elevation of a segment of the long wall that runs more than 200 metres from the structures near the southwestern landing to the south shore of the large pond on High Island, Co. Galway. The stones composing this wall are larger than those of any of the other remaining walls on the island. Drawing by G.D. Rourke.

Kinahan also described gateways leading into the monastic area at the north and south ends of the wall (marked no. 2 and no. 13 on his plan seen in Fig. 9); no sign of either entrance is visible today. Macalister (1896, 204) described it simply and more accurately as a wall running in

> *a curved course from an inlet in...the northern side to a similar inlet in the southern. It is interrupted by the larger lake in its way. There is a remarkable structure at either end...*

Both the larger pond and the monastery, which served as sufficient barriers themselves, interrupt the wall. At the northeast corner of the monastery the wall recommences and runs up to the structure(s) in the northern inlet (Fig. 12, no. 15; Fig. 22a); this section of the field wall has been largely removed and is only faintly visible, although the line of the wall is still clear. Both men were essentially correct, however, in stating that the wall divided the monastic area from the rest of the island, probably to keep herd animals, sheep and cattle, from invading the monastery and the monastery's kitchen garden and grain fields. This wall was part of a medieval field system and it is similar to the remnants of other stone walls on the island in that they appear to have run across the width of the island (Fig. 22a). Peaty gley soils are inherently weak soils in their structure, although capable of producing high grass yields if they are not overgrazed. Overgrazing causes severe damage to the soil structure and productivity, therefore prudent soil management would have required the island inhabitants to shift their grazing animals constantly from area to area in order to preserve the soil (Mytum 1992, 169, 183). Since High Island had a single owner, walls running across the narrow width of the island provided a practical solution to this problem, although it is not typical of what little we know of field systems on the mainland (see Mytum 1992, 170–180).

Midway along this wall, the remains of a small circular structure (Fig. 12, no. 23; Fig. 22a; Fig. 25) become visible across the way, some 35m west of the wall, just north of the small pond. Although much of this structure is missing or damaged, the

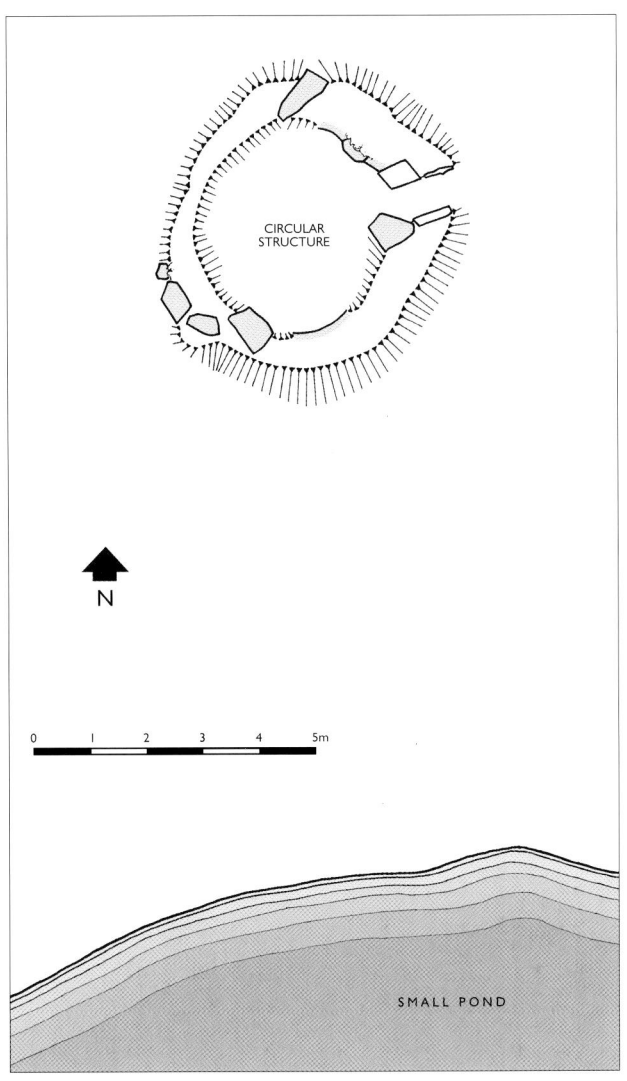

Figure 25

Plan of the small circular structure located north of the small pond on High Island, Co. Galway. This structure has a diameter of 3–3.5m and encloses an area of 8sq.m. On the more intact eastern side the wall thickness measures 1.2m. Drawing by G.D. Rourke.

entrance on the east side, 0.6m wide, is still defined. Large stones, reminiscent in size of the stones in the wall running up the valley, were used in its construction, among them blocks of pink granite, a few of which were incorporated as wall faces.

In construction, this structure, with its use of large stone blocks for base stones, is dissimilar to the two round cells in the monastery. However, it might be the base of a round building dating to a different period. It is possible, although unlikely, that the remains here formed a small circular enclosure rather than a building, but it is highly improbable that these remains were built as a penitential station on High Island (cf. Herity 1990, 83; 85).

At the southern end of the large pond, the large field wall curves into the pond and then continues underwater for 3.5 metres. This submerged section of walling clearly shows that the size of the pond changed after the building of the wall; most likely it was expanded to increase water volume when the mill was built. Both ponds, located in the valley on flat terrain lying lower than that on both its eastern and western boundaries, were natural collecting areas for ground run water, particularly the substantial quantities coming down the eastern hills from Brian Boru's Well. The larger pond, with its excellent location near the monastery and near the western cliffs, would have been relatively easy to turn into a millpond (see chapter 10).[57]

The presence of the substantial wall before the construction of the watermill demonstrates an early interest in closing off the western end of the island to grazing animals. The sizeable acreage thus sealed, far more than a small monastery would need for its dwellings, church and kitchen gardens, strongly suggests that cereal crops were being raised in this area before the watermill was built. The substantial size and evident duration of this wall fits easily into O'Corráin's translation and explanation of one of the Irish law tracts on fencing, the late seventh-century *Bretha Comaithchesa*, in which the stone wall is defined as a permanent wall erected in the *nochtmachaire*, the bare plain or, according to O'Corráin, the arable (O'Corráin 1983, 247–251). The stone wall should be three feet thick and four feet high and be 'a wall of three stones', which Fergus Kelly in his recent book on Irish farming in seventh- and eighth-century law tracts interprets as being a wall of three rough courses. The flimsier stone walls used for field division on High Island relate more readily to the use of oak fences or post-and-wattle fences on the mainland, fences more easily set up (Kelly 1998, 372–378).

Past the wall the approach to the monastery continues along the eastern border of the larger pond. The edge of a flagged pathway appears some 12m past the wall at the point where a little rivulet runs down the hill into it (Fig. 22a; Fig. 26). Originally this pathway must have been set back somewhat, but the constant flow of water, from the hills to the east has eroded the edge of the pond here; one flagstone has already fallen into the water, while others are now balanced on the edge. Petrie (1845, 421) described this pathway as running down to the (rectangular) structure near the southwestern landing:

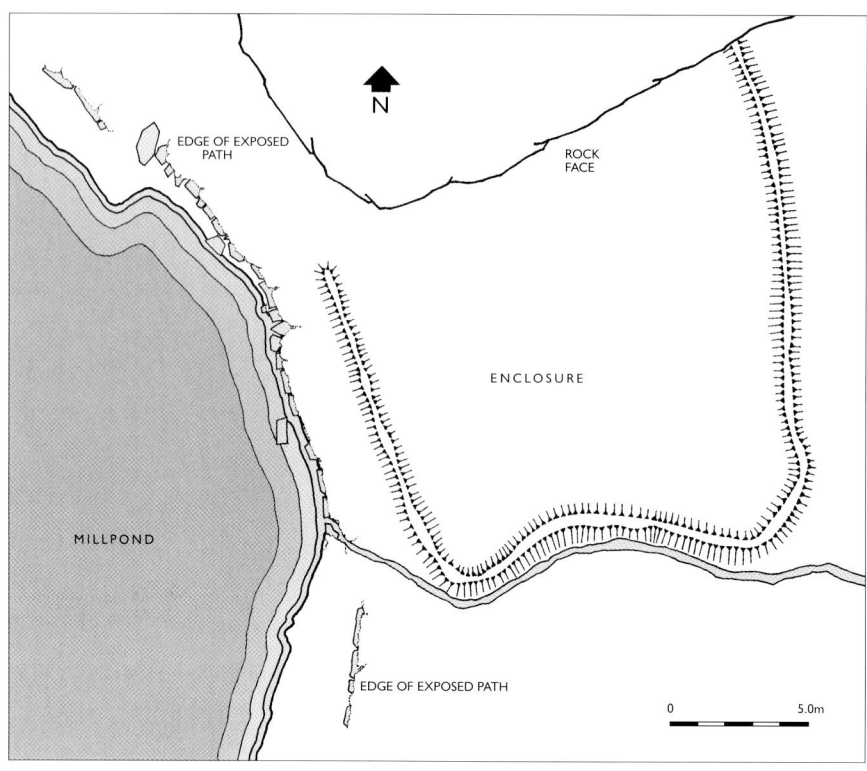

Figure 26
Plan showing the exposed edges of large flagstones forming the path on the eastern border of the large pond, and the remains of an enclosure to the east. Petrie said this path was 220 yards (approximately 200m), but today only the edge of a small section, (approximately 27m long), shows. More, however, lies concealed under growth, and there are faint indications that the path may shift to run on the eastern side of the large field wall towards the southwestern landing. Plan G.D. Rourke.

> *along the west side of this lake, there is an artificial stone path or causeway, two hundred and twenty yards [203m] in length, which leads to another stone cell or house, of an oval form, at the south side of the valley in which the monastery is situated.*

If Petrie was correct and this path ran the entire length, it indicates greater use of the path approaching the monastery from the southwestern landing than the present condition of the climb from the sea to the cliffs suggests. Water run-off from the hills east of the path frequently makes the ground in this area wet and muddy, a condition that would be continually exacerbated if this were the main entrance to the monastery. The millpond itself is also stone revetted (faced with consolidating masonry for additional support) on the side of the pond west of this path, further strong evidence of continual concern about water erosion in this area. A stone pathway to facilitate the passage of people and provisions would be a sensible, practical remedy for the problem, a problem that may have been particularly important after the construction of the horizontal watermill.

On the slope of the hills east of the rivulet are traces of a water reservoir whose primary remains consist of two different types of walling, one of orthostats and one of

Pilgrim's Path to the Monastery

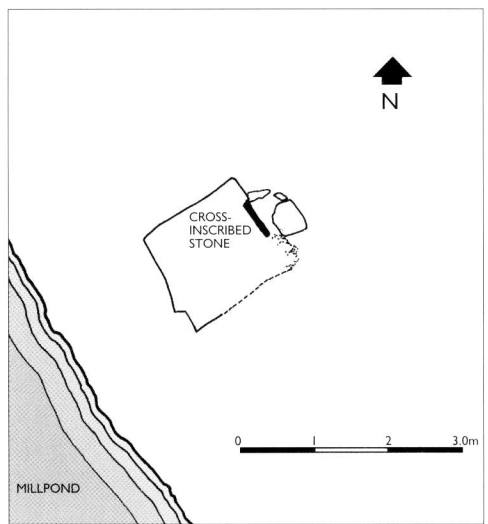

Figure 27

Plan of leacht *by the large pond. The leacht (1.55m by 1.45m) had a standard wall face with the stones set one on top of the other, unlike the upright placement of the stones of the* leacht *by the southwestern landing. Plan G.D. Rourke.*

Figure 28

Photo of the large cross stone leaning against the leacht *located east of the large pond outside the southeastern entry to the monastery on High Island, Co. Galway. In 1869 Kinahan described this cross somewhat fancifully as 'a long slab, in which, on both sides, were cut four holes in the form of rude crosses' (Kinahan 1869, 555). Photo J.W. Marshall.*

simple field walls (Fig. 12, nos. 19/20/21; Fig. 22a). The orthostats were part of a gravity dam, a system to control water run-off from a hillside reservoir into the lake for the horizontal mill. When the mill was in use, water would be released to flow down the hill along a single channel (which is marked today by the little rivulet), across the stone pathway into the millpond. The other walling may have been to prevent animals from entering the area, which would have been particularly important in view of the second important use of this water management system. Aerial photographs show the remains of cultivation ridges in this area; the water flowing down these western-facing hills to the millpond also irrigated crops[58] (for a more detailed description of the horizontal watermill, see chapter 10).

Continuing north along the lake toward the monastery there is another *leacht*, with a shaped cross, roughly 'man-shaped', positioned against it (Fig. 12, no. 17; Fig. 22a; Figs. 27 and 28). Neither Petrie nor O'Donovan referred to this *leacht* but its position was marked 'station' on the Ordnance Survey Fair Plan of 1839 (Fig. 5). Kinahan described the cross as a recently broken cross which he found in the monastic enclosure and placed upright '...at the station by the lake shore a little south-east of the cashel...' (Kinahan 1869, 555) (Fig 28).[59] The southeastern entrance to the monastery is only 30m beyond this feature.

Notes

40 Some 160 metres due north of this point, on the far side of this northeastern peninsula, are the stone remains of a now unidentifiable structure of uncertain date.

41 Personal communication on 21 August 1992 by Michael O'Sullivan, geologist. These round holes are identical to those seen on Skellig Michael on the rocks next to the path blasted by the engineers who built the path to the lighthouses in the 1820s. Blasting powder was probably used for the copper-mining shaft as well.

42 Personal communication, Richard Murphy, 1994. Murphy also added the upper stonework to the miners' well.

43 See Cowman 1983, 10–19 and Cowman 1980 on the life and conditions of miners in nineteenth-century Ireland. Our special thanks to Tom Wallace of Kill, near Clifden, Co. Galway, who told us about a local man who still owned the miners' tools used on High Island by his ancestor.

44 The first southeastern segment runs for almost 50m followed by a 40m break before walling resumes on the northwestern side of the island for another 37m.

45 This is Herity's Station 7 (Herity 1990, 85).

46 No comprehensive archaeological studies have been made of these structures, consequently their function and chronological placement is as amorphous as their definition. On one site, Skellig Michael, Co. Kerry, a primary *leacht*, too small for burials, contains human bones; on Illaunloughan, Co. Kerry, the primary *leacht* covers part of two earlier burials and is unlikely to be either a reliquary or a specific burial marker. (Horn, Marshall and Rourke 1990 and Marshall and Walsh, forthcoming.) On Omey Island, Co. Galway, a *leacht* in an excavated cemetery also cuts through and disturbs two earlier burials (Tadhg O'Keefe, lecture, IAPA Conference, 1994).

47 Petrie may have had a broader definition of penitential stations as he also noted that the altar in the church was 'covered with offerings, such as nails, buttons, and shell, but chiefly fishing hooks, the most characteristic tributes of the calling of the votaries' (Petrie 1845, 420).

48 The structure faces 40° south of west and the open end is 2.5m wide. At widest, it is 4m and at longest 7m. This is Herity's House 4 (Herity 1990, 82–83).

49 Personal communication to Grellan D. Rourke, 1996.

50 The structure, located 52m above sea level, is Herity's House 3 (Herity 1990, 82). Another small structure, about 60m southeast of the well, near the highest point on the island (63.3m), is a pile of stones set up perhaps as a marker by and for fisherman.

51 Report from Michael O'Sullivan, 21 August 1992. National Monument Service field report.

[52] See the descriptions in the seventh-century *Vita St. Columbae* for typical placement of auxiliary buildings.

[53] Small-scale post-monastic occupation is also possible, for whereas there are no structures identifiable as medieval on the island, excavations at Church Island, (O'Kelly 1958) and Illaunloughan (Marshall and Walsh 1994) have shown small-scale occupation in the medieval period. At High Island, the buildings were still in excellent condition in the early nineteenth-century. To date, excavation has revealed no long-term or extensive occupation of the island after the monks left.

[54] Some eight of us landed on and departed from the island in a rubber inflatable at this landing in 1982. Although we managed the climb, we were uncomfortable and have not been up or down here since.

[55] This is Herity's House 2. Herity describes this structure as standing 'within a ruined rectangular enclosure which is 17m north south by 22.5m east west, the south wall of the building close to the south wall of the enclosure. This seems to have been a house with two small gardens created by subdividing the enclosure, a wall from the northeast corner of the house running to the north wall of the enclosure' (Herity 1990, 82).

[56] Macalister (1896, 205) reviewed earlier comments but added no new information.

[57] There was also probably a similar mill on Inishbofin, Co. Galway, at St. Colman's monastery. A pond, once considerably larger, is located at the bottom of Knock Hill and a stream flows from it past the monastery. This pond was also bordered on its original edge with large stones on the hill side of the pond in a manner reminiscent of High Island, although when this was done is unknown.

[58] Either deliberately during the operative period of the mill or afterwards, after it was no longer in use.

[59] Kinahan likens this cross to two on St Macdara's Island, Co. Galway. Macalister (1896, 207) also describes the *leacht* and points out that two of the four notches in the cross are cut through and two are only depressions.

Chapter Four

The Monastic Enclosure Wall

Dark mounds of mica schist,
A lake, mill and chapel,
Roofless, one gable smashed,
Lie ringed with rubble.

Richard Murphy, **High Island**.

Irish monasteries, like those of the Continent and Britain, were based on the general architectural form of vernacular prototypes, which were then modified by Christian dogma and liturgical requirements. On the Continent, Benedictine monasteries, as typified by the Plan of St Gall, developed from provincial Roman villas, whereas Ireland, never part of the Roman Empire, had different vernacular models. Here, the monastic enclosure was an adoption of the Irish ringfort known variously as *rath*, *lios* or *cashel*, and the round dwelling cells of the clerics were identical to those of lay people.

Extant remains of thousands of ringforts demonstrate that the vast majority of them are curvilinear, circular or ovoid in shape and are believed to have been the home of prosperous farmers and other members of society with high status. Indeed, while enclosure walls may have served several purposes, one of the principal reasons for them in a society that was, according to the legal tracts, highly stratified, may have been as territorial markers and visible status symbols.⁶⁰ Two main early Irish texts on status, the *Uraiccecht Becc* and the *Crith Gablach*, mention enclosure walls as a measure of the king's status. The *Uraiccecht Becc* asks:

> *What is the due of a king who is always in residence at the head of his tuath? Seven score feet of perfect feet are the measure of his stockade on every side. Seven feet are the thickness of its earthwork, and twelve feet its depth. It is then that he is a king when ramparts of vassalage surround him. (MacNeill, 1923, 305)*

Churchmen were accorded high status in Irish society and enclosure walls may have served them also as status symbols. Even small communities were obliged, according to the *Rule of Patrick*, to provide their priests with a house and enclosure, as well as a milk cow every quarter, a sack of grain, and food on festival days.⁶¹ For an Irish ecclesiastic, however, there was an important religious significance to enclosure walls, because they separated the sacred and the secular world.⁶² For a monk, the enclosure wall safeguarded monastic desire for separation and seclusion; inside the enclosure wall or the cloister, monks could be free of worldly distraction. The monk, as the exemplar of the spiritual life, belonged exclusively to the sacred rather than the secular world. Monks everywhere, not just in Ireland, sought refuge behind enclosure walls and, indeed, enclosure could serve practically and symbolically as retreat from the world in a crowded city. When the Anglo-Saxon monk St Cuthbert built his hermitage on Farne Island he built his wall higher than 'a man standing upright' so that he

> *…could see nothing except the sky from his dwelling, thus restraining both the lust of the eyes and the thoughts and lifting the whole bent of his mind to higher things.*
> *(Bede, ed. Colgrave and Mynor 1969, 214–217)*

In Italy, St Benedict insisted that a monastery enclosure should contain all necessary things for monastic existence, even kitchen gardens and mills (*Benedicti regula*, McCann 1952, 156). Abbots, such as St Columbanus in *Regula Monachorum*, firmly discouraged their monks from idle wandering by imposing penalties: '…or if he has gone outside the wall, that is, outside the bounds of the monastery, without asking, with an imposition' (*Sancti Columbani Opera*, ed. Walker 1957, 154–155).

The High Island enclosure wall is an ovoid, whose internal diameter varies from 24m to 37m (Fig. 29a). The shape of the wall appears, in part, to be the result of its position abutting the steep slope of the hill on the east and the lake on the south. The deliberate positioning of an enclosure wall directly against and into the hill is highly unusual and clearly reduces any defensive intent in its construction. The topography would have permitted centering the enclosure in the valley; however, such a position

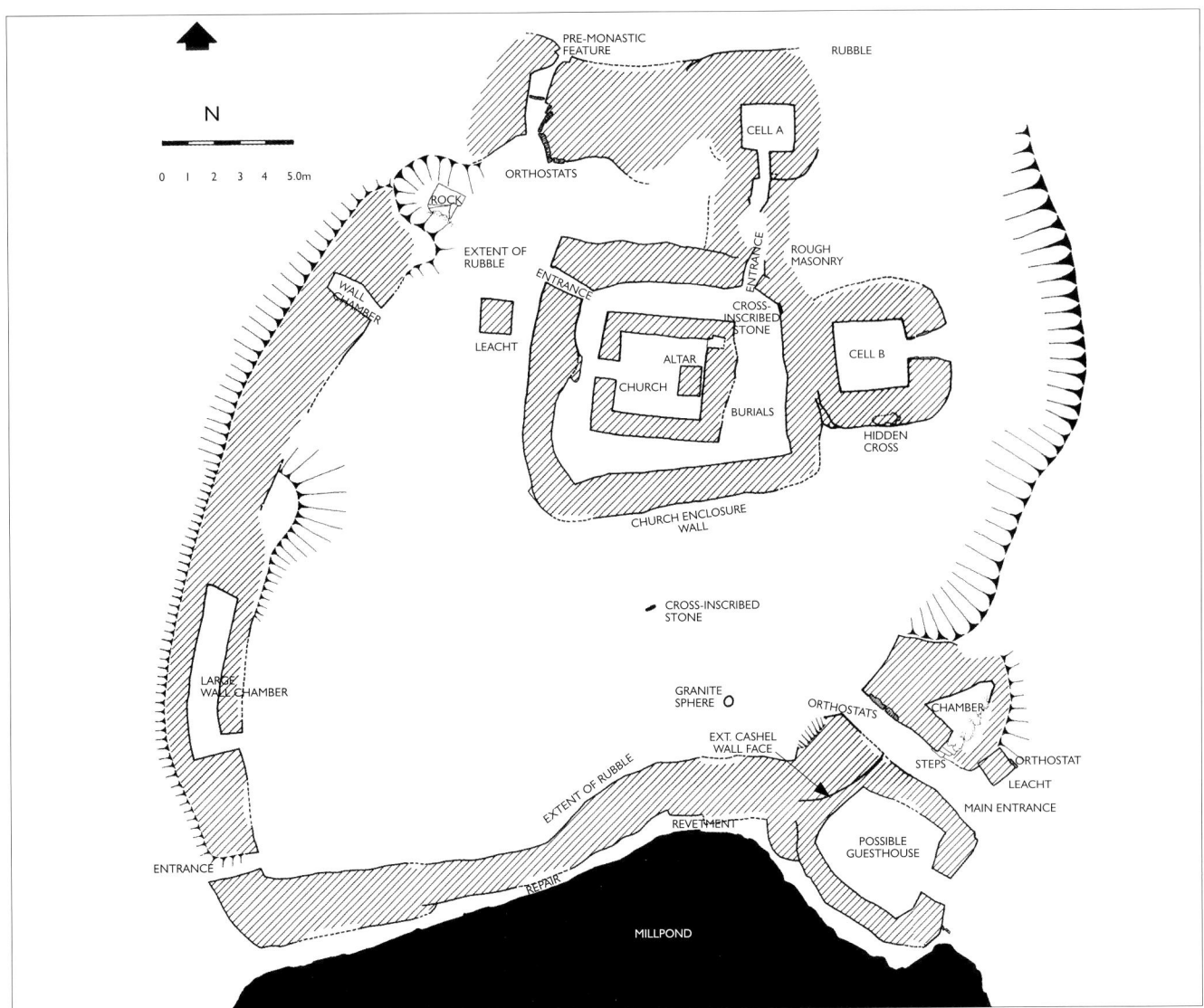

Figure 29a

Plan of the monastery on High Island, Co. Galway. The solid line equals definite wall faces, whereas dotted lines indicate conjectural ones. Plan G.D. Rourke.

would have left only a narrow passage around the exterior on both the eastern and western sides, whereas its present position allows ample space to the west. Maximum protection from the weather, convenient access to water, and other practical domestic considerations appear to have dictated the location of the enclosure wall and, to a certain extent, its shape.

Another unusual feature of the location of this enclosure is that it would have been possible to walk directly around the exterior of the enclosure only on its northern and western sides. Practical convenience thus required more than one entry into the enclosure.

Petrie's description of the enclosure wall in 1820 did not indicate its condition at that time: 'an uncemented stone wall, nearly circular, enclosing an area of one hundred and eight feet in diameter'. But Petrie (1845, 419) did describe the monastery

HIGH ISLAND

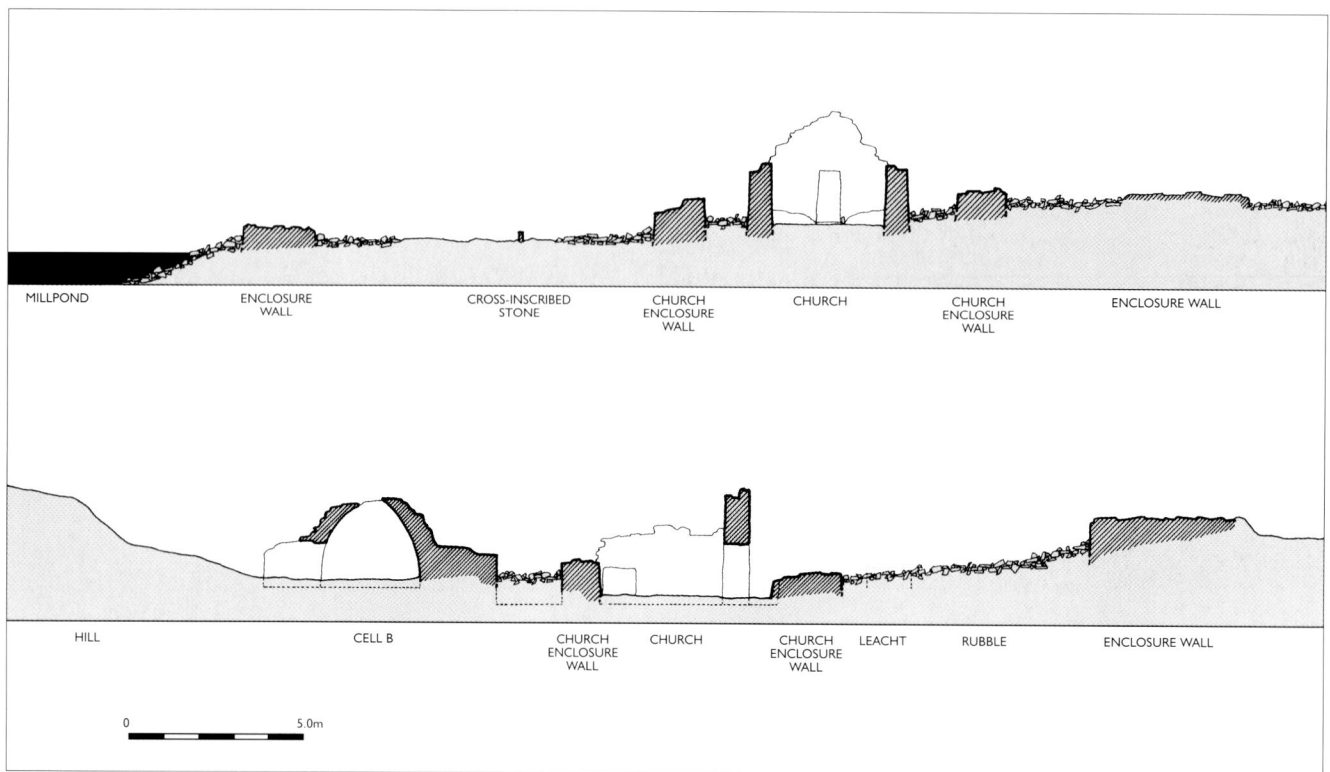

Figure 29b
Two site sections through the monastery on High Island, Co. Galway. The upper runs south-north and the lower runs east-west. Sections by G.D. Rourke.

in general as 'among the best preserved in Ireland, or perhaps in Europe', which might imply that the enclosure wall was in reasonably good condition. When O'Donovan visited High Island in 1839, he described an enclosure wall in sad condition:

> *The large round wall...is now very much dilapidated... It is nearly an oblong, measuring in length, from north to south, 38 yards [35m], and in breadth, from east to west, 23 yards [21.2m]. The wall is, in many places, level with the earth, especially on the north side, but a few feet of its height remain on the east, south, and west sides. Its thickness, as well as I could ascertain, from the most perfect part of its length, near the NW corner, was about 10 feet (more or less by a few inches) [3.07m]. (OSL, Galway, 1839, Vol.3: 80)*

Had the wall deteriorated between the time of Petrie's visit in 1820 and O'Donovan's in 1839? Even though there is only Petrie's vague description to compare to O'Donovan's more careful, detailed description, it seems likely that it had suffered in the nineteen years between the two visits. The wall now, almost entirely missing on much of the eastern and northern sides, is in a bad state of collapse. The quantity of missing stone on these two sides indicates not only natural deterioration but deliberate removal as well. Within the enclosure, not just natural deterioration and collapse of structures have caused the jumble of stone; clearly much of the wall and some

The Monastic Enclosure Wall

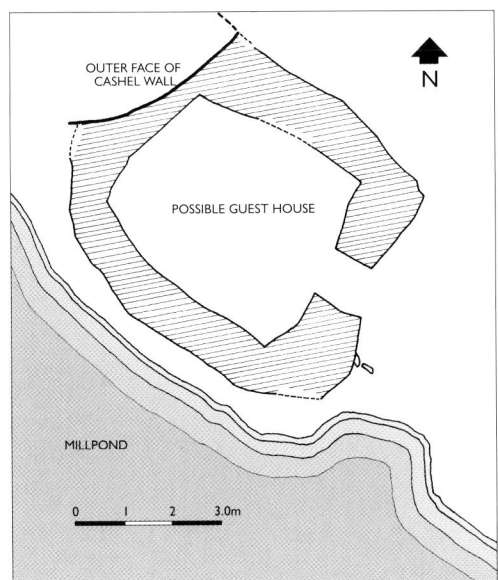

Figure 30

Plan of a possible guesthouse at the southeastern entrance to the monastery on High Island, Co Galway. Its dimensions are difficult to measure without excavation but the present width varies between 2.9 and 3.8m and the length between 3.7 and 4.3m. Its entrance was on the southeastern side of the structure. Plan G.D. Rourke.

structures have been deliberately dismantled. It seems likely that the copper miners who moved to the island in 1828 did some of this damage in their search for suitable building stones for house construction and field walls.

Southeastern Entrance of the Monastic Enclosure

The entrance at the southeastern corner of the monastery was clearly the main entrance to the monastery (Fig. 29a). Its size, 1.2m wide and 7m long, and the small cluster of structures, two buildings and a *leacht* on the exterior, all indicate that this was the most important entrance to the monastery. The easiest route across the island from the two landings on the eastern side of the island, moreover, leads to this entry, as does the flagstoned path, coming up from the southwestern landing (Figs. 12 and 22a).[63]

Structures Attached to the Main Entrance

Three structures outside the wall help to form a long entrance passage into the enclosure. On the right-hand (northeastern) side of the entrance there are remnants of two small structures, a small chamber with steps leading up to it and a small rectangular *leacht*-like structure built against it; on the left-hand (southwestern) side bordering the lake, there are the remains of a large rectangular structure (Fig. 29a; Fig. 30). Petrie (1845, 420–421) described two of these structures as 'circular buildings, probably intended for the use of pilgrims; but though what remains of them is of stone, they do not appear to have been roofed with that material'.

Three steps lead up to the small chamber from the entrance passage (Fig. 29a). Its interior walls, clearly evident on only two sides, now enclose an area of only three square metres. This chamber appears triangular in shape, but collapsed material on the eastern side of the chamber obscures the original walling; the original chamber may have been slightly bigger and more quadrangular in shape. Petrie, however, was inaccurate when he described this as a circular structure.

The function of this chamber must have been related to its location just outside the monastery's main entry.[64] Herity (1990, 73) logically speculates that it was used as a gatekeeper's lodge. Gatehouses to regulate traffic-flow into and out of the monastery were necessary at large monasteries, which often had more than one, such as the six gatehouses shown on Prior Wibert's plan, c.1160, of Christ Church, Canterbury (Fergusson 1990, 48). So important were they that a Cistercian document of c.1119, the *Summa cartae caritatis*, stipulates that a gatehouse along with '…an oratory, a refectory, a dormitory, a guest house…' needed to be constructed before the monks moved into a new monastery.[65] This is, nevertheless, an unusual structure for an Irish island monastery, with no known parallels, but unfortunately very little archaeological attention has been paid to these structures.

Built against this chamber is a small rectangular structure that is low, well built, and almost square (1.14m by 1.06m.) with white quartz stones lying on its surface; its height above the present ground surface is approximately 0.55m (Fig. 29a).[66] It is similar in scale and shape to the nearby *leacht* with the cross stone on the pond (Fig. 27). The fine masonry of this *leacht* is made up of small, horizontal stones tightly fitted together in a compact manner. It may have been built by pilgrims as a station, but the high quality of its stonework clearly shows the work of skilled masons, and thus it was more likely a monastic construction, perhaps used as a base for an entry cross.

Monastic Guesthouses

The remains of the third, a large structure, lie opposite on the other side of the entrance; it was built against, and hence later than the enclosure wall (Fig 30; Fig. 29a). Almost four metres of the enclosure wall were incorporated into the back wall of this building. The protection given the enclosure wall by the building explains the excellent and unusual preservation of this section of the external face of the enclosure wall, which still stands 0.7–0.75m above present ground level (Fig. 31). The original height of the enclosure wall is unknown but was certainly considerably higher than this remaining section.[67]

Although most of this structure has collapsed, the outline of the walls is sufficiently intact to define a roughly shaped sub-rectangular (trapezoidal) space, which Kinahan described as 'the site of a structure about fifteen feet square — it was probably a clochaun'. The thin walls and large size of the structure, however, suggest that the roof of this building was of timber construction, as Petrie suggested, rather than of corbelled stone.

The edge of the pond cuts neatly around this structure on two sides, which does not appear natural but rather tailored to fit the structure (Fig. 19). A logical explanation is that the land in this area was cut back in order to enlarge the pond, except for the space occupied by this already existing building. This is the second indication that the holding capacity of the pond was increased, again presumably done at the time of the construction of the horizontal watermill (see the field wall running into the lake, Fig. 22a, and chapter 10). It is probable that the entire eastern edge of the pond was expanded, from the point where the field wall runs into the water up to this structure outside the monastery, in order to create the millpond. The hills to the east constrained expansion eastwards, however, as further enlargement of the pond on this side would have eliminated the path to the monastery; equally, the presence of the monastic enclosure wall constrained expansion of the northern, upper side of the pond.

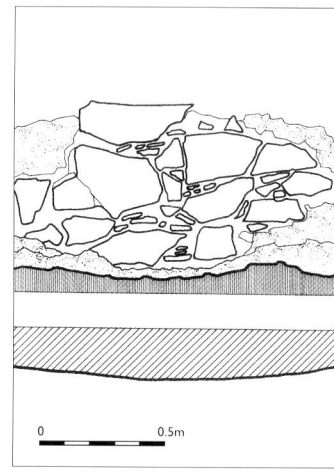

Figure 31
Plan and elevation of the monastic enclosure wall behind the rear wall of the possible guesthouse on High Island, Co. Galway. This is the best preserved section of the monastic enclosure wall. Plan and elevation by G.D. Rourke.

Because of its size and location just outside the main entrance to the monastery, this last-mentioned trapezoidal structure was probably used as a guesthouse. Inns were scarce in Ireland's medieval rural economy but everyone warmly welcomed guests. Indeed, the law tracts specifically state that a monastery refusing hospitality lost its legal status, its right to compensation in case of damage to its buildings (Kelly 1988, 140). All monasteries expected to provide hospitality for visitors, many of whom were other monks or priests, as a matter of Christian charity and also as a welcome opportunity for news and messages from other areas.[68] The *Canones Hibernenses* strongly cautioned ecclesiastics upon the particular importance of extending hospitality to other ecclesiastics:

> *Let the wise man observe what benefits Abraham and Lot received for their kindness in receiving Strangers; but let him likewise be aware what punishment Sodom brought upon itself by rejecting them and for the wicked deed.*[69]

Even island monasteries received a considerable number of visitors, as the constant references to guests in the seventh-century *Life of St Columba* vividly illustrates. Guests needed to be lodged conveniently close to the monastery, and yet somewhat removed, so that they would not interfere with the daily life of the monks. Although the *hospitium* or *tech n-oíged* was generally a separate building within the monastic enclosure in large monasteries, few small monasteries had enough room inside the enclosure for a separate guesthouse. The *Vitae Sanctorum Hiberniae* mentions guesthouses outside the enclosure at the monastery of Luchen and Odran (Plummer 1910, 209), and this was presumably a common arrangement in many monasteries.

Archaeological evidence for guesthouses can only be inferred from their position relative to the other monastic structures; in material remains they are identical to those of other dwellings. In 1958 Michael O'Kelly excavated a structure similar to the one at High Island on Church Island, County Kerry, with the same general dimensions (of 5.5m by 3.8m) and shape as the one on High Island (Fig. 32).

This house, also located on the outside of the monastic enclosure wall, had a flagstone path leading from the door of the guesthouse through a special entry into the monastic enclosure, and then around the interior of the monastery close to the enclosure wall, terminating at the western door of the church. The spatial layout clearly demonstrates the importance of respecting the monks' privacy, even from honoured guests.[70]

Round and Rectangular Dwellings in Early Medieval Ireland

Archaeological and literary evidence both indicate that Irish houses were round in the beginning of the early medieval period, unlike those of most of its neighbours in

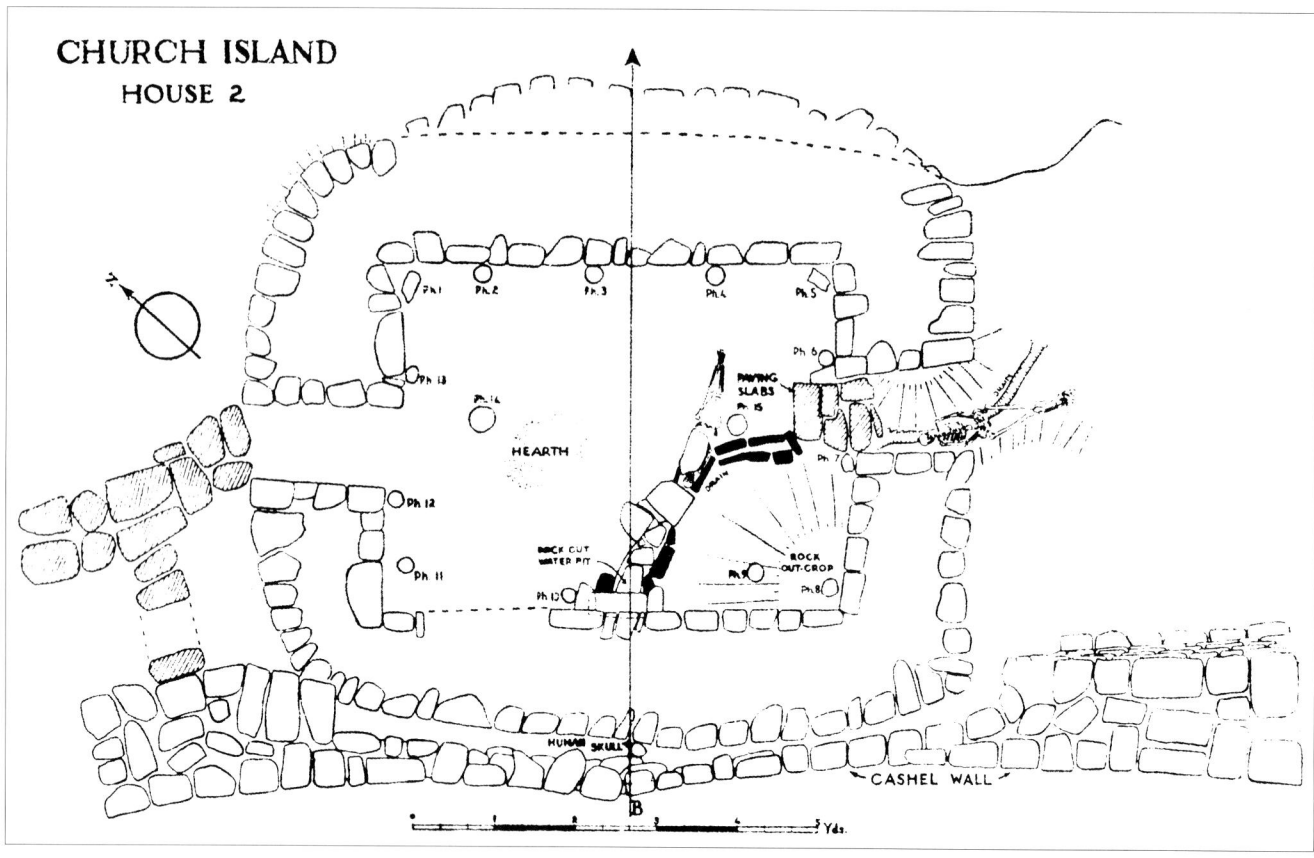

Figure 32

Plan of the possible guesthouse on Church Island, Co. Kerry, showing the same rounded external corners and rectangular interior plan as the one on High Island, Co. Galway (O'Kelly 1958, 72, Fig. 4). Courtesy the Royal Irish Academy.

Britain, Scandinavia and the Continent. Oratories and churches, however, were always quadrangular, evidently an architectural element brought in by the first Christian missionaries from Romanised Britain and the Continent.[71] At some point during this period, most vernacular houses also shifted from round to rectangular structures. The question of the time when this shift took place and why it happened continues to concern archaeologists.

The shape of the guesthouses on High Island and Church island, rectangular on the interior (on plan) and on the exterior as well, except that most of the exterior corners are rounded off, are, therefore, particularly interesting, as this shape may prove to be one with chronological implications, an in-between stage in the shift from round to rectangular structures. For centuries after the arrival of Christianity in Ireland in the fifth century, quadrangular structures are associated with churches. Rectangular structures on ecclesiastical sites, other than churches, are generally late buildings, such as the 'Fire House' at Inishmurray (Fig. 136).[72]

The introduction of a new religion along with an associated new structure into Irish society would have certainly drawn the attention of the Irish to the rectangularity of it and 'glamorised' it; indeed, it is possible that quadrangular structures became symbolic of the sacred. The spiritual aura attached to church architecture may have

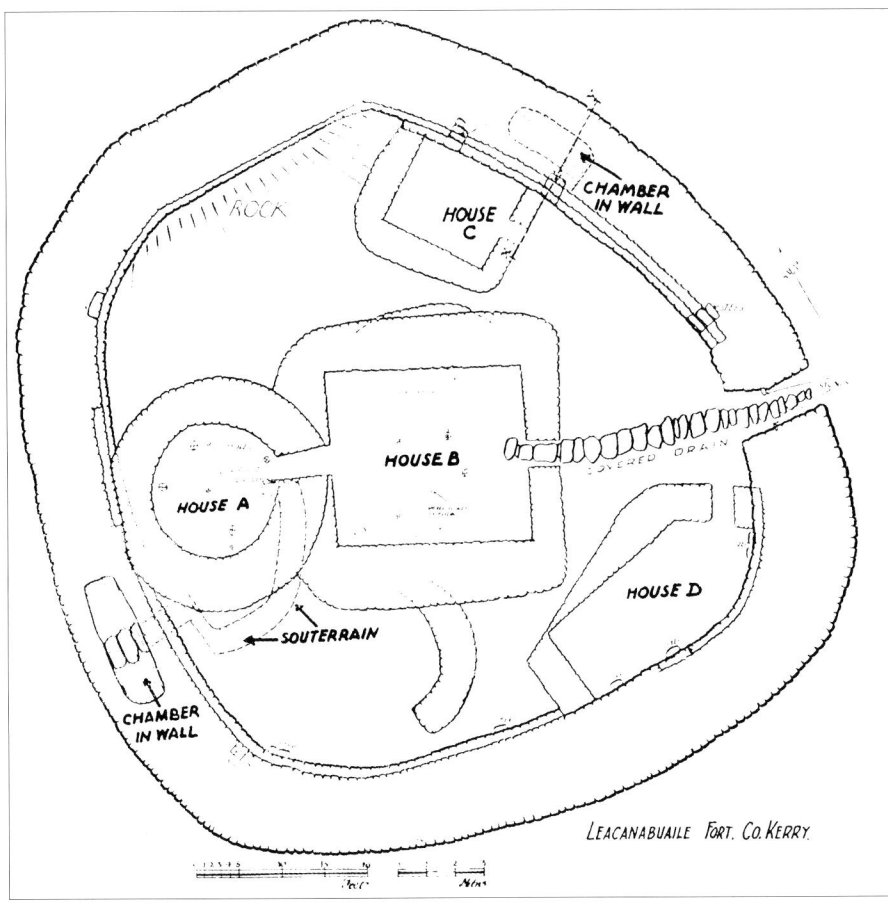

Figure 33

Plan of Leacanabuaile, Co. Kerry. Excavation in 1941 showed that the round house preceded the quadrangular, but gave no indication of the date of construction for either (after Ó Ríordáin and Foy 1941, 84). Courtesy Cork Historical and Archaeological Society Journal.

made the Church particularly reluctant to adopt them for mundane activities at first. Over the next few centuries, in any case, the Irish became thoroughly familiar with rectangular structures and with their construction techniques.

When did Irish vernacular houses become rectangular and what caused them to change? Was the change a purely local development based on centuries of church construction, or was it based on external influences such as the founding of the Viking trade-towns of Dublin, Wicklow and Cork?[73] No one has yet shown plausible specific causation for their adoption and they may eventually prove to be the result of a number of rather amorphous factors, such as increased familiarity and perception of them as desirable. No particular economic, technological or climatic advantage underlies either the Viking use of rectangular or the Irish use of round dwellings in this period, and the change from one to the other may have been a matter of slowly adopting cultural customs to those most commonly used elsewhere. Increased excavation and the advent of radiocarbon dating, however, have enabled archaeologists to make some progress in answering questions regarding the date of their adoption. C.J. Lynn has been able to demonstrate that, at least in eastern Ulster, there was a change from round to rectangular houses sometime between the eighth and ninth centuries, a transition particularly well documented at Rathmullan (Lynn 1983). Another similar structure comes from the marshland habitation site near Larne in County Antrim, where the second phase of construction was a rectangular structure with rounded external corners, which has an uncalibrated radiocarbon date of AD 730 plus or minus 45 (Waterman 1971, 65–76).[74]

In western Ireland as well there was a transition from circular to rectangular houses, a transition well demonstrated in two prestigious secular sites by Ó Ríordáin at Leacanabuaile, County Kerry (Fig. 33) and by O'Flaherty at Loher, County Kerry. On both sites the rectangular structures were built later than the round ones, but the dating of this changeover has not been as well substantiated in Kerry as on the Ulster sites. Occupation of Leacanabuaile was dated only generally to the ninth and tenth centuries because its finds resembled those found on other better-dated sites. Nor was O'Kelly's later excavation able to clarify the matter, although, he, too, was able to determine that the rectangular house on Church Island was built later than the church and the round dwelling cell. He was unable to establish a precise date for any individual structure, although he suggested a date between 650 and 750 for the founding of the site.

Current ongoing excavations on Bray Head, out on the western end of Valencia Island, County Kerry, by Hayden and Walsh will be the first to establish chronological guidelines for this part of Munster. Here, a small group of families lived for centuries raising cereal crops on the broad south-facing slope that runs down to the sea. Evidence of their homes and associated domestic structures mingles with traces of earlier ones, offering invaluable evidence for changing customs in vernacular architecture over time. Their first dates for some of the houses where rectangular buildings interrupt earlier round ones fit well within Lynn's recent estimates of a general time-range for this structural shift in the country.[75] Lynn believes he can generally propose that 'round houses were normal at the beginning of the period (up to about AD 800) and rectangular houses were normal at the end (after about AD 1000) (Lynn 1994, 85). While we suspect that future evidence will show that there was considerable variation from region to region in the time of adoption of rectangular structures, this estimate is broad enough to use as a working range until future excavations can refine it. On this basis the rectangular structure outside the southeastern entrance on High Island was not likely to have been an early structure from the sixth or seventh centuries but might possibly have been built sometime in the ninth century.

We believe that the holding capacity of the millpond was expanded when the watermill was constructed by cutting back the borders of the millpond. The straight lines of the pond's edge on the southern border of the monastery and around the possible guesthouse on the northeastern corner of the pond are not natural pond borders, which would be more irregular and curved. Instead, these edges are an indication that the pond itself was expanded, and further, that the builders respected the already existing structures of the monastic enclosure wall and the guesthouse. If this is correct, then the watermill was built later than the guesthouse.

There is evidence now establishing the construction of horizontal mills throughout the entire medieval period, rather than a more tightly bound period of time, particularly on the western seaboard (Rynne 1998a, 76–77 and 1998b, 90–91). It is, consequently, impossible to establish a sure date for the construction of the High Island mill. However Michael Baillie, Ireland's leading dendrochronologist, notes that 56 per cent of the mills dated by tree rings were built with timbers cut between AD 770 and AD 850 (Baillie 1995, 126). The end of the eighth century and the first half of the ninth was, therefore, a particularly active period for mill building. Since we believe that the earlier guesthouse was unlikely to have been built before the ninth century, the innovative High Island mill may have been built a little later, possibly sometime between the mid-ninth and the mid-tenth century, a suspicion that further work on the mill promises to resolve.

Monastic Enclosure Wall on the South

The southern wall of the monastic enclosure runs along the edge of the lake (Figs.19 and 29a). A central section of the southern wall, approximately 10m long, shows evidence of repair or rebuilding. This section of the wall is thinner (1.3m) than the wall on either side (2.5m), which shows in a set-back on the pond side; possibly the wall fell out because of erosion and then was reconstructed set back from the edge of the pond, or perhaps a narrower wall was considered adequate at a later date. The straight-edged border of land on the southern side of the monastic enclosure appears as artificial as the border around the 'guesthouse'; it is probable that here, too, the boundaries of the pond were expanded to the edge of the enclosure wall, an already existing structure. If so, the monastic enclosure wall originally stood slightly further away from the pond.

The land bordering the millpond on the east is the only side of the pond that becomes waterlogged during wet periods; here, water constantly runs down the hills. The monks' concern about this side collapsing into the pond is evidenced by the stone revetments placed underwater here, and the flagstoned path covering this wet area. Water run-off through the alternate millrace was adequate enough to ensure that the pond's other borders, which are surrounded by relatively level land, were not in danger of being seriously undermined or inundated by water, but remained firm, as they still are today.

The Southwestern Entrance and the Western Wall

The second entrance into the monastery is on the southwestern corner of the enclosure wall, one that must be approached from the western side of the pond (Fig. 29a). The entry passage is both narrower (0.6m wide on the interior) and shorter (2.1m long) than that of the southeastern entrance. The entry, still clearly visible on its interior southern jamb, is composed of large blocks of stone, as is much of the fallen debris in the entrance.[76] There is some indication that this secondary entrance may splay outward; however, the amount of collapsed material prevents accurate recording.[77] The substantial pond on the south would have blocked convenient access to the mill and the terrain to the west from the main, southeastern, entry to the monastery once the horizontal watermill was in use; a second entry on the southwestern side may have been added at this time as a practical solution to this problem.

The collapsed outline of the enclosure wall is evident on the western side, but very few wall faces are now intact above present ground level. There are still, nevertheless, two wall chambers in this length of walling (Fig. 29a).

The Large Wall chamber

The large wall chamber, some four metres north of the southwestern entrance, is still clearly evident (Fig. 34). Petrie mentioned it only briefly, calling it 'a covered gallery or passage, twenty-four feet [7.38m] long, four feet [1.23m] wide, and four feet six inches [1.38m] high' (Petrie 1845, 420). In 1869 Kinahan studied it in more detail, made a cross-section of it (Fig. 35) and arrived at surprisingly different measurements from Petrie:

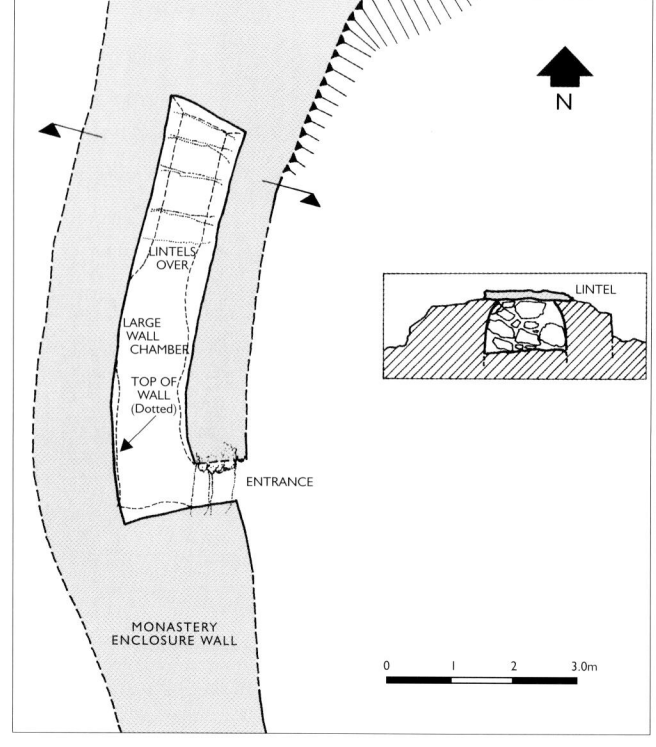

It is about thirty-two feet [9.8m] long, by four feet [1.2m] wide at the bottom, and coving into three feet [0.9m] wide at the top of the walls; the roof being formed of long, narrow, thick flags. It was entered from the church enclosure by a doorway at its south end, about three feet [0.9m] high, and two and a half wide [0.77m]. This, apparently, was a chamber for the doorkeeper; however, it is locally called 'The prison'. It is similar in construction to the wall chambers in the stoneforts [cahers and doons] in other parts of Ireland.[78]

Since both ends of the chamber are still intact it is hard to understand how Kinahan's figure was so exaggerated. Macalister noticed the discrepancy between Petrie's figures and those of Kinahan and looked for this chamber. Although a member of his party photographed the chamber (Fig. 36), Macalister believed he could not find the large wall chamber and that the photograph depicts another, smaller, wall chamber described by Kinahan. Macalister's confusion was due to his acceptance of Kinahan's dimension of 9.8m, whereas the actual length, 6.3m [20.47 feet], is close to Petrie's figure.

The entrance to the wall chamber at the southern end is narrow, only 0.65–0.67m wide. In 1987, when our original survey of the monastic enclosure was completed, there were two lintels over

Figure 34

Plan and section through the large wall chamber in the enclosure wall of the monastery on High Island, Co. Galway. The walls markedly cove at the top. At unexcavated ground level the chamber was 1.3m wide, whereas at lintel level it is only 0.8m. The height of the chamber above present ground level is 0.74 to 0.8m. Plan and section by G.D. Rourke.

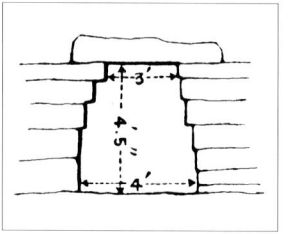

Figure 35

Cross-section made by George Kinahan in 1869 of the large wall chamber in the enclosure wall of the monastery on High Island, Co. Galway (1869, Plate XLVI). Courtesy Royal Irish Academy.

the entrance; now, however, only one lintel remains. The entrance lintels are at a lower level than those of the chamber, which forced an entrant to crawl in but gave more head room once inside. The chamber itself, still clearly defined with most of its walls intact, has only four of the original heavy lintels left, all at the northern end of the chamber, whereas in 1895 Macalister (1896, 204) noted that there were still six or seven roof lintels. This wall chamber is among the most impressive in western Ireland in its length of 6.5m and in its use of massive stones, many over 1m long, to form the chamber walls; only the wall chamber at Illauntannig, Co. Kerry, surpasses it in length. Only substantial enclosure walls may contain wall chambers, but even so they are not commonly found there. The reasons for their presence or absence remain mysterious, as does their function, although they are probably related to storage. In 1997 the clearance of a trench running from the large chamber to the church enclosure wall revealed very little stone

Figure 36a

Photo taken in 1895, during the visit of the Royal Society of Antiquaries, of the large wall chamber in the enclosure wall of the monastery on High Island, Co. Galway. Macalister mistakenly labelled it 'Entrance to Souterrain'. He also measured only the section of the wall chamber that ran back from the 'entrance'; consequently, he thought it was only 9 feet long (2.7m) (Macalister 1896, 203). Courtesy Royal Society of Antiquaries of Ireland.

collapse from the enclosure wall down into the monastic grounds, compared to areas adjoining the trench. Had the stones above the large wall chamber already been taken down and used by the monks for other structures?

Wall faces, both interior and exterior, are impossible to locate on the collapsed section of the wall north of the large chamber without excavation; consequently, we can only roughly estimate the wall thickness here at approximately 3.2m. O'Donovan's remarks indicate a dimension like this in 1839 when the northwestern section of wall was in better condition:

> *Its thickness, as well as I could ascertain from the most perfect part of it near the NW corner, was about 10 feet (more or less by a few inches) [3.07m].*[79]

There is a 1.7m length of walling on the interior between the two wall chambers, which is set back from where the internal face of the enclosure wall ought to be (Fig. 29a). This may indicate that the enclosure wall itself was stepped, or it may be the remains of a structure built into the wall.

The Small Wall Chamber

The inner face of the enclosure wall is visible at the location of the small wall chamber (Fig. 29a), although the external face is conjectural. The second wall chamber, in more ruinous condition than the first, is almost coffin-shaped, with an opening 0.6m, that widens to 0.95m, then narrows back to 0.65m wide in the back. The chamber runs into the wall for 2.2m.

In 1820 Petrie had described seeing several structures in this general area, each approximately the same size as the small wall chamber:

> *On the other side of the chapel are a number of smaller cells, which were only large enough to contain each a single person. They are but six feet [1.85m] long, three feet [0.9m] wide, and four feet [1.23m] high, and most of them are now covered with rubbish. (Petrie 1845, 420)*

And Kinahan in 1869 saw a building no one else saw, which he placed just west of the Abbot's Cell and described as:

> *A detached ruin about nine feet square apparently an* Oileac *(or stone building) built with flat stones except the doorway, which was formed of large flags pitched on end. This structure is now so much dilapidated that nothing more can be learned about it. (Kinahan 1869, 553)*

Figure 36b
Photo of the large wall chamber in 1980, showing its condition shortly after one of the remaining lintels had been dislodged. Photo Walter Horn.

North of the wall chamber for five metres, we were unable to find evidence of any wall face or structures. It is important to note that Petrie does not say that the small cells he saw were built into the wall. In 1839, however, O'Donovan remarked briefly that 'north and by west of the church in the wall there was another *cloghan* [cell], but level with the ground'. Did O'Donovan see another structure in this now-ruined section of wall, or was he talking about the small wall chamber? Were Petrie and O'Donovan talking about the same structure(s)?[80] There is one odd feature in this section of walling, an enormous stone sitting in a circular depression, which is now impossible to identify as anything specific.

It is unlikely that O'Donovan was describing the small wall chamber because thirty years later, in 1869, Kinahan measured a single wall chamber in this location (see Fig. 8) that was still relatively intact, and certainly not level to the ground:

> *A rectangular chamber, nine feet [2.76m] long by four and a half feet [1.38m] wide. It is in, and extends nearly across, the thickness of the cashel wall. It appears to have been about four feet [1.23m] high, and was covered by large flags. It was entered from the cashel by a doorway two and a half feet [.77m] high by three feet [0.9m] wide. (Kinahan 1869, 553)*

There certainly must have been other dwelling cells within the monastic enclosure; the remaining two small cells would hardly have housed enough monks to build and maintain the monastic structures that remain. Colgan, moreover, listed the names of ten other men apparently associated with Gormgal in the early eleventh century. The extensive rubble debris in this northwestern section may easily conceal other structures, but the question of what they were — Petrie's small cells and/or O'Donovan's *clochán* in the wall or Kinahan's *Oileac* — must remain a puzzle, one that future excavation may solve.

In the northwestern corner of the enclosure wall is another enigmatic feature whose remains are only visible at ground level (Fig. 29a). There is, nevertheless, some sort of break in the wall that may be the remains of another entrance into the enclosure, although there are no large facing stones here as at the other two entrances. The configuration of the opening is also somewhat distorted, possibly because of collapsed stone. At its widest point in the centre, 0.7 metres, a vertically set stone projects slightly above ground level. Assuming some collapse here, the thickness of the enclosure wall in this area was in the region of 3.2m.[81] Thus the monastic enclosure wall in its original condition varied between 2.5m and 3.2m.

Cell A or the Abbot's Cell

About 8m further east along the north wall is a cell, now roofless but originally corbelled (resembling an arch but composed of successive courses of masonry projecting inwards until they meet at the top) and built into the enclosure wall, which we have labelled Cell A (Fig. 29a; Fig. 81). While the enclosure wall is difficult to locate precisely here, it is nevertheless apparent that Cell A was set well into the enclosure wall, as the face of the interior rear wall of the cell is approximately 2m from the exterior enclosure wall face. Consequently, the enclosure wall in this area was dismantled in order to clear space for this cell (see ch. 7 for detailed discussion of this cell). Evidently the monks themselves were responsible for some of the destruction of the enclosure wall. A similar situation was found at Reask, Co. Kerry (Fig. 78), where the archaeologist Thomas Fanning (1981, 90–92; 153) noted that several of the cells, which he was able to date generally between the eighth to eleventh centuries, were also built against or into the enclosure wall, or in the case of conjoined structures A and B, directly on top of a dismantled enclosure wall with a new flimsier section of enclosure wall built around them.

Beyond Cell A the wall disappears altogether; there are no wall faces, only scattered stones along the northeastern and eastern sides until shortly before the main entrance to the monastic enclosure. In 1839, however, O'Donovan (1839, 83) mentioned an entrance to the monastery in the northeastern corner. He commented on three entrances to the monastery, one on the western side, 22 inches [0.56m] wide, one on the southeastern side, 2 feet 8 inches [0.82m] wide, and a third entrance

> near the northeast corner. It is 6.0 feet [1.85] wide on the outside and 4ft.3in. [1.3m] on the inside. Immediately to the south of this passage there was another cloghan which appears from its foundations to have been 15ft. 0in.[1.61m] long and 12 ft. 0 in. [3.69m] broad.

Twenty-two inches (0.56m) is convincing for the southwestern entrance; 0.82m is too small for the southeastern entrance (1.2m). However, this entrance could hardly have been missed. Where, then, was the extremely wide northeastern entrance O'Donovan measured? It is probable that O'Donovan's notes were erroneous and that he consequently mistook the structure in the northern inlet for a third entrance into the monastic enclosure. So much of the monastic enclosure is missing on the northern and eastern sides that he may have confused the field wall running up to this northern inlet structure with the outer monastic wall.

Herity (1990, 74) also noted a northeastern entrance into the monastery, '2.1m long and much ruined'. Although there may well have been another entrance to the monastery here, we could find no trace of the facing stones common to entrances. In this area there is simply a blank space into which stones have collapsed; however, we believe the monks tampered with the northern section of the wall in order to build Cell A and it is possible they also constructed a simple entry here.

The Eastern Side of the Monastic Enclosure Wall

Along the eastern side of the enclosure the hill had been cut back in order to place the stone enclosure wall directly against its flanks. Most of the enclosure wall has been removed along the escarpment and now there is only a bank of stone debris until the wall resumes for a length of 3m before the main entrance.

Structures North of the Monastery

There are traces of structures to the north and northeast of the monastic enclosure that, if used by the monks, would have justified another exit on this side of the enclosure wall. It would have provided both an alternate entrance into the monastery to monks coming over the island from the east, almost a backdoor, as well as quick access to the structures from the monastery itself. Because of the immediate relationship to them of a possible exit here, they will be described briefly.

The Monastic Enclosure Wall

On his map Kinahan drew a long wall that separates the monastic valley from the rest of the island running from the southern inlet — near the southwestern landing — to the larger of the two ponds (Fig. 9). Kinahan shows the wall interrupted by the pond but resuming again just outside the southeastern entry to the monastic enclosure and swinging around the monastery to the east as it continues to the inlet in the northern end of the valley.[82] In fact, no such wall could run around the monastic enclosure on the east side; moreover, it would be unnecessary because the monastic enclosure wall itself served, like the millpond, as sufficient barrier. Instead, the line of a wall, much damaged and interrupted now, picks up again at the northeastern corner of the enclosure wall (Fig. 22a) and runs northwest toward the inlet.

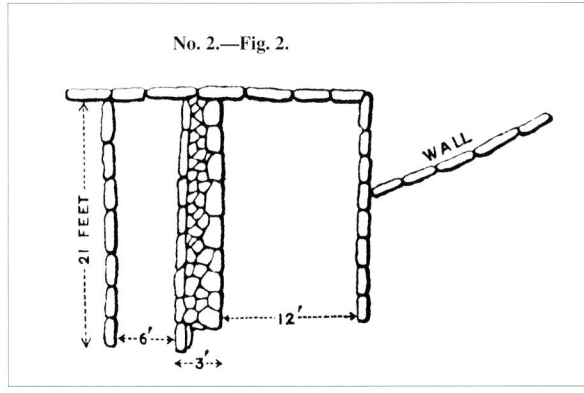

Figure 37a

Sketch made in 1869 by G.F. Kinahan of the structures in the northern inlet on High Island, Co. Galway. Nothing this definite exists today (Kinahan 1869, Plate XLVI, Fig. 2). Courtesy Royal Irish Academy.

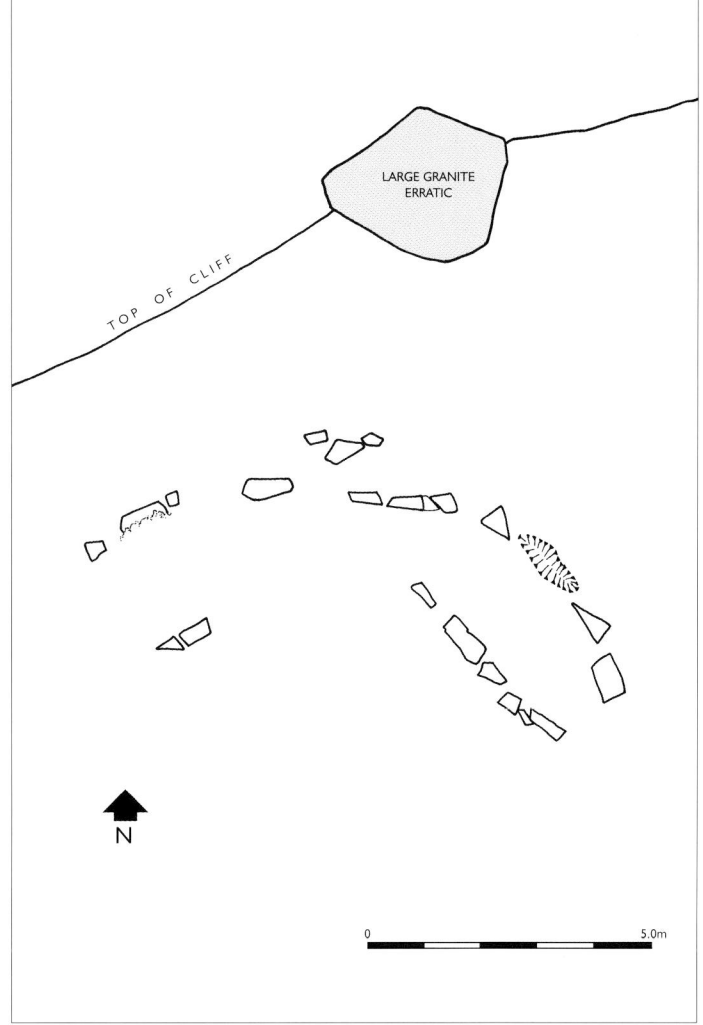

Figure 37b

Plan of the structure(s) north of the monastery on High Island, Co. Galway, as it exists today, showing its location almost at the northern cliff edge, close to a large boulder. Excavation might help explain the original nature and function of these stones, which at present form no recognisable pattern but are certainly not random. Plan G.D. Rourke.

Macalister was the first of the nineteenth-century antiquaries to disentangle this wall from the monastic enclosure wall and to describe it reasonably accurately:

The...wall runs in a curved course from an inlet in the precipitous flank of the island on the northern side to a similar inlet in the southern. It is interrupted by the larger lake in its way. There is a remarkable structure at either end: that at the northern end...was a two-chambered building... (1896, 204)

The two-chambered structure Macalister mentioned had also been described earlier and drawn by Kinahan in 1869. Kinahan's measurements appear correct, but his plan was more compactly organised than the present remains are (Fig. 12, no. 15; Figs. 37a and 37b). Kinahan described this structure in detail:

The northern one was twenty-one feet [6.4m] long by six feet [1.83m] wide, and appears to have been a typical fosleac *[dwelling built of flags], as the flags used in the construction of its walls were pitched...not built, apparently; originally it was also covered with flags. The south chamber seems to have been about two feet shorter than the other, but it was twelve feet wide. Its south and east walls were also made with pitched flags; but the north wall, which was three feet thick at the base, including the thickness of the flags forming the south side of the north chamber, was built, the stones being laid flat. Running oblique from the south wall of this structure extends the outer enclosing wall; but of it all that now remains in position is a line of upright flags (1869, 552).*

Kinahan believed there was an entrance through the wall into the area to the north of this structure between it and the large granite boulder on the edge of the cliff.[83] Herity (1990, 80) also believes there is the remains of 'a 8m long corridor opening to the southeast' some 1.0m to 1.5m wide in this area. Herity speculates that: 'This may be an entrance to control access to this end of the island'.

We do not know exactly what this structure(s) was, but an entrance here seems unlikely. In some areas the double row of orthostats is reminiscent of the sod structures at Illaunloughan, Co. Kerry, where such vertically set stones kept the sod walls from slipping, except that the distance between the two lines of orthostats is greater here. In their present condition, however, the structure or structures and their function remain enigmatic.

Barely visible in the ground today are indications that the wall may not have ended at Kinahan's two-chambered structure, but curved back to the monastery, forming a triangular enclosure adjacent to the monastery (Fig. 38). Such an enclosure might have been used as an animal corral or as a kitchen garden; however, there is so little left that any such use had probably ended long before the end of the monastery.[84]

The Monastic Enclosure Wall

Figure 38

Aerial photo from the northeast of the structures north of the monastery on High Island, Co. Galway, showing the spatial relationship between the monastery and these structures. The large field wall recommences at the monastic enclosure and curves north to end at the enigmatic structure(s) near the cliff edge. Faint traces of a wall can be barely detected running back to the monastery on the west. Photo Con Brogan. Courtesy Dúchas The Heritage Service.

Arcing around to the east some 30m are the remains of a very large subcircular structure that must have enclosed an area of roughly 50sq.m (Fig. 12, no. 14; Fig. 39a).

O'Donovan was the first to mention this structure and he noted that in 1839 'local people called [it] the Pound, from an idea that it was used as such by the saints of the Island' (OS Letters, Galway, 67). Kinahan (1869, 552) was the only other nineteenth-century antiquary to describe this structure, which he believed was a beehive cell. He also noted that there was a two-foot-wide [0.61m] doorway opening on the southwest (see Fig. 39b).

There is no sign of an entrance now; a large gap on the northeastern side probably marks the location of the entrance. The diameter, moreover, was too large for

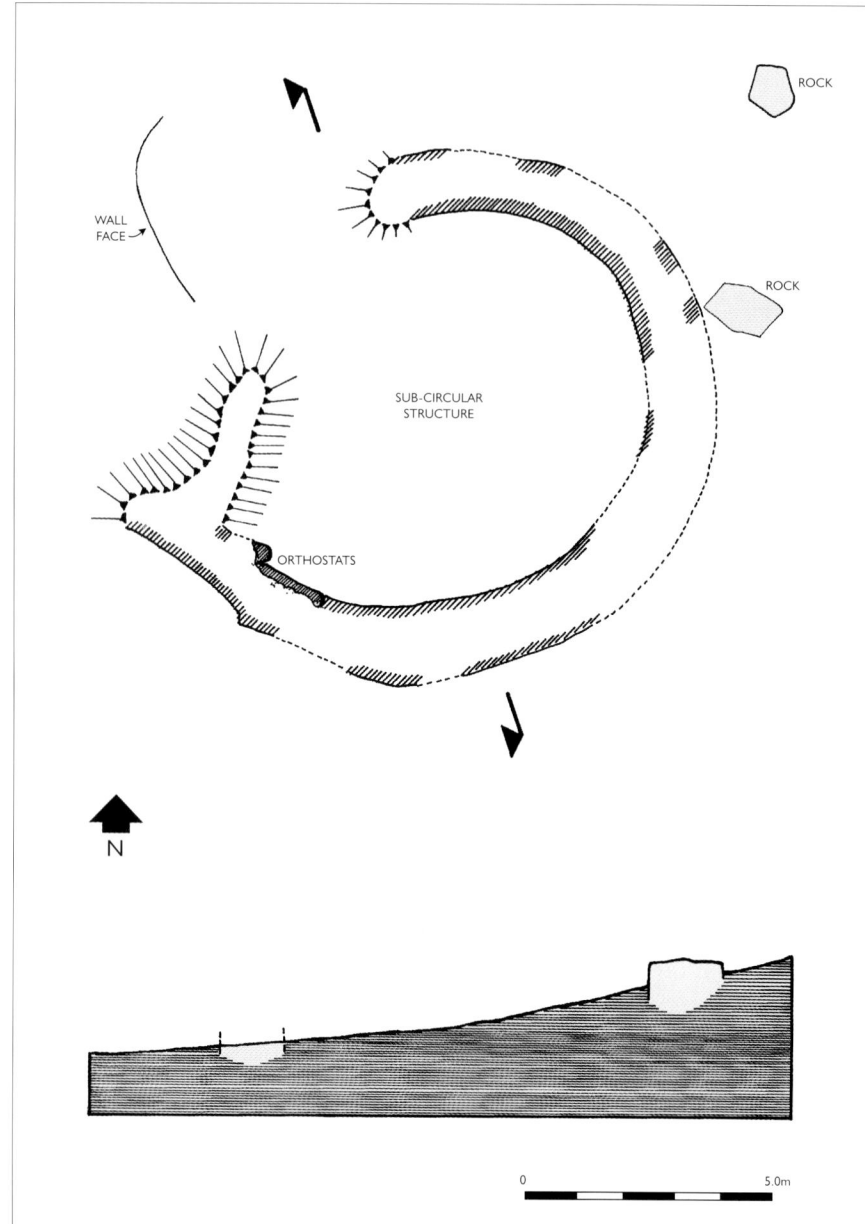

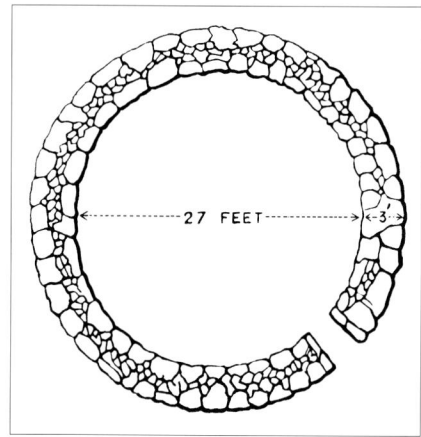

Figure 39a

Plan and cross-section of the large subcircular structure, formerly called 'the pound', located northeast of the monastery on High Island, Co. Galway. Large granite boulders form some of the base stones in this structure. If the original structure was ovoid, its dimensions may have been 7.5m by 9m. Plan and section by G.D. Rourke.

Figure 39b

Plan made by G.F. Kinahan in 1869 of the 'pound' on High Island, Co. Galway. Kinahan tidied up his structures, making them more symmetrical and more ordered than they could possibly ever have been (Kinahan 1869, Plate XLVI, Fig.1). Courtesy Royal Irish Academy.

a corbelled stone cell, although it might have been timber-roofed.[85] The original function of this structure is uncertain, but it was probably built as a habitation structure. The walls (1.15m to 1.5m) are very wide, indeed they are wider than most field walls; such substantial walls suggest a roof structure.

This ovoid structure is only 55m from the monastic enclosure. If there were a northeast entrance into the monastic enclosure, monks would have found it easier to get to this area; otherwise they would have had to walk around from one of the southern entrances. This large structure would have also been a convenient size and location for monastic tenants.

Notes

60. See Stout 1997 for an extensive treatment of the ringfort's defensive nature. For a more practical, but not incompatible, argument about the ringfort as a settlement type appearing in Early Christian times as a protection from cattle-raiding in a period of agricultural advance, leading to a major increase in population and prosperity and, eventually, increased stress and intensive cattle-raiding, see McCormick 1995, 33–37.

61. O'Keeffe 1904, 220; see also O'Corráin 1981, 327–341, on status of clergy and organisation of the early Irish Church.

62. For more on enclosures, see Doherty 1984, 45–49, and Bitel [1990] 1993, Ch. 2.

63. Petrie (1845, 420) described this entry, the only one he apparently saw, as 21 feet long and 3 feet wide, which is substantially correct if counting the full length of the longest structure outside the entry (1.2m wide and 7m long). O'Donovan and Kinahan both estimated only its width in close agreement with Petrie.

64. A small piece of iron slag was found during survey work in 1987.

65. From Bouton and Van Damme 1974, 121, as cited in Peter Fergusson 1990, 51.

66. Its present height above the turf is only 0.43m so it must be at least 0.5m in height.

67. Herity (1990, 73) believes the wall was originally 1.6m high, although we are not sure why.

68. Hospitality was not owed to everyone and was also measured according to rank. On the law tracts, see Kelly 1988, 139–140. In general, see Adomnán, *Life of St Columba*, ed. Anderson and Anderson 1964, 270–272, 296–298; Simm 1978, 67–100; Bitel 1990, 196–202.

69. 'Abraham et Loth de sua benignitate in acceptione hospitum sapiens amiaduertat quae bona acceperunt; Sodoma vero quam penan meruerat de iectione eorum et opere nefando similiter sciat.' *The Irish Penitentials,* ed. Bieler [1963] 1975, 173.

70. At Church Island, however, O'Kelly was able to demonstrate that the enclosure wall was built later than the rectangular house (O'Kelly 1958, 77).

71. See Horn 1973, 23–30 and Lynn 1978a. For a contrary interpretation of some of the literary evidence on round houses, see Murray 1979. The quadrangular may have been a sacred form, perhaps related to the shape of the codex, itself a newly introduced object (Horn, personal communication, 1980), or see Thomas 1981a for an alternative explanation of the rectangle as a religious shape. For an anthropological view of socio-cultural factors underlying architectural forms, see Rappaport 1969 and McGuire and Schiffer 1983, 277–303.

72. Hamlin 1985, 288 points out that excavation evidence of ecclesiastical sites has revealed few rectilinear structures, except for the 'school house' at Nendrum, Co. Down.

[73] For an excellent discussion of this, see Wallace 1992, 1: chapter 6, and Lynn 1994, 81–94.

[74] Lynn 1978a. Waterman also noted similar houses in an undated rath at Ballymacash in County Antrim, and a cashel, the White Fort at Drumaroad in Couny Down. The latter has a date of AD 1050 plus or minus 120 (Waterman 1956, 73–86; Radiocarbon 3 (1961), 36). We agree, however, with Wallace 1992, 1:71 that the changeover may not have been complete and that a few round dwellings continued to be built even in seventeenth-century Ulster (see also Robinson 1979, 3). Fanning's (1981, 94–96) excavation of Reask turned up a structure, E, that is quite similar to that at High Island, but was, unfortunately, unable to date it.

[75] See Hayden 1997; O'Kelly 1958, 73–76; O'Flaherty 1986, 26–27; Ó Ríordáin and Foy 1941, 85–99. Barry's excavation of Dunbeg, County Kerry also dated the first period of occupation of the drystone structure, which was square on the inside and round on the outside, to the tenth/eleventh centuries. UB 2217 990±100. This structure, 7.5m in diameter, was probably not corbelled. Barry 1981, 314.

[76] The stones here vary in size from 0.25m by 0.17m to 0.70 m by 0.32m, with the average around 0.50 by 0.39m. This is considerably bigger than those of the 'guesthouse', which tend to be at largest 0.54 by 0.34m and are considerably smaller on the interior base.

[77] O'Donovan's (1839, 83) dimension for the width of the entrance was 22 inches (0.56m). Kinahan (1869, 554) measured it at two and a half feet wide (0.769m). Herity (1990, 74) arrived at 0.9m. at the outer end, tapering down to 0.70m at the inner end.

[78] Kinahan 1869, 553–554. O'Donovan also briefly mentioned this chamber; his measurements are closer to those of Petrie.

[79] O'Donovan 1839, 80. Herity 1990, 74 states that 'north of there [the large wall chamber] the wall is apparently at its widest extent, 5.4 m wide'.

[80] But cf. Herity, who believes he may have found O'Donovan's *clochán* a short distance north of the small chamber: 'At this point the wall curves east, its north face enclosing a horseshoe-shaped space marked on the north-west by three large stones deeply embedded, its axis about 3.5m north-east to south-west, the floor area covered with spalled stone. It seems that there was a building here which may have opened on the east into the space within the enclosure' (Herity 1990, 74). This space is marked as conjectural on Herity's plan (fig. 32) and we were unable to find any evidence of a structure here.

[81] cf. Herity (1990, 74) who considers this a definite entrance and estimates the maximum length of the entrance passage at 3.9m and its outer width 0.7m and the inner 1.1m.

[82] O'Donovan does not mention this wall but he does confuse it with the monastic enclosure wall, as we have already mentioned.

83 Herity (1990, 80) describes this structure as 'a jumble of stones covering an area 9m by 4m'.

84 However, see Herity's (1990, 80) opinion: 'There was not enough soil for a garden and it has more the appearance of an open private area, possibly for recreation'.

85 Near the northwestern section there are five large blocks of stone forming a curve, which appears to lead towards the enclosure. This is Herity's Enclosure 1, 'Pound' (Herity 1990, 82).

Chapter Five

The Church in the Monastery

An older calm,
The kiss of rock and grass,
Pink thrift and white sea-campion,
Flowers in the dead place.

Richard Murphy, *High Island.*

The most important building in an ecclesiastical settlement, the church, was not based on Irish architectural prototypes, which were round, but on the simple rectangular structures common in the Roman Empire, where Christianity began. Modifications were continually made to this fundamental shape, according to Christian doctrinal and liturgical requirements and regional preferences. Nevertheless, a simple one-room rectangular structure that was orientated (aligned longitudinally east to west) could function as a Christian church anywhere. By the eighth or ninth centuries, cemeteries, crosses and reliquary shrines were closely associated with churches; part of a universal Christian complex forming the sacred focus of all ecclesiastical sites.

The new spatial relationships found on Irish medieval ecclesiastical sites reflect the changes in Irish culture brought by the adoption of a new religion. In Ireland the finished form of the church and its associated structures, their architectural

Figure 40

Photo of the west façade of the church on High Island, Co. Galway, in 1984. A comparison of this with the photo published by Macalister in 1896 (Fig. 10) and the drawing done by Wakeman in 1839 (Fig. 8) shows how little this part of the church has changed in the last 150 years. Photo Walter Horn 1984.

extensions, decorative elements, materials used, and a multitude of other details, were naturally modelled on local customs and resources, and then further modified and transformed over time by both Irish and imported ideas into a blend uniquely recognisable as Irish. The pattern of the church and its associated structures form an architectural unit on High Island, which is generally typical of many Irish ecclesiastical sites, but which also has some surprising elements that may be unique, features bearing strong witness to the faith and ascetic devotion of the monks who lived there.

The Church

The church, built with island schist stone, as are almost all the High Island structures, is the largest and best preserved, and hence most easily recognised, building within the monastic enclosure (Fig. 40).[86]

It was common during this period for prestigious Irish ecclesiastical sites, as well as English sites like Canterbury and Monkwearmouth, to have multiple churches, each built at a different time and each dedicated to a particular saint. In early centuries church regulations required only one altar per church, although by the sixth century the Mediterranean Church found this to be too restrictive. The custom of one altar for

The Church in the Monastery

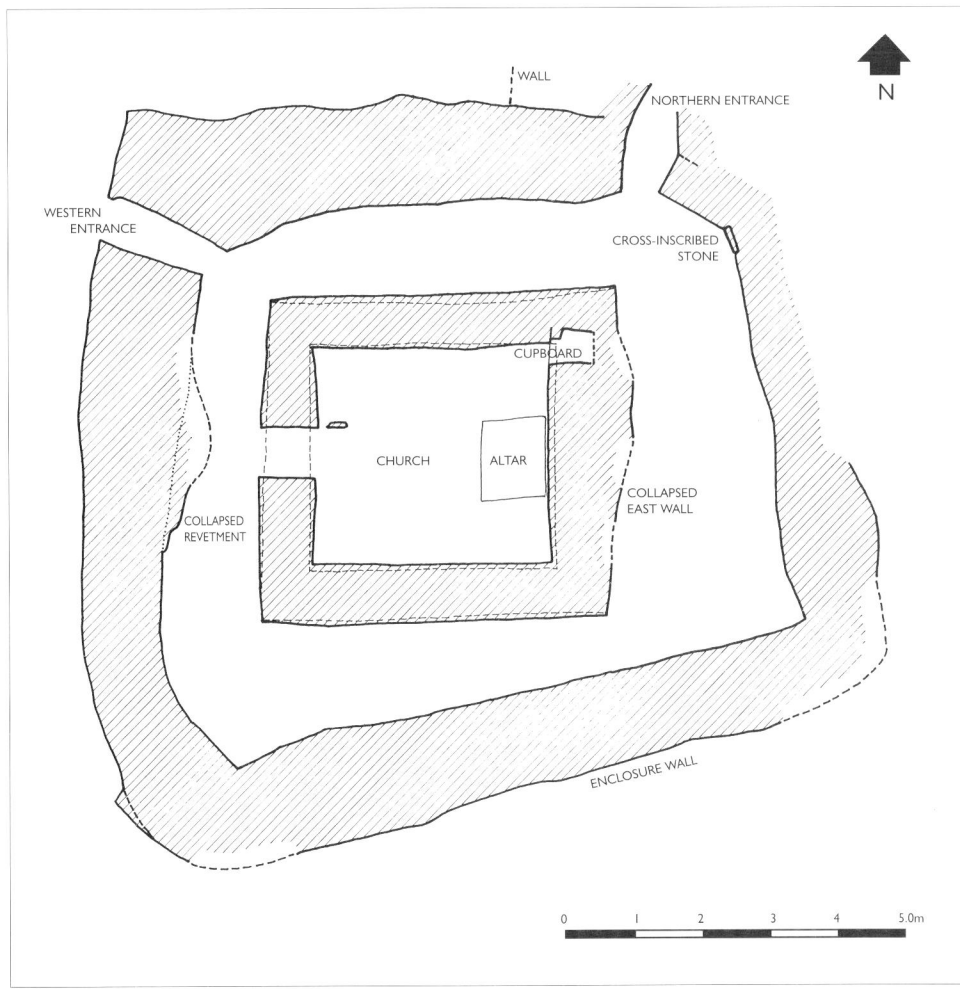

Figure 41

Pre-excavation plan of the church and the church enclosure wall on High Island, Co. Galway, showing the entrance into the enclosure at the northwestern corner, another entrance in the northeastern corner, and the location of the cross-inscribed stone embedded in the enclosure wall just east of the passage entrance. The altar and the cupboard in the eastern wall of the church are also shown. Plan G.D. Rourke.

one church dedicated to one saint appears to have lasted longer in Britain and Ireland, however. The late seventh-century hagiography of Bishop Wilfrid, written by his friend Eddius Stephanus, noted that the bishop built three churches at Hexham, starting first with the abbey church dedicated to the Apostle Andrew, and then later adding one dedicated to St Peter and one to St Mary.[87] A number of other reasons for building several churches existed, such as churches for special purposes like baptism and particular processional and liturgical requirements, and consequently multiple churches continued to be common on large Christian ecclesiastical sites.[88]

The Atlantic island monasteries off Ireland's western coast, however, rarely have more than one church. Only a few of these, most notably Inishmurray, County Sligo, Inishglora, County Mayo and Skellig Michael, County Kerry, have multiple churches. The presence of several churches at these sites may be related to their fame and longevity as well as to a fortuitous state of preservation.

The mound of rubble surrounding the High Island church belonged mostly to the sizeable wall, its upper levels now largely collapsed, that enclosed the church. The small stone church stood within the stone debris, roofless, but with most of its western gable wall and northern and southern walls intact. In design it is an unadorned, simple one-room structure with a door centred in its western side (Fig. 41). Originally, according to Petrie and O'Donovan, it also had a solitary window in its upper eastern gable wall, which had vanished by the time Kinahan came to the island in 1869.

The building is orientated, as were most Christian churches in this era.[89] The church threshold and part of the interior are paved with large, irregular but well-laid mica schist flagstones. The church interior, 3.15m NS by 3.50m EW enclosing an

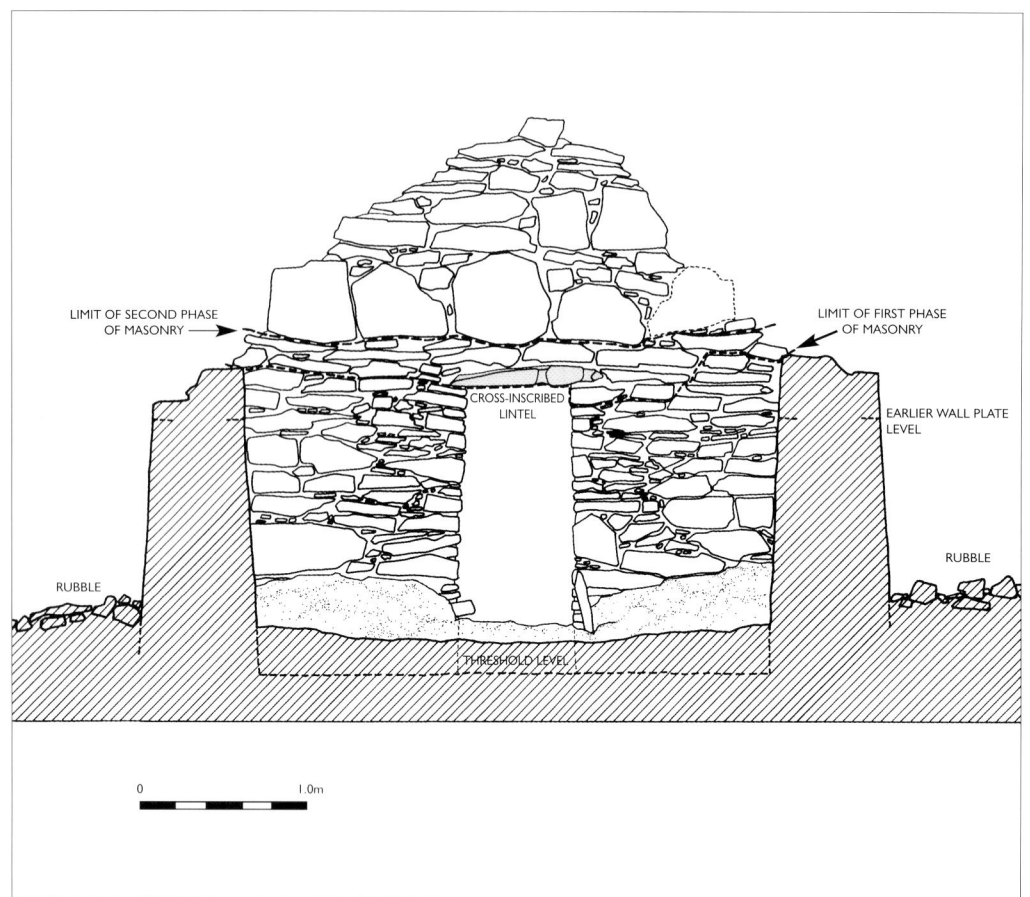

Figure 42
Pre-excavation western internal elevation of the church on High Island, Co. Galway, showing the threshold level and the location of the cross-inscribed lintel. Dotted lines separate the second masonry style at lintel level from the first and third; these styles probably correspond to three different periods of roof construction. Drawing by G.D. Rourke.

area of 11sq.m, is small, among the smallest mortared masonry churches found on islands.[90]

In plan, size, location and type of door and window, the church on High Island belongs to the most common style of Early Christian churches in Ireland.[91] Simple rectangular church plans of one to two cells, moreover, such as were found at the seventh-century monastic site of Nivelles and at Saint-Denis on the Continent, and the late ninth- early tenth-century Anglo-Saxon field chapel of Raunds Furnell, appear to have been common throughout northwestern Europe during the early centuries of Christianisation.[92] All the stone oratories and churches on the Atlantic monastic islands consist of one-cell plans, which is understandable on island sites supporting small communities. Few stone churches in Ireland during this period, however, are more complex than a two-celled nave and chancel church, even in the large mainland monasteries, unlike those of Britain and the Continent. Because of the simplicity of Irish stone architecture and the plentiful quantity of wood, a number of archaeologists are convinced, therefore, that most Irish churches were built in timber, and that mortared stone churches were rare before the tenth century, found mostly on prestigious sites (Harbison 1982, 618–629; Hamlin 1984, 117–126).

The Church in the Monastery

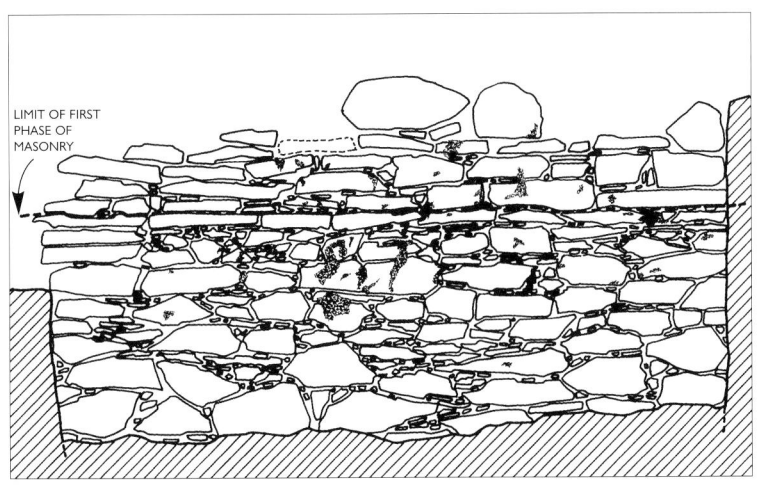

Figure 43a

Pre-excavation elevation of the southern internal wall at High Island, Co. Galway, showing two stages of construction. The base for a wall plate, located 1.5m above the church threshold level, is where the first roof began (see dotted line), and the masonry above the wall plate shows that the roof was raised in the second building phase. The two block-like stones on top of the wall may be all that remains of a third masonry style corresponding to the western gable wall. Most of the remaining interior church plaster is shown marked on the drawing. Drawing by G.D. Rourke.

Architectural examination of the church on High Island shows, however, that what appears to be a simple structure is actually more complex. The present church was not built as a unified whole but is a composite building, with various parts of it built during different periods; rebuilding, repairs and alterations are common for most churches that were used over a substantial period of time, as this one was. The eastern wall is the earliest part of the present church, all that remains of an earlier stone church. The eastern wall, or at least much of the base of it, was retained and incorporated into the building of a new church, which is itself visible now only in the lower northern, western and southern walls. Later, while the lower section of the church remained intact, the upper gables and roof were rebuilt twice.

Masonry Styles

None of the church fabric consists of coursed ashlar but most of it is of tightly fitting, well-placed island stone, which was occasionally lightly dressed. Evidence of the last two changes to the upper walls and gable is detectable in the change of masonry styles seen on the western, northern and southern walls. These changes are most clearly visible on the interior western façade (Fig. 42), which is harmonious until just below lintel level, where a band of masonry incorporating the lintel is similar but slightly different from that of the lower wall; this secondary style is contained between dotted lines on Figure 42. Finally, the upper gable's construction is distinctly different from the two lower sections of masonry.

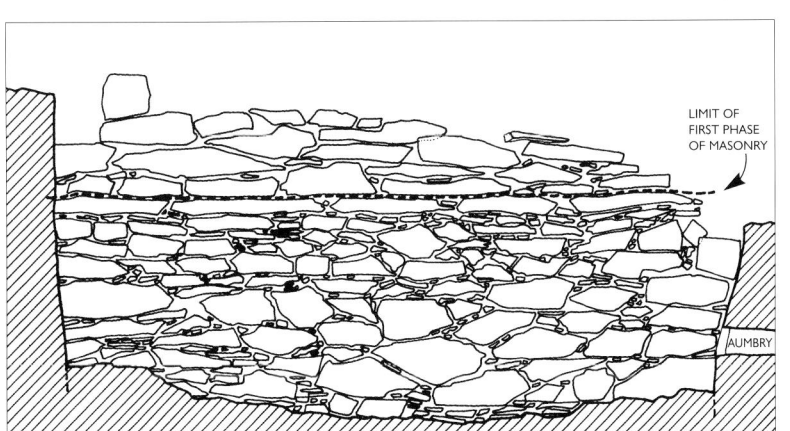

Figure 43b

Pre-excavation elevation of the northern internal wall of the church at High Island, Co. Galway, showing corresponding phases, with only one large stone remaining on top of the wall, which might be part of the third phase. Drawing by G.D. Rourke.

As we were reluctant to base conclusive statements about building periods on architectural analysis alone, and were also particularly concerned to distinguish the secondary masonry style from that of the first and third styles, samples of mortar from each of these areas were taken from within the wall and sent off for analysis.[93] According to the report[94] all three samples are lime mortars. The predominant aggregate for all three, the hard materials added to a lime binding material in mortar, was gneiss and schist together with quartz and mica. Small amounts of pozzolanic ash, probably ash from fires used to make the quicklime and shells, were also detected in the samples. Essentially, local stone material was used for the aggregate, possibly along with some crushed mica schist or sand from either the mainland or Omey Island.

The binder material was lime, completely carbonated to microcrystalline calcite. This is the result of burning and slaking limestone or seashells. Neither limestone nor shells are found on High Island so this material had to be imported; shells are the most likely material used as they were readily available in quantity on the mainland beaches and, in addition, were present in some of the samples. Most importantly, detailed mortar analysis reinforced the masonry style analysis, as the report concluded that it was possible that the mortar from under the lintel [H2] was made at a different time than the lower and upper masonry, as 'the mortar appears to be significantly different to both that of the lower walls (H1) and that of the upper western gable (H3) as it contains shells and the aggregate is better sorted than the other two mortars'.

Two distinct masonry styles are also seen in the northern and southern walls (Figs. 43a and 43b).

Only fragments of a third phase corresponding to that of the western upper gable are seen in the two blocky stones lying on top of the interior southern wall, and one on the northern wall. The first style is found in the lower part of the walls from the base up to a band of long flat stones; this relates to the masonry seen at approximately this level in the western façade. The band of long flat stones appears to be the base for the wall plates of the roof of the initial building phase of the two lateral walls (see dotted line on Figs. 43a and 43b); wall plates anchor the bottom of the roof rafters and are, therefore, an integral part of wooden roof structures. The church walls, moreover, are not strong enough to have supported the lateral thrust of a stone roof; the pressure would have caused their outward collapse. A wooden rather than a stone roof is further suggested by the small amount of stone debris found in the church's interior during excavation in 1995–1996. A conjectural reconstruction of the phase of the church represented by the lower southern, northern and western walls, using a simple rafter construction for its roof, is shown in Fig. 44.

The second masonry style consists of the narrow horizontal band of stones above the first wall plate (more or less level with the second level of the interior western

Figure 44

Conjectural reconstruction of the church on High Island, Co. Galway, during its first phase, showing a steeply pitched, but low, timber roof using wooden shingles. Wooden shingles are mentioned in the early Irish law tracts (Kelly 1998, 362f.11). It is also possible that slate or thatch was used for the roof. Reconstruction by G.D. Rourke.

masonry (Figs. 43a and 43b). That new masonry was inserted at this level means that there was a major reconstruction of much of the gable wall. It would not have been necessary to rebuild the entire upper gable if the sole purpose had been to raise the roof. It could simply be raised in height. Even a moderately unstable upper gable would not need to be rebuilt from lintel level. The inevitable conclusion is that the lintel (or lintels) was itself part of the problem. The lintel carries the heaviest burden of any single stone in the church and is, consequently, a structural weak point. A possible explanation for the replacement of the entire lintel is that upper gable movement cracked a lintel, thereby arousing fear that the entire section was in danger of imminent collapse.

The cross-decorated inner lintel was probably inserted at this time and it is also possible that the height of the door was raised. The roof was clearly raised some 0.40m then, because this is the distance between the first and the second wall plate levels, which are still clearly visible on the southern wall (Fig. 43a). The upper gable built for this second phase no longer exists, from which it can be deduced that it, too, eventually became unstable.

During the third masonry phase the upper gable was once again replaced. It is possible that the height of the roof was not changed this time but, instead, the wall plate position was moved to the outer face of the church. At this point the inner face of the lateral walls would have had to be raised somewhat; the two large remaining stones on the southern wall may be remnants of this inner face.

The masonry of the upper western gable is large and unwieldy by comparison to that of the lower walls. A different set of masons must have constructed it because the masonry is fundamentally different, being far less competent and aesthetically pleasing than that of the lower walls. In addition, the gable stones are also less homogeneous, with greater variation in size and shape than those of the lower walls. Some of the blocky stones are surprisingly large, with smooth faces similar to those used at the southern entrances to the monastery enclosure. There is no structural or practical reason to use such large stones, which, moreover, must have been inordinately difficult to position at this height, requiring the construction of stout scaffolding. Even with scaffolding, the present height of the gable, 3.44m from threshold level, made lifting these stones so difficult that some particular reason may have motivated their use. Possibly they were part of a nearby ruined structure, perhaps one with a special significance to the monks.

The impression created by this gable is no doubt the reason for Petrie's (1845, 419) comment that the church '…is among the rudest of the ancient edifices…', a statement that certainly is not applicable to the lower church walls. We are in perfect sympathy with Macalister's description of this gable:

> *Instead of being made of neatly fitted, small-sized, carefully selected stones, it [west gable] is formed of large, rough, irregular stones, thrown together in the clumsiest manner. (1896, 200)*

The Entry to the Church

The doorway in the western façade is high, 1.67m above threshold level (at midway), with slightly inclined jambs and flat-headed;[95] its threshold is paved with two large mica schist flagstones that run under the walls of the church (Fig. 57). The corners of the doorway are sharply defined as the stones were chosen to create the sharp arrises, sharp edges at the meeting of two planes, common to ashlar masonry (using squared blocks of stone), and the jamb stones, which show evidence of light working, are well fitted together, needing very few spawls (small packing stones). Three of these jamb stones are long enough to run through the full width from the exterior to the interior.

Two lintels, modest in size (both roughly 10cm thick) form the top of the door. The inner lintel is a reused cross stone, which was shaped by curved notches cut on each side into a short-armed cross, like many other stones on High Island. The stone

The Church in the Monastery

Figure 45

Part of the masonry at Cahergal, Co. Kerry, showing the use of polygonal-shaped stones to create a masonry style remarkably similar to that used in the north wall of the church on High Island, Co. Galway. Photo G.D. Rourke.

is also inscribed on one face with a cross design that consists of a circle containing a cross with forked terminals (see Fig. 95).[96] Crosses are occasionally inscribed on the entry lintel of churches as a sign of blessing; however, this is not the case here, as part of the design is concealed within the wall. Instead this is a secondary use of the cross stone. The cross design, moreover, although now in a well-protected spot, is badly weathered and had likely been located in the open for a considerable time before being used as a lintel.

There is neither decoration nor recessed rebates on the doorway. The simple door is cut straight through the wall, which most likely means that the door was hung on the inside face of the wall, as current evidence indicates was commonly done for this doorway style both in Ireland and in Anglo-Saxon England (Taylor [1978] 1984, 3:813). There is no concrete evidence for this, however, outside of a possible posthole just north of the entry. An inner door would have had to be lower than the inner lintel that projects into the church a few centimetres.

Church Walls

The lateral walls of the church have a distinct batter, narrowing as they rise from 0.72m at the base to 0.56–0.58m wide at the top.[97] The masonry of the lower walls is particularly beautiful, with great care taken in the choice of the mica schist stones (Fig. 43b), many of which are strikingly polygonal in shape. The stones are tightly fitting and needed surprisingly few spawls, so that the overall impression is of a very smooth, finished surface. There is no real coursing in the lower part of the church, although there is a skilful use of stone that creates a levelling effect at intervals. Some of the finest masonry of the early medieval period is displayed on the lower part of the interior north wall. It is particularly reminiscent of that seen at Cahergal Fort in County Kerry (Fig. 45), although at Cahergal the masonry is drystone, whereas the church at High Island is mortared.

The masonry at the base of the walls on the northern, southern and western sides, uncovered by excavation in 1996, while similar in style with well-interlocked and tightly fitted stones, is sharply different in size from the masonry above. The base level of stones is much larger, with faces that are markedly higher and wider than the stones above them (Fig. 46). They are indeed more reminiscent of the size and shape of the stones used in the church enclosure wall and are possibly stones reused from an earlier stone church (see discussion on the east wall, p. 80). Reusing these stones would be an efficient use of time and material because stones as large as these are not easy to prise out from rock and, moreover, their use here creates a solid base for the

Figure 46a

Post-excavation external elevation of the western church wall on High Island, Co. Galway. The three different masonry styles show clearly on this façade, demarcated by dotted lines. Drawing by G.D Rourke.

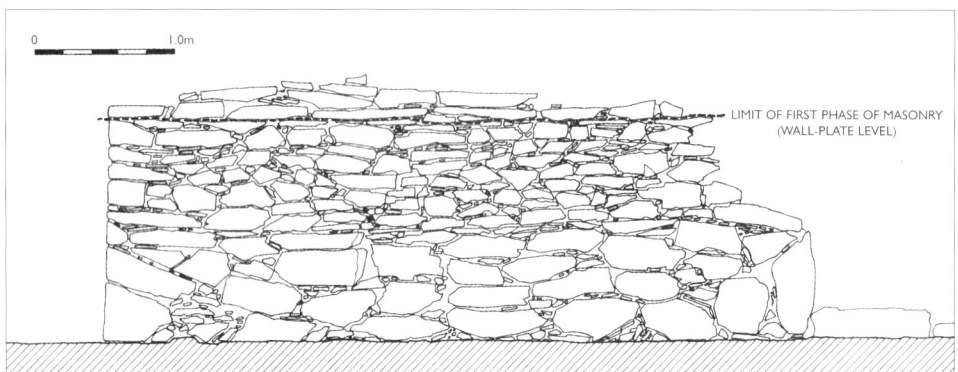

Figure 46b

Post-excavation elevation of the external northern wall of the church on High Island, Co. Galway, running east to west. A dotted line separates the two masonry styles. Drawing by G.D Rourke.

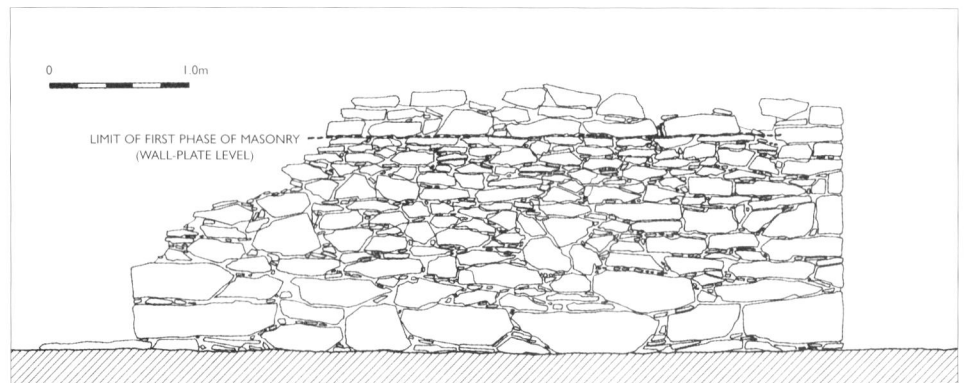

Figure 46c

Post-excavation elevation of the external southern wall of the church on High Island, Co. Galway. The base stones of this church are noticeably larger than those of the upper levels of masonry. Drawing by G.D. Rourke.

walls. Examples of similar reuse ... tone are abundant, as at Raunds Furnell in England, where the foundation of ... nancel used stones taken away from the eastern wall during the creation of the cha... arch (Boddington 1996, 19).[98]

The eastern wall, in contrast to the substantially intact other walls, has been badly damaged and is now almost gone. Its external face has also deteriorated considerably; it has slipped back and has little external face showing. When Petrie saw the church in 1820 the gable was still largely intact and contained a window, which he described as: 'semi-circular-headed and is but one foot high and six inches wide [0.35m by 0.15m]'. He also noted that the height of the church was 10 feet (3.07m) [Petrie 1845, 419–420]. By 1839, however, the eastern gable had been damaged, for John O'Donovan reported that the eastern gable was nearly destroyed except for 'a fragment of the window' that still remained, a quick sketch of which he included in his report (Fig. 47) (O'Donovan 1839, 82).

Evidently, more of the eastern gable fell after O'Donovan's visit, because in 1869 Kinahan made no mention of an east window, and in 1895 Macalister noted that 'the east end of the church is practically destroyed, and with it the window'. By 1995 the eastern wall stood only 0.87m [2 feet 10 inches] above threshold level on the interior. In 1995, a fragment of the east window, its arched upper stone, was found during excavation behind the eastern end of the church. In 1996 the lower sill was also found in debris from the same area; a conjectural reconstruction of the entire eastern window is shown in Figs. 48a and 48b.

A small semicircular-headed window in the eastern gable is a common style for windows in early medieval churches; their splayed jambs and base allowed more light to enter the church, while limiting weather exposure from windows that may have had timber shutters but were probably not glazed. St Molua's at Killaloe has a window almost identical to that of High Island, with one semicircular stone forming the head and a stepped embrasure (Macalister 1929, 130–136).

Very few structural elements of the wall remain. A large orthostat or vertical stone stands in each of the two corners of this wall; only one other similar orthostat, located in the northwestern corner, is used in the church interior. Orthostats placed like this served no function other than decoration; they are found occasionally in the interiors of early medieval circular dwellings but are not common in churches. The only other feature in the eastern wall is a recess, probably a cupboard or aumbry, in the northeastern corner (Fig. 49).

Although aumbries are seen in some Anglo-Saxon churches such as Barnack in Northamptonshire, they are most unusual in Irish churches until the later medieval period. They are common, however, in circular drystone dwellings of the early medieval period, where they were made with well-defined lintels, jambs and base stones, such as that seen in Cell A of Skellig Michael. The High Island cupboard was not as sharply delineated; it appeared to have modest lintels and short jamb stones, with its side and back walls built of small stonewalling. It also appeared to have been damaged at the back and only one sill stone remained of its base. The recess or

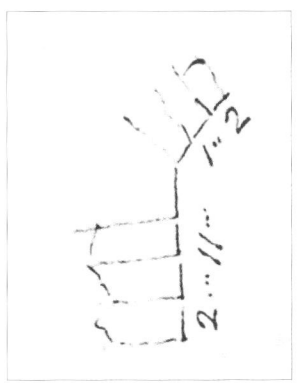

Figure 47
1839 sketch of the remaining fragment of the east window of the church on High Island, Co. Galway, made by O'Donovan (Ordnance Survey Letters, Galway, 3:82). This is the only visual record of this section of the window. It is clear given Petrie's dimension of the external ope in 1820 and the fragment of it found in excavation, that O'Donovan's sketch and dimensions refer to the northern jamb of the interior opening. He recorded it as 2 feet 11 inches high with 1 foot 2 inches of the collapsed head still intact. O'Donovan's sketch was a quick schematic drawing, so that it is likely the window had a more arched head. Courtesy Royal Irish Academy.

cupboard extends into the wall approximately 0.65m and is 0.5m wide at its widest (Fig. 50), although the opening is only 0.36m.[99] The height of the cupboard is comparatively low at 0.17m. Later investigation, however, showed that the cupboard was larger and more complex (see below).

There are a few reasons for believing that the eastern wall is earlier than the other church walls. The most distinctive evidence centres on the construction of the cupboard. The northern wall of the church was built against the eastern one so that it concealed almost 40 per cent of the cupboard, including 6cm of its opening. As a consequence, the knitted joint that commonly unites and strengthens the intersection where two walls run together is absent here, although clearly visible in the church's other three corners. Instead, there is a straight joint in the corner where the eastern wall runs beyond the interior northeastern corner for at least 0.26m, before the northern wall finally knits into the eastern wall. Early medieval builders usually laid out the base of the corners and openings (doors) first, and then, by using a taut string, filled in the base of the walls. Such a large miscalculation in the alignment of the northeastern corner, therefore, is not probable, particularly in a small simple structure.

Figure 48a
Conjectural reconstruction of the interior eastern window in the church at High Island, Co. Galway, based on the fragment found in 1995. Petrie's reported dimensions and the O'Donovan sketch. The stepped embrasure depicted here is not based on recorded information about the High Island church but it was a very common feature of early medieval windows. Reconstruction by G.D. Rourke.

Figure 48b
Reconstruction of the exterior eastern window in the church at High Island, Co. Galway, showing the original locations of the upper and lower window stones, found during excavation in 1995 and 1996; the jambs are conjectural. Reconstruction by G.D. Rourke.

Figure 49

Elevation of the recess or cupboard in the eastern wall of the church on High Island, Co. Galway. The cupboard is located 0.59m above the threshold level; the overall width of the cupboard is 0.5m, but only 0.3m now show, and the aumbry opening steps back 6cm behind the north wall, and then the side wall steps back a further 14cm (see Fig. 41). Drawing by G.D. Rourke.

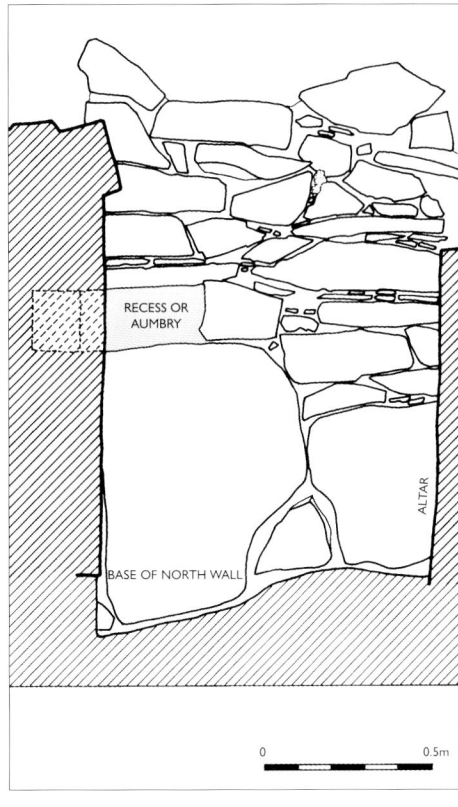

Figure 50

Plan and section of the recess in the eastern wall of the church on High Island. Drawing by G.D. Rourke based on the survey of John O'Brien. Courtesy Dúchas The Heritage Service.

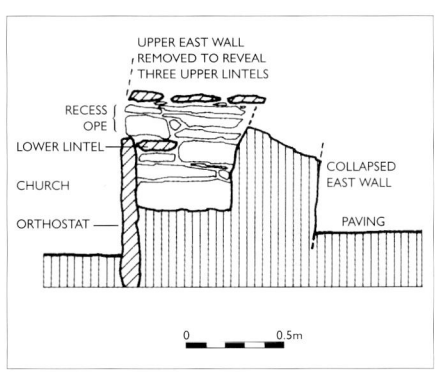
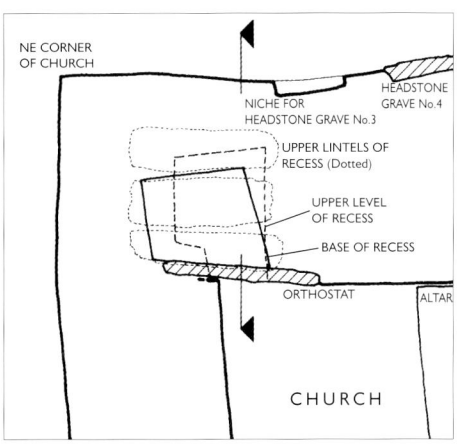

In June 1997 another puzzling section of this cupboard was revealed when masonry above the cupboard was removed, along with its three small lintel stones. Clearance of soil filling the cupboard's base exposed a stone-lined cavity, extending some 0.35m below the upper cupboard (Fig. 50). At this point it could be seen that the cupboard's overall shape is trapezoidal, partly due to structural deformities when the eastern wall fell back and the southern section of the cupboard pulled to the north from its original straight alignment.

The lower cavity was quite deliberately formed; a single large stone defines each of the northern, southern and eastern sides of its base, with small stone masonry seen above. Its western side was left open but is covered by the large orthostat in the church's north-eastern corner, probably an indication that they were constructed at the same time. This lower cavity is exactly the same width, 0.50m, as that of the upper cupboard, another indication that it was purposely constructed. Only the sill stone of the upper section separates the upper and lower sections of the cupboard. Oddly, there was no finished stone base here either so that the bottom of the cupboard is rough stone, probably the rubble fill between the wall faces.

If the purpose of this lower cavity was to keep precious items concealed, such as mass vessels and relics, they would have had to be fairly small and well wrapped in leather. It would, nevertheless, be extremely awkward to pull a paten and chalice out of a concealed recess, 0.35m deep and 0.50m wide, into a much smaller space only 0.17m high and 0.36m wide.

Cupboards or aumbries are fairly common in Anglo-Saxon churches, where they are generally located in walls near the altar, and hence were primarily used for liturgical ware, communion vessels, altar furnishings and, more rarely, relics associated with the altar.[100] The Rites of Durham specifically lay out the function of these simple recesses: 'In the north side of the quire there is an Almerye, near to the High Altar, fastened in the wall, for to lay anything pertaining to the High Altar. Likewise there is another Almerye in the south wall of the quire, nigh the High Altar, enclosed in the wall, to set the chalices, the basons and the crewetts in...' (Bond 1916, 207–208). These simple square or rectangular recesses often had stone or wooden shelves and were closed by wooden doors (Bond 1916, 210). Although there is no indication that a door or shelf ever existed at High Island, it is possible that a thin wooden board slid in and out of the upper cavity, which rested on the upper cupboard stone sill and effectively concealed the presence of the lower cavity.

Aumbries may be rare in the early medieval period because simple freestanding wooden cupboards or chests placed near the altar served as containers for liturgical ware instead. Although no studies have been made of aumbries, they probably appeared in only a few churches late in the period. The chancel of St Molua's church, near Killaloe, which probably dates to late in the early medieval period, had two small aumbries. These aumbries, one on the northern wall and one on the southern close to their juncture with the eastern wall, are unusual in their height, placed some 1.83m above the floor level (Leask 1929, 26–29). The stone church at St Vogue's in Carnsore, County Wexford, had a simple one in its eastern wall north of the altar; however, it is probably later than the one on High Island, as O'Kelly, in the absence of conclusive evidence, tentatively dated it no earlier than the twelfth century and possibly as late as the fifteenth century (O'Kelly 1975, 27; plate 5). Nothing quite as unusual as an aumbry with a concealed section is known to exist elsewhere.

Reasons for believing that the eastern wall was part of an earlier church do not rest solely on the relative position of the cupboard to the north wall. Another reason for believing the eastern wall is earlier than the others is that it is wider, measuring between 0.98 and 1.02m, than the other three walls, which are consistent with each other in a range between 0.72 and 0.85m.[101] Since most of the eastern wall is destroyed, it is impossible to know how much of the eastern wall was retained at the time of the building of a new church, although much of it appears to have gone. The section of the eastern wall containing the aumbry was retained but, judging by the line of the wall, the earlier northeastern corner appears to have been dismantled and rebuilt when the present north wall was built.

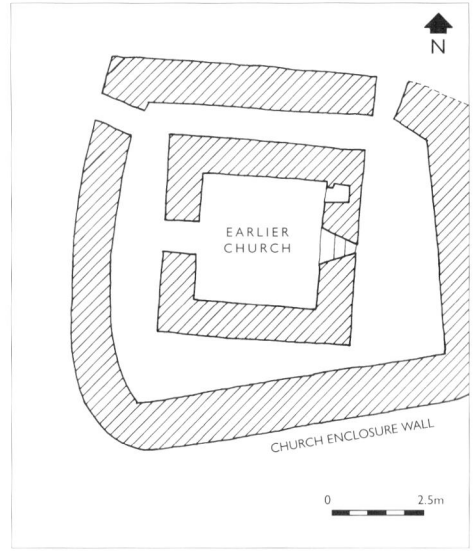

Figure 51

Conjectural drawing showing a church based on the width and location of the remaining eastern wall of the church on High Island, Co. Galway. The wider northern wall, located slightly to the north of the present wall, allows room for the aumbry. Drawing by G.D. Rourke.

Effectively, they created a new outer and inner corner by reconstructing the northern wall further to the south and making it thinner in the process to match the other new walls (Fig. 51).

The external southwestern corner was also certainly laid down at the same time as the new southern wall, although there is one stone, the upright stone on the corner, that may have been reused in this position. The position of the internal southeastern corner, however, does not appear to have been moved. It is likely, since walls are commonly built the same general width, that the earlier southern wall extended further south also. The older church for which the eastern wall was built, therefore, was in the same position as the present church, but it was a little wider.

And yet there was no evident practical or structural reason to save what clearly proved to be the weakest wall in the church. What was so important about this wall that its existence continued to define the general size and orientation of the successive stages of the church? In 1995 the enigma was resolved when excavation of the area behind the eastern end of the church revealed the special, perhaps unique, nature of this wall that made its preservation of great spiritual importance to the monks of High Island (see chapter 6, The Church Enclosure Wall).

The Altar

The altar is the primary focus of any Christian church because the Eucharist, the symbolic sacrifice of Christ, is celebrated there. In 1820 Petrie (1845, 420) commented that the church altar on High Island was covered with 'offerings, such as nails, buttons, and shells, but chiefly fishing hooks, the most characteristic tributes of the calling of the votaries'. In 1895 Macalister (1896, 201) noted that it was no longer covered with these objects (Fig. 52).

None of the nineteenth-century antiquaries commented on the elaborately carved cross slab that forms the southern side of the altar, nor is it among the crosses that Wakeman sketched (Fig. 53).[102] Lying on the altar in the church at the beginning of excavation were two stone objects, a hollowed-out stone that may have been used as a holy water font and a U-shaped stone that may have held a door-post in place (Figs. 54a and 54b).[103]

The top part of the altar was rebuilt by Richard Murphy's brother in 1972; he added a few stones found inside the church to the disturbed structure to give it a more intact appearance, thereby raising its height a little.[104] Its base is old, however, and may be roughly dated to the last use of the church by the monastery, because excavation

Figure 52

Photo of the altar in the church on High Island, Co. Galway. The altar is 0.95m high above threshold level, 0.95m wide and 1.15m deep. The top part of this altar was rebuilt in the 1970s by Richard Murphy's brother. The altar, originally covered with plaster identical to that remaining on the southern walls and doorway lintel, is quite old and sits at roughly the same level as the upper paving in the church. Photo G.D. Rourke.

Figure 53

The cross stone attatched to the southern side of the altar in the church on High Island, Co. Galway. The decoration on this stone, an elaborate version of an expansional cross, is a style seen on other crosses on the island. Photo by Con Brogan. Courtesy Dúchas The Heritage Service.

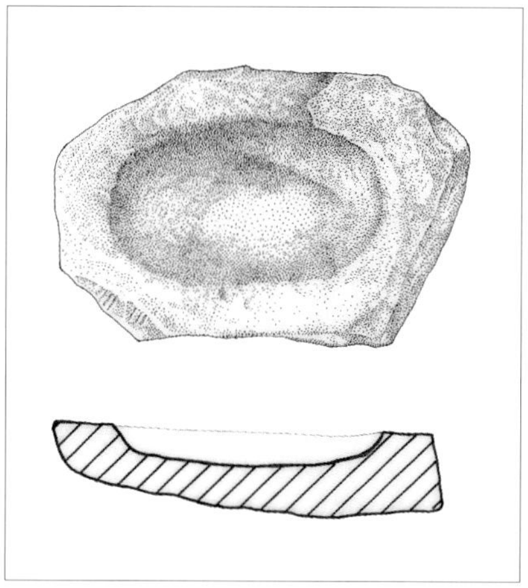

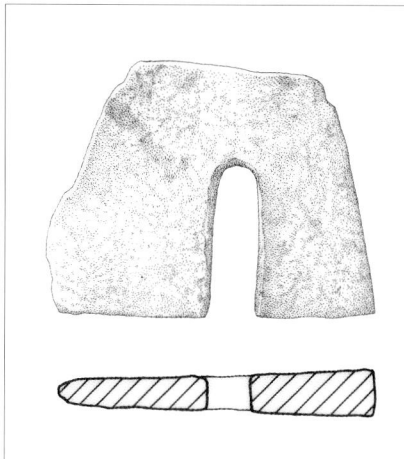

Figure 54a

Hollowed-out stone found on the altar in the church on High Island, Co. Galway, which was probably used as a holy water font.

Figure 54b

U-shaped stone found on the altar in the church on High Island, Co. Galway, which might have served to hold the door post in position. Cross section of this stone below. Drawings by Patricia Johnson. Courtesy Dúchas The Heritage Service.

revealed that the altar lies at the same level as the church's upper level of paving. The altar, moreover, was covered with the same plaster found on the church walls (see below, church floor and plaster).

The altar is rectangular and, although its original height is unknown, it is certain that its plan is original. This may have been a common shape, one among several different styles, for an Irish altar of this period but, unfortunately, information about Irish altars is scarce. Most altars are missing from early medieval churches and, commonly built directly upon the floor surface, they have rarely left archaeological traces behind them; furthermore, they are not described in the literature of the period. It is known, nevertheless, that simple stone altars shaped like chests or boxes were common throughout the Christian world during the early medieval period (Pochnee 1963, 38–39; Bond 1916, 6). All were not made of stone, of course, and many must have been wooden or had wooden bases with stone tops. Excavation has revealed one stone rectangular altar of monastic age still existing at St Vogue's in Carnsore, County Wexford. This altar had the base of its rectangular altar still in place and, similar to the one at High Island, it sat directly on earlier burned material (O'Kelly 1975, 27).[105] The unexcavated altar at Illauntannig, County Kerry, is square but of uncertain date.

A few altars remain in place elsewhere in Europe, such as the one in Abbot Mellebaude's seventh-century tomb-oratory, the Hypogeum of the Dunes, in Poitiers, and the three altars in the twelfth-century Norwegian church of Hopperstad. Manuscript illustrations and ivories demonstrate that chest-like altars were used in Anglo-Saxon England at least until the twelfth century, although excavation evidence here too has only yielded traces of one altar base in the Old Minster at Winchester. The altar at High Island thus fits into a venerable old tradition and may be one of the few surviving altars of the period in Ireland.[106]

Plaster

The interior of the church was plastered or rendered, as small areas of the material may still be seen on surfaces in the interior of the church in those areas best protected from weathering, i.e. on the door jambs, on the underside of the door lintels and in random patches on the interior southern and northern walls. The exterior of the church, most exposed to the elements, has only minute traces of plaster left, the largest being near the base of the northern wall at its western corner. In 1995 excavation revealed that plaster also originally covered the altar. Substantial patches remained in areas protected by dirt accumulating around the altar base on the northern side and trace amounts were still visible on the cross-inscribed stone that forms the altar's southern side. The altar and the cross stone attached to it are, therefore, quite old and date at least to the time when the plaster was applied. The eastern wall behind the altar is also plastered, which could not have been done with the altar in place. Either the altar was built and plastered sometime (shortly?) after the plastering of the eastern wall, or the plastering behind the altar belongs to an earlier phase of plastering.[107] Parts of the altar may be older still, reused from an earlier one the monks wished to preserve.

One hundred and fifty years ago, when Wakeman and Petrie visited High Island, there may have been considerably more plaster on the sides of the altar, which might explain why neither of these astute observers mentioned this decorated cross stone.

There is substantial evidence indicating that plastering was common early in Britain at Whithorn and Monkwearmouth, Repton and Jarrow. However, its use in Ireland in the early medieval period has not been documented or studied.[108] Plaster, nevertheless, was in use during the early medieval period, although the origin of its use remains unknown. In 1929–1930 Macalister and Leask dismantled St Molua's church on Friar's Island in the Shannon before it was moved to Killaloe, County Clare. When the small chancel was detached from the nave, it was discovered that the chancel had been added to an earlier church, as represented by the nave. Traces of plaster on what had been the earlier church's external eastern wall had been protected and preserved by the abutting western wall of the chancel.[109] Although there is no specific date for this church, all its features indicate that it belongs to the early medieval period.

A more definitely dated example, although in a broad range, is the original south wall of Clonmacnoise cathedral. Conleth Manning, senior archaeologist with the National Monuments Service, recently published an article in which he convincingly demonstrated when various sections of the cathedral were built (1995, 30–33). The original south wall of the cathedral, some 2m south of the present wall, was excavated, although unrecognised as such in the 1950s. The photograph taken at the time of excavation shows this wall with a thick coat of plaster. According to Manning's analysis, this wall was built in AD 909 and lasted until the late thirteenth century, when it was taken down. The plaster on the now-reburied south wall must have been applied sometime in this period.[110]

The material used for plaster in the church on High Island was identical to the mortar samples used to bind the church wall together; all were lime mortars with aggregates of mica-schist and quartz with small amounts of mica. The coarse texture of this material had not been refined at all for its different, more visible, role as plaster.[111]

Church Floor

Over a period of centuries after the collapse of the last roof of the church, 0.20–0.30m of material accumulated on the church floor, topped off by grassy sod. Visible in this material now is a mixture of small stones and soil, along with small amounts of collapsed stone and minute flakes of plaster from the walls of the church; doubtless it also contains decayed roof rafters and roofing material as well as the remainder of the plaster fallen from the wall.

Under this debris some interior paving of large, well-fitted but irregularly shaped mica-schist flagstones still existed (Fig. 57). A few paving stones in the threshold lie under the church's western wall, which means that the paving is most likely contemporaneous with the building of this wall.

Inside the church the paving consists of only a short section leading into the church through the door that ends unevenly, considerably short of the altar (Fig. 57). The ragged edges of the church paving and the amount of effort expended paving outside the church at the same time both suggest paving originally covered the entire church interior, paving that has since been disturbed and removed.

Excavations in 1997 revealed yet another layer of paving stones some 0.20m below the upper. This lower paving is visible now because it projects a few stones eastwards beyond the upper; it appears to continue westwards toward the church door under the upper paving. A few scattered stones elsewhere in the church may also belong to this paving, notably one that runs under the northwest corner of the altar.

Logically, this lower paving should constitute additional evidence that another church once stood in this location. The paving averages 9–11cm below the present church walls and so is not likely to be related to them.[112] The 0.20m of soil layer between the two sets of paving is, therefore, particularly important, as it should yield some information about the events and time intervals between their construction. Much of the material between the two layers of paving appears to consist of a layer of orange ash mixed with small particles of charcoal. This layer of orange ash extended generally throughout the entire church interior, apart from areas of later disturbance. In areas, the northern, southern and western walls were set directly upon it, but it does not appear to run under the eastern wall and is not present east of the wall in the area of the graves. The layer varies considerably in depth but is thicker in the centre of the church than on the northern and southern sides. In the centre the ash ranges from 7cm up to 10^+cm whereas on the sides it varies from 2–4cm. Initially this material appeared to be burned debris, possibly part of an earlier church, such as a timber roof. There is, moreover, precedent for building a church directly on top of the ash of a burned earlier structure. At St Vogue's church in Carnsore the eastern, northern and southern walls and the altar were built immediately on top of the burnt layers of the earlier phase (O'Kelly 1975, 27).

The situation became more complex and confusing, however, when radiocarbon dates on the charcoal in this orange ash material were run. Two separate radiocarbon dates run on this charcoal, each taken from a different area in the church, consistently produced virtually identical Iron Age dates that ranged between 300 BC to AD 20.[113] Analysis of the material, moreover, has revealed the presence of five different species of trees, small amounts of burnt bone, much of it from pigs, and unburnt fish bone and shell.[114] This information eliminates any idea that this material could have been part of an earlier church. To eliminate the possibility that peat was affecting the date, a third date was run on carefully selected charcoal fragments that were positively identified as wood. When this date also yielded the same dates, this layer was conceded to be Iron Age in date.[115] It may safely be concluded from this that there was Iron Age occupation of High Island by people who may have brought pigs and firewood with them and also ate birds and fish. Does this mean that the church was built on top of an Iron Age structure and that the lower paving was part of an Iron Age structure?

There are several reasons to suspect that this is unlikely and that the layer of Iron Age ash is actually sandwiched between two levels of early medieval paving. The two levels of paving are similar to each other and both appear to begin at the entry and run parallel into the church interior, which is somewhat unlikely if a church were accidentally built on top of the remnants of an Iron Age structure, particularly since paved Iron Age structures are exceptionally rare.[116] More importantly, very little material, only a paving 'foundation deposit' 0.1–0.15cm thick, separates the upper paving from the orange ash material (Scally 1996, 22). The altar sits directly on top of this ash and, in places, the northern and southern church walls also appear to do the same. There is no possible way that roughly 1000 years passed between the deposition of this ashy deposit and the construction of the paving, walls and altar of the succeeding church. The church, furthermore, is the last of at least three churches constructed in this area. If this orange ash is of Iron Age date, then it must be redeposited material that the monks found and brought into the church to spread across the interior, probably as bedding for the upper paving stones.

This is not as strange or unusual a concept as it first appears. The fourth layer of floors and occupation within the first Anglo-Saxon church at Raunds Furnell was of white plaster and contained a Roman coin, two late neolithic/early Bronze Age arrowheads and a fragment of an eleventh-century knife. Boddington, the excavator, concluded that the layer consisted of reused material 'debris from a replastering or reflooring operation' (Boddington 1996, 19–21). This situation, however, provokes a number of unanswerable questions about the original location and discovery of this Iron Age material and points towards future ideas for the ongoing excavations.

The last argument against the lower paving stones being Iron Age, however, is the presence of another deposit that appears sporadically beneath the orange ash. This deposit, pale grey in colour with a fine, gritty, cohesive texture, is found in several places in random patches both inside and outside the church, as well as in Cell A. The most substantial amounts of it are found inside the church, primarily in the northeastern corner where there are two sizeable areas, one against the eastern wall between the altar and the northern wall and the second in a strip running along the northern wall. Small portions of it were also found around the altar and on either side of the remaining paving.[117] When it was found in conjunction with the orange ash inside the church, the grey material was always below the ash, and is, therefore, the earlier layer.

Years of experience in dealing with mortar of the early medieval period convinces the authors that this is a form of lime mortar, although far more finely textured than most. This would provide an excellent bed in which to set the paving stones, presumably the lower paving, as this material is well below the upper paving stones and is further separated from them by the orange ash material. This would help hold the paving stones in place and yet allow some movement. Under the church's northern wall lies a particularly clearly preserved sequence of orange ash, what we suppose to be grey mortar and a dark organic layer of soil. It appears, therefore, that it was used under the walls of the church in places, although it would not have been particularly effective except for levelling the ground surface.[118]

The Church in the Monastery

If this material is mortar, it must be early medieval in date, as mortared stone construction came into Ireland no earlier than the seventh century. Although the Irish had occasionally built in drystone for many centuries, as witnessed by the 4000-year-old megalithic tombs, wood was more readily available and a more flexible material than stone. Despite their certain knowledge of Roman mortared buildings in Britain and on the Continent, the Irish long continued to build in wood, as did most people who lived in forested regions.

The main components of this grey material clearly consist primarily of finely textured mica-schist and quartz, which raises some intriguing possibilities about its origin. Although both are common island stones, finely textured mica-schist and quartz does not occur in large quantities on or around the island. There are, however, several layered piles of crushed bedrock visible near the mill close to the edge of the mill stream, each layer interspersed by a thin dark layer (soil).[119] This is clearly an artificial, rather than a natural deposit, possibly laid down intermittently and completely different from any soil or rock deposits here or indeed anywhere on the island. This is not debris from the working of the mill to grind grain, as millstones were commonly made of sandstone and, further, millstones would not have caused such an outward spread of debris.[120] It does, however, appear likely that the neat pile of layered crushed bedrock was derived from using the mill.

Could the monks have ground up local stone to make a finely textured aggregate for mortar? There is no known precedent for this in Ireland, but use of mills to grind stone, ore from mines, goes back before the birth of Christ on the Continent and new documentary studies in France demonstrate the use of watermills for this purpose from at least the twelfth century on (Domergue et al. 1997, 48–61; Benoit, Bailly-Maître and Dubois 1997, 62–78). Although we lack definitive evidence to establish that this is what happened, the technological information could easily have been available to the High Island monks and such an innovative use of it would also have been characteristic of these monks (see below, chapter 10).

There is no natural sand or gravel around the island to use as a bedding surface for the interior paving, materials that have been used on other sites under structures. In their absence, the monks here improvised by either manufacturing a bedding material or finding a cohesive substance such as the ancient ash. Mortar this finely textured is not commonly found and is certainly not the type of mortar used in walls. One of the consequences of its texture and location on the ground is that it remained soft, adherent and pliable, all qualities that were vital for a successful bedding under paving stones. The substance used must help hold the stones in place and yet allow movement of them; consequently, this would be a very sophisticated use of mortar. It is known, however, that mortar in some form was occasionally used for flooring in this period. It was primarily known in Anglo-Saxon England as *opus signinum*, 'a strong mortar set on a surface of flints with a polished red surface of cement and powdered brick', seen at Reculver, St Augustine's abbey and Glastonbury among others (Taylor 1978 [1984], 3:1061). A more exact analogy is found in the floors in the crossing/choir of the church at Bordesley Abbey. Floors in this area were made of tiles set upon a mortar or, perhaps more accurately, a lime-based putty, from at least AD 1200 on.[121]

On High Island the use of mortar under flagstones and walls might date to the construction of a church that, at earliest, took place in the second quarter of the eleventh century. Does this mean that the monks of High Island were using mortar-based bedding for floor surfaces sooner than Cistercian monks in England? It is more probable that this apparent disparity is due to poorly preserved evidence for flooring surfaces in the early medieval as well as in the later medieval period, and that use of mortar or lime putty to hold flagstones, tiles, etc. began earlier in both Ireland and England than was previously suspected.[122] It is interesting that mortar appears to have been used for the paved floors of Cell A, and likely for Cell B as well, perhaps its first known use in domestic structures.

A dark brown mud layer streaked with charcoal and a few shells underlies the grey mortar material throughout the church and possibly extends beyond it into the northeastern corner of the burials. This layer appears to have an organic component in it also and may have been a mixture of redeposited midden material and clay, spread to create a bedding for a thin layer of mortar underlying the paving stones, or perhaps it was a separate floor surface. Was diluted mortar mixed with it as well? If so, it would be somewhat analogous to the first floor found in the chancel at Raunds Furnell, which was 'grey-brown clay mixed with about 40% plaster'.[123]

As a final comment on the lower paving stones, it should be noted that paving stones, facing stones and corner stones are always the first to go in a derelict building as they are the most valuable, i.e. the hardest to find or fashion. The lower paving stones would have been lifted by the monks themselves to reuse when they built a new church, although for some reason they left a central strip running through the doorway, and perhaps a few others they didn't want or need.

Foundations

Several of the walls appear to sit immediately on top of the orange ash, which suggests that the church was constructed without foundations. This possibility was reinforced by excavation in 1997 directly behind and below the eastern church wall, clearly revealing that there were no foundations under this wall. Excavation elsewhere has shown that stone Anglo-Saxon and continental churches had substantial foundations of varying materials such as gravel, chalk, stone rubble, sand or crushed mortar.[124] The first church at Raunds Furnell in Northamptonshire, built in the late ninth/early tenth century as a field chapel, a private proprietary church, is an excellent comparative example. This small one-celled church, similar in size to High Island, had a foundation composed of two layers of cornbrash limestone some 0.4m deep, set in a narrow construction trench 0.35–0.43m wide (Boddington 1996, 16, 25). Traditional foundations were not common, however, in Irish medieval churches; often they were entirely absent or, if present, were comparatively slight. Sometimes they consisted of a layer of gravel simply laid down to provide a level base, or a plinth, a single layer of stones, was used for a more substantial foundation, which also helped to spread the weight of the walls.

In the 1990s, excavation at Ardfert cathedral revealed no substantial foundation but a single stone laid under the tenth/eleventh-century walls (F. Moore, personal communication to G. Rourke, December 1997). A similar system to that of Ardfert was visible at St Vogue's in Co. Wexford (O'Kelly 1975, 26) where there was no foundation, but a single layer of rough stones formed a plinth. A classic example of a substantial internal and external plinth is strikingly visible today on Inishglora, County Mayo. Here the sea has washed away most of the eastern wall of the Saint's Church, thereby exposing the southern wall in section set upon a single layer of massive stones that project beyond the church walls.

Irish builders were aware that special situations required more preparation of the ground under their structures and they used a variety of ingenious solutions. When the damming of the Shannon River in the late 1920s made it necessary to move St Molua's, the church on Friar's Island, R.A.S. Macalister and H.G. Leask worked together to excavate and record the nave and chancel of the church before moving it. They discovered that concern about periodic flooding of the Shannon caused the builders of the nave, the first church, to construct the church on a platform of loose stone and clay that raised the structure 0.46m. When the considerably heavier stone-roofed chancel was added, it was placed on a sturdier platform of 'lime concrete and rough stones'.[125] These foundations were not limited to the walls, like most foundations, but were true foundation platforms, both being somewhat larger than the full extent of the structures.

The lack of a foundation does not appear to have affected the stability of the sturdy little church at High Island, perhaps because bedrock is close to the surface here and the ground is well compacted beneath it. It should also be noted, however, that even in areas where churches had foundations, many English, French and German stone-built villages of the thirteenth to fifteenth centuries were also built directly on the ground, without foundations (Chapelot and Fossier 1985, 252).

Burial in the Church

Further investigation under the existing paving in the church in 1995 revealed the burial of a man in the northeastern corner between the altar and the northern wall, laid with his feet at the eastern wall. Post-excavation analysis revealed that the skeleton was that of a young male, twenty to thirty years old, who had died between AD 1169 and 1221.[126]

From the fourth century, reverence for the tombs of the saints inspired the construction of churches over the sacred graves, but burials inside the church for all others was strongly discouraged by the early Church. A compelling desire to be buried *ad sanctos*, close to the saints, nevertheless persisted over the centuries, slowly eroding the old prohibition. By 658 the Council of Nantes issued a reaffirmation that 'no bodies whatsoever are to be buried in church, but in the atrium or in a porticus or outside the church' (Grabar 1943–1946, I: 550). In the early eighth century, nevertheless, the Venerable Bede casually related that archbishops Theodore and Bertwald were buried in the church, 'no space remaining in the porch' (Bede, *A History of the English Church and People,* ed. Sherley-Price 1968[1955], 105). By the second half of the seventh century, venerated ecclesiastics were also qualified as saints shortly after their deaths and then quickly reburied in the church. In England Bede mentions St Cuthbert, followed shortly by his successor Bishop Eadbert and St Chad, among others who were brought into the church shortly after death to be buried near the altar.[127] The lives of St Gall, who died in 630 at Sankt-Gallen, and of St Fursa, who died in Peronne in 645, indicate that Irish missionary saints were also being buried near the altars of their churches at this time. The sole mention of a similar burial in Ireland in the hagiographies is in Cogitosus' seventh-century *Vita S. Brigidae*, which described the elaborate tombs of St Brigit and Bishop Conláed at Kildare, one on each side of the altar.[128]

From these saints' Lives it appears that the Irish were following the prevailing customs of the time. However, archaeological evidence completely contradicts this, at least in Irish stone churches. Was Kildare an exceptional case, an unusual imitation of continental customs? Present evidence generally shows that the Irish maintained earlier church traditions of no burial inside churches, not even for saints.[129] Princes of the church and secular princes alike are found in the graveyards around the churches in this period, as the inscribed gravestones from Clonmacnoise show. When burial did begin within Irish churches in the later medieval period, it followed the normal European pattern of élite burials; saints, bishops and kings were offered the special privilege, not ordinary citizens. Nothing about the grave inside the church indicates that this was a special man, for it was the simplest of graves, dug with no cists or markers distinguishing it, totally unlike the treatment of the graves behind the church (see next chapter).

Buried with him, however, were two simple artifacts, one on each shoulder: a hone stone and a line-net sinker. This evidence leads to the conclusion that he was not a monk, but a fisherman. So far, this is the only burial at High Island that contains any form of grave deposition. Burial with artifacts or personal goods, other than the occasional religious insignia for a ranking ecclesiastic, was unusual for most Christians. The church, however, did not expressly forbid burial with personal objects (Bullough 1983, 185; Salin 1951, 2: 233–236; Treffort 1996, 180) and there were some notable exceptions to the common tradition among the descendants of Germanic tribes. Christianised Merovingians and Anglo-Saxons continued to be buried with personal objects such as weapons, jewellery, etc., a custom that disappeared by the end of the seventh century.

Vikings, as well, typically buried their dead with personal items identified with the individual, as well as with more general grave goods. However, Irish Christians of Viking descent had assimilated and adopted Irish customs by the end of the twelfth century. Burial with personal objects was never common among Irish laymen, but two stone weights that may have been line sinkers or net weights were found in phase 2 burials, *circa* AD 550–855, at the early medieval church at Skeam West in County Cork (Cotter 1995, 73).[130] Irish ecclesiastics, however, were never buried with personal secular objects.[131]

The man buried within the church could not have been a monk. Further, his burial must have taken place after the monks were no longer in full-time residence on the island, for they hardly would have sanctioned a burial practice they avoided for themselves. A fisherman who died accidentally at High Island would surely be taken home to his family, and the island is too difficult of access to have been attractive as a *cillín*, an unauthorised burial site. The young man may have been a drowned stranger found by fishermen floating off the island, who took him ashore to bury him or, perhaps more likely, he was a member of a family living on the island during the late twelfth or early thirteenth century, perhaps as a custodial family for the monks. In the absence of a priest or official service, the people who buried him improvised the most Christian burial possible by placing him in holy ground in the heart of the derelict church.

Notes

[86] Excavation in the area of the church was started in 1995, organised by Marshall in search of more detailed information about the church area for this book. Dúchas The Heritage Service aided financially in the excavation that first year, and in subsequent years took over the funding and planning of the excavation, with Scally as director. Our approach here is a more general one, which only covers work done through 1997. Archaeologists may refer to Scally's interim reports of 1996, 1997, 1998, etc. and the final report (forthcoming) on file at Dúchas The Heritage Service. Marshall and Rourke are solely responsible for the opinions and facts cited in the text unless otherwise attributed.

[87] See *The Life of Bishop Wilfrid*, ed. Colgrave, 1927.

88 Taylor [1978] 1984, 1020; Lehmann 1962. Multiple churches were also customary on continental sites such as Jumieges and St Riquier; excavation at St Pierre in Geneva revealed three churches from the seventh to the eleventh century (Bonnet 1993).

89 In this case the orientation is 5° north of west. Orientation varied.

90 In fact, St Benen, Inishmore, Co. Galway, Teampull Dhiarmaid, Incleraun, Co. Longford, and Teach Molaise, Inishmurray, Co. Sligo, are smaller, but they are auxiliary structures to other larger churches.

91 For plans, see Leask 1955, 1:49–75. For discussion, see Harbison 1982, 618–619.

92 Hubert, Porcher and Volbach 1969, 31; Boddington, et al., 1996, 8; Taylor [1978] 1984, 3:969; Lehmann 1958: 291–292.

93 The three mortar samples were taken from: HI-C-9601, the interior west wall lower section in first phase; HI-C-9602, the interior west wall below lintel in second phase; HI-C-9603, the upper gable in last phase. All taken from within wall. The plaster sample (HI-C-1904A) was taken from the interior west wall, near base of wall on either side of entrance.

94 Report on the composition of bedding mortar and plaster samples of the Church of High Island, County Galway, prepared for Dúchas The Heritage Service, by Carrig Conservation Engineering, October 1995. The mortar of the upper western gable was also submitted to the XRF facility at Queen's University Belfast for analysis. See Report by Dr. F.G. Mc Cormac from samples collected 8 August, 1995. The two reports are consistent and show the same results.

95 The door has a slight splay: its width on the interior is 0.61m at the top and 0.69m at the bottom. On the exterior the width is 0.56m at the top and 0.66m on the bottom. O'Donovan's measurement for the width of the entrance was 22 inches (0.56m). Herity (1990, 74) arrived at 0.9m for the outer end, narrowing down to 0.70m at the inner end.

96 Petrie was the first to notice this cross stone (1845, 419); Macalister (1896, 206) was the first to describe it, although he missed part of the design.

97 Measured midway along their length. The thickness of the western wall varies considerably along its base, from 0.7 to 0.87m; the wall thickens on either side of the door opening.

98 At ten out of nineteen extant Anglo-Saxon churches identified by H.E. Taylor, there is clear evidence for reuse of stone by either architectural components or inscription. Morris 1988, 192.

99 The width, however, tapers to 0.45m at the rear, which is broken away.

[100] Parsons 1986, 107–108 notes that they are found generally in the north wall of the chancel in Anglo-Saxon churches, but a few are found in the eastern wall behind the altar; see also Cox 1923, 274–275; Bond 1916, ch. 8 also notes that the same word is used for a wooden cupboard standing free, which may have been more common in earlier centuries. Parsons considers an aumbry to be one of those church furnishings whose position can be used as evidence for the original position of an altar.

[101] The eastern wall was measured, carefully avoiding areas where the wall has pushed out.

[102] Herity 1987, 141–142, believes that this cross stone originally formed part of a tomb described by Petrie in 1820 as being behind the church's east wall. The plaster remaining on this stone makes that impossible.

[103] Identification of this object as a water font is owed to Michael Moore, archaeologist with the Archaeological Survey, Dúchas The Heritage Service. Personal communication to G.D. Rourke, 1 August 1997.

[104] Personal communication, Richard Murphy to G.D. Rourke, January 1998.

[105] O'Sullivan and James 1998, 9–10; 22–23 found a rectangular stone altar to be of second stage construction on Inishmurray, Co. Sligo, of uncertain date. It was preceded by a cell and the remnants of a small area of paving that supported a post; possibly a post for either a table altar or a cross in the primary phase.

[106] Parsons 1986, 105–120. For Winchester, see Biddle 1971, 315. On position of altars, see Taylor 1973, 52–58; for manuscript illustrations of English altars, see Hope 1899. See also Hubert, Porcher and Volbach 1969, 56–61; Pochnees 1923, p. 27; 38–39. The most complete book on altars remains that of Braun [1924] 1932.

[107] Plaster or mortar was found in varying amounts in the grave behind the church, an indication that an earlier mortared stone church existed here.

[108] Taylor [1978] 1984, 3:1063–1064; Cramp 1976b, 231; Cramp 1976a, 225; Radford 1950, 85–126; *Whithorn and St Ninian: The Excavation of a Monastic Town, 1984–91,* ed. Hill 1997, 27–8, 81, 470–471.

[109] Leask 1930, 130–136. Reference to this plaster was pointed out to us by C. Manning.

[110] Letter to J.W. Marshall from C. Manning, 5 November 1996; now published in *Clonmacnoise Studies I*, ed. H. King, 1998, 57–86. We are grateful to Manning for sharing this material with us and also for showing us the excavation photo of the southern wall. See also O'Sullivan 1994b, where the render was probably added later to a clay-bonded church stratigraphically dated to the early medieval period at Iona.

[111] Report prepared for Dúchas The Heritage Service in October 1995 by Carrig Conservation Engineering. See also XRF analysis done by Dr F.G. McCormac at Queen's University Belfast on similar samples, Autumn 1995.

112 Based on levels taken by John O'Brien, architectural assistant, Dúchas The Heritage Service, on 27 June 1997 and on 22 Sept. 1998, as well as our own observations.

113 The first sample taken in the northeastern corner, UB-4001, was 2072±51BP, the second taken on the south side of the church UB4157 was ±45Bp. Both calibrate at two sigma BC 336–AD 20.

114 Personal communication, Niamh O'Callaghan, 8 July 1997 and Dr F.G. McCormac, July 1998.

115 The third date, UB– 4264, was 2127 ±23 years BP, which calibrated to two sigma is BC 338–AD 103. Personal communication from Dr F.G. McCormac, 5 August 1998.

116 Unfortunately little is known about Iron Age domestic structures (Raftery 1994, 113) so there are no comparatives.

117 These smaller patches near the altar and the paving stones are slightly darker in colour, perhaps mixed with mud. This layer probably was widespread across the interior but has been much disturbed, first by the monks building the upper paving and later by an intrusive burial and rabbits. On the exterior of the church, almost directly opposite the main interior deposit in the northeastern corner, between graves nos. 5 and 6 and also tightly against the wall, is a small fragment of this deposit. Several tiny spots were also found wedged against big rocks in grave no. 6 at the lowest level this grave was excavated in 1997. Two minute pieces of this material were also found near the footstone of grave no. 3, only 0.07 to 0.08m above the skeleton. Finally, a sizeable portion was found in Cell A lying against the rear, northern wall and under the flagstone paving.

118 In view of the disturbance of the church floor, the only certain method of determining if the mortar was used under the paving would be to lift the remaining paving stones.

119 A sample of this material was identified as crushed mica-schist by Carrig Conservation Engineering, Report on the composition of Bedding Mortar and Plaster samples, October 1995, 3.

120 Personal communication, Colin Rynne, September 1998. Stone debris from the millstones ended up in the ground grain; this, in cereals of the time, caused considerable damage to people's teeth.

121 Hirst, Walsh and Wright 1983, 39. For floors, see 29–57. For analysis of this material by Evans and Biek, see 130–134. There were earlier phase one (1140s) lime beddings, perhaps a temporary floor level.

122 See Stalley 1988, 211–214 on the uncertain evidence for the origin of the use of tiled floors in medieval churches.

123 Boddington 1996, 19. This chancel was added to the first church probably sometime in the tenth century.

124 Great efforts were made at all Anglo-Saxon churches, from the simple solution used at Rivenhall and Hadstock of digging a foundation trench approximately a metre deep and filling it with rammed hoggin, a mixture of clay and gravel (Rodwell and Rodwell 1973, 225;1976, 59), to more elaborate systems sunk even deeper and involving flints and mortar at Winchester (Taylor 1984 (1978), 3:761).

125 See Macalister 1929, 16–25; Leask 1929, 26–28; Leask 1930, 130–136.

126 UB–4000 849±16. This high precision date was calibrated to two sigma, which means that the probability that the date falls within the given calendrical range is 95 per cent. Accurate high-precision dates give the narrowest calendrical date ranges of radiocarbon dating methods and consequently are the best for archaeological purposes (McCormac and Baillie 1993, 311–316),

127 Bede, *A History of the English Church and People*, ed. Sherley-Price 1983 [1955], Book IV, ch. 29 and 30, 265–267; Book IV, ch. 3, 212. The large cathedrals were already changing the old customs. The trend was started earlier at St Augustine's, where the chapel of St Mary, east of St Peter and St Paul, the cathedral, was built in the mid-seventh century for burial of kings and abbots. Biddle 1986, 13. We are not attempting to present an absolute chronology but rather demonstrate a general progression taking place outside of Ireland at this time. There continued to be conflicting views on the subject for some time and in the ninth and tenth centuries a number of prominent French churchmen again banned burial in the church (Treffort 1996, 137–141).

128 Strabo *S. Galli*, II, 2 (MGH, SRM 4,314); *Vita S. Fursei*, c.10 (MGH, SRM 4,439) and also Bede, Ibid Book 3, ch. 19, 175; On Brigit, see Doherty 1989, 2:89–101. Irish hagiographies rarely mention where a saint was buried, although St Baire of Cork was buried in front of his church (Bethada Náem nÉrenn, ed. Plummer, 1997 [19222], 2:17) and Aidan of Iona was buried in the cemetery there (Bede, *A History of the English Church and People,* ed. Sherley-Price 1983 [1955), 168). On Brigit, see Doherty 1989, 2:89–101. Doherty's interpretation of the meaning of the word basilica as tomb and church (1984, 303–315) means the written sources warrant more investigation.

129 It is possible that future excavation may yet demonstrate that important ecclesiastics were occasionally buried inside the church. Excavation knowledge, particularly about the large wooden churches, is still very sparse. The large wooden building (church?) at Dunmisk, with burials within its eastern end (Ivens 1989, 17–64), may be the beginning of a reassessment of this position. There is also some reason to believe that at important monasteries small churches were eventually built to contain the relics or possibly even to cover the burial of important saints, following a tradition common to the Continent and England, see St Swithin at Winchester (Biddle 1986, 22–24; Herity 1984, 105–113; Marshall 1989, 193–197).

[130] O'Brien cautioned us that there may also be a practical function for the line sinker and hone stone. We are deeply grateful to Dr O'Brien for her gracious and generous sharing of her enclyclopaedic information and references on the subject of burials. We also owe Fionnbarr Moore many thanks for sharing his expert opinion on this subject. Moore noted that he found one secular burial with a comb at Ardfert cathedral. Personal communication, 16 June 1997.

[131] O'Brien noted that whenever personal objects, not grave goods, but objects that were part of their burial attire, such as buckles, knives, rings, etc., are found in early medieval burials in Ireland, she suspects they are Anglo-Saxon burials, rather than Irish. Personal communication, 21 August 1998. For Irish burials, see O'Brien 1992 and 1997; Marshall and Walsh, forthcoming; Howells 1941; Ivens 1989, among others. For Merovingians, see Halsall 1995; Wood 1994; Picard 1984, 9–12; Young 1984. For Anglo-Saxon burials, see O'Brien (forthcoming); Geake 1997; Bullough 1983; Boddington 1990, 188–190, Morris 1983, 49–62.

Chapter Six

The Church Enclosure Wall: Burials

Day keeps lit a flare
Round the north pole all night.
Like brushing long wavy hair
Petrels quiver in flight.

Richard Murphy, *High Island*.

The Church Enclosure Wall

A substantial drystone wall surrounds the church, but collapsed stone largely concealed most of it until stone clearance in 1995 exposed its lower courses and two openings still intact at base level. The main narrow entrance into the enclosure from the monastic grounds, 0.45m to 0.65m wide, is located in the northwestern corner of the wall (Fig. 29a). Stone rubble here so filled the space between the wall and the church that visitors never noticed either wall or entrance but simply climbed over the collapsed debris in front of the church door to enter the church. Wakeman's sketch of the church (Fig. 8) indicates that much of the damage to the wall had already occurred by 1839. Outside of the entrance to the west is another small square structure, 1.25m by 1.25m (Fig. 29a). This structure, built in similar fashion to that at the southeast entrance to the monastic enclosure and the one by the millpond, resembles a *leacht*. Is this one of the two structures labelled as 'stations' near the annotation 'Abbey' on the Ordnance Survey Fair Plan seen in Figure 5?

In 1995/6 clearance of rubble around the church revealed that all of the lower section of the enclosure wall, composed of large stone blocks, survives, as do the lower jambs of the two openings in the wall; most damage is on the northern side, where only the base level is wholly intact and stable. On the southern side the wall rises to a height of 1.10m and on the eastern to 1.35m. The wall is also irregular in width, varying from 1.15m at the northeast entrance to the enclosure wall to about 1.0m at the entrance to the enclosure itself.

Judging by the amount of stone collapse, the wall must have been quite high originally. The surviving revetments that buttress sections of the western wall are evidence of past problems with stability. One sizeable external revetment is located near the southwestern corner where the wall curves around to the south and ends snugly braced against a large boulder; a second, more flimsy, revetment was on the inner side of the wall just in front of the church. This last revetment, built on a few centimetres of accumulated soil above the flagstones, was likely a late addition added by pilgrims as the wall began collapsing inwards, threatening to block the door to the church.

Garnet schist and blue mica-schist paving similar to the paving within the church covers the entire area between the church and its enclosure wall, at the same level as that of the upper-level paving in the church's interior (Fig. 57). The church's external northern and southern walls also sit upon some of these paving stones, another sign that the external paving dates to the same period as that within the church. All the paving, therefore, was doubtless laid down contemporaneously with the first phase of the building of the present church.[132] Another lower set of paving may run underneath the present paving around the church's exterior, corresponding with a second lower set of paving revealed in the church (see p. 86). If the monks had not paved this area it would have become muddy and slippery immediately during rainy periods. Lengthy paving on the eastern border of the millpond illustrates that the High Island monks were well aware of the problems created by mud in narrow, restricted areas that were highly travelled. Paved paths probably also existed within the monastic enclosure, leading from the entries to the church and possibly running between the interior structures as well. Sections of

Figure 55a
A photo of the cross stone in the northeastern corner of the church enclosure wall on High Island, Co. Galway, taken by J.W. Marshall in 1996.

The Church Enclosure Wall: Burials

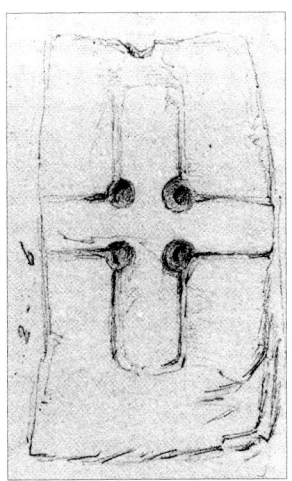

Figure 55b

Drawing made of this stone by W.F. Wakeman in 1839, showing the stone intact at that time (RIA MS 12 T9, 43). Courtesy Royal Irish Academy.

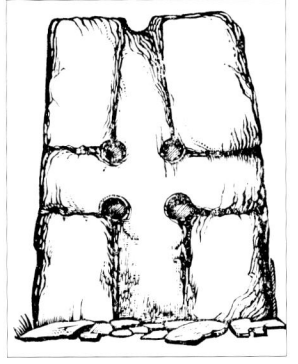

Figure 55c

Woodcut made by Robert Gibbings after a trip to High Island in the early 1940s(?) for his book Lovely is the Lee. *This drawing, more realistic than that of Wakeman, shows very clearly how the missing upper-right side of the cross looked (Gibbings 1945, 104).*

such paved pathways survive at simpler monasteries such as Church Island and Illaunloughan in County Kerry, and more extensive areas of pavement cover the ground at more complex sites such as Skellig Michael. Paving must have been a normal and necessary requirement on Irish sites, done to facilitate and expedite the daily routine of the monastery.

Silt and mud seep gradually into the area behind the church from the soil around Cell B. Excavation in this section revealed that there were several layers of soil alternating with rough paving on top of the monastic paving here and markedly different in quality from the monastic paving. These stones were carelessly laid with no discernible concern about their size and fit; no spawls were placed between stones to make them fit neatly and closely together on a level surface, such as were used for the monastic paving. Pilgrims and visitors to the burials behind the church probably hastily threw down these crude layers over mud that accumulated in this area after the monks had left the monastery.

Excavation also revealed the full extent of another cross-inscribed stone embedded in the church enclosure wall behind the church (Figs. 55a and 55b); W.F. Wakeman had sketched this cross in 1839. In his sketch of the church's western façade, a cross-inscribed stone appears behind the church to the east, which looks like this cross but appears to be freestanding (Fig. 8). On another sheet he made another detailed drawing of it that shows its excellent condition at that time (Fig. 55b).

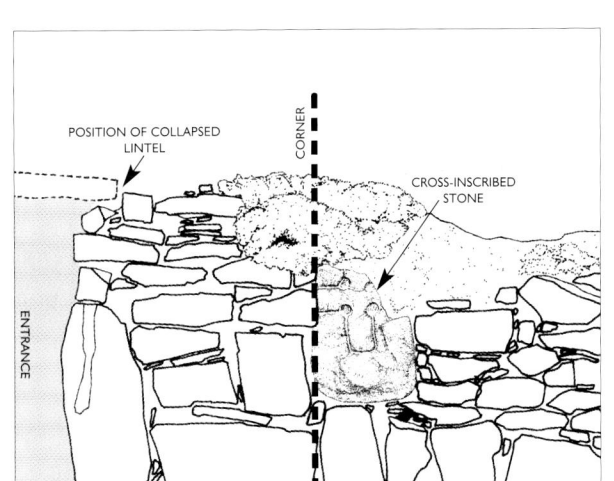

Figure 55d

Drawing of the cross stone in place in the northeastern corner of the church enclosure wall in 1996. Drawing by G.D. Rourke.

This stone, now broken along the top and upper right-hand side, is in the same position as when Wakeman drew it, except that it is set into the church enclosure wall. Was this artistic licence on the part of Wakeman or had he not noticed the wall? The cross stone must have been deliberately inserted here when the wall was built. Unlike the cross stones used as lintels, the stone serves no structural purpose here; on the contrary, it is awkward. Was this a stone the monks found nearby and placed here or did it serve a symbolic purpose now unclear to us? This stone was intact until sometime in the 1940s (Fig. 55c). By 1980 the stone was not visible, but hidden behind stone rubble.

Burials Behind the Church

The church enclosure wall encompasses an irregular space; the wall runs close to the church on the northern and southern sides until it reaches the eastern area. There the area between church and wall widens noticeably, suggesting that the monks had either planned to use this space for burial or that the burials were already there when the enclosure wall was built.

Nineteenth-century scholars noted the presence of graves here; the first report was that of Petrie, who in 1820 described only one grave behind the church:

> *On the east side of the chapel is an ancient stone sepulchre, like a pagan kistvaen, composed of large mica slates, with a cover of limestone. The stones at the ends are rudely sculptured with ornamental crosses and a human figure, and the covering slab was also carved, and probably was inscribed with his name but its surface is now much-effaced. (Petrie 1845, 420)*

In 1839 O'Donovan did not mention the area east of the church at all. Wakeman, however, made sketches of crosses that apparently disappeared shortly afterwards and are no longer visible on the site. One of them appears to confirm Petrie's description of end stones 'rudely sculptured with ornamental crosses and a human figure' (Fig. 56).

Wakeman filed no written report to the Ordnance Survey, but decades later he wrote two articles about the High Island ruins. In 1863, in one of these articles, he described a number of tombs accompanied by crosses in the area east of the church:

> *Within the shadow of the eastern gable, ranged side by side, are a number of little enclosures, about seven feet long by two in breadth, made, like the pagan kistloaen, of flags placed edgeways and forming an oblong. These are evidently graves of the earliest Christian period, and at the time of our visit several appeared to have been recently opened and in the stone forming the western end of the enclosure we could, in each instance, discover the tracings of a cross within a circle... (1863, 220).*

Figure 56

Sketch made by Wakeman in 1839 of an anthropomorphic stone on High Island, Co. Galway. This sketch is found on a sheet bearing the handwritten inscription 'Ancient stones near the church on High Island, Omey Parish' (RIA MS 12T9, 43). Courtesy Royal Irish Academy.

The Church Enclosure Wall: Burials

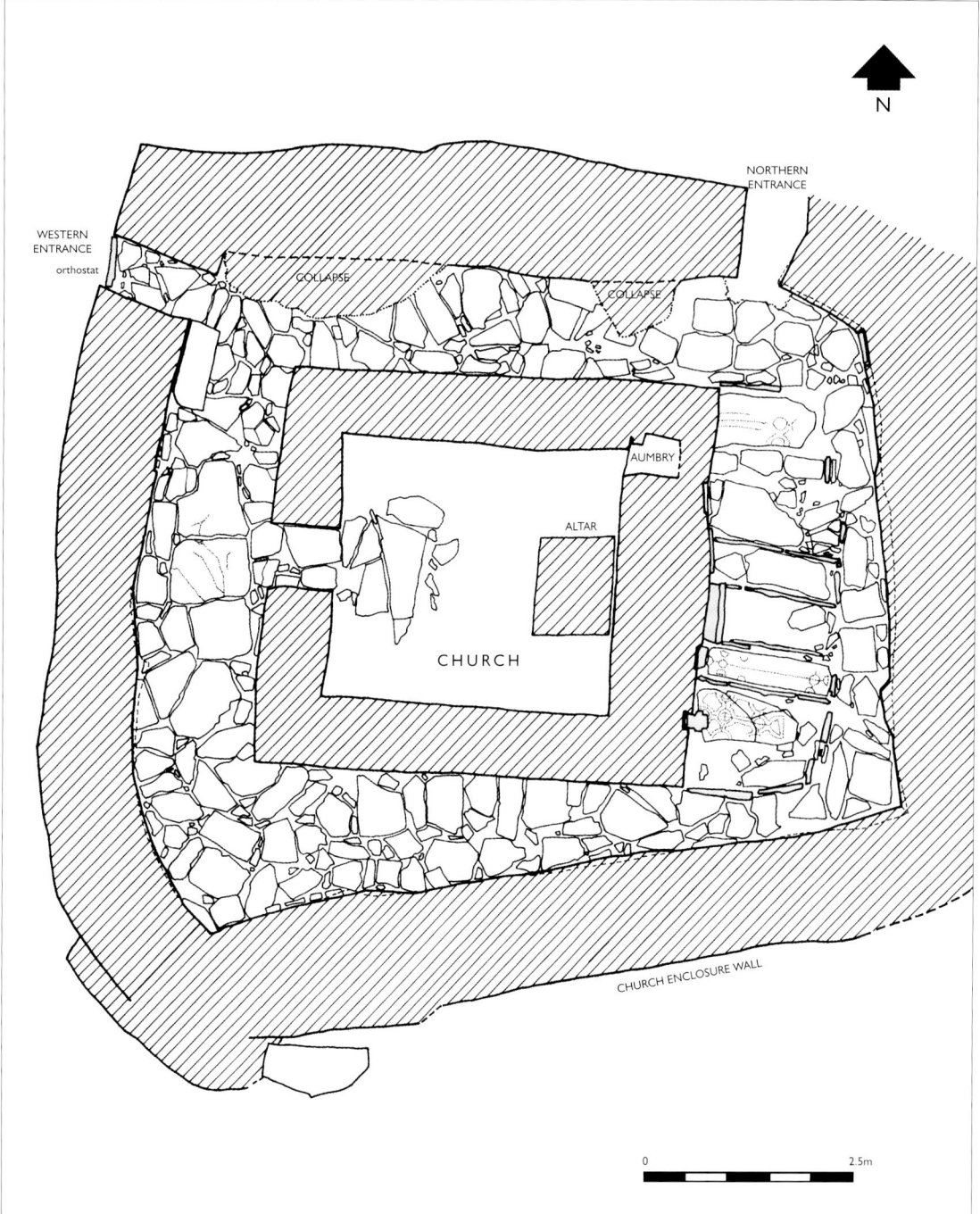

Figure 57
Drawing showing the upper paving in the church on High Island, Co. Galway, the paving around the church and the burials behind the church. Drawing by G.D. Rourke based partly on plans of paving contributed by Scally of 1996, excavations, partly on photos by Marshall, 1996, and finally by on-site checking.

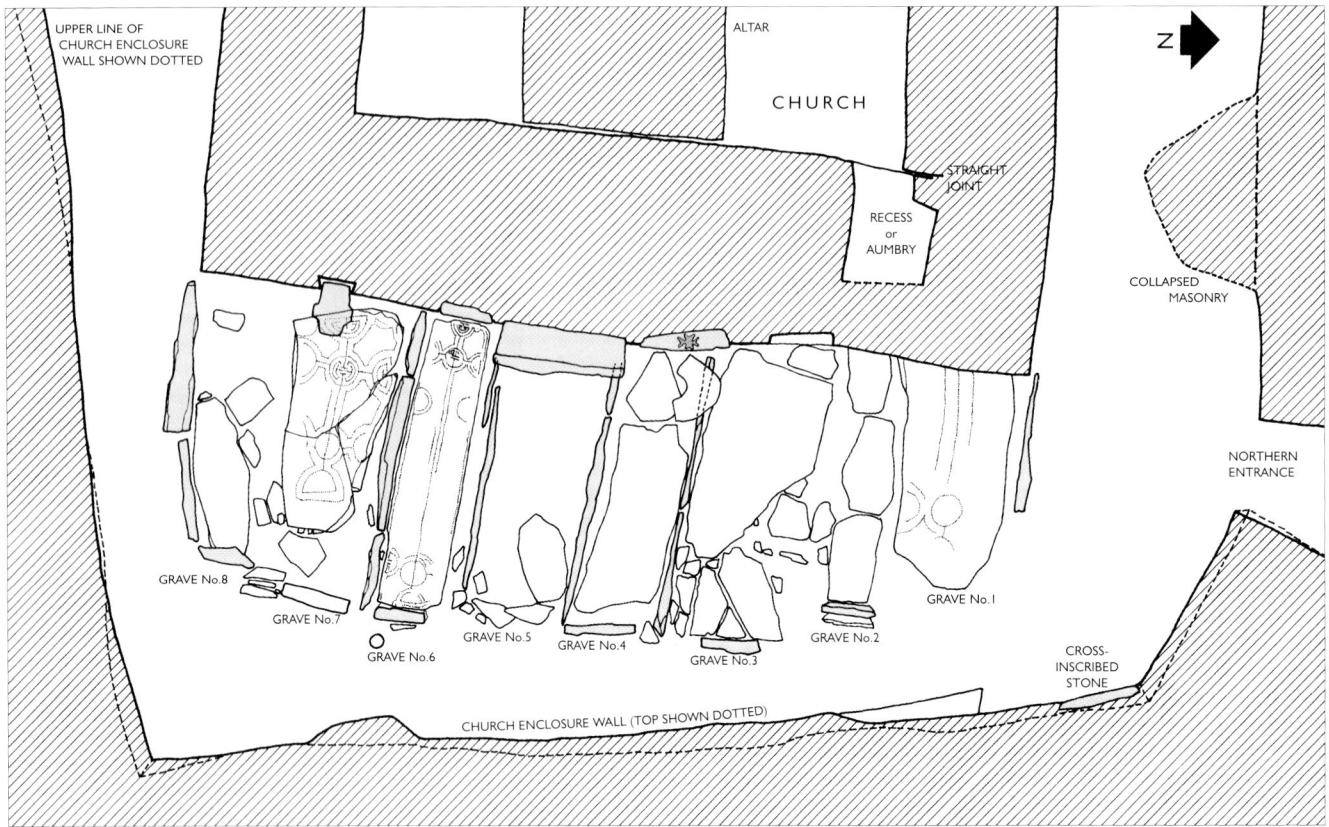

From Wakeman's description of these burials we assumed the burials ran east-west, with an inscribed cross as a headstone, a typical Christian burial pattern in this period. These burials, placed in the limited space east of the church, were likely to be those of important monks. In 1869 the next written account of a visitor to High Island, made by George Kinahan, said nothing about tombs or crosses east of the church. None of the reports written after 1869 mentioned anything east of the church; clearly, the continued collapse of the eastern gable wall and the enclosure wall had finally concealed all trace of them sometime between 1839 and 1869. One of the main reasons for excavation in 1995 was to determine if these burials were still there. The first season's work revealed that Petrie and Wakeman's reports had been substantially accurate, but seriously inadequate, even misleading, because they failed to describe so much.

Under the collapse of the two walls there appeared to be eight tombs, several of which were carefully constructed with long stone side walls looking, as Wakeman had noted, like 'pagan kistloaen' (Figs. 57 and 58).

The tombs, however, were far more embellished than his remarks indicated; indeed, they are among the most elaborate burials known in Ireland in this period. Four of the burials have decorated headstones, six have decorated footstones and three of the tombs have decorated recumbent stones.[133] The decorated cross stones forming

Figure 58a

Plan showing details of the eight graves east of the church on High Island, Co. Galway. Both 58a and 58b are composite drawings based on excavation during 1995 and 1996 in order to show the appearance of the recumbent stones and headstones before excavation of the graves. Plan G.D. Rourke.

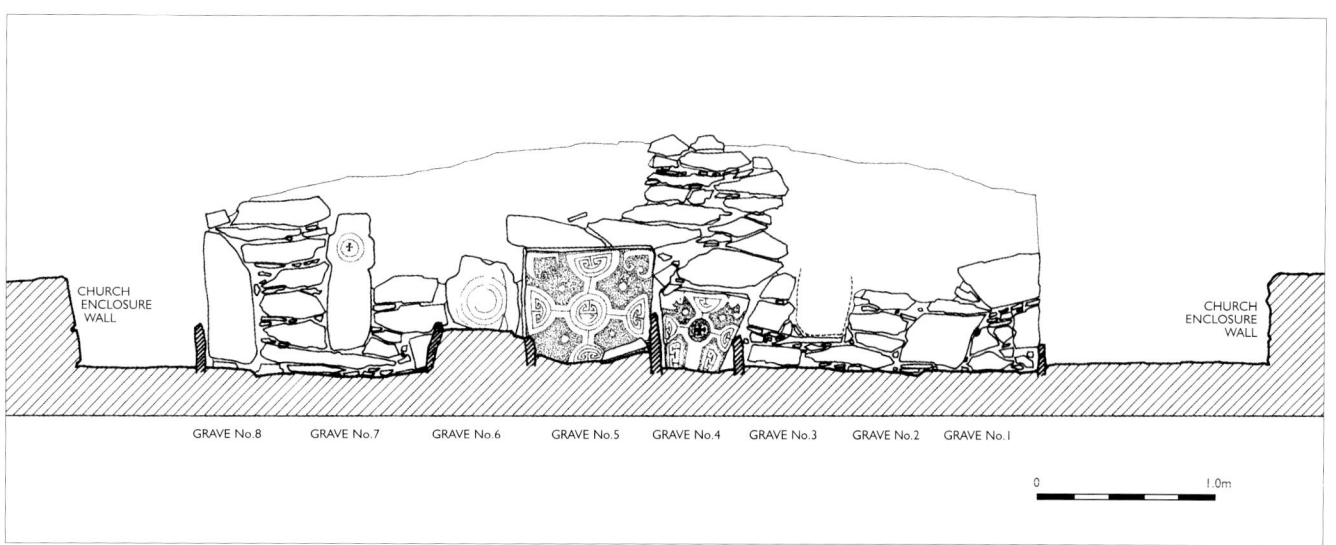

Figure 58b

Elevation showing headstones of the burials east of the church on High Island, Co. Galway. Drawing by G.D. Rourke.

part of the burials doubled the number of decorated cross stones previously recorded on High Island. Excavation also showed that a number of stones are missing: originally seven of the graves had footstones, five had headstones, and one recumbent stone may also be missing.

The style of several of the graves here is essentially an elaborate variation of lintel-cist graves. Long stones set on their sides form the sides of these graves, stones that often project above ground, and a stone lintel or recumbent stone covers the top of five graves. Lintel-cist graves appear in Scotland around the fifth century (Dalland 1993, 327–444) and are believed by some Scottish archaeologists to be found in Scotland between the fifth to eighth centuries. This type of grave is also common during this period in Ireland at sites such as Ballyshannon, County Donegal (O'Brien 1997), Reask, County Kerry (Fanning 1981, 79–84) and Illaunloughan, County Kerry (Marshall and Walsh, forthcoming) but, while the dates are hard to determine at other Irish sites, the style may have begun earlier and lasted longer than in Scotland.[134] The embellishment of this early simple style into graves with decorated recumbent stones and decorated head and footstones was probably common at many prestigious Irish monasteries as it was in Anglo-Saxon England, but little evidence of this survives in Ireland because these were the monasteries that suffered the most damage to their cemeteries. Something reminiscent of the High Island graves is found in the cist graves and graves with decorated recumbent stones preserved at Inish Cealtra. Lionard also (1961, 149–150) noted the presence of nineteen cist graves at Glendalough with decorated recumbent stones, which also have small socket holes at the head or foot of the grave, meant to hold small stone crosses or cross-decorated stones. The presence of these graves on High Island is, therefore, most likely owed to the exceptional state of preservation of the early medieval remains here rather than to their unique qualities.

Initially we were inclined to number the graves from left to right in normal reading style, which is a simple, natural manner in which to number the graves. However, excavation showed that the burial order was the opposite. We have, therefore, numbered them by starting with the grave in the northeastern corner as no. 1. Excavation also revealed differences in the construction, geology and, oddly, even in the content of the graves.

The most striking aspect of these burials, one that may be singular, is that when the eastern church wall was constructed, the headstones of five already existing graves were incorporated into the church wall. The wall must have been built, therefore, after the latest grave with a headstone was completed. Unfortunately, there is no datable evidence for this one, which was burial no. 7. It must, however, have been completed after burial no. 6, which was dated AD 980–1025 and before burial no. 8 (AD 1030–1166), which has no headstone and is the only burial that might have been placed here after the wall was built. The eastern wall, therefore, was most likely built sometime in the eleventh century. Two other headstones were set in niches in the wall, which were clearly created and shaped especially for them. Cross stones were commonly reused in other structures on a number of early medieval ecclesiastical sites, as lintels for churches or dwelling structures, as sidestones for graves, etc. Reused cross stones are even commonly found in the fabric of churches, in Irish churches such as the foundation stones of the church of Gallen Priory or in many Anglo-Saxon churches such as Ormesby (Kendrick 1939, 1–20; Morris 1983, 79; Gem 1983, 79). In all cases these cross stones were detached from their original context and significance, but clearly more was intended on High Island than the preservation of the cross stones. Most of these headstones, moreover, under enormous pressure from the weight of the eastern wall, had been pushed downwards and outwards; stones placed vertically offer smaller weight-bearing surfaces and are, therefore, inherently less stable. Constructional solidity, however, was secondary to the main purpose in building this wall, because the monks clearly planned to incorporate the headstones into the church for spiritual reasons. The visible bonding of the two is an architectural statement easily understood by Christian pilgrims, a signal that distinctly marks the men buried here as saints.

From the beginning the first two or three graves appeared to be the earliest: the church wall lies directly upon part of the decorated recumbent stone of grave no. 1 and also lies on one of the small covering stones of grave no. 2; in addition, these two graves were on a level some 0.25m lower than the other graves. In 1997 uncompleted excavation of graves nos. 2 and 3, however, indicated that they, along with grave no. 1, had possibly never actually been graves. An extensive spread of a dark charcoal-laden soil, similar to that under the grey mortar-like material in the southeastern interior corner of the church, suggests that this exterior charcoal layer may be a continuation of the one inside the church. If so, any burial in this area would have to predate the activity that created these layers and would of necessity be comparatively early.[135] They would also have to be earlier than burial no. 4, which was dated to the late ninth to late tenth century. And yet great efforts had been made to create the appearance of graves, although the visible side stones characteristic of the five cist graves are absent here, except for the burial-area boundary stones north of grave no. 1. Christianity is the religion of sacred graves so we do not believe that these graves were simply decorative accessories created to even up the appearance of this area. These were deliberately, not casually, constructed, for a serious purpose. It is possible that these were cenotaphs or memorials for beloved men (abbots?) previously buried elsewhere in the mosastery, lost at sea, or otherwise unable to be brought home for burial.[136]

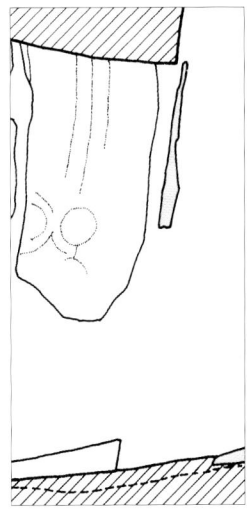

Figure 59
Drawing of Grave no. 1 behind the church on High Island, Co. Galway (taken from the plan in Fig. 58a).

Grave no. 1

The first grave in the northeastern corner, no. 1 (Scally's F30), has a decorated recumbent stone, now badly effaced (Fig. 59). This grave will never be excavated because of its position under the northeastern corner of the church wall.

Grave no. 2

Grave no. 2 (Scally's F34) appeared to be the least likely to be a grave because of its narrow width, but it did have a decorated footstone (Fig. 60).

Figure 60
Drawing of Grave no. 2 behind the church on High Island, Co. Galway (taken from the plan in Figure 58a).

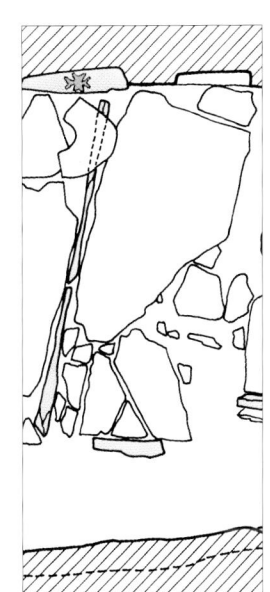

Grave no. 3

Grave no. 3 (Scally's burial F25) had a simple undecorated recumbent stone, a decorated footstone, and, in addition, a niche, now empty, had been constructed in the base of the eastern church wall for its headstone (Fig. 61).[137]

The large irregular-shaped undecorated recumbent stone had been placed close to the eastern wall of the church. A fill similar to that found in grave no. 4 lay under the recumbent stone, consisting of small fish bones, quartz stones and small fragments of mortar. A sizeable

Figure 61
Grave no. 3 behind the church on High Island, Co. Galway (taken from the plan shown in Fig. 58a).

pocket of mortar, some pieces with small stones still clinging to it, lay under the centre of the recumbent stones. This material stopped at a layer of large stones, consisting primarily of three long ones, which lay diagonally across no. 3, extending into grave no. 2.[138] It is most likely that the material lying between the recumbent stone and the lower diagonal stones was added when grave no. 4 was constructed in order to equalise the levels of the two graves. The grave level of no. 3 needed to be raised in order to brace the northern sidestones of grave no. 4 and prevent them from slipping out of place. The installation of grave sidestones provides an excellent practical reason both for raising the level of this grave and leaving graves nos. 1 and 2, which had no sidestones, at their original levels.

Under the second layer of stones was a deposit that may be identical to the material in the interior northeastern corner of the church, a dark layer containing charcoal. At the base of the eastern wall just north of the sidestone of grave no. 4, there was also a small patch of grey material, roughly 4cm long and 2 cm thick, that appears identical to the mortar-like material found inside the church. Occasional drop-sized pieces of this mortar-like material were found at random at the lowest excavation level, most notably clinging to several large stones. The dark charcoal layer extends more fully into grave no. 2 and under the recumbent stone of grave no. 1. Excavation in this area ceased at this point as there was no sign of grave fill at this level, and the strong possibility existed that these layers were identical to those on the other side of the church wall.

Grave no. 4

Grave no. 4 (Scally's F23), the first of the cist graves, had a decorated footstone, a large undecorated irregular-shaped recumbent stone and an elaborately decorated headstone that was part of the base level of the eastern church wall (see Fig. 62). Much of the small but sturdy headstone was below ground level and several courses of the eastern wall remained intact and in place directly above it.

Two sidestones on each side form the northern and southern borders of this grave. On the northern side the second long stone, the one furthest away from the church, is a reused erect cross stone approx. 0.76m long, now placed on its side. On the exterior northern face of this stone is a design of a cross in a circle with terminals that bifurcate outside the circle (Fig. 112 in chapter 8). Multiple layers of large, thin stone packing lay under the grave fill, protecting the burial of an older man, approximately fifty-five years old. Radiocarbon analysis placed his date of death between AD 881 and 977.[139]

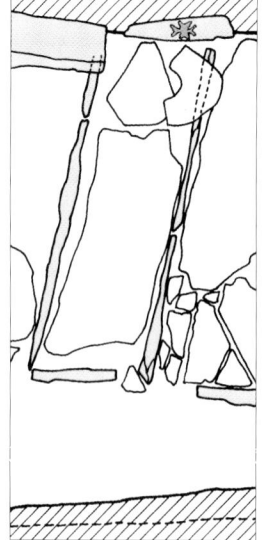

Figure 62

Grave no. 4 behind the church on High Island, Co. Galway (taken from the plan in Fig. 58a.).

The Church Enclosure Wall: Burials

Figure 63

Grave no. 4 behind the church on High Island, Co. Galway, showing clearly that the headstone formed the base course of the church's eastern wall. Also visible are the grave's sidestones. Photo J.W. Marshall, 1995.

Figure 64

Grave no. 5 behind the church on High Island, Co. Galway (taken from the plan in Figure 58a).

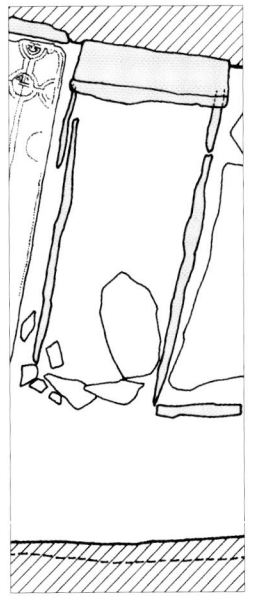

Grave no. 5

Grave no. 5 (Scally's burial F21) had the largest, most impressive headstone, one that is elaborately decorated with a variation of the expansional cross design seen on the headstone of no. 4 (Figs. 64 and 65). The headstone, which was also part of the base of the eastern wall, still had several courses of stone balanced precariously above it, although everything had been pushed forward away from the wall face as the eastern gable collapsed (see Fig. 63). This headstone was set deeply into the ground so that little more than one half of its surface could be seen; this view uncovered by excavation is precisely the one drawn by Wakeman in 1839 (Fig. 66).

A large rectangular stone at the base, just behind the skeleton's head, helped to hold the headstone in place and also provided an end stone for the grave. Originally there must have been a footstone for this grave because excavation revealed an empty socket for it still in place at the end of the grave; the socket was formed by two stones and several small wedge stones. No recumbent stone nor, indeed, any large stone covers this grave, but it is probable that a grave with such an elaborate headstone did have some sort of recumbent stone. Wakeman had noted that 'at the time of our visit several [graves] appeared to have been recently opened…' Some disturbance of the graves had clearly taken place, as one headstone and one footstone are definitely missing and one recumbent stone was broken. Perhaps it was these surface signs of disturbance that provoked Wakeman's comments, because excavation showed that only one grave had ever been opened, and its disturbance only became apparent after excavation.

Figure 65
1996 excavation of grave no. 5 on High Island, Co. Galway. Photo was taken before removal of the skeleton; three quartz stones laid between his legs may be seen resting on the flagstone-lined grave. The empty socket for a footstone may also be seen in the foreground. Photo J.W. Marshall.

No stone packing was used in grave no. 5 to protect the body; the grave fill, similar to that of several of the graves, consisted of a damp brown clay mixed in places with small stones, flecks of charcoal, tiny fish and bird bones and mortar pieces. This grave was well built with sturdy side stones and, in addition, a stone cover placed on the lower side stones to protect the head.

On High Island each of the three complete cist graves appeared to have its own lower sidestones, which defined the grave itself, but they shared the upper sidestones. It is extremely unusual for graves to have a double layer of sidestones; however, grave no. 4 is the sole burial that has a single layer of sidestones, the only one of the three here that conforms to standard grave construction. When the adjacent grave, no. 5, was constructed, the grave was dug to a deeper level. Consequently, its sidestones are below those of no. 4, on the north. It thus appeared that no. 5 had a double set of sidestones on this side. For some reason, perhaps to match and balance the levels, the monks then added a thin set of upper sidestones on its other, southern side. These upper southern sidestones were in turn used by the next burial, no. 6; they also acted as a placement guide for the next grave. This is a rational and efficient method of constructing graves in a restricted area if it is necessary or desirable to have double-layered sidestones.[140]

Figure 66
1839 sketch of the headstone for grave no. 5 on High Island, Co. Galway by W. F. Wakeman, showing half of the stone as it still looked set in place in 1995 (RIA MS 12T9, 43). Courtesy Royal Irish Academy.

The monk in grave no. 5 received very careful and special treatment in several respects. The bottom of the grave was carefully lined with flat, thin stones the width of the grave, which, while not common, had been done for centuries with some graves (O'Brien 1997). More unusual still, fine sand sparkling with minute fragments of crushed shell was poured on top of the stones, perhaps to provide a cushion for the body, and then, after deposition, another layer of this fine sand must have been poured on top, as substantial remnants were still attached to the skeleton. Fine sand like this cannot be found on High Island, but there are several beaches on Omey Island where it is plentiful.[141] White quartz stones, deliberately placed around the body, three between the legs some 15cm below the pelvis and four more around the ankles, are another distinctive element of this burial. White quartz stones were found scattered in quantity on top of all the graves east of the church, probably brought by pilgrims; however, substantial amounts of white quartz were also used by the monks as part of the grave fill under the recumbent stones. This High Island burial, however, is the first known early medieval burial in Ireland where white quartz was placed around or on top of the body.[142] Radiocarbon dating places the death of this monk between AD 980 and 1023. These dates, which show no overlap with the date of death for the adjoining monk, also confirm original intuitive estimates that burial order ran from north to south.[143]

With increased excavations of early medieval sites, it is becoming evident that the monks of this period, as well as pilgrims, considered white quartz to have important spiritual meaning. There is no specific reference to white quartz in the literary sources of the time; however, its significance likely relates to its colour because it is a plentiful, readily available stone. White has traditionally been the Christian colour of purity, innocence and a holy life (Ferguson [1954] 1972, 152). The *Leabhar Breac*, a volume of passions, homilies and sermons based on Latin texts, mentions white precisely in these terms. The mystical significance of colours in the vestments of priests discusses the meaning of white in one sermon: 'What the white is intended for when the priest looks upon it is, that he should blush at with sensitiveness and shame if he should not be chaste and pure in heart and mind, …or like the color of the swan before the sun, without any kind of sin remaining in his heart'.[144] Christ wore white after his Resurrection, as did the angel of the Lord who rolled back the stone from the door of Christ's tomb:

> *'His countenance was like lightning, and his raiment white as snow' (Matthew 28:3). Irish monks wore white to celebrate mass on special days as early as the seventh century, for Adomnán mentions a special mass St Columba ordered to honour the death of St Colmán: '…they went with the saint to the church, clothed in white, as on a solemn feast-day'.* (Adomnán's Life of Columbus, ed. Anderson 1991, iii:12)

The careful, elaborate construction of the grave, the fine sand poured under and over the body, and the quartz pebbles carefully placed around it, distinguish this burial from that of grave no. 5 and suggest that the monk buried here was a particularly well loved and holy man.

Grave no. 6

The construction of Grave no. 6 (Scally's F18) is unusual, although some details, particularly in the manner of burial, are strikingly similar to those of no. 5. This grave has a decorated headstone, decorated recumbent stone and decorated footstone (see Fig. 67). Its headstone, a reused cross stone decorated on both sides, was set as part of the base of the eastern wall; as in grave no. 5, a large stone was placed at its base behind the grave. Neither the recumbent stone nor footstone are of island stone, as all the other monastic structures and features are; they are limestone. Limestone is not found closer than Clew Bay, County Mayo or the Aran Islands, both approximately eighty kilometres away. The quality of the stone allowed the recumbent stone to be finely tapered and cut for the grave and also contributed to the elegance of the cross design, a variation of the expansional cross design seen on the recumbent stones of grave no. 1 and grave no. 7, and the headstone of graves nos. 4 and 5. It must have been extremely heavy and awkward to get this stone onto the island, even though we assume the stone was at least roughly cut to reduce its weight before transporting it; indeed, because of the elegance of its carving, it was probably entirely carved to High Island specifications at its point of origin. When the recumbent stone was moved in 1997, it took four men to lift and move it a short distance (Fig. 68). As Edwards notes (1998, 102), local stone was generally used for carving because of transportation problems.

Figure 67

Grave no. 6 behind the church on High Island, Co. Galway (taken from the plan in Figure 58a).

Figure 68

Men moving the heavy limestone recumbent stone for grave no. 6 behind the church on High Island, Co. Galway. This recumbent stone is made from a beautiful dark blue-grey limestone with 'ostrea' fossils. Photo J.W. Marshall, 1997.

The Church Enclosure Wall: Burials

It would have taken special equipment to lift this stone up the cliffs at the southwestern landing. The effort involved in bringing this stone to the island gives us some idea of the monks' determination to use this particular stone for the grave of a special monk.

The footstone was found broken in place; the top had sheared away from its base. The head had a cross in a circle design inscribed on it, whereas a small figurative design decorated the shaft of the cross (Fig. 69). The shaft of the cross was sunk into the ground to hold the cross upright; consequently, the figurative design necessarily remained hidden until excavation. Was it never intended to show? Another odd feature of this cross is that the design faces west instead of east like the others, making it harder for a visitor to the grave to see (see discussion on this, p. 149). Could this stone have been turned around at some point?

Under the limestone recumbent stone, there was a thick layer of stone rubble mixed with many pieces of white quartz and some dry, loose soil, instead of the usual grave-fill soil. Two large stones lay under the rubble layer; these stones

Figure 69

The footstone for grave no. 6 behind the church on High Island, Co. Galway, with its unusual figurative design, one of only two figurative designs among the decorated stones here. The small figure is holding aloft a gospel(?) book in each hand. Photo Con Brogan, 1997. Courtesy Dúchas The Heritage Service.

Figure 70

Grave no. 6 behind the church on High Island, Co. Galway, after excavation, with the base of the church's eastern wall resting in part on the grave's lintel, a clear indication that the church was built after the grave. The northern lower sidestone in the foreground, built for this grave, appears to have slipped south slightly. Sand covering the stone paving of the grave lies between the skeleton's legs.
Photo J.W. Marshall, 1997.

rested on the lower side stones and acted as lintels or covers for the grave. The smaller upper one resembles the stone head cover used in grave no. 5, but here the stone is firmly fixed by the church wall sitting on a few centimetres of it; a clear confirmation that the grave was here when the church wall was constructed (see Fig. 70). Another sign that the grave was earlier than the church is that both the lower sidestones near the church run under the church; this would have been extremely awkward and difficult to do after construction of the church.

Under the two large flagstones was a grave-fill of soil that contained fragmented bits of mortar debris as well as two tiny patches of the grey material, a type of mortar, found in the interior and exterior southeast corner of the church. The bed of the grave was at the same level as no. 5 and, also in similar fashion, was paved with stones. The six stones lining this grave are of greater dimension in every way than those of no. 5 and are reminiscent of the paving stones in the path around the church. The same fine sand used in grave no. 5, moreover, was laid over the flagstones under the body, and then also sprinkled on top of it.

Still another similarity to the neighbouring grave was that small white quartz stones, smaller and less conspicuous than the ones used in no. 5, were also found, one at the elbow and two at the ankle. Graves nos. 5 and 6 are the most similar in their burial depth and style, in their use of a lined stone base, an end stone placed behind the head of the monk and in white quartz placed near the body, and fine sand laid as a bed on the base of the grave. None of the other High Island burials were treated this way so it was not surprising to learn that these two men had probably known each other, perhaps even died within a few years of each other. The radiocarbon dates of the skeleton covers exactly the same narrow range of time, from AD 980 to 1025, as those of the neighbouring monk in grave no. 5.[145]

There is another unusual aspect about the setting of the grave's upper and lower sidestones, however, besides

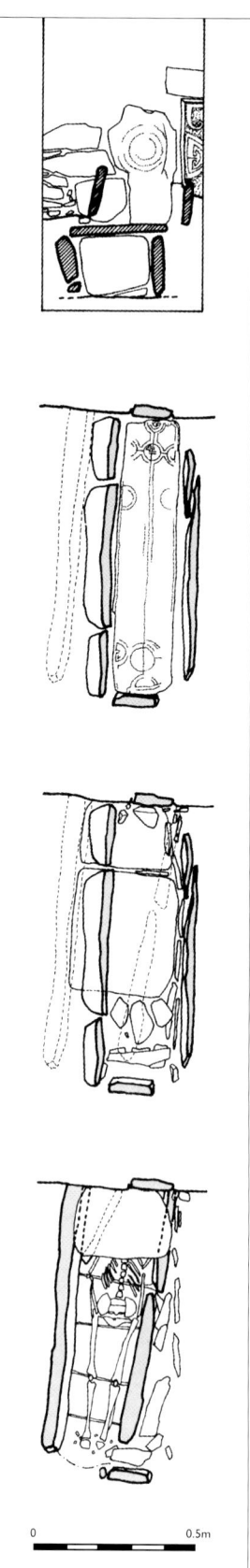

Figure 71a
Section through grave no. 6 behind the church on High Island, Co. Galway, showing the relative position of the headstone. Drawing by G.D. Rourke based on photographs and survey by Marshall, Rourke and Scally, 1997.

Figures 71b, 71c and 71d
Plans of grave no. 6 on High Island, Co. Galway, before, during and after excavation, showing the relationship of the skeleton to grave components. Drawings by G.D. Rourke.

their being double-layered. Before excavation this grave appeared reasonably straight and parallel with no. 5, with its head and footstones aligned with each other and set in the centre of the grave (see Fig. 71b).

After excavation, however, it became apparent that the lower sidestones forming the grave itself actually were not straight like those of the other graves, but tilt diagonally towards grave no. 7, to the south.[146] More important, the head and footstones were not centred on the grave but set on its northern side; indeed, the footstone is altogether off-line with the feet (Fig. 71).

We do not understand why the lower sidestones slant diagonally but we can present a logical explanation for the odd positioning of the upper sections of this grave. The explanation relates to the inclusion of the headstones in the construction of the eastern church wall and the necessity to fit five of them into the centre of the wall. The monks may well have feared that headstones on or too near the corners might have seriously endangered the corners of the church, which by necessity need to be robust. The upper sidestone to the right was really the upper sidestone for grave no. 5 and didn't need to be moved at all. The headstone, footstone, recumbent stone and the upper southern sidestone, however, needed to be moved slightly towards grave no. 5 in order to fit the headstone close to its neighbours and leave space to build a niche for grave no. 7 before the corner. In short, they realigned the grave so that it appeared straight. This necessitated moving the headstone and footstone more than the recumbent stone; the distance involved was not great, perhaps only 12 to 15cm.[147]

Limestone was used only for this one structure on the island. Was it a gift? Was the monk here originally from a limestone region? It certainly is a particular mark of distinction for this monk as it represents an enormous investment in time and labour to get this stone onto the island. Athough the stone came a long way, the designs on the recumbent stone and footstone are so clearly related to other High Island designs that the stone must have been carved on the island or perhaps, more likely, made to the order of the High Island monks at its point of origination. The sand could easily be acquired, especially if Omey belonged to the same *Féchín paruchia*. Is it possible these two monks were originally from Omey Island, or was this a reverent gesture and a similar burial style for two men who died contemporaneously?

Petrie's Special Tomb

Petrie described a special tomb that had ornamental crosses and a human figure on the end stones and a decorated but badly effaced limestone cover. No one grave behind the church now fits this description, indeed, only graves nos. 5 and 6 each contain one of the elements Petrie mentions. The most distinctive, easily recognisable features of Petrie's tomb are the limestone recumbent stone and the end stone with a human figure carved on it. We only know of two figurative cross stones on High Island, the one on the footstone of grave no. 6 and the decorated stone that Wakeman drew in 1839, a stone that is no longer visible at High Island (Fig. 56). Wakeman's drawing, on which he annotated the stone's size as 2 feet, 6 inches (0.76m), similar in size and shape to the other footstones, was further annotated 'Ancient stones near the Church at High Island'. It is possible that this was the missing footstone for grave no. 5.

If Petrie was describing no. 5, which has the most ornamental cross of all, it is necessary to assume that its missing recumbent stone must have also been limestone and its footstone the stone that Wakeman drew. If Wakeman's drawing was that of a footstone, the figure would have been difficult to see while properly set in the ground, but it may have already been out of place at that time.

Grave no. 6 does have a badly effaced limestone recumbent stone and a figurative design on its footstone, although it is difficult to understand how Petrie could have seen the figure on the shaft of its footstone. The little figure on the shaft was covered by the grave and the footstone itself tightly wedged in against the paving by the recumbent stone. Presumably, this stone would have been difficult to take out and put back in again unless the recumbent stone were also moved, which in view of its weight seems unlikely. Petrie was probably describing one of these two graves, but it is not possible to decide confidently which one it was, based on the present evidence.

Grave no. 7

Grave no. 7 (Scally's burial F14), like grave no. 6, had a decorated head and footstone and a decorated recumbent stone (Fig. 72). The headstone, like that of grave no. 6, did not form the base level of the church, but was set into a shallow niche constructed for it. The niche itself rested on a sizeable base stone for the church wall; the cross was set into a narrow slot (natural or cut?) in this stone. Above the base stone the wall face was recessed or set back 6cm and the sides of the recess were also grooved or cut back so that the headstone, which was slightly wider above than below, would fit as it rose into the wall face and be held in place (Fig. 73).

Both the head and footstones were reused stones, as they were decorated on both sides (see discussion pp. 147, 148, Figs. 99 and 100). The design on the recumbent stone is, like the recumbent stone next to it on grave no. 6, that of an Expansional cross, expanded into mirror images, only the work is more crude here than on the limestone (see Fig. 105). At some time, unfortunately, the recumbent stone broke into three pieces, probably when the eastern gable of the church began collapsing, or earlier, when the grave was disturbed.

There were several unusual elements about this grave. There appeared to be no lower sidestones constructed for this otherwise carefully built grave. On the northern side the extremely long stone that served grave no. 6 as its southern side, a stone 1.62m

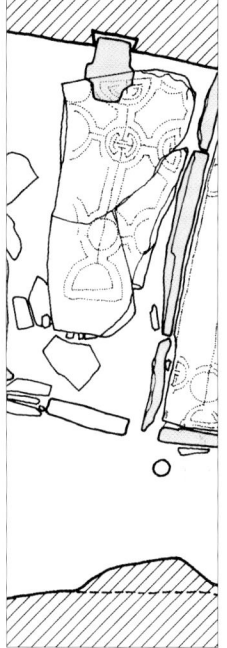

Figure 72

Grave no. 7 behind the church on High Island, Co. Galway (taken from the plan on Fig. 58a).

Figure 73
The niche constructed for the headstone for grave no. 7 behind the church on High Island, Co. Galway. The niche, 0.50m high, is located on the base stone of the church wall and space was tailored for it in the wall face. The church's wall face was recessed slightly to allow the stone to fit and grooves were carved in the surrounding stone to accommodate and hold the headstone. Photo J.W. Marshall, 1996.

long, as much as 0.23m high and 0.12m thick, was used on the bottom (Fig. 70). The southern sidestones were not sidestones for a cist grave but were simply three large blocks of stone casually separated from each other (Fig. 74). These stones may also relate to the most surprising aspect of this grave, which is the absence of any trace of a body.

There is every reason to believe that there was a skeleton here originally, not only because this is one of the most decorated graves but also because the soil contained within it was not natural boulder clay, but rather consisted of redeposited material, resembling grave-fill taken from a midden with a great deal of charcoal. The top layer consisted of broken stone mixed with grey clay. Underneath the top layer was more clay mixed with small stones and stone fragments, small quartz stones, a few fragmented animal bones and small lumps of mortar. A rough layer of stone packing running the length of the grave lay below this. Underneath the stone packing was more soil, some 12 to 15cm deep, some areas of which (near the church) contained tiny fish bones, small pieces of quartz and fragmented mortar.

Figure 74
Graves nos. 7 and 8 behind the church on High Island, Co. Galway. Grave no. 7 clearly used the upper and the lower sidestones for grave no. 6 as its northern sidestones, but evidently the three large rocks to the south substituted for its southern sidestones. The burial in this grave was mysteriously missing, although there was every reason to believe there had been one there originally. Visible in this photo are the footstones for Graves nos. 7 and 8. Photo J.W. Marshall, 1996.

It would have been impossible to place burial no. 7 in the area designated for him by his three sidestones, which rested on the grave's lowest soil layer, because Figure 74 shows that the ranging rod barely fits in. Due to the odd alignment of grave no. 6, grave no. 7 must have been placed at least 0.30–0.40m further to the south, filling the space now occupied by the three sidestones. It is possible that this grave may also have been realigned at the time of building the eastern church wall. The monks may have originally planned grave no. 7 to be the last burial behind the church, as the level of bedrock begins to rise here. One more burial, however, was fitted in.

Grave no. 8

Grave no. 8 (Scally's burial F11) in the southeastern corner is the last grave and marked only by a decorated footstone (see Fig. 74). The simplest and the most poorly constructed, it is also the shallowest of the graves. The northern sidestones have already been discussed above as particularly ineffective; the southern sidestones are, like their counterparts at the northeastern corner, primarily border or boundary markers, shallowly placed stones used to define the edge of the burial area as a whole, rather than forming the side of the grave.

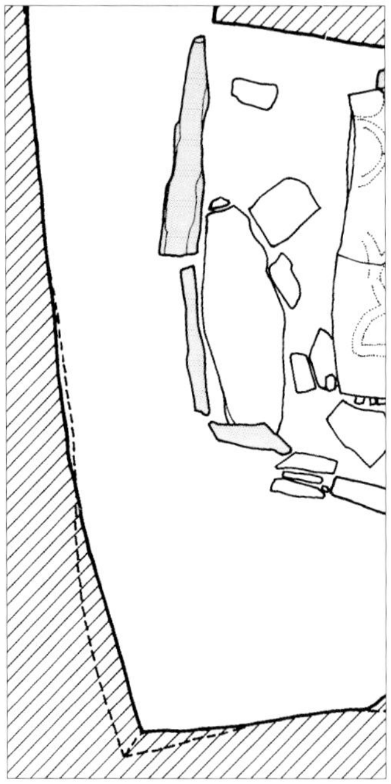

The upper fill of the grave was a layer of grey clay which lay on top of a layer of mixed irregularly placed and sized stone with some quartz in it; the whole grave fill and packing appeared carelessly done. The burial was so shallow that the skull and the feet of the skeleton lay a few centimetres above the paving level of the church enclosure and the pelvis was only a few centimetres below paving level. Another anomaly about this grave was that it was too short for its skeleton; his head was pressed up against the wall of the church and his legs had to be crossed in order to force him to fit. This grave and the church wall have no necessary relationship like that of the other graves, so that it might have been placed in here at any time after the church was built, a thought further encouraged by radiocarbon dating, which yielded a time of death somewhere between AD 1030 and 1166.[148]

We suspect that the absence of a skeleton in grave no. 7 and the cramped burial of no. 8 may be related in the following manner. A long time after the construction of the church that encompassed the burials behind this church, when the monks had long forgotten that graves nos. 6 and 7 had been somewhat realigned in order to consolidate their headstones within the wall, they tried to fit one more distinguished monk into

figure 75

Grave no. 8 behind the church on High Island, Co. Galway (taken from the plan on Fig. 58a).

this space. As they dug out the space for his grave, they discovered that grave no. 7 was occupying much of the space and, further, that bedrock was not far down in this space. The bones of no. 7 had to be moved and they may have taken up the original sidestones as well and quickly substituted the more irregular rocks to hold up the replaced recumbent stone of grave no. 7.

Ordinarily, an entire skeleton would not be taken out, but some of the bones, particularly the skull, simply moved to accommodate the new burial. Were these bones then deliberately taken for relics? The grave itself would naturally be restored. St Swithin was moved at Winchester from his original burial ground and redeposited into two different reliquaries in two different sections of the main church. His original grave, although empty, remained a holy site and maintained its status as a reliquary shrine. Alternatively, the monks may have removed no. 7 at an earlier time, again most likely for relics. Because the decoration on his recumbent stone closely resembles that of the recumbent stone of grave no. 6 and the headstone of grave no. 5, it is probable that he was buried in the same general period, sometime in the eleventh century.

The Saints and Church Architecture

The burials behind the church at High Island vividly demonstrate one of many ways in which Christian veneration of the saintly dead influenced church architecture. Christians believed that the physical remains of the saint, in part or in whole, and his possessions, indeed even objects that came into later contact with his bodily remains or possessions, continued to contain the saint's potent spiritual power. These relics or remains of the saints were, thus, carefully treated and displayed in reliquaries. Reliquaries and pilgrimages of the faithful to them became an essential driving force in the early Christian Church.

Decades ago André Grabar established that the cult of relics in European churches centred on the high altar, a practice whose origins were probably formed by two customs dating back to the early centuries of Christianity. Early Christians traditionally met at the tombs of the martyrs to celebrate their feast day and their day of death and also, during periods of persecutions, secretly gathered around the tombs of the martyrs in the catacombs, where mass was celebrated using the stone lid of the martyr's coffin for an altar. A natural parallel was drawn between the sacrifice of the martyr as a lesser human version of the greater divine sacrifice of Christ; the saint's grave and the celebration of the Eucharist became permanently connected. After the fourth-century legalisation of Christianity, this bond was expressed by building churches over the saint's tomb, with the altar generally over or close to the tomb; a famous example of this was the reburial of St Peter under the altar of St Peter's in Rome.[149] Early Christians may have been influenced as well by a sentence from Revelations (vi. 9): 'I saw under the altar the souls of them that had been slain for the word of God'.

With the geographic and numerical expansion of Christianity, it was soon no longer practical to build a church over the burial of a martyr or saint. The underlying theme, nevertheless, was only modified rather than eliminated. In the sixth century the letters of Pope Gregory the Great show that it had become customary to consecrate a church by placing relics in or under the altar(s) of the church, and in 787 the second Council of Nicaea explicitly obliged that relics be placed in altars for church consecration.[150] The continuous development of the cult of relics, with a consequent increase of pilgrims, was one of the primary motivations for the expanding evolution and development of the Church in Europe.

These architectural changes were most noticeable in the eastern end of the church, which commonly took the form of a crypt under the main altar or under the chancel, with a passageway or ambulatory for access to the relics running behind, with subsidiary altars, each with its own relics, in apses that radiated off the ambulatory (Grabar 1943–1946; Conant [1959] 1966, 26–29; Taylor 1984, 972–973).[151] These modifications in church plans evolved on the Continent and were most common there. Continental church architecture, however, was only tentatively adopted in Britain and Ireland; in England some churches used part of this pattern. In Ireland, outside of adoption of the chancel, few of these particular architectural alterations related to relics were constructed in early medieval stone churches. Indeed, as mentioned earlier (see pp. 91-93) the Irish apparently did not generally rebury a saint near the altar of the main church, although the association between relics and altars was certainly as strong as elsewhere. From documentary sources as early as the seventh century, when Adomnán mentions that St Columba's tunic and books were placed on the altar at Iona, to the 1143 AD reference in *The Annals of the Four Masters* to the great altar of Clomacnoise as 'the altar of Ciarán, with its relics…', relics were placed on or in altars.[152] The faithful went on pilgrimage to them, vows were sworn on them, they were carried into battle, and kings placed themselves under their protection.

The annexation of the headstones in the eastern wall of the High Island church appears, therefore, to belong to this general European pattern of expansion and construction of churches to encompass saintly relics or burials close to the altar, but was also adapted to adhere to the ancient restrictions against burial in churches still favoured in Ireland. The monks of High Island succeeded in bringing their saints into the church near the altar symbolically, while still keeping their bodies physically outside the church. This imaginative modification was also appropriate for this simple church with its severe space limitations. The particular variation seen here may be unique, as it is now unknown elsewhere.

The monks would naturally have wished to preserve this wall with its headstones, or at least its base, in a new stone church. The reason for the architectural and constructional discrepancies between the eastern wall and the other walls now becomes clear. And the instability created by these headstones and burials may also explain why the eastern gable collapsed whereas the rest of the church still remains relatively intact. Although the eastern gable wall proved to be the weakest of the walls it was, nevertheless, a robust wall that substantially survived until the nineteenth-century, some hundreds of years after the monks left the monastery.

Conclusions About the Church, Burials and Enclosure Wall

Petrie (1845), Wakeman (1863), and Herity (1987; 1990) have all believed that the tomb (or tombs) behind the eastern wall dated to a very early period; however, calibrated radiocarbon dates from these burials revealed that no burial was earlier than the late ninth century, with most of them at least a century later than that. What the visitor to High Island sees today in the remains of the church is part of the late centuries of monastic occupation, not part of its early period. There is, moreover, reason to believe that the present church is the last of at least three different churches in this area. The first church or churches would have been the one(s) behind which the present burials were located. The only indications for its existence except for the burials is the mortar found in all the burials, and possibly the lower paving inside the church. Excavation inside the church, moreover, had not as of 1997 exposed any trace of earlier walls. From this we conclude that the first church was probably in almost the same location as the present one. Mortar fragments found in the graves indicate that this church was also a mortared (and plastered?) stone church. Judging by the radiocarbon dates of burials nos. 4 to 7 this church, or these churches, lasted a long time, possibly from the ninth until the mid-eleventh century.

The second church, represented today only by the base of the eastern wall, was doubtless not built until after grave no. 7 had been constructed sometime in the eleventh century. The third church represented by the lower sections of the three other walls is of unknown date but is possibly mid to late eleventh or even perhaps early twelfth century; its gable walls and roof were then later remodelled twice.

The present upper western gable represents the last major remodelling of the church. Another radiocarbon date for the charcoal in the mortar of this gable reveals a date range for this last constructional phase. The mortar sample, taken on the western exterior, 0.6m above the lintel on the southern side, came out, when calibrated to a calendrical scale, to a broad range of AD 690–1210. Clearly this broad range is not precise enough to state more than that the last construction on the church took place no later than the end of the twelfth century or the beginning of the thirteenth century.[153]

Continued excavation may uncover the vestiges of churches that are earlier still in or near this same area, because this is the most desirable, protected location within the monastic enclosure. The limited space within the monastic enclosure, as well as

Figure 76
Aerial photo of Caher Island, Co. Mayo, from the west, showing the church inside a rectangular enclosure wall in the centre of the photograph. Photo Con Brogan. Courtesy Dúchas The Heritage Service.

within the church enclosure wall, constrained the types of changes possible, i.e. enlargement and complicated additions to the church were not possible.

There are several factors suggesting that the church enclosure wall is earlier than today's visible church. An interesting, although certainly not conclusive, case for this is presented here solely as conjecture and as a hypothesis for future investigation. The basis for the argument relates to the church's orientation relative to that of the church enclosure wall and to the paving outside the church.

Ordinarily, a church enclosure wall would be built after the church and its walls would be coordinated with those of the church, such as the rectangular stone enclosure walls around churches at Caher Island, County Mayo, Carrownaseer, County Galway and the Norse church on the Brough of Deerness in Orkney; here the walls are parallel with the church and allow reasonable space within the enclosure (Fig. 76).[154]

At High Island, however, there is a striking misalignment of the axes, particularly evident in the church's southern and eastern walls. These are not at all parallel with the present church, thereby creating awkward spaces in these areas between the church and its enclosure wall. The western and northern walls, moreover, are parallel to the church but not with the two other walls, which only adds to the strange effect. Early medieval construction was not precise; however, no matter what the construction sequence or how crude the buildings, the axes and the orientation of the structures should coincide. A number of excavators have used burial alignment as a prime indicator for another church. Among the relatively few sites where there is a rectangular church enclosure wall, all three, burials, church and enclosure wall, should align if constructed concurrently (see O'Brien 1996 on importance of burial alignment).

The difference in alignment between two walls of the enclosure with the other two walls and with the church creates a significant structural anomaly. When the monastic site of Kiltiernan, County Galway, was excavated, the excavator found a church enclosure wall that was not parallel to the church; here his suspicion that the misalignment indicated an earlier no-longer visible church was buttressed by the discovery of graves that were aligned with the church enclosure wall but not with the church (Duigan 1951, 73–75). Although excavation at High Island has been more limited than that at Kiltiernan, the burials here do not imply that the earlier church associated with them, the so-called first church, was orientated differently. On the contrary, the manner in which the eastern wall of the church sits squarely on the recumbent stone of grave no. 1 and on part of grave no. 2 suggests that the eastern wall of this church was set back and that this church was probably, therefore, smaller than the present one, but oriented exactly the same way. The second church was wider than the present church (see discussion above on original width of the east wall, pp. 80–82) but its orientation was the same. The walls of the church enclosure make no sense, nevertheless, if they were built contemporaneously with any of the three churches we are certain were in this location, all orientated the same way. What had caused the peculiar arrangement of the church enclosure wall?

It seems likely there must have been another church or churches earlier still than any previously noted. If this was a smaller church within a smaller enclosure wall, with its east-west axis rotated 14° more to the north, the present western and southern walls would make sense (Fig. 77).

If the monks decided to build a slightly bigger church with its present orientation, the new church would not have fit within the old enclosure's eastern and northern walls. These walls would have had to be changed. The new walls were now automatically aligned with the

Figure 77

Conjectural drawing showing a church on High Island, Co. Galway, showing the northern and western enclosure walls turned slightly so that they are in conformity with the existing southern and eastern enclosure walls. Drawing by G.D. Rourke.

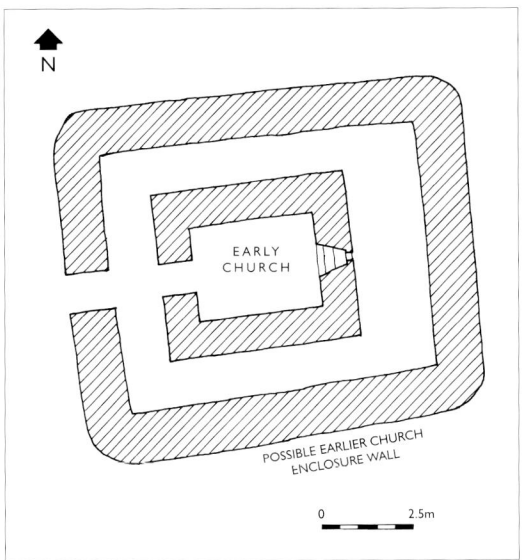

new church but, since the old western and southern walls did not hinder its construction, that section of the enclosure wall was left in its original position.

The change in orientation of churches here could be due to a number of reasons, either practical or liturgical. It might be as simple as beginning construction at a different time of the year when the sun rises in a different part of the sky, or the dedication of the church changed and they wished to begin construction on the memorial-death day of this saint, or possibly the method of defining east-west orientation changed.[155] Orientation of the church was important, but clearly alignment of the enclosure wall with the church, while desirable, was not as important.

The second reason for suspecting that the enclosure wall predates the present church concerns the mica-schist paving that extends from the church interior through the threshold of the church and continues to fill the area between the church and the enclosure wall. The paving runs under some part of three of the walls of the church but stops short at the church enclosure wall, except for one stone in the entry to the church enclosure wall. Its absence under the enclosure wall suggests that the wall was already in place when the present church and its paving were built.

Notes

[132] The present church as represented by the lower northern and southern walls. The paving is not all at exactly the same level, as inevitably certain sections have been repaired since or are under heavier loads. The levels are, nevertheless, remarkably homogeneous, varying only a few centimetres. See O'Brien's levels, 22 September 1998.

[133] Two of the tombs have undecorated stones serving as recumbent stones, although the fit is far from perfect.

[134] Cist graves may have been used earlier in Ireland than in Scotland: see Bray Head burials, Co. Wicklow (Edwards 1990). O'Brien excavated a fifth-century lintel-cist grave with a stone-lined floor in Ballyshannon, Co. Donegal, in 1997. O'Brien notes that this style of grave is seen on Romano-British fourth- and fifth-century sites and spread to Ireland from there. Personal communication, 21 August 1998. For possible later continuation of cist graves after the eighth century, see Moyne, Co. Mayo (Manning 1984, 37–68); Millockstown, Co. Louth (Manning 1986, 144–7); Boolies Little, Co. Meath (Sweetman, 1992–3). Cist graves may have lasted longer in Scotland as well (see RCAHMS 1982, 114, 137, 244).

[135] Grave no. 1 cannot be excavated, but the same dark charcoal soil does run under its recumbent stone. Presumably graves nos. 2 and 3 will be dug out to settle the question.

[136] We owe this suggestion to E. O'Brian, who also noted the only instance she knew of a false grave, in Scotland, where only chain mail was found in a grave. Ms O'Brian also agrees with us that this was not a decorative or casual construction but one with a serious purpose. Personal communication, 23 July 1997.

137 The niche was 0.33m high, 0.32m wide and quite shallow at.0.07m deep.

138 This second layer of stones, at the same level as graves nos. 1 and 2, indicates that graves nos. 2 and 3 may have been sealed at the same time.

139 UB 3992 1126 ±22; all skeletons were dated by high-precision radiocarbon methods at Queen's University, Belfast, where they were then calibrated to two sigma (Stuiver and Pearson, 1986). For complete pathological details about this skeleton, see Scally 1996, 31–34 for Barra Ó Donnabháin's report.

140 The level of grave no. 4 varies in depth but is nowhere as deep as nos. 5 and 6, which are the deepest graves in this area and are at the same level. The difference in level between the skeletons varies considerably, as do a number of other elements, such as the presence in no. 4 only of 'earmuffs', a stone placed one on each side of the head to hold the head in place.

141 Personal communication from Feichin Mulkerrin, present owner of the island and life-time resident of Omey Island and Claddaduff, Co. Galway. This sand may have been brought to the island for more practical reasons, such as making mortar, but it was used in only two graves.

142 But use of white quartz should probably be considered throughout Britain and Ireland, see Whithorn graves that also had white quartz in them at early levels and were also cist graves, in *Whithorn and St Ninian: Excavation of a Medieval Town, 1984–91,* ed. Hill 1997, 472–473 and Crowe 1982, 413–315 for the Isle of Man.

143 UB 4255 1027±19.

144 See Kenny [1929] 1993, 739–740; the translation of this section of *Leabhear Breac* (fol. 54, now fol. 44) in Petrie 1845, 346. See also the reference in a poem about St Mochua of Balla: 'To do the will of the white pure cleric', *Lives of Saints from the Book of Lismore,* ed. Stokes [1890] 1989, 143, 287.

145 UB–4266 was 1023±21 yr. BP or calibrated to two sigma AD 980–1025.

146 Nor does it seem likely that these stones have shifted, although the lower sidestone furthest away from the church, on the north, has moved a couple of centimetres south as the stone presses against the skeleton. The lower sidestones nearest the church are well anchored under the church and have not moved.

147 It has been suggested that the headstones were inserted in the wall and the graves built in advance and then the bodies inserted when a likely candidate died. To the best of our knowledge, graves were not dug in this manner. The closest analogy would be the occasional gift of an elaborate sarcophagus to an important cleric; these, however, sat on top of the church floor so that insertion of the body was simple. Advance construction of graves in the ground, especially if the church wall sits on a lintel cover, makes later burial awkward, if not impossible. It seems evident that if all these graves had been built at the same time, they would not show the small individual differences in construction and depths that they do show.

[148] UB 4256 913±19.

[149] Brown 1981; Hermann-Mascard 1975, ch. 3. A rule in the *Liber Pontificalis*, attributed to Pope Felix in the third century, required the celebration of mass either on or near the tombs of the martyrs. Duchesne, 1886–1892, L.P. I:158.

[150] For Gregory, see Epistolae, in MGH, ed. Ewald and Hartmann, L.I. 54; L.VI, 22 and 45. For the council of Nicaea, see Mansi 1901, XIII, col. 428, and see also Herrmann-Mascard, 1975, 149. Nevertheless, if relics were not available, the sacrament of the Eucharist was sufficient for church consecration. See Pochnee 1923, 40–41 for specific examples.

[151] Between 971 and 994 Winchester expanded both to the east and to the west because of a desire to display more relics. First the westward expansion incorporated the church over the tomb of St Swithin into the main church, while shortly afterwards the small eastern end of the church was replaced by a large eastern end with a crypt and semicircular northern side chamber (Cherry [1976] 1986, 186; Taylor [1978] 1984, 3: 743–745; Biddle 1975; 1976).

[152] *Vita S. Columbae*, Anderson and Anderson, 1961, ii, 45; *Annals of the Four Masters*, ed. O'Donovan, AD 1143, 'altóir ciarain co na miondaibh…' Ó Floinn 1997, 139 notes that some of the reliquary shrines contained corporeal remains. We are indebted to Ó Floinn for bringing these two references to altars to our attention.

[153] At 2 sd cal., this sample, UCLA 2792 2792 ±105, was taken by Dr Rainier Berger, head of the Isotope Laboratory at the Institute of Geophysics at UCLA.

[154] On the church at the Brough of Deerness, see Morris and Ernery, 1986, 301–374. The excavators believed this church to be eleventh-century or possibly later, and the enclosure wall had rounded external corners like those at High Island. On Caher Island, see Henry, 1947, 23–38; on Carrownaseer, see *An Archaeological Survey of County Galway. Vol. I*, ed. Gosling 1993, and personal communication and sketch from J. Higgins, 1988.

[155] It is obviously very difficult to establish these death-dates. However, Morris (1983, 68) believes that Benson's results for 237 medieval churches in Oxfordshire were helpful. See also Rahtz 1982, 2.

Chapter Seven

The Cells

There's no comfort inside me, only a small
Hart's-tongue sprouting square, with pyramidal headroom
For one man alone kneeling down: a smell
Of peregrine mutes and eremitical boredom.

Richard Murphy, *Beehive Cell.*

Passage to Cell A, known as the Abbot's Cell, from the Church Enclosure

The most sacred part of an ecclesiastical site centred on the church, cemetery and reliquary shrines, the area in which sacraments were performed and in which the saints were buried. The symbolic gravity of the area is usually readily distinguished from more ordinary structures by special attention to the architecture of the church, by special reliquaries in or outside the church, and by the placement of special crosses. In a number of the sites left on Ireland's western coast in the early medieval period, the sacred area was spatially separated from domestic structures by a low drystone wall. Walls such as these are seen at Reask and Gallarus in County Kerry and also at Kiltieran East and Carrownaseer Graveyard in County Galway (Fig. 78, Reask).[156]

When no separation wall is present there is often a discrete space between the most sacred area and the dwelling cells, which also served as a communal gathering

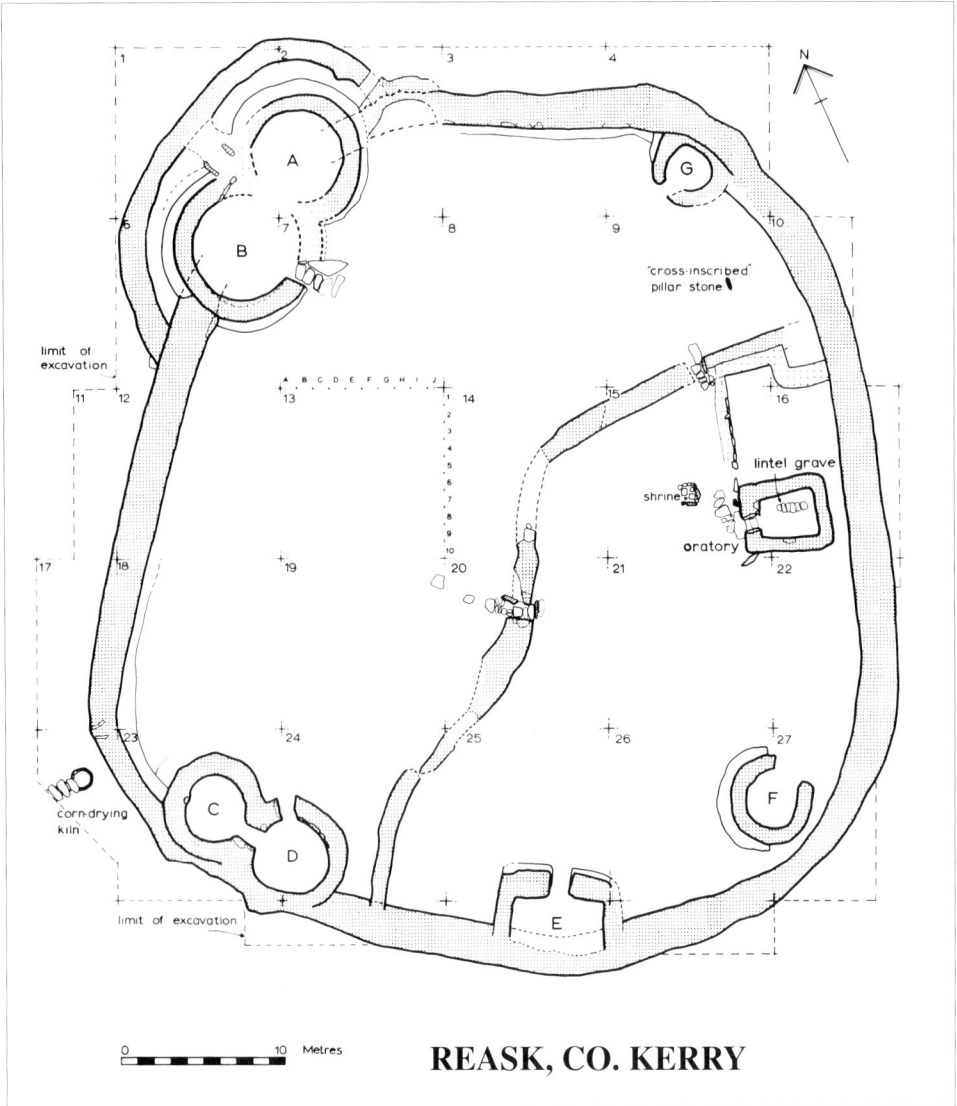

Figure 78

Plan of Reask, Co. Kerry, showing the meandering wall that separated the church and its cemetery from the main part of the enclosure. This wall is typical of those seen at many early medieval ecclesiastical sites (Fanning 1981, 71, Fig. 2). Courtesy Royal Irish Academy.

place.[157] A wall enclosing only the church is unusual, although a similar wall exists at nearby Caher Island in County Mayo, where the church enclosure wall is also closely restricted to the church.[158] At High Island the wall runs so close to the church that the main monastic cemetery could not possibly have been within the enclosure. Thus, the church must have been separated from most of the graves and from the cells within the monastic enclosure.

A second opening, in the northeastern corner of the enclosure wall, was believed to lead to a passage to Cell A (Fig. 57). This lintelled opening, the same narrow width as the main entrance, was still clearly visible until 1991, when one of the stone lintels of the entrance to the passage collapsed (Fig. 79).

In 1820 Petrie (1845, 420) described it: 'from this [church], a covered passage, about fifteen feet long, by three feet wide, leads to a cell, which was probably the

Figure 79

Photo of the doorway that once led out of the church enclosure wall on High Island, Co. Galway; the lintels over the doorway have now collapsed. The ruins of Cell A are in the background. Photo Walter Horn, 1983.

abbot's habitation'. O'Donovan mentioned neither the opening in the enclosure wall nor the passage leading from it, but by 1869, when George Kinahan visited High Island, he noted:

> there are the ruins of a passage about three feet wide, with walls of pitched flags, which seem to have led to a doorway in the wall of the cashel [i.e., the church enclosure wall]. In confirmation of this idea, it may be mentioned that an old fisherman, who was met with at the ruins, appeared to say he remembered them so joined before the passage was broken down.[159]

By 1895 Macalister simply stated that the passage was destroyed (1896, 202).

In view of the nineteenth-century antiquarian descriptions of this passage, particularly that of Petrie, the most reliable and specific of them all, there was no reason to doubt that a passage linking Cell A and the church enclosure wall had existed. Excavation in 1998 and 1999 showed, however, that a short section of walling built against the western side of the entry to the church enclosure curves eastwards in front of the entry. A direct covered passage from the church enclosure to Cell A was, therefore, unlikely at the time Petrie described it. What was it that Petrie and Kinahan saw? We may never know. It is interesting that this curving wall was built against, and hence later than, the church enclosure wall. The entrance would appear to be a later insertion in the church enclosure wall; the masonry styles are quite different.

The Cells

In the nineteenth century Petrie, O'Donovan and Kinahan all reported cells, of varying location and size, in ruinous condition west and north of the church, near Cells A and B. Cell A, a tiny cell, could have held no more than one monk, possibly the abbot who traditionally had his own cell. Larger Cell B might have held two to three monks. There must have been more cells for monks because a monastery the size of High Island certainly housed more than four monks and it is likely that this area, the furthest removed from the main entrance, was the domestic area of the monastic enclosure (Herity 1984). Cells A and B are similar in style, plan and construction technique and were probably built at about the same time, whereas, judging by the nineteenth-century descriptions, the other cells appear to have been different in style and possibly in date of construction.

Cell A

In 1820 Petrie (1845, 420) described this cell as 'nearly circular and dome-roofed'. It is difficult to assess the general condition of the cell from Petrie's few words, nor was O'Donovan's brief description in 1839 particularly helpful. In 1869 Kinahan remarked: 'On account of its ruined condition, the original outward form cannot be seen; however, tradition says that it was bee-hive shaped...' (1869, 552). He made a plan and a sketch of the cell, which, although somewhat inaccurate in their dimensions, nevertheless show a domed beehive cell with an intact inner skin (Figs. 80a and 80b) in considerably better condition than it is today when no trace of a dome remains.

Figures 80a and 80b
1869 drawing and plan of Cell A on High Island, Co. Galway, made by G.F. Kinahan, showing the inner dome of the cell still intact but with the outer layer of the dome missing. Kinahan's sketch implies that the cell was rectangular externally up to plinth level (Kinahan 1869, Plate XLVII). Courtesy Royal Irish Academy.

Cell A is a corbelled drystone structure, rectangular on plan but probably circular on the exterior above lintel level (Fig. 81a). The outer face of the cell is largely destroyed, and apparently the outer skin was stripped away; only traces are still visible on the southeastern quadrant at the base of the wall. At the base here there are also the remains of a possible plinth or offset, 0.18m wide. There are traces of external walling on the north side of the cell, but this appears to be part of the monastic enclosure wall rather than the cell.

The door, located on the south side, is placed slightly west of centre. The entry here is narrow: 0.65m on the outside tapering down to 0.5m on the inside, pre-excavation, and to 0.56m after excavation. Its height above the stone debris blocking it was only 0.68m until excavation, when the actual height of the entry was determined to be slightly over 1.0m. Only one lintel, the interior one, survives and it is in bad condition; it has a fracture and is also broken over the opening (see sections, Figs. 81b and 81c).[160]

The Cells

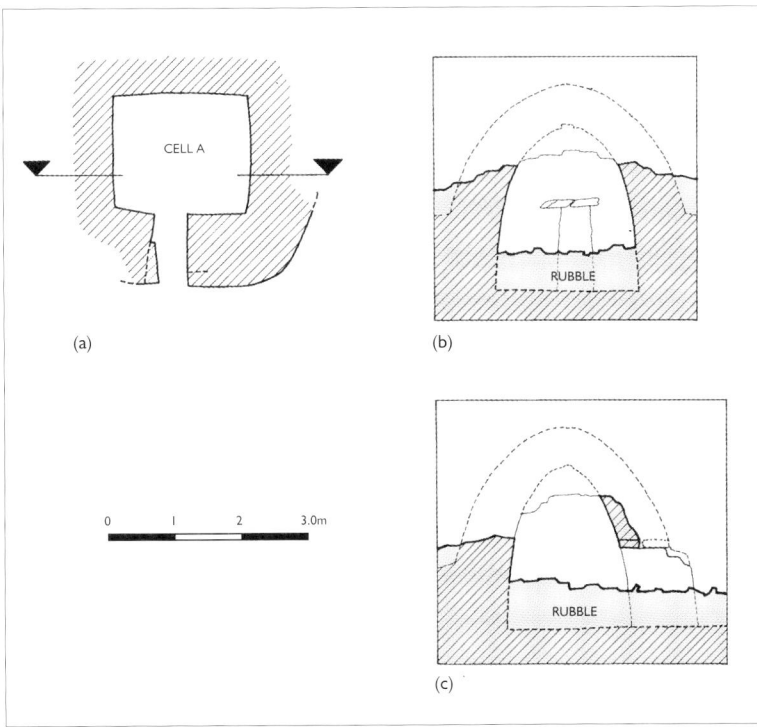

Figure 81a
Pre-excavation plan of Cell A in the monastery on High Island, Co. Galway. The possible original configuration of the cell showed in dotted lines. Because the west jamb of the entry has fallen in, the entry into Cell A appears to be only 0.42m on the exterior. The wall thickness at the entry is 1.1m. Plan and sections by G.D. Rourke.

Figure 81b
Pre-excavation cross-section of Cell A on High Island, Co. Galway.

Figure 81c
Pre-excavation long-section of Cell A on High Island, Co. Galway.

The interior masonry style is similar to that of the other cell but not as finely built; the stones here are shorter and blockier without the overall horizontal pattern of Cell B. The stones are well fitted together, to create a reasonably smooth surface which gently inclines inwards, but the surfaces were not tooled as they are in Cell B. The best masonry can be seen on the northern and western walls, while that of the southern side above the lintel is much rougher, perhaps due to movement. Cell A is small inside, with dimensions of 2.1m EW by 1.90m NS, with a total space of 3.99m (after the 1997 season of excavation), barely big enough to hold one person. The rectangular shape is kept as the walls rise, for there is no sign of the corners rounding as they approach the dome. The simple, bare interior has no signs of windows or hanging pegs. There is a possible cupboard in the western wall, which is in a bad state, particularly at the rear; it is equally possible that this cupboard is an illusion created by a missing stone.

Excavation in 1997 revealed a base layer of disturbed flagstones with material similar to the mortar found in the church against the walls and extending into the cell a short distance. It may have been used to level the ground or to set the flagged floor of the cell. In general, more elaborate attention was paid to churches than to other monastic structures. This may be the first known instance of the use of mortar as one of the bedding materials for a monk's cell in Ireland. At present, radiocarbon dating of the charcoal fraction in mortar appears to centre between the eighth and ninth centuries as an indication of the earliest widespread use of mortar in Irish stone churches on ecclesiastical sites (Berger 1995); its use in cells would be later still. It is probable that Cells A and B belonged to a later period in the monastery, possibly even the same period in which mortar was used under flagstones in the church, but it all remains speculative for the moment.

Although the cell is open to the sky now, in 1839 O'Donovan said that the apex of the cell was sealed by only one stone and the height of the cell was 7 feet 6 inches (2.29m). Kinahan's comments let us know that this cell was still covered in 1869, although he counted a different number of apex stones — 'crowned by three large flags...'[161] O'Donovan and Kinahan give different figures for the number of stones forming the apex of Cell B as well, but it is unlikely that there was a serious change in

131

the apex between the two visits because Kinahan's drawing shows a capped dome; the two men were simply using different methods of calculating the capstones.

A corbelled drystone beehive cell is typically built of two skins, and they are remarkably stable as long as the cell is round internally and externally. Such beehive cells have been built for centuries in Ireland and continue in use in the remote parts of the country even now, although their use has changed from dwelling house to service shed or shepherd's hut. Cell A, however, is rectangular, almost square on the interior, which places uneven stresses on the walls; consequently, such a design is more prone to differential movement and subsequent collapse.

Figure 82
Cell B on High Island, Co. Galway, from the east. On the inner northern jamb there are two orthostats and there are probably two on the inner southern jamb as well (one is less definite). Photo Walter Horn 1981.

Cell B

This cell, misleadingly called in local tradition the scriptorium, is built against the eastern side of the church's enclosure wall (Figs. 29a and 82). Like Cell A, the apex of the dome is missing, as well as most of the outer skin of the cell, except for a small amount at the base of the eastern and southern sides. In 1839 O'Donovan noted that the apex was closed by two overlapping capstones. His only critique of the cell's exterior was to say that 'The architecture is very smooth on the inside though without cement, but on the outside it looks as irregular as Carn Ceasrach on the summit of Knock Meádha' (O'Donovan 1839, 80–81). Can we assume from this description that much of the outer skin was missing? Wakeman made a sketch of this cell, which O'Donovan claimed would 'give some idea of the [cell's] external appearance' (Fig. 83a). Although the drawing is impressionistic, Wakeman depicts individual stones at the base, whereas above the lintel the graphic representation is more vague, perhaps an indication that this section of the cell had greatly deteriorated.

In 1869 Kinahan described Cell B and sketched it (Fig. 83b):

> *The outside of this clochaun is in a similar deplorable condition to that of the clochaun [Cell A] just now described; fortunately, however, the interior has been spared by the barbarians who have ruined the rest of the settlement, and displays a beautifully finished chamber, in good proportions, coved in on all sides from the floor to the roof, a height of over 9 feet [2.74m], the apex being covered by three flags placed in steps...* (Kinahan 1869, 553)

The Cells

Figure 83a

Sketch made by W.F. Wakeman in 1839 of Cell B on High Island, Co. Galway. This appealing sketch was also used by Petrie for his book on ecclesiastical architecture (1845, 128). Courtesy Royal Irish Academy.

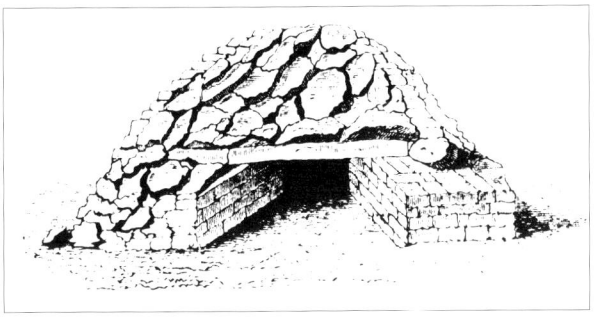

Figure 83b

G.F. Kinahan's sketch in 1869 of Cell B on High Island, Co. Galway, showing a startling brick-like construction (Kinahan 1869, Plate XVIII)

By 1895 Macalister wrote that Cells A and B were missing their apex stones and that they had been:

> *so to speak skinned; the outermost stones have been nearly all removed, and holes are broken in the sides and the roof: this gives them a forlorn and shapeless appearance (1896, 201–202).*

Macalister's word 'skinned' is very apt, for the decay of these cells can be attributed not to natural collapse, but rather to a deliberate removal of the outer facing of stone. The removal of such a large amount of facing stone can possibly be attributed to the miners who needed such stone to construct their cottages on the far side of the island, where there was not a readily available source of stone. A drawing by Robert Gibbings in the 1940s allows us to know that Cell B retained its inner dome fifty years ago (Fig. 83c).[162]

The removal of the outer layer allows a clear view of the construction of the inside of the cell's wall. Projecting stones spaced at intervals were used to tie the inner and outer layers together, a typical corbelled drystone construction technique. The walls at the base of the cell are so thick that there must have been a plinth or offset. On the southern side some of the actual plinth stones may still be in position; conjectural reconstruction suggests an offset of roughly 0.35m (see dots on the long section and Figs. 84b and 84c).

While Cell B's external shape is rounded, the interior plan is almost square, averaging 2.63m EW and 2.74m NS, with a maximum height of 2.16m pre-excavation (Fig. 84b).[163] The entrance has a pronounced splay running from 1.4m wide on the outside to only 0.66m wide on the interior and the

Figure 83c

Woodcut based on a sketch made by Robert Gibbings at the time of his visit to High Island sometime before 1944, showing the dome on Cell B still intact at that time. Gibbing's account of the monastery in his book, Lovely is the Lee, *is highly romanticised, but he does confirm this: 'For the most part the buildings on the island are in ruins, but one of the cells still retains its domed roof' (Gibbings 1945, 102).*

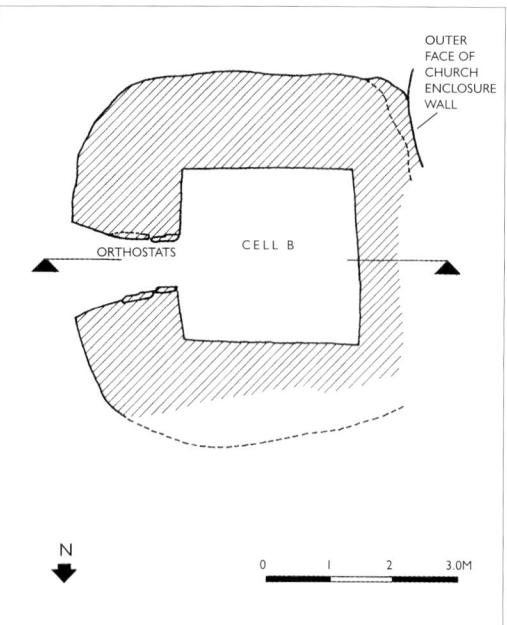

Figure 84a

Pre-excavation plan of Cell B on High Island, Co. Galway. The external rear wall is concealed but it appears to have been built against the church enclosure wall. Plan G.D. Rourke.

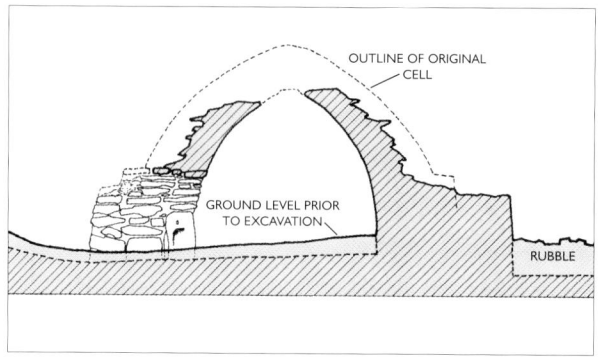

threshold was paved with flagstones.¹⁶⁴ There are orthostats at the base of both jambs (Fig. 84d). There are three lintels remaining but originally there must have been one more lintel on the exterior of the entry.¹⁶⁵

The broken innermost lintel has a simple cross inscribed on its underside (Fig. 96) identical to the one incised on the lateral arm of the southeastern landing cross (Fig. 87c). This cross was not inscribed in place as a blessing sign because part of the cross design disappears into the wall on the south side; it is another reused cross slab and a sign that this cell was not part of the original monastic foundation. Nor can we

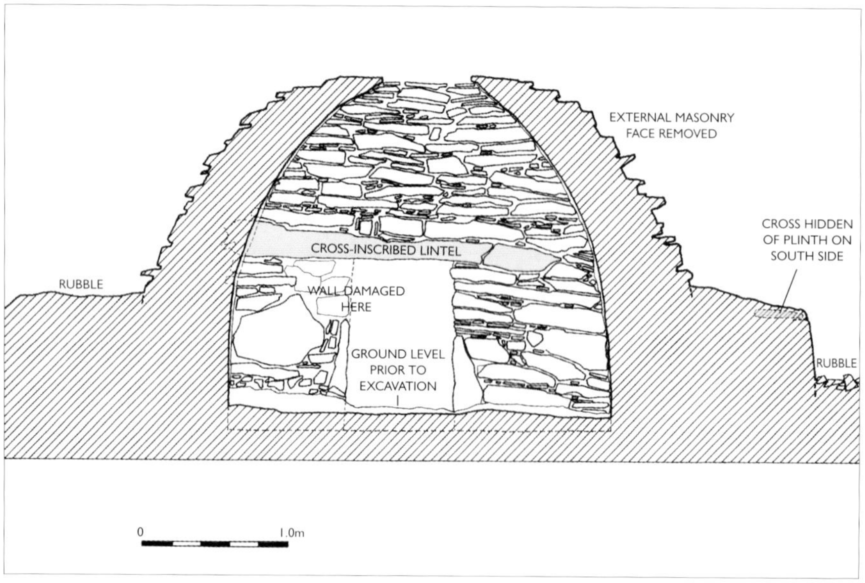

Figure 84b

Pre-excavation long section of Cell B on High Island, Co. Galway. The possible original configuration of this cell is shown in dotted lines. This cell, like Cell A, is rectangular on the inside. Drawing by G.D. Rourke.

Figure 84c

Pre-excavation cross-section of Cell B on High Island, Co. Galway, showing an elevation of the internal eastern wall with the cross-inscribed lintel stone, now broken in place. The outline of a cross is shown lying on the plinth on the southern side where some unknown visitor had placed it to preserve it (See Fig. 93). Drawing by G.D. Rourke.

The Cells

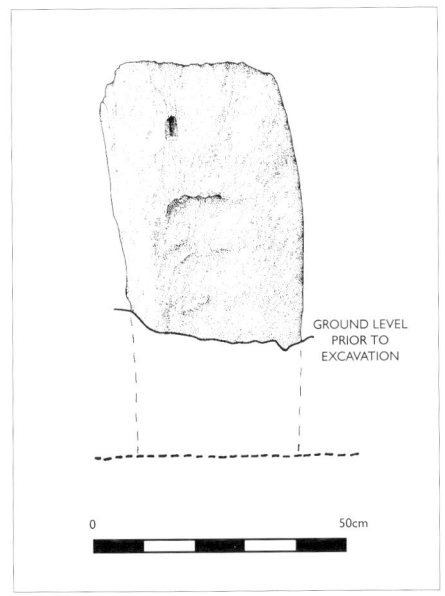

Figure 84d

The orthostat on the southern jamb has evidence of working on it, a small rectangular hollow (20cm by 30cm) near the top of the orthostat, which may have been a receiver for a metal bar on a door. Beneath the hollow the stone has been cut back and smoothed. Drawing by G.D. Rourke.

date the design on the cross stone, although it is a style that apparently came into use in the beginning of the Early Christian period.[166] This is the tallest incised stone extant on High Island and its height probably indicates it was used for something other than a burial marker and set upright.

Viewed from the inside, the cell is beautifully built. On the back wall each course consists of two or three thin stones of unusual length for a corbelled cell. As the walls rise, the sharp corners bow gracefully inwards and retain their shape to the apex. This construction is similar to that of cells B and C on Skellig Michael. The apex stone(s) is unfortunately no longer present and the empty space where it was measures 0.7m square. For the most part, the building stones were chosen so that their faces slope in slightly; however, there is evidence that some of the stones were also worked to shape their surfaces. This is particularly clear on a series of stones on the northern interior side, where pointed chisels left a toothed pattern on the stones (Fig. 85) (O'Sullivan, 1992).

A breach in the cell's northeastern corner was further enlarged in the early 1990s by sheep, illegally placed on the island, using the cell for shelter. Excavation in 1997 showed that both cells had been used for temporary shelter many times over the centuries; the interior was excavated 0.55m down and was still not entirely completed, although the base appears to be badly disturbed paving. Its north-south dimensions as of 1997 were 2.68m NS and 2.7m EW, giving an internal area of 7.5 sq.m, almost twice the internal space of Cell A.

Cell B was designated the scriptorium by local fishermen in the nineteenth century, but there is no reason to believe that a small dark stone cell like this would have been used as a scriptorium.[167] It is, moreover, too small to have been used as a refectory or communal meeting cell and has no windows, cupboards or stone pegs on

Figure 85

Photo of chisel marks on two stones on the northern wall of Cell B. The rough, jagged marks are clearly seen on the first and third stones from the bottom. These marks are similar to those seen on the lintel of the eastern window in the miners' cottage, which was clearly a stone taken from the monastery. Photo G.D. Rourke, 1990.

which to hang things like those in the Skellig Michael cells, although it may have had wooden pegs. It was most likely a dwelling cell for two to three monks.

Cell B's location, directly east of the church, is unusual. There are generally no structures east of a church other than burials, an occasional *leacht*, or, because of restricted space, two churches almost in line with each other as on Skellig Michael. All structures were positioned carefully around the spiritual focus of the church, so as not to distract from its importance. Here the presence of the church enclosure wall as a barrier may have permitted an exception. Space for cells, moreover, is restricted within the monastic enclosure, as is seen in the tight fit of the cell against the church enclosure wall. The monks may have taken down a large section of the monastic enclosure wall (cashel) when they constructed this cell in order to improve passage around the east side and to gain entry to the cell, just as they removed some of this wall to construct Cell A.

Examination of the junction between Cell B and the church enclosure wall revealed that the rear of the cell was built tightly against this wall. The cell's rear wall is much thinner than those of its other three sides and obviously does not have a smoothly finished external face at the lower level; the enclosure wall itself acts as a buttress to the cell at this level. Consequently, it is clear that the cell was built later than the church enclosure wall.[168] Because of the close similarity of their internal square plan, construction and interior masonry styles, the two cells were likely built contemporaneously, although considerably more effort was spent on the construction of Cell B.

Notes

[156] Irish canons called for separation; Collectio; *Die Irische Kononensammlung*, ed. Wasserschleben 1885. See Doherty 1984b, 45–75 for a discussion of these canons.

[157] See Herity 1984 for an explanation of the communal area in front of the church.

[158] Similar use of a rectangular wall with externally rounded corners to enclose the church was found on the Brough of Deeness, Orkney. The excavators roughly dated this small Norse church to the eleventh century, or possibly later (Morris and Ernery 1986, 301–374).

[159] Kinahan had confused the cashel wall with the church enclosure wall at this point (Kinahan 1869, 552, 553).

[160] This lintel is 0.97m long, 0.14m high, and the depth into the doorway is 0.27m.

[161] O'Donovan 1839, 81; Kinahan 1869, 552,553.

[162] We are grateful to Finbar McCormick for bringing this book to our attention.

[163] The thickness of the wall at the entry is 1.65m.

164 A rabbit burrowing by the south jamb orthostat uncovered a small portion of this pavement.

165 The outer two lintels are 1.25m above threshold level, while the innermost lintel is slightly stepped down (8cm lower). The remaining lintels are long stones; the outermost one is 2.3m long and the innermost one 2.15m long and broken in places by the weight of the stone pressing on it.

166 Nash-Williams 1950, 17–18, 20, fig. 6, nos. 20 and 21. Nash-Williams dated this style to the seventh–ninth century in Wales in areas of strong Irish influence. Nash-Williams warned that the dating remains problematical because of the lack of direct evidence, but typologically and historically they fit here.

167 See Horn 1986 and Hughes 1958 for sensible appraisals of their special requirements.

168 Cf. Herity (1990, 80) who believes Cell B and the church enclosure wall might be contemporary.

Chapter Eight

The Cemetery and Cross Stones

Waif of the afterglow
On summer nights to meet your mate you jink
Over sea-cliff and graveyard,
Creeping underground
To hatch an egg in a hermit's skull.

Richard Murphy, **Stormpetrel**.

The cross is the most potent symbol in Christianity, reminding Christians of Christ's sacrifice and the promise of salvation and resurrection, of atonement and life everlasting. Crosses were carved on stone for many purposes other than for burial markers; they were also used at or near the church, at pilgrimage stations, on altars, as ecclesiastical boundary-markers, and as dedicatory or memorial crosses to special saints or events.[169]

Cross stones are easily moved about, reused in new locations, covered over by new growth, or even removed from ecclesiastical sites. It is not surprising, therefore, that today we find no visible trace of the monastic cemetery on High Island, and that a number of cross stones are scattered inside the monastic enclosure, incorporated into later monastic structures, or even found a considerable distance away from the enclosure on penitential stations around the island. Their original locations remain unknown, although many were likely burial markers in the cemetery. If the location of the present church was reused many times for church buildings over the centuries, burials may have been on any side of the church. Burials in this period were around a sacred focus, usually a church, but also occasionally around a shrine, as at Illaunloughan, County Kerry. Expediency rather than rules appears to have determined which side of the church or shrine was used for burial, although burial to the east may have been a customary first choice. At High Island the most spacious available area is on the southern side of the monastic enclosure. The two main entries to the monastery are on this side and it is, therefore, more likely that this space was better suited for multiple-purpose use than for dwelling cells. Shortage of space inside the enclosure may also have mandated reuse of burial space over the centuries, although excavation of the burials behind the church offers no evidence of multiple use. This restricted area was special, however, and clearly reserved for monks of particular importance, most likely revered abbots.

At present only one cross stone (Fig. 86a) and a large granite sphere are visible in the area south of the church, although others have been found in this area (see below, illustrated cross slabs).

Some cross stones have disappeared since the nineteenth century, although they may still be on the island, broken or buried under rubble; all we know about some of these crosses comes from the sketches made by W.F. Wakeman in 1839. All of the known crosses as of 1997 are shown on the next few pages, with a brief description of their location, size and style. All dimensions given are maximum sizes. The crosses were all made of mica-schist, the island stone, except for the recumbent stone and footstone of one burial behind the church, grave no. 6. All cross illustrations courtesy of Dúchas The Heritage Service.

Figure 86a
Cross stone south of the church on High Island, Co. Galway. Photo G.D. Rourke.

Figure 86b
When Wakeman drew this stone in 1839 enough of the upper right quadrant remained to show another boss in it (Wakeman RIA MS 12T9). Courtesy Royal Irish Academy.

Figure 87
Cross Stone no. 1 — Garnet-Schist
Location: *East of the southeastern landing.*
Size: *0.73m high, 0.53m wide, 0.07m thick.*

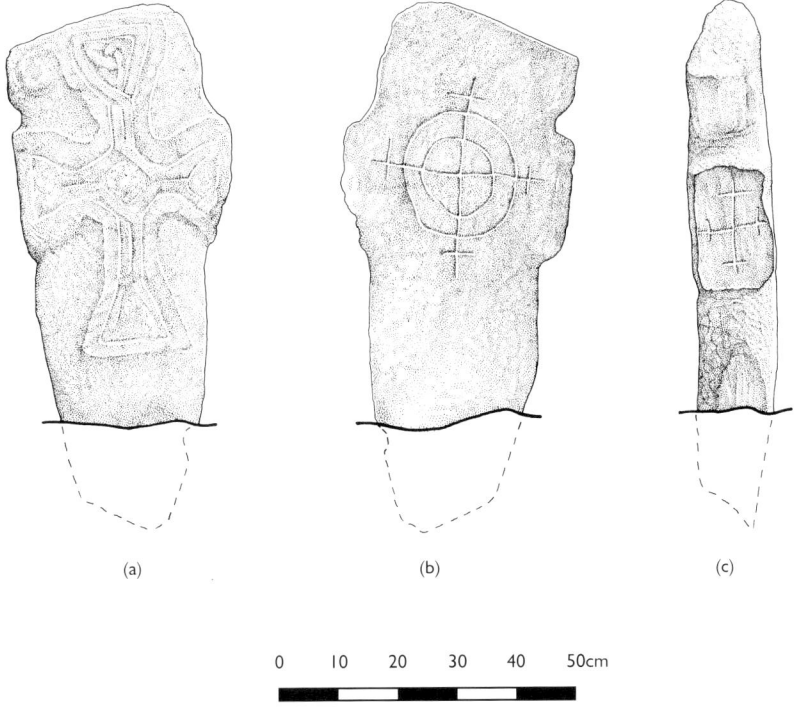

This cross is inscribed with crosses on three faces; the stone itself was also lightly cross-shaped, with short arms formed by notches carved out of the stone; this shape is clearest on the reverse side (87c).

87a bears a Latin cross with expanded terminals carved in high relief. More design decorates the interior, as incised bands repeat the line of the cross; the band forms a diamond or lozenge in the centre, which contains badly weathered knotwork. In the upper arm, bands surround a triquetra (a triangular-shaped decoration formed of three interlaced arcs). The lateral and lower cross arms are badly weathered and part of the right arm has broken off. No pattern other than traces of incised banding is now visible but it is possible that each arm held a triquetra, as Macalister showed for the left lateral terminal (1896, 206, cross A). In the upper left quadrant a carved band arcs off the top of the cross and loops into a coil.[170]

For the triquetra as the symbol of the Trinity, see Ferguson ([1954] 1972, 153; Higgins 1987, I: 121). For the symbolic meaning of the lozenge, see Richardson, who believes that 'Where the lozenge occurs alone it seems probable that it stands for Christ, the second person of the Trinity, the Logos' (1984, 32–45; see also Cabrol-Leclerc: Lozenge). This cross was drawn by Kinahan 1869, Fig. 1 on Plate XLIX.

87b. The reverse side has a lightly incised linear cross with short linear cross bars near the end of each arm. The cross is set within two concentric circles. The entire design, particularly the central circles, is badly weathered and hard to see; it is clearest on the left-hand side.

87c. On the left-hand face of the cross arm is a small incised linear cross with each arm intersected by a short cross bar near the ends.[171] Drawings by P. Johnson.

Figure 88

Cross no. 2 — Garnet-Schist

Location: *Standing south of Brian Boru's Well. This cross was moved here sometime after 1839, when Wakeman drew one side (88b) on a sheet marked 'Ancient stones near the church on High Island, Omey Ph.' (RIA MS 12T9, 43) and the other side (88a) on another sheet (RIA 12T9, 44), on which he had also written 'At the church on High Island'. In 1869, however, Kinahan noted it as at the well (1869, 555; Fig. 2 on Plate XLIX). This stone is similar in both size and style to the footstones of the graves east of the church; certainly Wakeman sketched it on the same two sheets as other stones east and south of the church (also drawn by Macalister 1896, cross B on p.206).*

Size: *0.73m high, 0.53m wide, 0.07m thick.*

This cross stone carries an inscribed cross on two faces.

Fig. 88a. An incised linear cross set within a roundel with broadly splayed terminals formed by slightly raised bands.

Fig. 88b. A simple linear cross with expanded or splayed linear terminals. Drawings by P. Johnson.

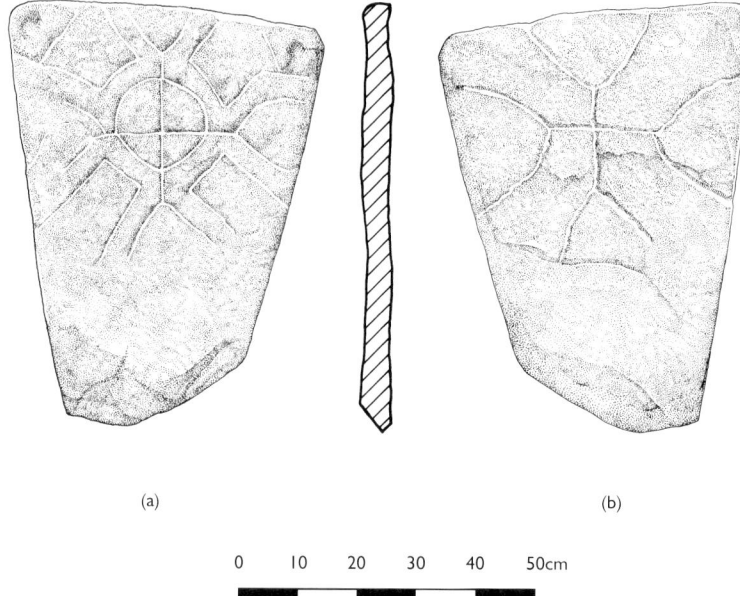

Figure 89

Cross no. 3 — Mica-Schist

Location: *Found in the trench at Brian Boru's Well.*
Size: *0.28m high, 0.32m wide, 0.07m thick.*

The head of a small cross, the lower terminal broken off, found by men cleaning/digging the overflow trench for Brian Boru's Well in 1972. The stone, like a number of the High Island crosses, was slightly cross-shaped. Carved in relief on the stone is a cross with a central roundel which contains a linear cross; the terminals, incised into bands, curve out and bifurcate at the end. Four bosses, one in each quadrant of the cross, were placed close to the central roundel. Drawing by P. Johnson.

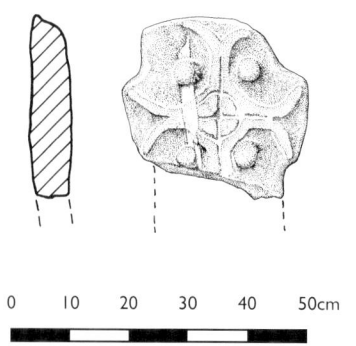

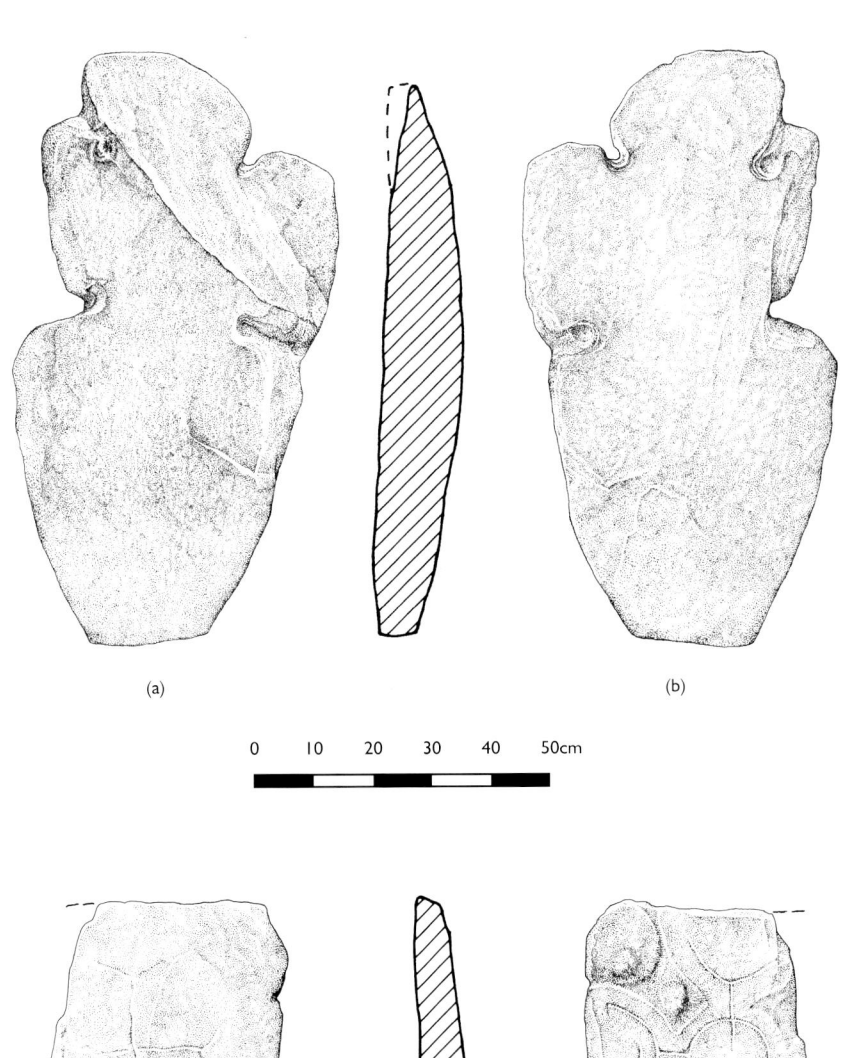

Figure 90

Cross no. 4 — Garnet-Schist

Location: *On the* leacht *by the large lake, near the southeastern entry to the monastery.*

Size: *1.0m high, 0.5m wide, 0.14m thick.*

The stone bears no design but has been roughly worked to create a cross shape. Four notches were cut, forming a head and short arms; this may be an unfinished cross stone as two of the holes were not cut through the stone. On one side (Fig. 90a) a section has fractured off on the top. Possibly drawn by Wakeman in 1839 (MS 12T9, 45). Drawings by P. Johnson.

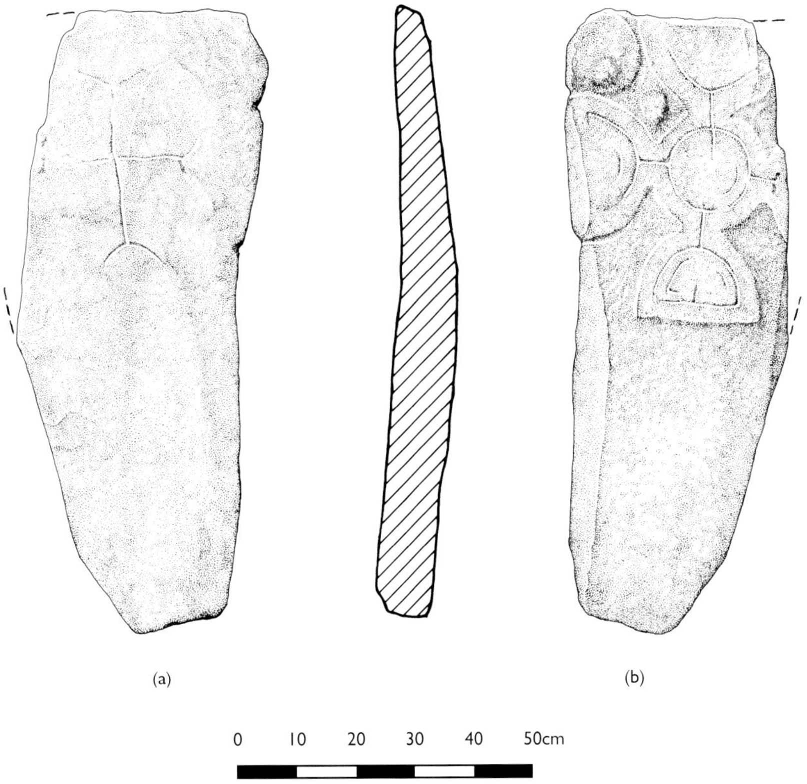

Figure 91

Cross no. 5 — Garnet-Schist

Location: *Standing south of the church within the monastic enclosure. In 1869 Kinahan found this cross lying down within the enclosure and he 'placed [it] upright at the east side of the station between the S. W. and S. E. doorways of the cashel...' Kinahan 1869, 554–555). Today there is no station here.*

Size: *1.09m high, 0.385m wide, 0.11m thick.*

This tall cross stone bears a design on two faces.

    91a. The reverse side of the stone bears a crude, lightly incised linear cross with bifurcated terminals.

    91b. Carved in relief is a cross formed of a central roundel with traces of a second narrower roundel within; the cross has expanded D-shaped terminals. Hints of interior design survive in the badly weathered cross design; the lower terminal has traces of a repeated D-shape in banded relief, and still fainter traces of a similar design are visible in the upper left arm. This pattern may have originally existed in all the arms, but no trace of interior design is visible in the weathered upper arm and the right arm has sheared off. In the upper left quadrant of the cross is a small boss with a larger shape (not quite a boss) above it.

In 1839 Wakeman's drawing of this cross showed that the right-hand terminal was sheared off at this time but that there was a small boss in the right-hand quadrant to match the one in the left-hand quadrant (RIA MS 1279, 44. See Fig. 86b). The central roundel may have contained a linear cross and the lower arm contained clear fretwork, as shown by Macalister (1896, cross C on 207). Macalister's photo (1896, 199) shows some evidence of this, but little is now visible. Wakeman's earlier sketch does not show this fretwork as clearly. Drawing by P. Johnson.

Figure 92

Cross no. 6 — Garnet-Schist

Location: *Lying flat on the southwestern side of the church.*
Size: *0.51m high, 0.31m wide, 0.07m thick.*

This is a small tapered cross stone with a simple incised linear cross enclosed by a subrectangular line. Drawing by P. Johnson.

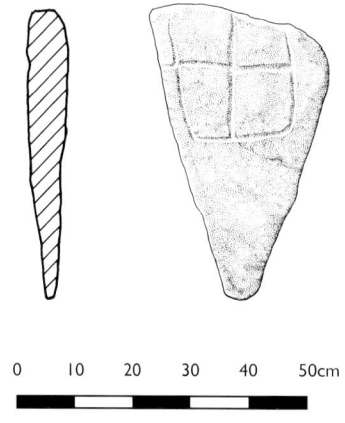

Figure 93

Cross no. 7 — Garnet-Schist with Dispersed Quartz Eyes

Location: *Lying face down on the plinth on the southern side of Cell B.*
Size: *1.08m high, 0.43m wide, 0.12m thick.*

This cross has not been reported or described by any earlier writers on High Island, although obviously placed at Cell B for protection by some visitor to the island and discovered by the authors during survey. The stone is shaped like a cross with short arms, although only the left-hand arm is visible now

as the right arm has been damaged and partly broken off. The design, carved in relief on the stone, is of a Latin cross with slightly expanded terminals. The Latin cross design is repeated within the cross. The upper and left-hand terminals appear incomplete, probably because of weathering and damage. Drawing by P. Johnson.

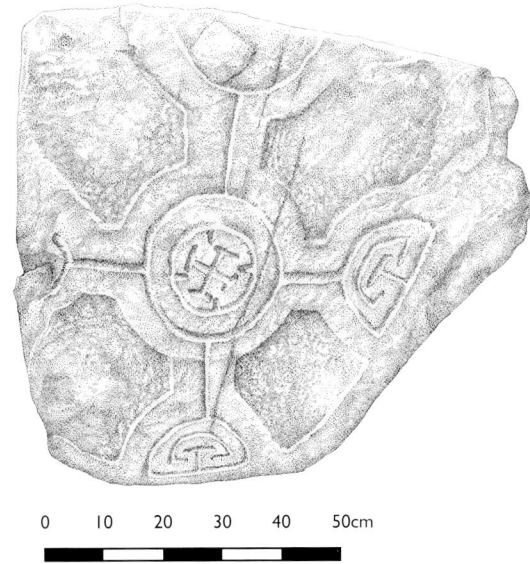

Figure 94

Cross no. 8 — Garnet-Schist

Location: *Forms the southern side of the altar in the church.*
Size: *0.75m high, 0.82m wide, 0.12m thick.*

This is one of the best preserved cross stones on High Island and still clearly shows the depth of the carving in relief. The design is unusual in that it fits the stone so badly that the design is unbalanced, set askew and, of necessity, incomplete in areas. The arm terminals could never have been equal (even if the left-hand terminal was intact); the upper terminal must have been left unfinished as it could never have fitted in the space, and the right terminal is twisted. This indifference to the spatial design of the cross stands in sharp contrast to the amount of effort spent in elaborate carving.

The design consists of a cross in relief with two central roundels formed by deeply incised bands with D-shaped expanded terminals. The central roundel contains an incised tilted cross with cross bars on its terminal ends. The cross terminals have short shafts formed by two bands and the lower and right-hand terminals each contain a type of fretwork consisting of repeated D-shapes, each set inside the other, with the inner Ds dividing into two in the centre and coiling away.

The design on this stone essentially covers the entire surface and the stone further lacks the tapered foot commonly used to anchor erect slabs in the ground. This stone may have been used as a recumbent slab. Drawing by P. Johnson.

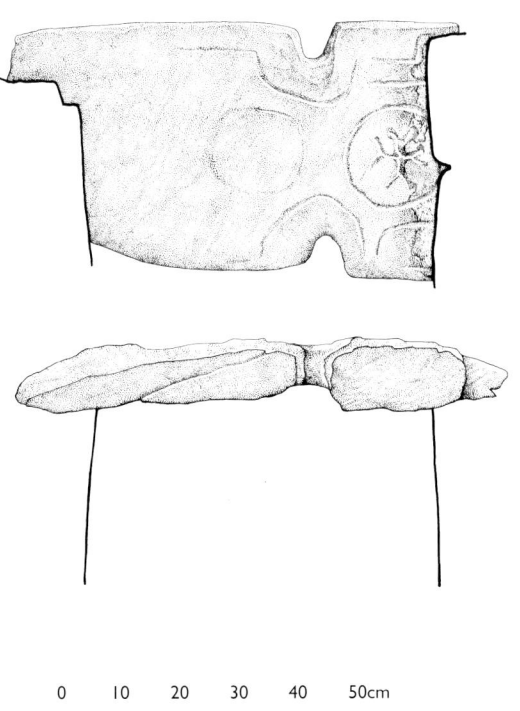

Figure 95

Cross no. 9 — Cross on Church Lintel — Garnet-Schist

Location: *The inner lintel of the church doorway.*
Size: *0.88m high, 0.44m wide, 0.10m thick.*

This stone, broken off at the top, is shaped into a short-armed cross by deeply carved notches, and the under side of the stone shows part of a cross design, some of which is hidden because of its position as a lintel. The design consists of the incised outline of a cross that appears to follow the shape of the stone. Within this outlined cross are two circles, one above the other; inside the upper circle is a cross with bifurcated terminals; the lower circle is fainter and free of design. This cross stone was greatly weathered before being placed here. Remnants of mortar remain on it. Drawings by P. Johnson.

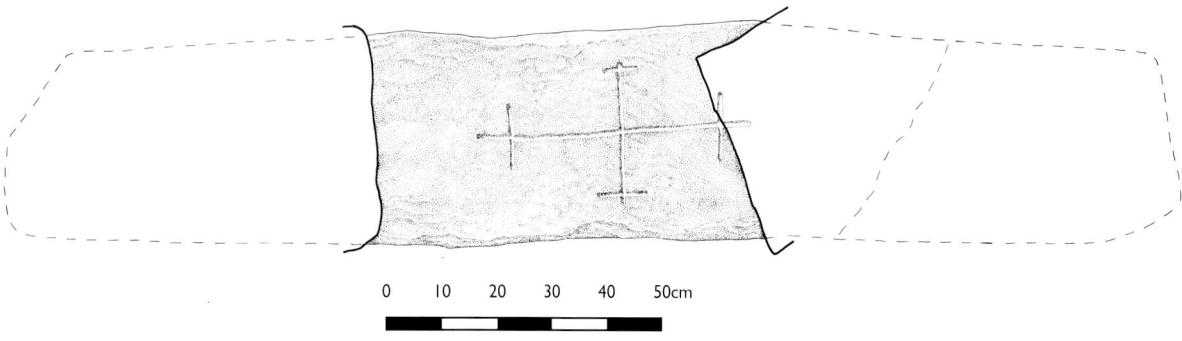

Figure 96

Cross no. 10 — Cross on Cell Lintel — Garnet-Schist

Location: *On the underside of the inner lintel of Cell B.*
Size: *2.15m long.*

This stone has a long linear incised cross with short cross bars near the end of each terminal, similar to the small cross on the edge of Cross no. 1 (Fig. 87b). Drawing by P. Johnson.

Figure 97

Cross no. 11 — Cross in Church Enclosure Wall — Garnet-Schist

Location: *At the base of the northeastern corner of the church enclosure wall.*
Size: *0.60m high, 0.45m wide.*

This cross was drawn twice in 1839 by W.F. Wakeman, once on a sheet marked 'near the church' (RIA MS 12T9, 43) and once in the background of a sketch of the church (RIA MS 12T16). The cross stone was in better shape when Wakeman sketched it; now most of the top and upper right side of the stone has broken away. The design is a deeply incised Latin cross, with four circular hollows at the crossing of the arms with the shaft of the cross. Drawing by P. Johnson.

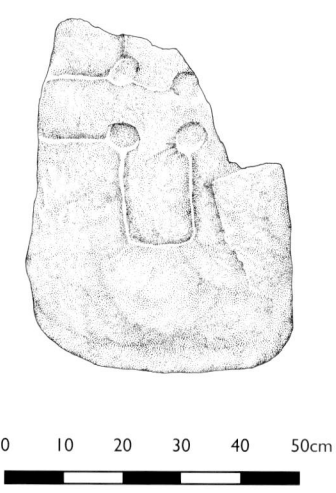

East face   *West face*

Figure 98

Cross no. 12 — Footstone from Grave no. 8 — Garnet-Schist

Location: *Behind the church.*
Size: *0.79m high, 0.30m wide, 0.03m thick.*

The footstone for grave no. 8 is inscribed on both faces and the stone itself is also slightly notched to form a rough short-armed cross shape on one side.

98a. East face: A linear cross with short crossbars at the end of the lateral arms, set inside a roundel. Four notches, not carved all the way through the stone, were cut on this face, forming a short-armed cross in relief; a small boss was set in each of the upper notches.

98b. West face: A badly weathered stone that has a roundel or possibly a double roundel in relief that contains a small linear cross whose upper and lower terminals are bifurcated. A semi-circular area was carved out under the roundel — remnants of another roundel? Photo Con Brogan.

East face   *West face*

Figure 99

Cross no. 13 — Footstone from Burial no. 7 — Blue Mica-Schist

Location: *Behind the eastern wall of the church.*
Size: *0.66m high, 0.39m wide, 0.07m thick.*

The footstone for burial no. 7 is inscribed on two faces.

99a. East face: An unusual cross design. A cross carved in relief consisting of double-banded arms with double-banded terminals that curve and expand outward at the ends. The upper quadrants contain geometric shapes in relief.

99b. West face: Similar to the east face but with four bosses, one in each quadrant, set close to the crossing of the arms, each with a hollowed dimple in its centre. In addition, there is another badly weathered boss in the upper left quadrant, and an odd mushroom or T-shape formed by a raised band sits below the cross.

This cross has several unusual features in that its base has been shaped into a tenon for fitting into a cross base. Although decorated on both sides, this is not a reused cross, as the design and carving techniques are the same on both sides; both sides were probably worked contemporaneously. The cross was probably intended, therefore, to be seen on both sides and may have been set up on an altar or *leacht* before its present use as a footstone. The main face appears to be the east face. Photos Con Brogan.

Figure 100

Cross no. 14 — Headstone of Grave no. 7 — Garnet-Schist

Location: *Set into a niche in the church's eastern wall.*
Size: *0.78m high, 0.26m wide.*

This stone was shaped into a short-armed cross and inscribed on two faces.

100a. East face: A linear cross (?), badly effaced, set into a roundel.

100b. West face: A linear bifurcated cross that could not have been seen in its present position; a reused stone. Photos Con Brogan.

East face *West face*

Figure 101

Cross no. 15 — Recumbent Stone of Grave no. 7 — Garnet-Schist

Location: *on top of grave no. 7 behind the eastern wall of the church.*
Size: *1.2m long, 0.56m wide.*

Roughly shaped and weathered recumbent stone broken into three pieces; it is also fractured along the right-hand side. Near the top this stone has a carved central roundel filled with a fretwork cross and three D-shaped terminals. The upper and right-hand terminals are filled with repeating D-shaped fretwork; the left-hand terminal has no visible internal design. The lower shaft of the cross runs down in two bands to a mirror image of the upper pattern: a roundel with three D-shaped terminals. None of the lower terminals contains internal design; badly effaced. Photo Con Brogan.

The Cemetery and Cross Stones

West face

Figure 102
Cross no. 16 — Footstone for Grave no. 6 — Dark Blue-Grey Limestone with 'Ostrea' Fossils
Location: *Behind the east wall of the church.*
Size: *0.89m long, 0.32m wide, 0.09m thick.*

This footstone was found sheared off its base but still in position at the time of excavation in 1995; it was possibly damaged when the eastern gable fell. It is one of only two cross-inscribed stones on High Island made of imported limestone.

West face: Atypical in that the other footstones all have decoration on the eastern side, whereas this footstone is inscribed only on the west face (see Rahtz, 1982, 11, on typical placement of decorated stones). The stone is shaped into a short-armed cross. Incised lines then repeat the shape of the stone. A roundel within the carved cross contains a cross formed by a straight line with three centrally placed crossbars. The design may have been more complicated originally, as there are hints of a third concentric circle or possibly another incised cross outside the inner roundel.

An unusual feature of this cross is that the lower shaft of the stone is also decorated on the western side with a small religious figure standing within a linear frame. He wears a long robe and holds both arms up in an orans position, showing outstretched arms and palms up in a gesture of prayer; he also appears to be standing in something, possibly a boat or in water. Each hand also holds a square-shaped object (gospels/satchels?). This lightly incised figure and the more deeply cut cross design on the head of the stone were done by two different hands, most likely at two different times.

It is not traditional for orans figures to hold anything. A cross within a circle clearly decorates one of these books and it is possible in good light to see another cross on a somewhat larger book in his left hand.

The shape of the stone, with a tapering base, indicates that it was intended to be an erect stone; however, this means the little figure would always be hidden. Human figures are unusual on High Island, being found on only two stones. Orans figures have a long history in Christian art; seen on figures in the catacombs, they are believed to represent variously a position of prayer, of blessing, surrender of the soul to Christ, the cross and Christ's crucifixion, of Christ's suffering and victory over death, and a promise of future salvation (Ladner, 237). Farr, in addition, relates them to the 'vigil of the cross', an imitation of Christ's passion, assumed by many Irish monks as a penitential practice.[172]

An apostle or Christ holding up one book is one of the most common depictions in Christian art, but a figure in the orans position holding up two books (gospels?) is extremely rare. It is paralleled only by a small figure above the canon tables in the *Book of Kells* (f.4r) (Fig. 103). Photos Con Brogan.

Figure 103

Detail of St Matthew from the Book of Kells with a similar orans pose, holding up two gospel books. Courtesy Trinity College Library, Dublin.

A similar figure, but with arms crossed in front of him, is also found representing the apostle Matthew on the Evangelist symbols page of St John's Gospel (f.290v); (see Fig. 130), also in the *Book of Kells*.[173]

The composite iconography of the little figure is almost certainly related to salvation and resurrection through the Gospels, the Word of God. Extrapolating from Farr's interpretation, this figure may also be a reference to the benefits of severe ascetic practices in imitation of Christ's sacrifice, as practised by the particular monk buried here. Two different hands worked on this cross stone; possibly the figure design was carved later on the island for this particular monk.

Figure 104

Cross no. 17 — Headstone for Grave no. 6 — Garnet-Schist

Location: Set inside the eastern wall of the church.
Size: 0.92m high, 0.40 wide.

East face

West face

This headstone was part of the base of the church wall. The stone is lightly shaped and has a design inscribed on both faces. Part of the top of the cross has been broken off, as well as part of the right side of the eastern face.

104a. East face: this face is lightly shaped near the top of the left-hand side and probably was on the right as well, where now there is only a small notch on the damaged upper right arm. A badly effaced and weathered triple roundel was incised on this stone but the outer roundel is only visible along the bottom. A carved line can still be seen following the inward curve of the notched arms.

104b. West face: On this side four notches were cut on the side of stone. The notches were not cut all the way through the stone, but a band of stone was cut away from the notches back to the roundels in the centre of the stone; hollows were cut just outside the inner roundels. Two roundels, the outer one now partly effaced, contain a linear cross with cross bars at the end of each terminal, and a short diagonal runs into each quadrant from the roundel. This cross, the west face invisible in its position in the church, is a reused cross. Photos Con Brogan.

Figure 105

Cross no. 18 — Recumbent Stone for Grave no. 6
— Limestone with Oyster Shells, Fossils

Location: *Lying on top of grave no. 6 behind the church.*
Size: *1.62m long, 0.36m wide, 0.10m thick.*

This is the most elegantly carved of the three decorated recumbent slabs but now effaced so badly that much of the decoration is impossible to see. It is made of limestone, most probably from the Aran Islands.[174] Originally the stone was shaped into a smooth rectangle and had a narrow border carved around the edge of the stone. Much of this border has fragmented away; it is most visible on the right side of the stone.

Like its neighbouring recumbent stone, the basic design is of a central roundel containing remains of fretwork in the centre, and three D-shaped terminals also containing fretwork. This is best seen at the top of the stone, where a central roundel still shows inner fretwork of a cross pattern and the upper terminal still clearly shows a type of repeating D-fretwork. To the right of this upper terminal is an odd small boss with a hollow in the centre.

Two bands run the length of the stone down to the bottom, where the upper pattern, reversed in a mirror image, is repeated; now very faint, and internal design not visible. Very faint traces of incision indicate the possibility that a central roundel with two D-shaped terminals was also repeated once or twice more between the top and bottom of the stone.

The design on this stone, which so clearly relates to the other two recumbent stones at High Island, is also related to the design of crosses seen at Clonmacnoise (see discussion, p. 162). The patterned repletion of the cross design seen on the High Island recumbent slabs and the creation of a mirror image, however, has created a far more complex pattern than those used at Clonmacnoise; these are clearly a local variation, not seen exactly like this anywhere else. Photo Con Brogan.

Figure 106
Cross no. 19 — Headstone for Grave no. 5
— Blue Mica-Schist
Location: *Set as a base stone for the eastern wall of the church.*
Size: *0.90m high, 0.74m wide.*

East face: This is the largest of the headstones and one of the most elaborately carved stones on High Island. The cross carved in relief is in excellent condition and clearly shows the two central roundels with D-shaped terminals. The centre of the roundels contains a cross with fretwork (similar to that seen on the recumbent slab for burial no. 7), as do the terminals (repeating D pattern). The upper quadrants have peltas, a pair of facing looping coils, bands that curve down from the edges of the stone towards each other and then coil inwards as they approach each other. A boss is set below each pair close to the centre roundel. The lower quadrants contain only bosses close to the centre roundel.

This headstone and its neighbouring headstone for grave no. 4 to the north are unusually decorated for headstones, as the design covers the entire stone and, consequently, some of the design was hidden when it was used as an erect stone. Both of these cross stones and that of burial no. 6 must have been in their present position when the eastern wall was built on top of them, unlike the other two headstones, which were moved and set into niches in the church wall. Photo Con Brogan.

Figure 107
Cross no. 20 — Footstone for Grave no. 4 — Blue Schist
Location: *Behind the church.*
Size: *0.60m high, 0.39m wide, 0.05m thick.*

East face

East face: Cross in relief of three roundels with D-shaped terminals. The terminals are roughly D-shaped. In centre of roundel is a linear cross with short diagonal lines running into the quadrants from the roundel. Upper and lower terminals are bifurcated bands with a single line running down the centre of the terminal; lateral terminals have three bands running out to edge of stone. Photo Con Brogan.

East face

Top of cross stone

Figure 108
Cross no. 21 — Headstone for Grave no. 4
— Blue Schist

Location: *Used as a foundation stone in eastern wall of the church.*
Size: *0.68m high, 0.59m wide, 0.16m thick.*

108a. East face: This cross is as elaborately carved as its neighbouring headstone and resembles it in basic cross design. It has similar peltas in the upper quadrants, as well as bosses; here, however, the bosses have hollows (possibly with crosses carved into them). The cross in the central roundel is a raised Greek cross. The lower quadrants have lozenge-shaped panels filled with key or fretwork.

West face: A linear bifurcated cross. This face of the stone could not be seen once the church wall was built. This face has not been photographed.

108b. Top face of stone: has a small linear bifurcated cross, an equal-armed cross with the terminals beginning to separate almost immediately; it is similar to the cross under the lintel of the church. This may have been a reused cross stone. Ordinarily, a stone like this one and like its neighbouring headstone would be expected to be recumbent stones so that the whole complex design might be seen; however, both stones do have the tapered ends indicative of erect stones, and this headstone was clearly used previously as an erect stone. It is possible that we do not yet clearly understand medieval purpose and plan in the use of inscribed crosses. Because the designs used on these two headstones are so closely related to those on the recumbent stones for graves nos. 6 and 7, and because of their tapered stone ends, we believe that, although unusual, they were deliberately planned this way. Photo Con Brogan.

Figure 109

Cross no. 22 — Footstone to Grave no. 3 — Garnet-Schist

Location: behind the church.
Size: 0.067m high, 0.30m wide.

East face: Linear cross in a roundel, with terminals that surpass the roundel and bifurcate. Four bosses, one in each quadrant, in low relief, each with a cross incised into it. Photo Con Brogan.

East face

Figure 110

Cross no. 23 — Footstone to Burial no. 2 — Garnet-Schist

Location: Behind the church.
Size: 0.55m high, 0.26m wide.

East face: Linear cross in a roundel, with terminals that surpass the roundel and separate or bifurcate. Identical to footstone no. 3 without the bosses. Photo Con Brogan.

East face

Figure 111

Cross no. 24 — Recumbent Stone for Burial no. 1 — Blue Schist

Location: Behind the church in the northeastern corner.
Size: 1.2m long, 0.56m wide.

This stone is badly effaced and worn away and partly hidden, as the wall of the church sits on its upper end. Visible are traces of two bands running down from the wall face to a roundel and one D-shaped terminal on the left at the bottom of the stone. It is very badly worn on the right-hand side. A curving line under the roundel hints of another terminal. No interior decoration visible. Basic design similar to other recumbent stones. Photo Con Brogan.

The Cemetery and Cross Stones

Figure 112

Cross no. 25 — Reused Decorated Stone — Mica-Schist

Location: One of the northern sidestones for burial no. 4; the stone nearest the footstone.
Size: 0.72m long (still in the ground).

This stone was turned on its side for its secondary use as a sidestone for this burial. The design is a linear cross in a linear circle, whose arms surpass the circle; the lateral and lower arms bifurcate into broad semi-circles, while the upper arm bifurcates and then re-divides yet again. Photo J.W. Marshall.

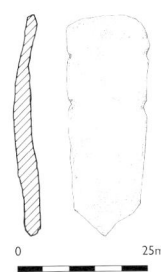

Figure 113

Cross no. 26 — Undecorated Cross — Garnet-Schist

Location: Found lying on ground east of the church near the graves during excavation, 1995.
Size: 0.40m high, 0.15m wide, 0.03m thick.

This small cross has four small notches cut into the sides of the stone, creating the faint semblance of a short-armed cross. The tapered foot shows it was intended to stand upright. Drawing by P. Johnson.

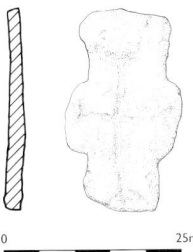

Figure 114

Cross no. 27 — Decorated Cross — Garnet-Schist

Location: Found lying on the ground east of the church near the graves during excavation, 1995.
Size: 0.27m high, 0.13m wide, 0.02m thick.

This small cross stone was roughly shaped into a short-armed cross with a linear cross incised on one face. The lateral and lower terminals bifurcate at the end and the upper terminal bifurcates into a broad U shape. Drawing by P. Johnson.

Figure 115

Cross no. 28 — Fragment of a Decorated Cross — Garnet-Schist

Location: Found lying on the ground east of the church near the graves during excavation, 1995.
Size: 0.25m high, 0.11m wide, 0.015m thick.

This small cross stone was decorated on two faces and was also shaped as a short-armed cross. The stone is broken or sheared off on the top and bottom.

    115a. A linear cross with terminals ending in short cross bars set within two roundels or three concentric circles. The outer circle shows best in the lower and right-hand part.

    115b. A roundel containing a linear cross whose arms bifurcate. Drawing by P. Johnson.

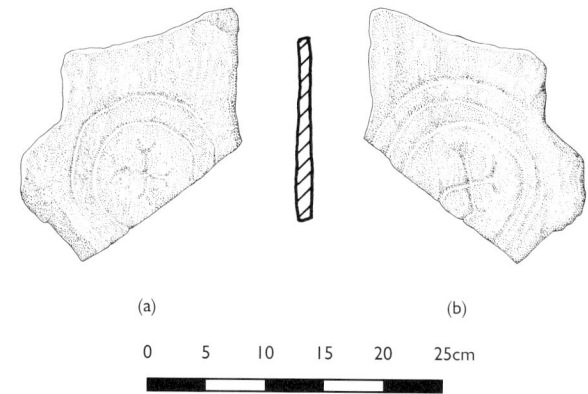

Figure 116

Cross no. 29 — A Ring Cross

Location: Found in the 1995 spoil from the southern side of the church enclosure wall, this cross was possibly also embedded in the church enclosure wall.
Size: 0.55m high, 0.29m wide.

A Latin cross set against a ring; the arms do not pass beyond the ring; four deep hollows at the intersections of the cross arms. Similar to the west face of the headstone for grave no. 6. Broken off on the upper left-hand side and on the top, and damaged on the right as well. Photo Con Brogan.

Figure 117

Cross no. 30 — Fragment of a Short-Armed Cross with a Simple Latin Cross Inscribed on it

Location: Unknown.
Size: 0.55m high, 0.24m wide.

Photo Con Brogan.

The Cemetery and Cross Stones

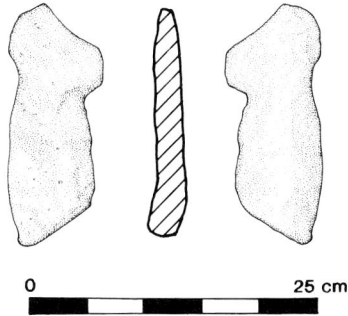

Figure 118

Cross no. 31 — Small Hand Cross — Mica-Schist

Size: *0.20m high, 0.083m wide, 0.025m thick.*
Location: *Southern border of the millpond.*

This is the only hand cross found on the island; it may have been dropped by a pilgrim. Drawing by P. Johnson.

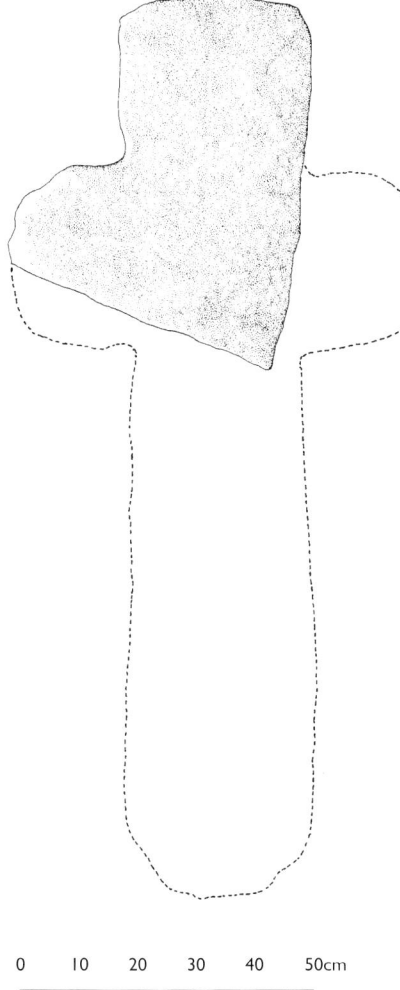

Figure 119

Cross no. 32 — Cross Fragment — Garnet-Schist

Location: *Lying outside the west façade of the church.*

This fragment of a small cross was found lying on the rubble on the western side of the church. This was probably a simple undecorated cross stone with notches cut to form a cross with short arms. Dotted lines show a possible reconstruction; it may have been up to 1.5m high. Drawing by P. Johnson.

Figure 120

Cross no. 33 — Cross Base and Cross Fragment — Garnet-Schist

Location: *At the* leacht *south of the small lake near the southwestern landing.*

120a. This is probably the slotted base for a cross built with a tongue (tenon in wood construction). Higgins notes that socket stones are rare in Galway but are found at Conwall, County Donegal, and at Inchagoill (Higgins 1987, 261). A variation of freestanding socket stones is seen at Glendalough, where some socket holes were cut into the recumbent slab itself (Lionard 1961, 149–150); Macalister (1916, Fig. 4 and Fig. 10) mentions similar recumbent slabs at Inishcealtra. Large socket stones were certainly used at Iona (Argyll, Vol. 4, 1982, 215–216), and they must have been fairly common at large monasteries.

120b. It may be the cross stem or tenon of the cross stone that fits into the base. At least one of Wakeman's drawings of High Island crosses, Cross 34 below, demonstrates the use of socket stones and bases. This particular cross base and cross fragment may be the remains of the cross that Petrie mentioned seeing here, 'a stone altar surmounted by a cross…' (Petrie 1845, 421).

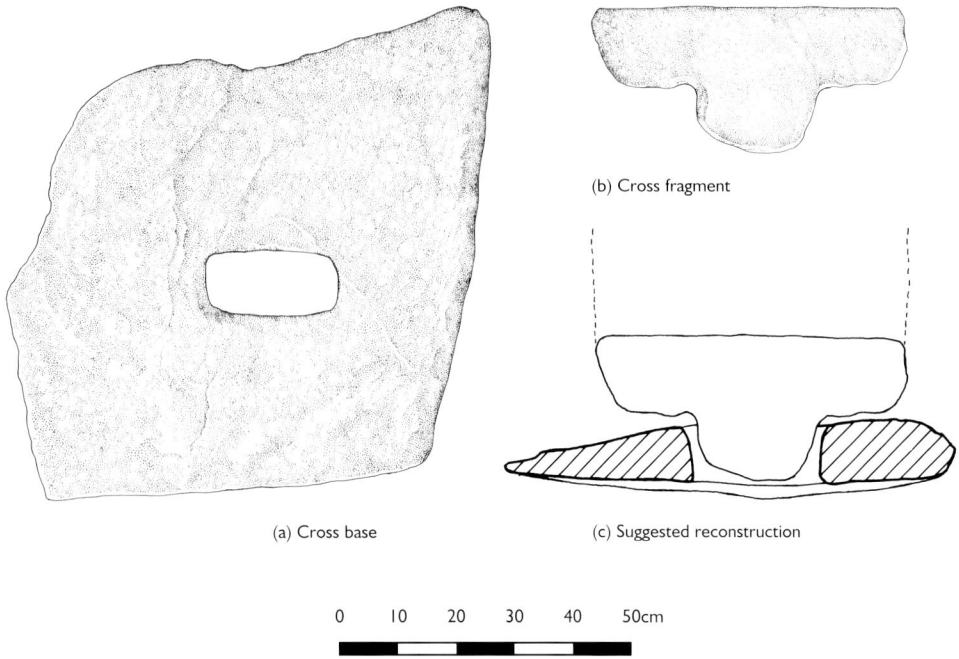

(b) Cross fragment

(a) Cross base

(c) Suggested reconstruction

120c. A drawing showing how the base and tenon were fitted together, and the close fit between these two, which would have been further supported by wedging stones. Drawings by P. Johnson.

Figure 121
Cross no. 34 — Latin Cross, Missing
Location: *Labelled in handwriting 'south of the church', so it was within the monastic enclosure.*
Size: *Unknown.*

Knowledge of this cross is owed to a pencil sketch made by W.F. Wakeman during his visit in 1839 (RIA MS 12T9, 45). This freestanding cross with an expanded lower shaft was apparently set in a slotted base similar to the cross in the figure above. This may be the cross standing in the background of a drawing Wakeman made of Cell B in 1839 (see Fig. 83a) and used by Petrie (1845, 128). Courtesy Royal Irish Academy.

The Cemetery and Cross Stones

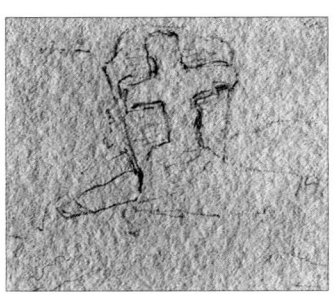

Figure 122

Cross no. 35 — Latin Cross Carved in Relief, Missing

Location: *A Latin cross carved in relief, drawn in pencil by Wakeman in 1839 (RIA MS 12T9, 45), who labelled it 'south of the church'.*

Size: *Wakeman annotated this drawing with the words: '2 feet three inches high' [0.68m].*

Courtesy Royal Irish Academy.

Figure 123

Cross no. 36 — Anthropomorphic Stone, Missing

Location: *This was drawn by W.F. Wakeman in 1839 on a sheet marked 'near the church' (RIA MS 12T9, 43).*

Size: *Wakeman wrote '2 feet 6 inches' [0.76m] next to this drawing.*

On this stone is a much weathered figure of a man (?) beneath a cross. The cross has a central circle, three plain D-shaped terminals, and an upper terminal that is a scroll/hat? Courtesy Royal Irish Academy.

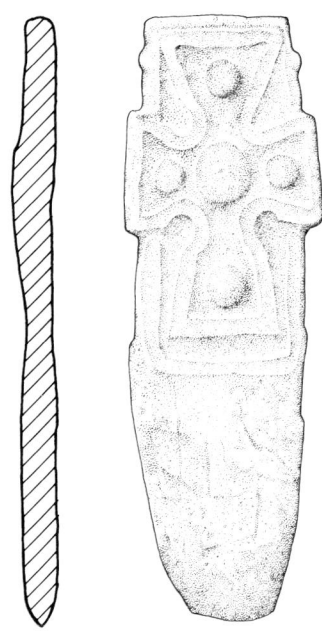

Figure 124

Cross no. 37 — Missing

Location: *A sketch made by Wakeman in 1839; this cross is missing (RIA 12.T.9, 45). Herity suggested (1990, 93) that it might be the cross standing on a* leacht *near the lake, but this is unlikely because of the easy recognition and identification of stones from Wakeman's drawings.*

Size: *Drawing was annotated '3 feet' [0.91m] by Wakeman.*

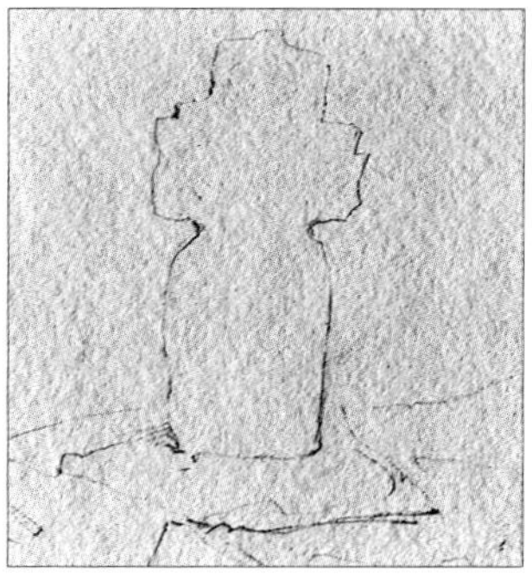

Courtesy Royal Irish Academy.

Figure 125

Cross at Kill Cemetery — Silt or Mudstone

Location: *In the cemetery of Kill church, a medieval church at Streamstown, near Clifden.*

Size: *1.0m high, 0.34m wide, 0.074m thick.*

This cross was reputedly taken by a fisherman from High Island for the grave of a local woman around the turn of the century, as reported by M. Gibbons; cross found by M. Gibbons and J. Higgins (see Higgins 1987, ii: fig. 66 and p.345). A brief conversation on 2 July, 1997 with the fisherman's daughter confirmed this account. The cross is lightly shaped into a short-armed cross, with a Latin cross set in a panel carved on it with four bosses, one in each arm surrounding a central boss. Two small protrusions or knobs, one on each edge of the stone, are found near the upper terminal. The design on this cross closely resembles the crosses on Caher Island, County Mayo, an island not too far from High Island that has easy access onto sandy beaches.

Geologically identified by Michael O'Sullivan as mudrock (personal communication, J.W. Marshall 1997); Caher Island has Derrylea formation mudrock among its components, a finely grained sedimentary rock composed mostly of clay, whereas High Island has none. This cross clearly originated on Caher Island rather than High Island (see Higgins 1987, i: fig. 29, who also agrees that this is possible). Drawing by P. Johnson.

Figure 126

Omey Island Cross — Missing

Location: *Women's Graveyard, Cruaghnaman, Omey Island.*
Size: *Unknown, but Higgins (1987, ii: 299–300) believes the stone may have measured 0.44m high and 0.26m wide.*

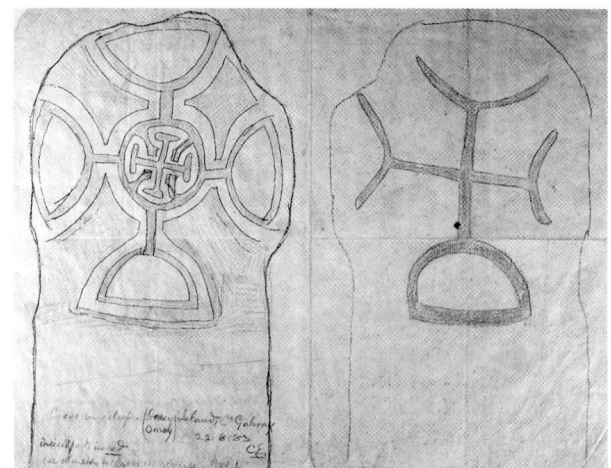

This cross is remarkably similar to the High Island crosses in both shape and decoration; one side is particularly close to the cross at Brian Boru's Well, while the other is an expanded version of it that has become an expansional cross. The cross itself is now missing, but two sketches of it are in the archives of Dúchas The Heritage Service. They were made in 1883 by an individual who signed his initials as 'CE' on both sides of the paper. On the page shown above, a handwritten inscription noted: 'Cross in relief Omey Island, Co. Galway, 22.8.83. Incised parts in red… See other side for Cross on reverse of Slab. CE'. On the reverse side (a duplicate of the simpler design seen on the right above) was written: 'Incised cross on Slab in Women's Graveyard, Omey Island, Co. Galway, 22.8.83. (Cruagh-on-ama=Women's Hillock). See other side for Cross on reverse of Slab. CE'.

Wakeman (1891, Plate 1, fig. 32, p. 354) also drew the simpler side of this cross and commented that the cross had already been sketched by C. Elcock.

The similarities to crosses on High Island are so striking that it is probable that either both monasteries employed the same craftsman/small workshop or that this stone was removed at some point from High Island.

The Cemetery and Cross Stones

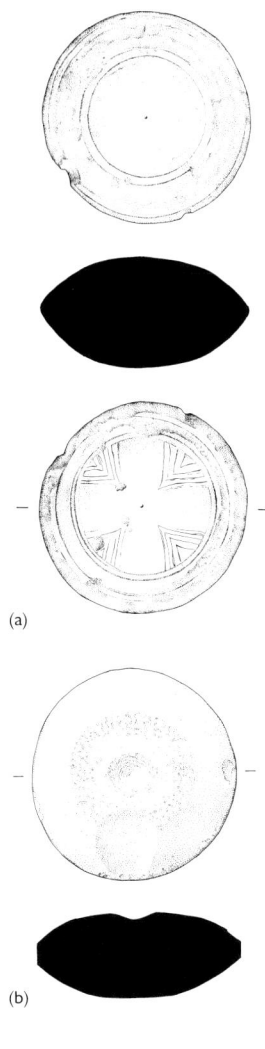

Figure 127

Decorated 'Pebble Stones' — Black Chert

Location: *Three of these, two of them decorated, were found near the footstones of the burials east of the church during excavation, 1995 and 1996.*
Size: *Small. All roughly 7–9cm wide.*

127a. Pebble stone with a small central indentation, like a compass point, from which several concentric circles were carved on the outer edge of the stone. The other side has a Latin cross cut upon it. It is made of chert or black flint, which is composed mostly of microcystalline quartz and tends to be deposited in nodules or layers amongst beds of limestone. It breaks in concoidal fractures and makes a good tool.

127b. Pebble stone with a Latin cross engraved upon it. Not geologically identified.

127c. Undecorated pebble stone. Not geologically identified. Not shown.

These round or oval stones have been water-rolled to their shape and have a smooth surface. Petrie (1847–50, 273–274) noted that on his first visit to Connemara 'stones of this kind were very frequently preserved upon the altars in the most ancient churches in that district ...' Also found on other coastal sites such as Inishmurray, County Sligo, and Iona, Argyll, Scotland (Argyll, vol. 4, 16, 184, 188). Believed to have been altar stones, cursing stones and/or cure stones; on High Island they were probably made by pilgrims who left them on the graves as offerings, as they did white quartz stones. They are of unknown date of origin and function but some were certainly made during the early medieval period. The stones at Inishmurray and Iona are much larger and more elaborately decorated (see Higgins 1987, i: 18–21 for more complete discussion. On painted pebbles in Scotland, see Ritchie 1971–71, 297–301).

The so-called decorated pebble stones are different from more utilitarian objects, such as the more elaborately inscribed stone lamp found in an eighth–tenth century grave in Temple Breccan on Inis Mór, County Galway. This had an inscription on it that read: 'pray for Bran the Pilgrim'. Drawings by P. Johnson.

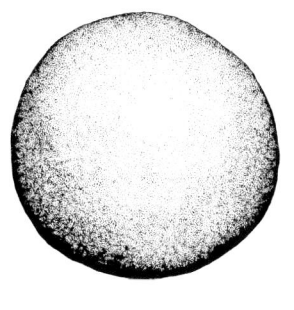

Figure 128

Granite Sphere

Location: *South of the Church.*
Size: *0.44m in diameter.*

A granite erratic, probably of stormbeach origin; possibly of some symbolic significance to the monks. Drawing by P. Johnson.

Discussion of Crosses

In 1996 an impressive number of cross stones still remained on the island, and High Island ranks among the largest island collections. The designs on the stones have a broad range, from very simple incised linear crosses to more elaborate, deeply carved forms. The simply worked crosses are typical of what one would expect on an island site without extensive artistic resources. A number of crosses, nevertheless, have surprisingly complex carved designs, more typical of large mainland sites with resident artisans.

There was clearly a High Island repertory of design and shape. A brief discussion of some of the more commonly used stone shapes, cross designs carved on the stones, and of one single element of cross design follows, with the intention of placing them in geographical and chronological contexts where possible.

Cross in Circle

Wakeman commented about the decoration of the cross stones behind the church in 1867: '…the western stone of these graves is usually carved with a cross within a circle, the emblem of eternity' (Wakeman 1867, 368). This is an accurate but oversimplified description, as the cross in circle only forms one element of the decoration on a number of the stones. He was, however, precisely accurate about the symbolism. This pattern has an ancient and widespread history in Christian art. It is indeed so common and widely commented on that little more needs to be said about it. The cross stands for Christ or his crucifixion, and the circle for universality, the world and life everlasting. As a symbol it reflects fundamental Christian thought, as reflected by Irenaeus: 'And because He is Himself the Word of God Almighty, who in his invisible form pervades us universally in the whole world…the son of God was also crucified in these, imprinted in the form of a cross on the universe…'[175]

Short-Armed Cross Stones

The most typical stone shape, found on twelve cross stones on the island, is that of a short-armed cross, the arms generally formed by carving notches in the sides of the stone. Some of these stones are undecorated, such as Fig. 90 by the millpond, but many also have cross designs inscribed on them, such as that on the reused lintel of the church (Fig. 95). Short-armed crosses are commonly found on other Irish sites such as Skellig Michael, County Kerry. They sometimes have a vaguely anthropomorphic appearance, particularly if the top of the vertical shaft is rounded. Crosses shaped like this are difficult to date and at present appear to have a wide chronological range; a few excavated examples have been dated as early as the eighth century (Thomas 1971, 121–123; Small, Thomas, Wilson, et al. 1973, 29), but Higgins (1987, I: 71–73) points out that there are numerous examples from the nineteenth and twentieth centuries.

Linear Crosses with Bifurcated Terminals

Linear crosses with forked or bifurcated terminals were the single most popular cross design. This is not surprising, for it is one of the simplest of cross designs. They are found by themselves or in more complicated designs set inside linear circles or roundels, sometimes with the terminals forking just outside the roundel; plain linear crosses with barred terminals were also popular on High Island. Bifurcated crosses are generally believed to be early, and Nash-Williams assigned them to the seventh to ninth century in Wales. Indeed, the few that have been dated have been early, such as the bifurcated cross attached to the initials in the sixth-century *Cathach of Saint Columba*, and another one at Iona dated by its inscription to the ninth century.

On High Island, this design can only be roughly placed relative to its use as part of other better-dated structures, such as on the cross stone reused for grave no. 4's sidestone (Fig. 112). The decorated sidestone was reused for this burial as the design was placed sideways and covered entirely by the grave fill; therefore, the design was used at an earlier time. For the same reason, the west face of the headstone for grave no. 4 is earlier than this grave, which was dated late ninth to late tenth century.

Simple bifurcated crosses like these had a widespread, centuries-old history of use in Christian contexts: they are found in Coptic Egypt, on Maronite churches in Libya and in northern Syria dating from the late fifth century. In Syria these crosses are closely associated with the small monastic sites that formed around the Syrian stylite hermits who, in imitation of St Simeon the Stylite, manifested their ascetic fervor by living on top of a column.[176] The presence of bifurcated crosses hundreds of years later in Ireland and Scotland evidences the longevity of this design, although its specific Syrian or Maronite symbolic content could easily have changed over the centuries. Extensive use of this cross form in Ireland and its simplicity of execution suggests that it may well have continued in use beyond the ninth century, especially on small remote sites without skilled artisans.

Outline Crosses with Hollows

Another simple cross design, dated by Nash-Williams to the seventh–ninth centuries in Wales, is that of an outline cross with circular hollows in the central angles, like the examples on High Island found on the stone at the base of the church enclosure wall (Fig. 97). Something similar without the outline cross but with the hollows is found on the west face of the headstone for grave no. 6 (Fig. 104b) and on the cross stone found in 1997 (Fig. 116). Lionard believed that this design may have originated in Northumbria and appeared in Ireland by at least the eighth century. More recent efforts to date these crosses confirm his beliefs.[177] The early origin of this design has been confirmed by dendrochronological evidence following its use on the coffin of St Cuthbert in the late seventh century at Lindisfarne; in addition, two ringed versions at

Iona have been dated by inscription to the eighth and ninth centuries.[178] The use of this cross design is probably early on High Island, certainly ninth century and perhaps as early as the eighth. The full time-range of these crosses has not been established. Strikingly similar Latin crosses with hollows in the crossing of the arms are found on two Scottish recumbent cross stones dated to the tenth century.[179] Two of the High Island stones, nevertheless, have been found in secondary contexts, which does mean that they are earlier than the structures, such as the eastern wall of the church and the church enclosure wall, in which they were found.

Bosses as an Element of Cross Design

Even distinctive single elements of cross design have an extensive and diverse tradition. One such element, common on the more elaborately decorated cross stones, is the round boss carved in relief. Bosses are not common on the Galway cross stones, although they are found on crosses on two nearby monastic islands, St MacDara's Island, County Galway and Caher Island, County Mayo.[180] Bosses as an element of design, however, have a long and geographically widespread history of use on Christian sculptured monuments. They are commonly seen, for instance, not only in Ireland, but also on early medieval crosses in Scotland and Wales, in Early Christian Egyptian and northern Syrian contexts and on fifth/sixth-century Merovingian sarcophagi.[181]

Bosses appear to have had no inherent symbolic meaning in themselves; however, it is highly unlikely that they were purely decorative. The driving purpose of early medieval religious art was the expression and reaffirmation of the sacred; to this end, artistic elements of line, form and colour were purposefully used. Christians transformed ordinary objects, animals, colours, plants and numbers, into metaphors of Christian doctrine and philosophy (see Ferguson [1954] 1972 and Krautheimer 1969). Hence naturalistic and even purely decorative elements were used in religious art, not just for their intrinsic artistic values but as the visual expressions of abstract spiritual thought, a sign and a message for the faithful. Over the centuries writings of many renowned Christian intellects such as St Augustine, Boethius and the ninth-century Irishman, John Scottus Eriugena, manifest a particular fascination with number symbolism. The translation of the world into a metaphysical, mathematical harmony derived from a combination of Pythagorean and Platonic ideas combined with the advice of Solomon (II.20) 'but thou hast ordered all things by measure and number and weight' to encourage Christian philosophers to believe in the sacred symbolism of number.[182] The significance of bosses may lie, therefore, in their number rather than in their form.

On High Island three cross stones — the small broken cross found near Brian Boru's well (Fig. 89), the footstone for grave no. 3 (Fig. 109) and the headstone for grave no. 5 (Fig. 106) — have four bosses, one in each quadrant of the cross. Four is commonly the number of the four evangelists, who themselves represent the core of Christian belief, the life of Christ, the Word Incarnate, as found in the four Gospels.[183] The figures illustrating the four evangelists, the man, the ox, the calf and the eagle, moreover, are frequently seen in the quadrants of a cross on the evangelist symbols page of illuminated Gospel books such as the *Book of Kells* (f. 27v and 129v), *Trier Gospels* (f.iv), *Macdurnan Gospels* (f. iv), *Lichfield Gospels* (p. 219), and an early ninth-century Gospel in Augsburg (f. 197 r, Bayerische Staatsbibliothek, Munich) (Fig. 129).

Similar evangelist symbols also occur in the cross quadrants on the elaborate metalwork covers of these books, such as the mid tenth-century *Gospel Book of Saint Gauzelin* (Cathedral Treasury, Nancy) and on the eighth-century *Soiscéal Molaise* book shrine from County Fermanagh. If number is the key symbolic element, then the four bosses in the quadrants of crosses on High Island stones are abstract symbols of the four evangelists' figures, in effect, symbols of symbols. Bosses may be a rough sculptural equivalent of the same number of small crosses, disks, etc. that appear in and around other cross designs in painting, book illustration and on metalwork pieces.[184]

Figure 129

Evangelist symbol page from the Gospel of John in the Book of Kells *(290v) showing each quadrant of the cross filled with the symbol of one evangelist. St Matthew holds up two books, one in each hand, in a gesture reminiscent of the figure on the footstone to grave no. 6. Courtesy Archives, Trinity College Library.*

Expansional Cross Designs

If simple linear bifurcated crosses and bosses are difficult to place chronologically, a time-period can be more confidently assigned to one group of designs on High Island. Seven stones on High Island are decorated with expansional cross designs, that is, crosses with central roundels and semi-circular or D-shaped terminals that often contain geometric designs. These seven are: the cross standing south of the church (Fig. 86), the cross forming the southern side of the altar (Fig. 94) and five stones used for the burials behind the church: the headstones for graves nos. 4 and 5, and the three decorated recumbent stones on graves nos. 1, 6 and 7 (Figs. 101, 105, 106, 108, 111).[185]

These are the most distinctive and elaborate cross designs on High Island. Expansional crosses like these are not found on any other Atlantic island site and, indeed, are extremely rare on Ireland's western coast; in Galway they are found at Inchagoill and Clonfert.

In 1961 Padraig Lionard did a typological and chronological study of designs on Irish recumbent gravestones. He found the expansional cross, a cross with semi-circular and circular terminals and centres, to be the design most commonly used and the one most reliably dated (Figs. 130 and 131). A number of the recumbent stones with expansional cross designs at Clonmacnoise had inscribed names, which enabled Lionard to develop a typology by correlating names inscribed on these burial or memorial stones with the death notices of prominent people, mostly ecclesiastics or princes, mentioned in the monastic annals, who were known to be buried at Clonmacnoise. Out of a total of 172 expansional cross stones in Ireland, Lionard was able to date twenty-five, or a statistically significant 14.5 per cent of the total. Lionard's typology thus allows us to group into this time-period stones with the same design.[186]

New styles, whether of art, music, architecture or speech, tend to be begin with slow acceptance, then grow more popular and common in use until boredom or new ideas cause them to pass out of fashion. Thus, one of the main principles of seriation typology used by archaeologists is that, barring variations in time and space, 'a graph of the popularity of any cultural trait will have a single peak.'[187] In any geographical area, then, in a single period, the use of an artistic motif, not a simple solitary design element but a complex design on a particular object, might be expected to become favoured, flourish, and then fade away. According to Lionard's typology this is exactly what happened with internally decorated expansional cross designs on recumbent stones. Recumbent stones decorated with this motif appeared late in the mid ninth century, beginning to replace the most popular motif of the ninth century, the ringed cross. Expansional crosses continued with greater, almost exclusive use in the tenth and eleventh centuries, then began to diminish in the first half of the twelfth century, and finally ceased to be used after the mid twelfth century. Dr Raghnall Ó'Floinn at the National Museum believes he can refine this hypothesis as follows: the dates of expansional cross designs centre on the later ninth century to the end of the tenth century, and only late survival variants can be dated as late as the eleventh or twelfth centuries (1994, 254).[188] Some of the High Island stones may be later than the late tenth century and may indeed be late survival variants, an opinion that fits well with our conviction that the design here would naturally be later than its use at Clonmacnoise.

Expansional cross designs are not original or unique to the Irish. Lionard felt they may have originated in Byzantine crosses with splayed ends or crosses ending in

Figure 130

An inscribed expansional cross from Clonmacnoise. Inscribed on it is 'Pray for Thuathal craftsman'. Courtesy Dúchas The Heritage Service.

The Cemetery and Cross Stones

Figure 131
An expansional cross from Clonmacnoise, without decoration. Courtesy Dúchas The Heritage Service.

discs, seen in Merovingian metalwork. An early example of a variant, however, is seen in the Roman catacombs in the first half of the second century.[189] Internally decorated expansional crosses, however, first appear in Insular manuscripts of the late seventh or early eighth century, primarily on the carpet pages, where crosses with round or rectangular terminals and expanded centres are filled with interlace, spirals and fretwork. Designs like this are seen in the *Book of Lindisfarne* and the *Book of Kells*, and on the four evangelist symbols cross-page in the *Trier Gospels* (Henderson 1987, 91).[190]

Simple forms of expansional crosses begin to be seen on stone on the 'pillow-stones', small stones less than one foot high, found at Irish foundations in England, particularly at Hartlepool and Lindisfarne. Because they often have inscriptions in Hiberno-Saxon runes, Lionard believed that these stones could date to the eighth century, after Irish influence had waned and before Viking raids caused these two foundations to be abandoned in 800 and 875 (Lionard 1961, 130–131). Similar cross designs are found on Inis Mór in the Aran Islands, and at Clonmacnoise, of uncertain date.

Lionard believed, however, that fully developed expansional crosses on stone, whose internal spaces are filled with geometric patterns, interlace, spiral or fretwork, were an Irish innovation. While he was able to date the use of certain specific ornaments, such as spirals, to a narrow range, Lionard found that the use of key and fretwork, the most common for expansional crosses, was also the longest lasting. Expansional crosses with these patterns occurred as early as the end of the ninth century and as late as the first quarter of the twelfth century.[191] Parallels to the type of fretwork seen in these crosses are found on thistle brooches dating from the late ninth to late tenth century and on decorated wood from tenth-century levels in Dublin.[192]

The decoration on the High Island stones is clearly that of developed expansional crosses with circular centres, with D-shaped arm terminals. Parts of the High Island designs are so badly weathered that they cannot be read entirely, but the primary internal decoration appears to be key or fretwork, with a cross generally in the centre of the roundel. Another aspect of the High Island designs closely resembling those of Clonmacnoise is the tendency to repeat the basic design within the design so that there is a circle within a circle and the D-shape of the terminal is echoed within the D-shape, creating a repeated linear rhythm. Macalister used this to distinguish the Clonmacnoise stones, calling them three-line and five-line crosses (Macalister 1909).

Lionard was working only with recumbent stones, but on High Island this design appears on both recumbent and erect stones. Indeed, while it is sometimes difficult to tell whether a stone was originally an erect or recumbent stone, apparently the only decorated expansional crosses on erect stones are on High Island.[193] There are other minor differences between the High Island stones and those of Clonmacnoise. The crosses on High Island are always equilateral crosses, whereas those at Clonmacnoise are more generally Latin crosses, i.e. those whose vertical shaft is longer than the cross arms.

None of the stones on High Island carry inscribed names, which are almost universal at Clonmacnoise. While the basic design of expansional crosses on High Island is virtually identical to those of Clonmacnoise, the design at High Island has frequently been elaborated with additional designs outside the expansional cross, such as looping coils, bosses, geometric designs as seen on the two headstones or with repetitions of the expansional design seen on the recumbent stones; these are the most sophisticated and complex elaboration of the expansional cross design on stone and they appear to be unique here. They required far more skill than the simpler cross designs and, with one exception, were all carved on island stone of mica-schist, and hence were likely carved on the island by either a resident stone-carver or perhaps by a travelling craftsman. These variations and elaborations appear to be those one might expect by artisans working in another region on a design that originated elsewhere.

Figure 132

Expansional cross at Inchagoill, Lough Corrib, Co. Galway. Courtesy Dúchas The Heritage Service.

Lionard noted that two-thirds of all the recumbent stones with expansional crosses (some 115) are found at Clonmacnoise. An additional twenty crosses are found nearby, from Gallen to the Lough Ree area; the others are distributed throughout the country. Even with the addition of the seven High Island stones to Lionard's total count, some 75 per cent of expansional crosses are found in a small area, all within a twenty-five-mile range.

Lionard included all expansional cross stones, both internally decorated and undecorated ones, in his data. If only the internally decorated expansional crosses are considered, however, the figures are even more interesting. Approximately sixty of the expansional crosses at Clonmacnoise were internally decorated. Of these crosses Lionard was able to correlate the inscriptions with eighteen obituary notices in the monastic annals; all eighteen were from Clonmacnoise. Approximately another twenty-four such crosses are found elsewhere in Ireland; outside of Clonmacnoise, Galway has the greatest number of these designs, with one at Clonfert and possibly a fragment of another at Inchagoill (Fig. 132), Lough Corrib, and an additional seven on High Island.[194]

Almost three-quarters of the known internally decorated expansional cross stones are found at Clonmacnoise, therefore it seems highly probable that the use of this design on stone originated at Clonmacnoise. From the tenth through to the twelfth century, Clonmacnoise was one of the most prestigious monasteries in Ireland, famous for its workshop of artisans, to whom, doubtless, other ecclesiastical establishments looked for inspiration.[195] High Island has the largest number of expansional cross stones outside of Clonmacnoise, which suggests there was a significant connection between the two.

Any dating of the stones on High Island must also consider Deetz and Dethlefsen's theory of the 'Doppler effect', which holds that types or motifs on artifacts will occur at sites further from the originating point at a later period.[196] Use of this motif on High Island is therefore apt to be later in the period than at Clonmacnoise, thus at a conservative estimate this design is unlikely to have been used on High Island before the tenth century.

According to Lionard's typology, the High Island crosses were most likely carved sometime between the tenth and the early twelfth centuries, a range that can be still further narrowed to a maximum on High Island by the radiocarbon dates of the burials, from the late ninth to the first quarter of the eleventh century. Someone on High Island, perhaps an abbot who designed the first stones or the skilled artisan who carved them, may have had close ties with Clonmacnoise. Even if we suspect that radiocarbon dates are actually broadening this chronological range too much, differences in burial dates clearly demonstrate that the crosses were carved over a fairly long time. One artisan, therefore, probably did not carve all the stones. The repetition of the unusual variants and elaborations of the design, designs that in their totality exist only on High Island, also shows that once a design was successfully used for a high status purpose it continued to be copied and used for similar positions. In time these designs may have taken on a special meaning for the monks, becoming an emblem symbolising their monastery as well as their saints.

Notes

[169] For a discussion of ways in which crosses might be used, see Higgins 1987, 1: 8–33; see also Bitel [1990] 1993, 64–66 for crosses as markers for gateways to heaven.

[170] All geological information and identification is owed to Dr Michael O'Sullivan of Cork, except for those crosses simply labelled 'mica-schist' by the authors, where circumstances prevented our consulting him.

[171] We have tried to develop a consistent terminology for these cross designs. We have used 'concentric circles' when the circular pattern is repeated more than once but the design is flat or relatively flat on the stone, and 'roundel' when the design is in relief. Occasionally, weathering created a dilemma.

172 See Farr 1997, 106–109 for an excellent detailed discussion of the orans figure and its particular importance in Ireland as the *crossfigell*, and its use in other parts of the *Book of Kells*.

173 We are indebted to Dr Peter Harbison who pointed out the similarity of the figure in the canon tables to us. Henry believed the second figure (f. 290v) derived from Osiris, the judge of the dead (Henry 1974, 190–191; see also Farr 1989, 65–66). On orans pose and the *Book of Kells*, see also O'Reilly 1993, 108–109.

174 Personal communication, Michael O'Sullivan, July 1996.

175 See Ladner 1995, chapter 8, esp. 99, 100, 110, among many others.

176 On their use in early Christian Coptic Egypt, although of uncertain dates, see Graves (1891, 346–349); for the Maronites, Sadar 1993; for Syria, see Peña, Castellan, and Fernandez, 1975. Fernandez believed the bifurcated cross is an archaic symbol of Judaic-Christian groups, p.203; Peña, Castellan and Fernandez 1987; Testa 1962, 331–334.

177 Lionard 1961, 115–117; fig. 11. He also believed that the design lasted until the twelfth century, which is less secure. Lionard noted crosses with hollowed angles, not in a circle, among them a recumbent slab of Muirgal, abbot of Clonmacnoise, possibly dated 789, and that a freestanding cross, the cross of Cathasach at Inish Cealtra, is dated 1111. Lionard also notes that four crosses of this type are found on the base of the south cross at Ahenny. The design is also present on a number of recumbent stones at Inish Cealtra, Co. Clare.

178 Bailey 1989, 238–43; RCAHMS 1982, 183–186. Henderson 1993, 209 discusses this briefly in relation to Pictish versions and notes that outline Latin crosses with rounded arm-pits, some of them ringed, are hard to date on Pictish crosses, or indeed generally.

179 One at Inchinnan and one at Govan, see Carwood, 1990, 118, ill. 16:3 and 4.

180 See Higgins 1987, I: 57–59 and Fig. 19. Higgins also notes their association with stones shaped into short-armed crosses. This is generally true on High Island, except for the two headstones for burials nos. 4 and 5.

181 Allen and Anderson 1993, 63–66, 75–80 and 381–193 among others; with spirals and serpents on the eighth-century High Crosses of Iona, such as St Oran's, St John's and St Martin's, RCAHMS 1982, 192–208; for other examples in Scotland and England, see Higgins 1987, I: figs. 36b and 37; Peña, Castellan and Fernandez 1987 and Sirat, Viellard-Troiekouroff and Chatel 1984, 3:44–47, pl XVI and XVII; Wessel 1965, 103–111.

182 See Ladner 1995, 103 for this example and the book in general for an historical, philosophical explanation of much of Christian symbolism.

183   Ferguson [1954] 1972, 154. The number eight represents the Resurrection, eight bosses that are frequently found surrounding an encircled cross on Merovingian sarcophagi and also surrounding the cross above the Tomb of Christ on the late sixth-century Palestinian ampulla at Bobbio (Sirat, Viellard-Troiekouroff and Chatel 1984, 3: 44–47; Grabar 1968, 124; fig. 295). Eight bosses are also seen on the west face of the bottom shaft of the South Cross at Clonmacnoise above a crucifixon scene. See Richardson (1984, 28–45) for a detailed discussion of eight and number symbolism in general. On the particular importance of the Gospels in Ireland and the British Isles, see McGurk 1961 and Henderson 1987, chapter one.

184   The headstone for burial no. 5 behind the church (Fig. 106) has only two bosses in the upper quadrants, with two geometric designs in the lower quadrants. The cross standing south of the church (Fig. 86a) also probably had two. The bosses (?) in the upper left quadrant of this cross were suggested by Macalister 1896, 207 as representing the sun and moon. See also Higgins (1987, i: 116–118) for a more detailed discussion of this motif. According to Ferguson, the sun and moon are associated with the Crucifixion or as attributes of the Virgin Mary; the number two more generally represents the two natures of Christ, human and divine. Ferguson [1954] 1972, 45, 154.

185   Lionard (1991, 128) found that for purposes of his typology, diamond and triangular expansions were a variational equivalent of the circular and semicircular expansions of the arm terminals. One of his examples, the 'ordo maelfinnia slab' dated to either 992 or 1056, has triangular-shaped terminals filled with triquetras, closely paralleling the High Island cross at the southeastern landing. Nevertheless, for purposes of clarity and simplicity we do not include the SE landing stone among our prime examples or the cross at Brian Boru's Well.

186   The validity of this statistical sampling was checked with Michael Mohr, Ph.D. candidate in the Department of Statistics at The University of California, Berkeley. Mohr also noted that Lionard was able to date other earlier (ninth-century) stones with different designs, the ringed cross, to known prominent people, thus helping to eliminate the possibility that the names related to the recumbent stones by accident, which enhances confidence in Lionard's typology. Occasionally there were two or more possibilities for a recumbent stone, such as no. 737 OR DO Gilluchrist, which could be the 1085 abbot of Clonmacnoise, the 1104 bishop of Clonmacnoise or the 1127 abbot of Clonmacnoise.

187   Deetz 1977, 67.

188   But see Swift 1995, 245–249 for arguments against the Lionard typology. Lionard's work needs modifying and correcting, probably following Ó'Floinn, but our radiocarbon dates show substantial agreement with his typology.

189   The painted ceiling of the crypt of Lucina in the Cemetery of Pricilla (Lowrie 1946, p. 14).

[190] Unpublished Ph.D thesis, Marshall, 1989 and a view shared by O'Floinn, personal communication November 29th, 1996. The place of the Berechtuine stone at Tullylease has yet to be precisely placed in this sequence. Lionard (1961,154,155 believed that the Tullylease cross was an anomaly among Irish crosses and not related to them. A more extensive study done by Henderson and Okasha (1992, 1–36) makes a strong case for considering the Tullylease stone within the context of insular cross carved stones, High Crosses and illuminated manuscripts.

[191] Lionard 1961, 131–136. At Clonmacnoise the use of plain expansional crosses, those with no internal decoration, dates between the late ninth to eleventh centuries.

[192] We are indebted to Dr Raghnall Ó'Floinn, Assistant Keeper of the National Museum of Ireland, for his help in this matter. Personal communication, 29 November, 1996 and Ó'Floinn 1994, 254.

[193] See Higgins' comments on this (1987, 1:97–98). Higgins, who did a valuable survey of Galway stones, is somewhat confusing in his description and drawing of his no. 67 (1987, 2:342; 2). We assume he is discussing the stone attached to the altar in the church.

[194] For these purposes we have left out expansional crosses with square or rectangular terminals such as the one at Templemurry, Kilmacduagh (see Higgins, 1987, 2: fig. 59) and the one at Durrow (Lionard's 592). Nearby Gallen Priory has two decorated expansional crosses (Kendrick 1939, 9), Fuerty (Roscommon) has one, Inishcealtra (Clare) has two, Durrow has one, Glendalough two. The High Island stones were unknown to Lionard.

[195] See Ó Floinn 1994, 251–259 for an article on the central position of Clonmacnoise in the early medieval period.

[196] Deetz, J. and E. Dethlefsen 1965, 196–206; Deetz 1977, 64–90; and Joseph W. Michaels 1973.

Chapter Nine

The Monastic Enclosure Wall

*A dry stone wall, of considerable strength and irregular height,
surrounds the whole group of buildings.
This is the cahir, or fortification, which was necessary,
no doubt, to preserve the old recluses from piratical attack…*

Wakeman, 1863.

In the surface remains of High Island there is no visible sign of large-scale or long-term occupation of High Island after the monastic period; the only post-monastic occupation is that evidenced by the short-term stay of the nineteenth-century copper miners. However, there is some reason for suspecting both secular ownership and secular occupation of the island before the foundation of the monastery. Certain structures among the remains generally assigned as monastic hint that the island was owned and occupied by a secular family before the foundation of the monastery. Among these structures, the monastic enclosure wall itself most clearly demonstrates elements suggesting its original construction for secular purposes during a pre-monastic period of uncertain date.

Evidence for early occupation of the Atlantic islands, while not abundant, exists. Food resources such as migratory birds, plentiful fish, and seals would have made the islands attractive to hunters and gatherers, at least, on a seasonal basis, perhaps as early

Figure 133

Aerial photo of the enclosure wall on High Island, Co. Galway, from the southwest. Photo Con Brogan. Courtesy Dúchas The Heritage Service.

as the mesolithic period. Neolithic peoples who brought domesticated, hence controlled, resources to supplement natural supplies, may have lived on a more permanent basis on Ireland's western islands, as they did on the Orkneys off the coast of Scotland. On the Aran Islands a number of wedge tombs indicates occupation of these islands possibly as early as 2000 BC (O'Connell 1994, 81). Additionally, an exciting new excavation within the innermost enclosure at Dún Aengus on Inishmore has revealed a Late Bronze Age settlement; hut sites and occupation debris date between 1300 BC and 800 BC (Cotter 1993, 1–11).

The introduction around AD 300 of new, more efficient agricultural tools, such as the mouldboard plough and watermills, resulted in significant agricultural expansion onto lands that had formerly been abandoned or unusable, and their use, particularly during this period of climatic improvement, clearly signals an expanding population as well.[197] By the early medieval period it is likely that all suitable land, including all of the islands lying close to the mainland, offering resources attractive to a pastoral economy, would be in use by or at least under the control of leading families. The repeated emphasis in early medieval hagiography on land donation prompts comments from historians that 'the obsession with donations and endowments [to monasteries] in all types of ecclesiastical literature suggests that monks and nuns were forced to seek land from those who already owned it' (Bitel 1986, 17; see also Bitel [1990] 1993, ch.1).

Kings and ruling families customarily gave property, cattle, land and raths to the Church, according to the lives of the saints, for reasons such as piety, or in exchange for miracles performed by the saint on their behalf, or because a family member joined the monastery. Accounts of endowment of land to the saints were promoted in monastic documents by lavish praise of the pious donor and equally fulsome threats to the grudging, uncharitable landowner. Indeed, saints, assisted by the Lord, didn't hesitate to apply severe sanctions to reluctant donors. In Muírchú's seventh-century *Vita S. Patricii*, King Dáire finally gave Patrick the land for his foundation at Armagh after Patrick had killed the king's horses and stricken him with an illness for refusing to give up his land. Muírchú, undisturbed by this saintly blackmail, enthusiastically encouraged such royal largesse by stating 'they went out together, holy Patrick and Dáire, to inspect the marvellous and pleasing gift that he had offered..'[198] On occasion, a king would make an even more munificent gift, such as the fort and its fields offered by the king who was overwhelmed by the Holy Spirit after hearing Saint Mochoemog:

> *I offer you, oh Servant of the Living Lord*
> *My fortress and all that is in it, and*
> *Its fields.*[199]

The most famous example of island donations is that of St Columba, who was probably given Iona by King Conall mac Comgaill of the Scottish Dál Riata.[200] The hagiographies also contain one miraculous reference to island donations, the gift of Sheep Island to St Declan by the king of the Deisi. Sheep Island, now known as Ardmore, has not been an island since St Declan, yielding to his monks' complaints about the terrible inconvenience of being on an island, drove the sea away by striking it a mighty blow with his crozier.[201] In the *Betha Mochuda*, the life of St Mochuda of Lismore, there are also references to island donations. St Mochuda is generally associated with eastern Ireland, the midlands, and County Waterford, but he also cured Cathal MacAodha, King of Munster, who was deaf, lame and blind, with his prayers. In gratitude:

> *... Cathal gave extensive lands to God and Mochuda for, scil: Oilean Cathail and Ros-Beg and Ros-Mor and Inis-Pic [Spike Island]... Mochuda himself commenced to build a church on Inis-Pic and he remained there a whole year... That island we have mentioned scil:-Inish-Pic, is a most holy place in which an exceedingly devout community constantly dwell.*[202]

The hypothesis that High Island was owned by a secular family before the monks came is a logical probability. But the extended proposition that the monastery's enclosure wall was not built by monks but by earlier secular occupants is bolder and less certain. Archaeologists have long suspected intuitively that the stone enclosures on a few island sites, such as Inishmurray, County Sligo, Nendrum, County Down and

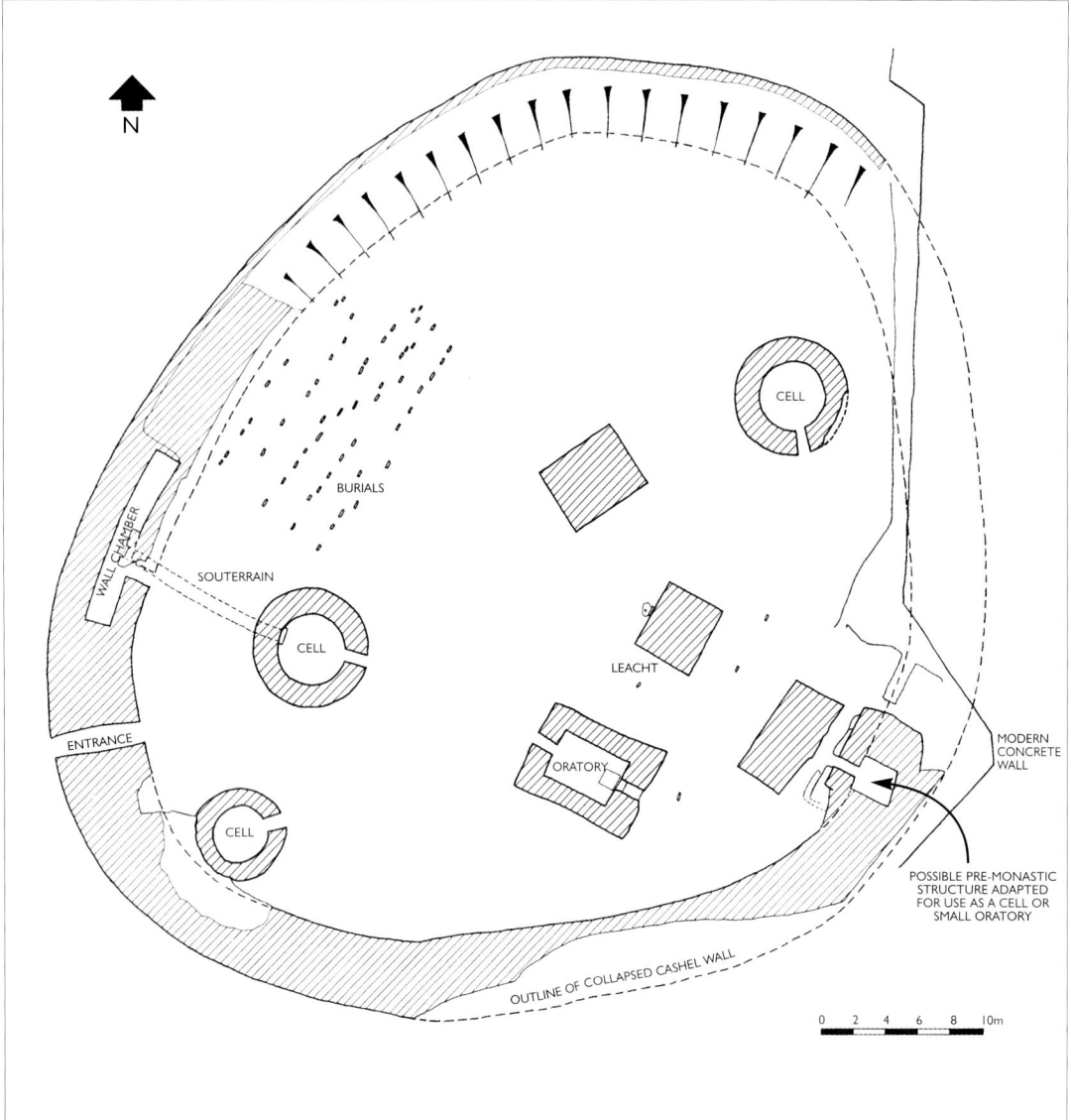

Figure 134
Plan of Illauntanning, Co. Kerry. The small chamber on the east side was later expanded, perhaps to use as a small oratory. Plan G.D. Rourke based on survey by Aighleann O'Shaughnessy and Richard Stapleton. Courtesy Dúchas The Heritage Service.

Illauntanning, County Kerry, were originally secular, gifts from local rulers similar to the more famous, well-documented example of King Muírchertach O'Brian's gift of Cashel, County Tipperary in AD 1101. Firm excavation evidence has been, and still is, lacking (Hamlin 1985, 283) for stone enclosures, although some recent excavation evidence shows that this was true for the vallum of the most famous Irish monastic island, Iona, in Argyll, Scotland. Finbar McCormick has revealed that the site of the monastery on Iona was occupied before the arrival of the monks and, more interesting still, that the rectangular shape of the monastic earthern enclosure bank on Iona, an uncommon shape for an Irish monastic enclosure, most likely results from monastic use of an already existing middle Iron Age western bank (McCormick 1993, 78–107; 1997, 49–51). In the absence of excavation evidence, the conjecture of pre-monastic

The Monastic Enclosure Wall

Figure 135

Aerial photo of Illauntanning, Co. Kerry, from the east. Photo W. Horn, 1980.

occupation of High Island is supported by arguments about the nature of ecclesiastical enclosure walls.

Much of the High Island enclosure wall is missing and what remains is now so badly collapsed that it has few discernible features left (Figs. 133 and 139). The construction of the wall places it among a small number of ecclesiastical and secular enclosures built entirely of stone; that is, it has stone facing externally and internally, with a core of stone rubble or stone mixed with earth. Besides its construction material, the two remaining features of the wall, its exceptional width and the presence within of wall chambers, distinguish it from more ordinary ecclesiastical stone enclosure walls.

Enclosure walls were more commonly built entirely of earthen banks or of earthen banks faced with stone. Stone ecclesiastical enclosures and stone secular sites, ringforts more generally called cashels, are almost exclusively found on Ireland's western coast, probably because of the greater availability of stone building material there.[203] Leo Swan, who made a study of ecclesiastical enclosures, noted that the stone enclosure walls of the early medieval period are massive in width, height and size of stone used at the base, as compared to the more flimsy stone walls of modern times.[204] Secular cashel walls of this period fit this general description as well; walling, both

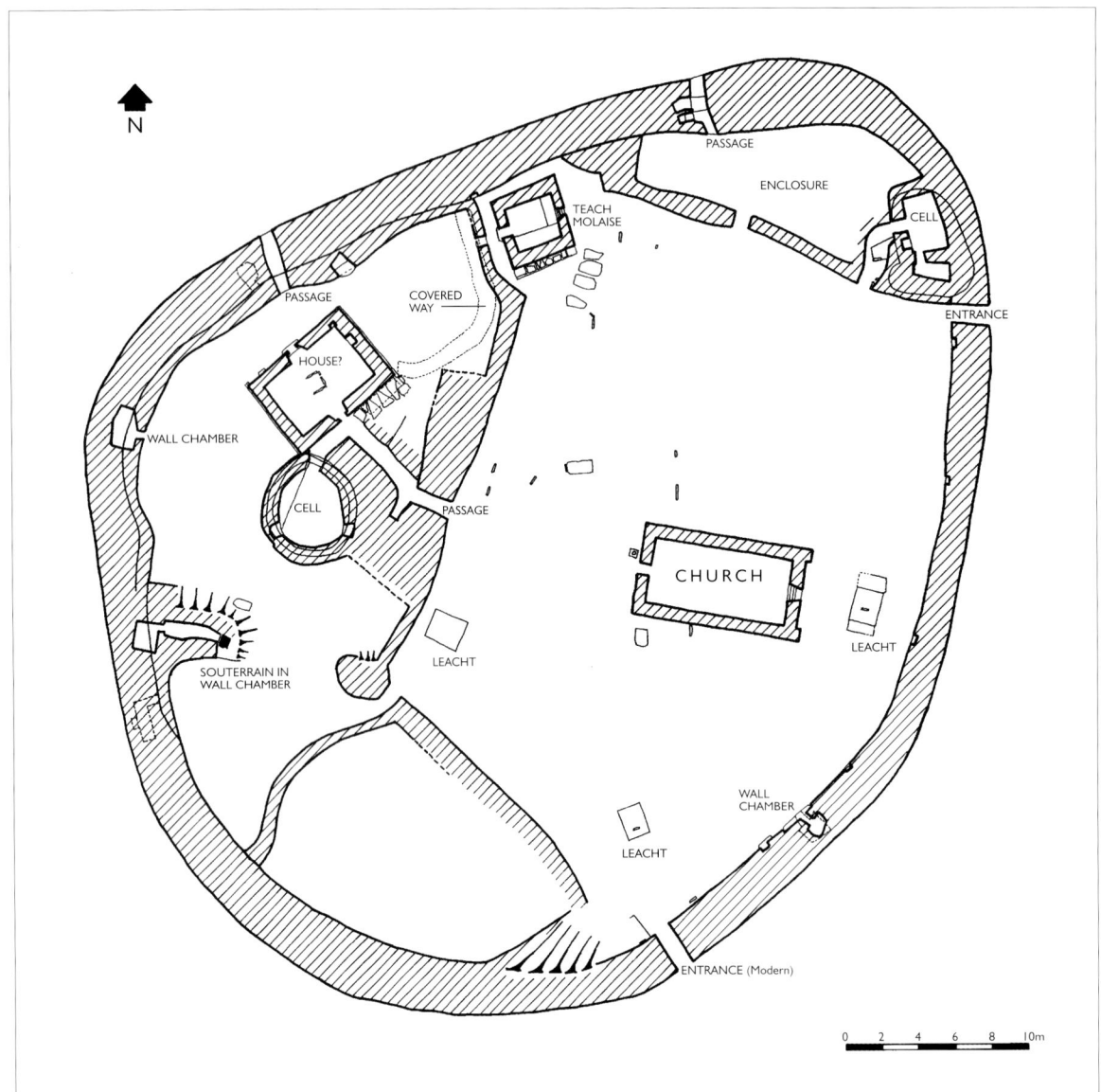

Figure 136

Plan of Inishmurray, Co. Sligo, showing the wall chambers and low entries in the wall. Plan G.D. Rourke based on the survey by J. O'Brien. Dúchas The Heritage Service.

stone and earthen, ecclesiastical and secular, was apparently built on a more substantial scale in the early medieval period than today. Archaeological surveys made in the last fifteen years have provided a broader range of quantitative evidence which now allows comparative studies of stone secular and ecclesiastical walls. High Island may now be compared to other ecclesiastical and secular sites in West Galway (Gosling 1993), and then further compared to Illauntanning, Co. Kerry, in the context of the far more abundant information in the Dingle Peninsula Survey (Cuppage 1986) and the Iveragh Survey (O'Sullivan and Sheehan 1996).[205] However, Illauntanning is of particular interest to our analysis because there is an additional structural reason, besides its unusual wall width (4.5–5.5m) and wall chambers (Figs. 134 and 135), for stating that it was initially a secular construction. There is one large oratory on Illauntanning and

Figure 137

Aerial photo of the monastery on Inishmurray, Co. Sligo, from the north. Photo Con Brogan. Courtesy Dúchas The Heritage Service.

a small wall chamber which was later remodelled and expanded. Because this rectangular structure was naturally oriented, it may have been expedient for the monks to use it as an oratory while building the larger one. Inishmurray, Co. Sligo (Figs. 136 and 137) also offers additional structural reasons, such as its unusual low entrances, which strongly suggest it was an earlier secular structure. However, the comparative survey data are currently lacking for this area. For this reason alone we have not included Inishmurray in the analysis.

The wall dimensions presented by each survey team, with a few exceptions, were accepted, although ecclesiastical sites recording unusual wall thickness of over 2.5m were verified. Invariably, minor recording errors had been made, such as the typographical error in the transcription of the archaeologist's field notes for Roscam, where the wall width was reported as 4.5m when the archaeologist had reported the entry to the monastery as being 4.5m wide. At Roscam the walls average slightly over 2m in width. All sites where field workers found only bands of stone collapse were eliminated in favour of sites where they, or nineteenth-century scholars, had measured wall width as determined by the presence of a section of wall that had intact internal and external wall faces. All wall widths naturally vary in these large enclosures, and only the maximum dimension was used.

When the resulting data indicated that a broad distinction could be made between secular and ecclesiastical walls, we then submitted the width data for statistical grouping to Professor David Hankin, analytical statistician at Humbolt State University in California. Professor Hankin compared the distributions of wall width measurements at known ecclesiastical sites (n=19 sites) with those at known secular sites (n=80 sites).

Hankin first calculated simple summaries of the quartile ranges of wall width measurements, each of which contains 25 per cent of the representations, for the two sets of known sites, excluding Illauntanning and High Island. He found that 50 per cent of the measured wall widths at known secular sites exceeded 2.65m, and 25 per cent of these secular wall widths exceeded 3.3m. In contrast, 50 per cent of the measured wall widths at known ecclesiastical sites were less than 2.2m, and none exceeded 2.5m (shown in simple graph form in Fig. 138). Thus wall widths at secular sites are, on average, substantially greater than those at ecclesiastical sites, and no wall widths at known secular sites in these two areas have exceeded 2.5m.

Because the wall widths measured at Illauntanning ranged from 4.5 to 5.5m, large even for a secular site, there seems little doubt that this site was originally a secular site. At High Island, original wall widths ranged from 2.5 to 3.2m and, in keeping with our wall width data summaries, we would report wall width as 5.5m for Illauntanning. On the basis of wall width alone, much greater statistical probability can, therefore, be placed on assigning the High Island site to the secular group although such an assignment would not be unequivocal.

Both Illauntanning and High Island possess, moreover, substantial wall chambers (Figs. 134 and 139), and the data for wall chambers provide additional striking evidence supporting their secular origin. None of the nineteen ecclesiastical sites, excluding Illauntanning and High Island, have wall chambers. Indeed, fewer than 10 per cent of the eighty-two known secular sites used for this study have wall chambers, and 75 per cent of those are found in sites where wall widths are 3.3m or more. Together, wall width and wall chamber data provide compelling evidence that Illauntanning was a secular site and very strong evidence that High Island was also a secular site.[206]

There are, therefore, convincing logical reasons to believe that Illauntanning and High Island were earlier secular sites resembling Steigue Fort, Cahergal and Leacanabuaile on the Iveragh Peninsula or Dún Fearbhaí on Inish Mór in the Aran Islands. It is also possible that High Island and Illauntanning were not cashels but belong to a group of sites being studied under the Western Stone Fort Project, one of

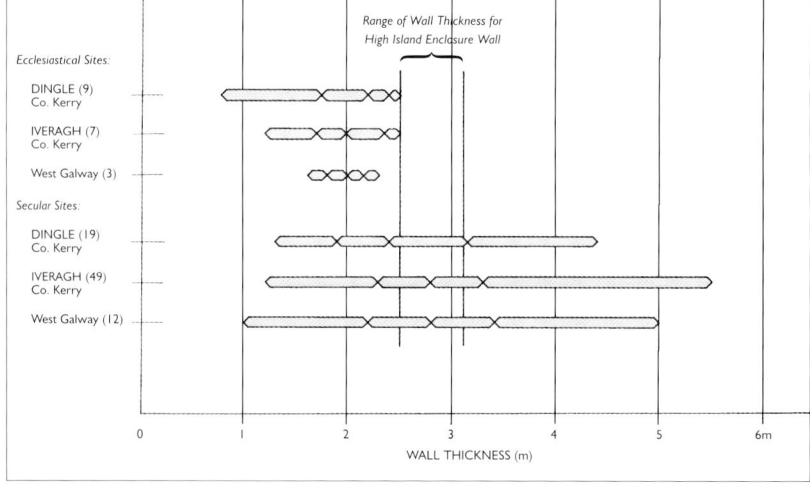

Figure 138

Graph showing the ranges of wall widths in secular and ecclesiastical sites on the Iveragh and Dingle peninsulas, Co. Kerry, and in western Co. Galway. Graph by G.D. Rourke, based on D. Hankin's analysis.

The Monastic Enclosure Wall

several major projects set up in 1991 under the Discovery Programme to investigate aspects of the Later Bronze Age and Iron Age. In 1992 when the project director, Claire Cotter, in the absence of studies and chronological information about these sites, drew up a working definition, she noted that: 'The main focus of the project is a group of large stone forts, which are distinguished from the majority of cashels, promontory forts etc. by the massiveness of their enclosing wall or walls and by a number of other architectural characteristics' (Cotter 1992, 2). Among the other characteristics of these forts, although few have all of them, Cotter listed interior terracing, mural steps, intramural chambers and *chevaux de frise*, angular sharp stones set upright in the ground to deter approaching enemies.

The groupings of data presented here do not explain the purpose and chronological placement of massive stone enclosure walls and wall chambers, or their location on islands as small as Illauntanning and High Island. Nor is it clear that they both served the same purpose in the same period. Even with excavation, however, a secular origin

Figure 139

Conjectural reconstruction of the enclosure wall at High Island, Co. Galway. The large wall chamber on the western side is an original feature of the enclosure wall; the small wall chamber north of it may be an original feature but Cell A is not original. Cell A could only have been built after the enclosure wall had been taken down. Reconstruction by G.D. Rourke.

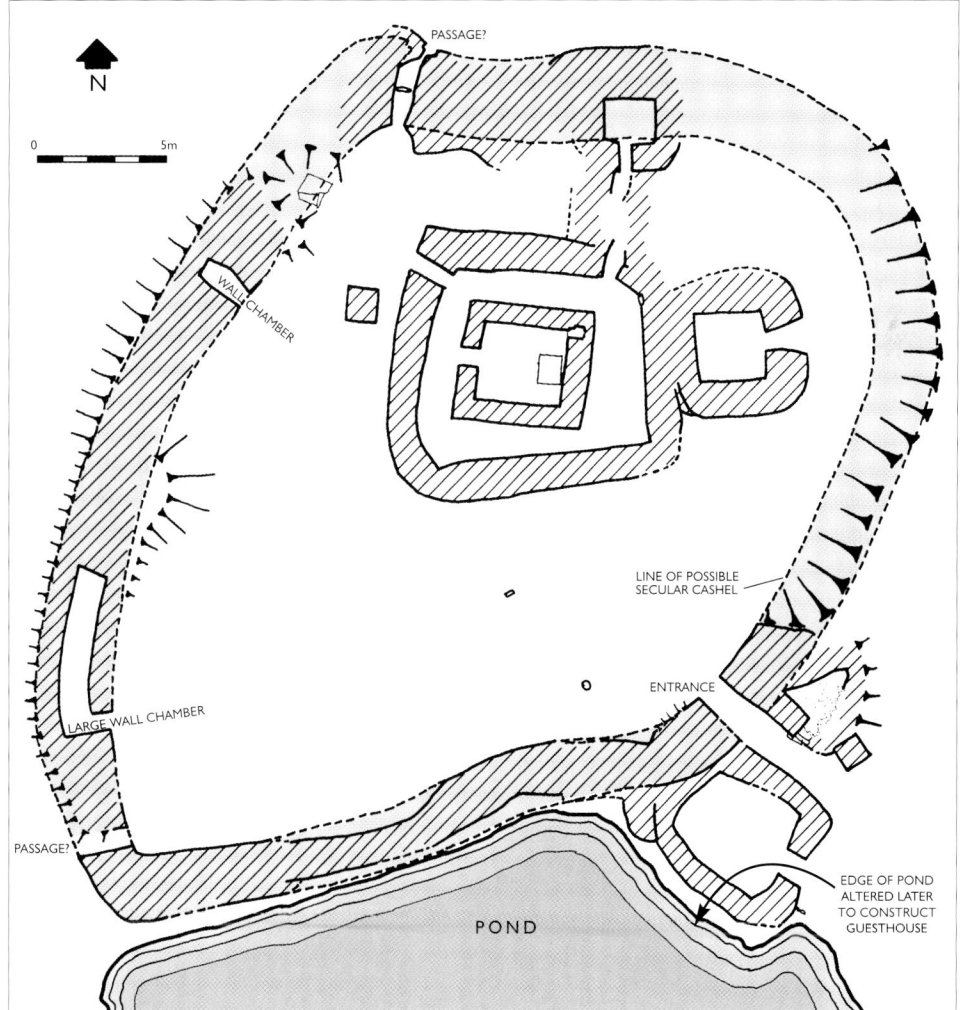

may be difficult to establish in most cases because of the problems in dating and relating enclosure walls to other structures and material remains. The results of the study show a high mathematical probability that these two were secular in origin (Fig. 139).

However, the data does argue persuasively for a new perspective on island monasticism, one that views it as part of Irish mainland monasticism and medieval culture. The romantic image of island monasticism has been that of ascetic monks setting forth for the islands on a heroic quest with a quixotic indifference to where they were going. Indeed, some evidence exists that this ideal existed and occasionally resulted in extreme behaviour, as in that recorded in 891 by *The Anglo-Saxon Chronicle*: 'And three Irishmen came to King Alfred in a boat without any oars from Ireland, whence they had stolen away, because they would be in a state of pilgrimage for the love of God, they recked not where' *(The Anglo-Saxon Chronicle*, ed. Garmonsway 1984, 82). It is also true that many Irish monks were seafaring adventurers. Early medieval voyage tales, the *Immrama*, which relate the adventures of wandering monks like St Brendan, contain some real elements of seafaring situations. The early ninth-century *De Mesura Orbis Terrae*, written by Dicuil, an Irish monk employed at the Carolingian court, demonstrated that Irish monks were in the Hebrides, the Shetlands, and even as far as Iceland, by the eighth century (Dicuil, ed. Letronne 1814). The island monks unquestionably demonstrated that spiritually they were the men 'to whom for Christ's sake the world is crucified and they to the world' (*Sancti Columbani Opera*, ed. Walker 1937, 127).

Few archaeologists today, however, would agree with Rev. Power that 'The more inaccessible or forbidding the island the more it was in request as a penitential retreat' (Power 1914, xiii).[207] Monks seeking to found permanent communities would be attracted to islands that were readily accessible from the mainland with known living conditions. They almost certainly carefully planned their settlements with the assistance of the mainland rulers or monasteries that owned the islands and who continued to retain an interest in these sites. Support of an ascetic island foundation offered advantages to everyone, including increased honour and status for a mainland clan or monastery through their support of the ideal monastic life. Mainland support increased the survival chances of the island monastery, particularly during periods of environmental crises, as well as offering access to necessary and desirable supplies from the mainland not available on small islands. Not surprisingly, the archaeological remains on islands tend to buttress this position, because most remains of monasteries exist on islands close to the mainland. The siting of the monastic structures indicates sensible, well-planned strategies in terms of protection from the elements and access to fresh water, landing locations, etc.

Practical necessity mandated that a small ascetic colony of monks maintain close connection with the mainland, even if they were completely self-sufficient in food and clothing. Early medieval monks needed many everyday and liturgical objects that could not be produced on the islands. Iron and wooden farm implements, knives, butter churns, bowls, as well as chalices and patens, bells and croziers, simple brass or iron brooches for fastening clothing, would all need to be imported. Bibles and Gospel books, moreover, were also required for study and worship, but few small islands could have supported scriptoria. Even the boats, called *currachs*, were made of materials, wood and cured cow hides, largely unavailable on islands and most likely produced by specialist craftsmen on the mainland. Early medieval monks were well aware of these troublesome supply problems, as displayed in the engaging story of St Declan's unhappy monks who begged the saint to make the sea recede from around Declan's new island monastery, Aiat-mBreasail, because: 'Many things are required (scil. from the mainland) and we must often go by boat to this island and there will be crossing more frequently when you have gone to heaven.'[208]

In most respects island monasticism was not a cultural anomaly, estranged from the main current of cultural affairs, but a natural and logical extension of mainland monasticism, well integrated with the large mainland monastic confederations and cultural patterns.[209] Indeed, it is probable, due to geographic proximity and the hagiographic references to St Féchín, that High Island was linked with Omey Island in a monastic confederation owing allegiance to St Féchín, and that a secular family, perhaps a member of the Conamaicne Mara ('the hound-sons of the sea'), the ruling family of the area at this time, donated the island for this use (Byrne [1973] 1987, 68).

Notes

[197] Mitchell and Ryan [1986] 1997, ch. 6. The increased emphasis on fencing, building ringforts, etc. indicates a strong drive for land control and need to mark ownership. See, among others, Ó'Corráin 1983; Mytum 1992.

[198] *Patrician Texts in the Book of Armagh*, ed. Bieler 1979, 110–111. 'Et exierunt ambo sanctus patricius et Daire ut considerarent mirabile oblationis et benepplacitum munus...'

[199] 'Seve Dei Viui, ecce offero tibi arcem meam regalem cum onmibus que in ea sunt, et aris suis.' *Vitae Sanctorum Hiberniae*, ed. Plummer [1910] 1968, 2:170. See the introduction for several other examples. See Bitel ([1990] 1993, ch. 1) for a discussion about monastic settlement. For similar continental examples, see the monastery of Columbanus at Annegray (Walker 1957, xxiiii). Sulpicius Severus mentions monks in a fort at Amboise (Hoare 1954, ch. 8).

[200] Contrary to the Venerable Bede's assertion that Iona was given to Columba by the Picts, Bede *HE*, ed. Sherley-Price, Book 3, chapters 3 and Book 4. But see Herbert 1988, 28–29.

[201] *Life of St Declan of Ardmore*, ed. and trans. Power 1914, 27–31.

[202] Power 1914, 108–109.

[203] As compared to the eastern regions of Ireland, where Moore (1987) noted there are only three stone ringforts in Co. Meath, and Buckley and Sweetman (1991) recorded none in Co. Louth. O'Sullivan and Sheehan (1995) found that 38 per cent of the ringforts on the Iveragh Peninsula in Co. Kerry were stone, and Lacy (1983) counted 210 cashels among the 444 ringforts extant in Co. Donegal.

[204] Swan 1983, 270. See also O'Ríordáin, 1979, 30 and Swan 1971; 1983, 269–280. While we agree generally with Swan about the nature of ecclesiastical walls, not all early medieval ecclesiastical walls were constructed with massive stones. Among four ecclesiastical sites whose walls have been excavated, two of them, Church Island and Illaunloughan, Co. Kerry, do not use large stones.

[205] John Sheehan kindly sent us the information on ecclesiastical sites and ringforts in advance of publication. We did not include other ecclesiastical sites such as Nendrum, Co. Down because of its distance from this region.

[206] All figures and much of the statistical language taken from the report of Professor Hankin, prepared for Marshall, December 1998.

[207] Archaeologists have begun to research this, beginning with Hurley's (1982) study of spatial distribution of mainland and island sites.

[208] *Life of St Declan of Ardmore*, ed. Power 1914, 29.

[209] For explicit references to the familial nature of the Irish Church and its strong ties with local families, see *The Patrician Texts in the Book of Armagh*, ed. Bieler 1979, 172–173. For a general discussion, see Hughes 1980; O'Corráin 1973, 1984; and Herbert, 1988.

Chapter Ten

The Early Medieval Monastic Watermill

by Colin Rynne

Once upon a time, because of the great labour of the monks in grinding their rations with a quern, Féchín proceeded to build a watermill.

Stokes 1890, 345, *Life of S. Féchín of Fore.*

The long association of the nearby cove and the watermill is clearly reflected in the Irish placename *Cuan a' Mhuilin*, but we may perhaps attach a deeper significance to O'Flaherty's identification of the mill. Mills of this type were very common throughout western Connaught in the seventeenth and eighteenth centuries (Rynne 1988, I, 238), and there can be little doubt that O'Flaherty would have instantly recognised the relationship between the pond, mill channels and building without having to call upon folk memory. Indeed, as late as the first half of the nineteenth century, similar mills were still used in Mayo, Roscommon (Deering 1857; Knox 1907) and parts of Connemara (Lucas 1953). Contemporary antiquaries, such as George Petrie, were fully aware of these survivals. The previous accounts of the island only make passing reference to the existence of the watermill. Indeed, in the most recent account (Herity 1990), the mill is described without reference to its likely mode of operation or of its significance in terms of other sites of the period. Apart from being the earliest surviving example of an Irish monastic mill, its very existence on the island calls into question the use of the term 'hermitage' in relation to the religious community on the island.

The Mill and its Water Supply

The water supply for the mill appears to have comprised three main elements. Firstly, a feeder pond established on the hillside to the east of the main millpond, impounded (or dammed) behind a gravity dam of earth and stone; secondly, a feeder stream that led from this to the main pond; and finally the millpond itself (Figs. 140 and 142). The island appears to have been too small to have sustained a free-flowing stream, although the basin-like areas to the south of the monastery clearly served as a natural collection point for water running off the high ground to the east of the millpond. There can be little doubt that the mill would not have been built if its water supply was considered in any way unreliable. Indeed, on present evidence early medieval Irish mill sites appear to have always been supplied by fast-flowing streams, often in upland areas, but almost invariably reliable over an entire year.

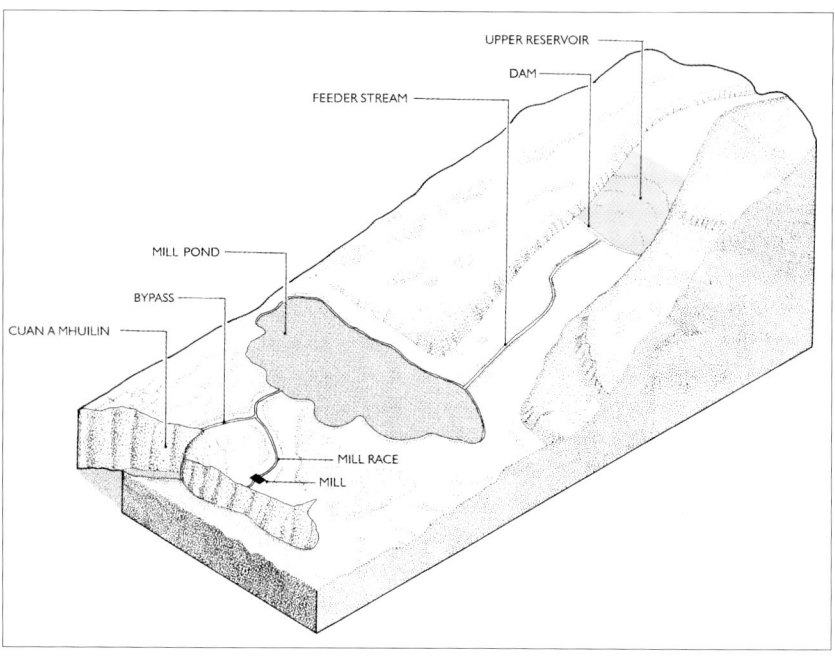

Figure 140

A schematic, three-dimensional view of the mill system in the terrain on High Island, Co. Galway. Drawing by C. Rynne.

The reasons for this are obvious enough. Firstly, the mill would be a substantial investment and should not remain idle, if possible, even during the summer months; although even the most reliable watercourse could potentially fail during hot summers. This possibility would have been foremost in the mind of the High Island millwright, where the purpose of the mill was to enable the island's population to be self-sufficient in terms of its milling needs. The second reason for ensuring the maximum operational period for the mill would have been the need to provide regular supplies of fresh flour and meal all year round. As will be seen below, the manufacture of flour using millstones greatly reduces its keeping qualities, and what is frequently overlooked is that while grain could often be stored for long periods, stone-ground flour could not. Therefore, households were obliged to produce fresh flour and meal on a very regular basis. On an island that would have been very often inaccessible during the winter months, complete self-sufficiency with regard to milling operations would therefore have been extremely important. To make the construction of a mill on a relatively small island with limited water resources a worthwhile investment, therefore, the most careful effort, along with great skill, had to be exercised by the millwright.

Figure 141

Typical sluice gate at Mashanaglass, Co. Cork, similar in principle to the one that must have been at High Island. Drawing by C. Rynne.

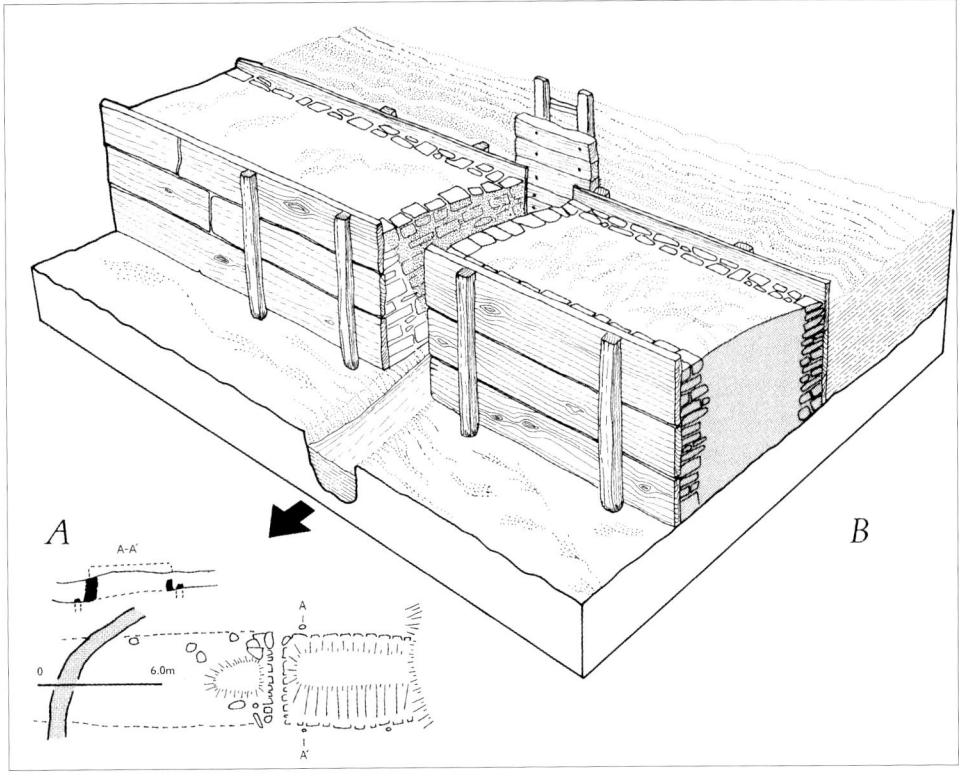

In the early medieval period millponds were generally formed by constructing a barrage across a suitable stream in such a way as to hold the inflowing water behind the dam. A sluice gate was generally positioned within the dam wall to regulate the intake of water into the mill's headrace or feeder channel, the flow of which would have been further regulated immediately in front of the penstock or feeder chute, which directed a jet of water onto the vanes of the waterwheel. The steep fall from the adjacent hillside, however, presented considerable difficulty for the millwright. To all intents and purposes, the unregulated flow of water down the side of the hill would not have allowed any measure of control over the filling of the millpond. Furthermore, during periods of heavy rainfall, excess water would have entered the millpond at several points, eventually undermining the sides of the pond and allowing the pathway leading to the monastery to become flooded. An examination of the pond's water supply, however, established that certain measures were taken to control the water intake into the millpond.

Two features set on a break on the hillside slope to the east of the millpond, set at right angles to the flow of the stream, appear to be the arms of a gravity dam. The arms of this dam, in contrast to the field walls found elsewhere on the island, are made of upright slabs, which revetted looser material (probably tamped earth clay and stones) and may have originally been faced on the east-facing side with planking or wickerwork (see Fig. 141).

HIGH ISLAND

Figure 142a

Figure 142b

Figure 142
A 1m-interval contour plan with side section of the horizontal mill landscape on High Island, Co. Galway. Drawings by G.D. Rourke.

The Early Medieval Monastic Watermill

In gravity dams the water is dammed by their mass, the weight of the filling material withstanding the pressure of the contained water. The dam marks a definite break in slope between a basin-like area to the east of the dam elements and the feeder channel for the main millpond at the bottom of the hillside (see contour plan of the area of the mill system, Fig. 142a). This basin-like area is defined by a sharp, upward change in slope to the north, the dam elements to the west and a natural rockface or bluff-line to the south. Surface examination of this basin indicated that the sloping sides at the base of the rockface to the south and the northern edge of the basin were caused by the deposition of silt: a common feature of primitive gravity dams after they fall into disuse. The northern and southern elements of the dam were actually divided by a narrow gap near the centre of the basin. The opposing extremities of each arm of the dam were splayed outwards in the direction of a feeder channel immediately to the west of the dam. This latter splay and the gap between the elements of the dam would appear to have accommodated a control gate, which would have regulated the flow of water from the pond into the feeder channel servicing the lower millpond. There are

Figure 143

Photo of the mill area on High Island, Co. Galway, from the west, showing the area of the uphill reservoir and its relationship to the millpond below. In the area of the reservoir the photo has picked up what appears to be ridges and furrows from the raising of cereal grains. Photo Con Brogan, 1996. Courtesy Dúchas The Heritage Service.

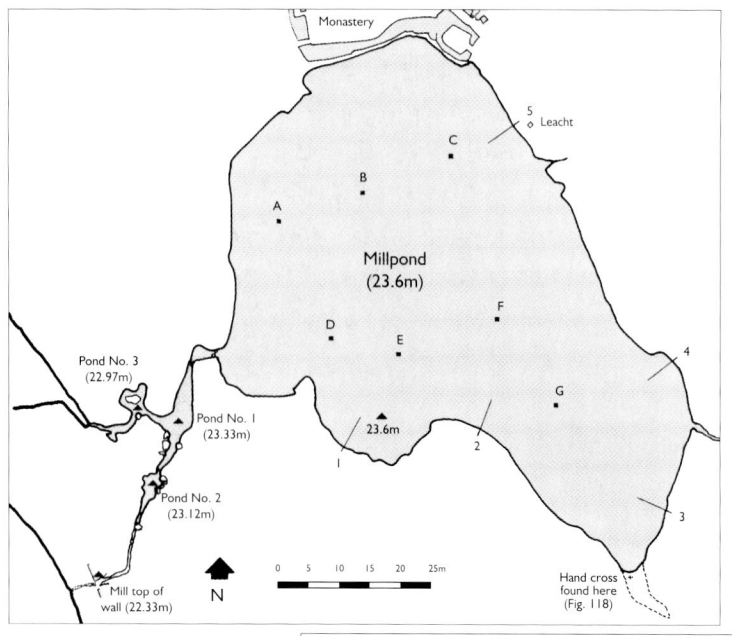

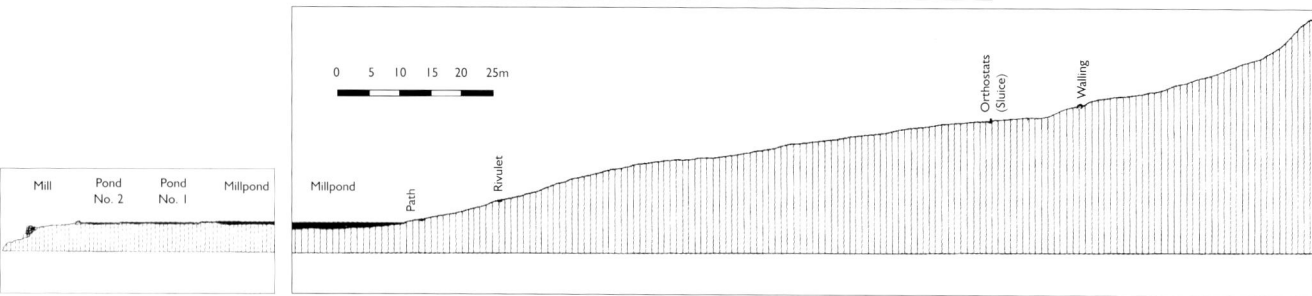

Figure 144a

The plan showing present depths in the millpond and the fall in level from the millpond to the mill building on High Island, Co. Galway. Plan G.D. Rourke.

Profiles at edge of millpond showing limit of stone base

Table showing depths (m) of water and peat in millpond

Point	Depth of water	Depth of peat beneath water
A	0.84	1.15
B	0.90	0.75
C	0.90	0.70
D	0.92	1.10
E	0.90	0.40
F	0.95	1.10
G	0.94	1.05

also clear indications of small-scale quarrying on the exposed rock outcrops immediately to the east of this reservoir, which would have been associated with its construction.

The remains of the outfall channel from this upper millpond can be traced on the hillside immediately below the dam (Fig. 143). The upper pond would have allowed a large measure of control over the filling of the lower millpond, particularly during crucial periods when the mill would have been in regular use. However, the water allowed to exit from the upper pond still had to be carefully marshalled down a steep slope, in such a way as not to erode the hillside or pose a danger to the integrity of the millpond immediately below it. The channel appears to follow the gentlest fall on its traverse to the lower millpond, and the likelihood is that it was excavated into bedrock when necessary. Its lower portion appears to have been embanked so that the flow of water could be contained within the channel at this crucial juncture. This measure appears to have been necessary to prevent the water-flow from fanning out; the loose stones near the juncture of this channel with the lower millpond seem likely to have formed part of a low revetment wall for the channel.

Figure 144b

Sections showing the drop from the hillside reservoir to the millpond, and from there to the mill on High Island, Co. Galway. Plan G.D. Rourke.

Aerial photographs of this channel indicate that it may have been also used to irrigate the terrace immediately below the dam (Fig. 143). Crop marks of three parallel channels are in evidence on the terrace and it may well be that this relatively flat area was cultivated in the early medieval period. This general area is free of large stones, and would have provided a small degree of shelter. Water from the settling pond may have been used to irrigate this area, where it seems likely that the monks would have cultivated some crops. It is possible, therefore, that the upper pond served two purposes: to regulate the flow to the main millpond and to irrigate a small area of cultivable land.

The Millpond

Roderic O'Flaherty's *Chorographical Description* of 1684 describes the larger of the two High Island ponds as 'a standing water [i.e. the pond], on the brook whereof was a mill'. Petrie believed that the lake was man-made, although later accounts by Healy (1890) and Herity (1990) suggest that it was not. Both hypotheses are half true. This is clearly a natural lake, but one that has been modified and probably extended to serve as a storage reservoir for the operation of a watermill. An ancient field boundary on the eastern side of the lake appears to have been deliberately submerged at its western extremity by the millpond (see Fig. 142a). Closer examination also revealed that most sides of the pond were originally revetted with large stones, the collapse of which was caused by erosion subsequent to the pond falling into disuse. These stones are clearly visible around the edges of the lake (see Fig. 142a). There are no indications of serious flood damage to the pond and it seems likely that the overflow or bypass channel to the west of the pond would have easily facilitated excess run-off during periods of heavy rainfall.

The original eastern edge of the pond is delineated by the stone slab footpath, which was clearly built to respect the edge of the millpool. Unfortunately, the intake point into the headrace channel for the mill is badly disturbed by later (but apparently early medieval) quarrying activity; but it seems likely that an intake control sluice would have originally been positioned at the juncture of the outfall channel from the millpond into the headrace/bypass channel complex for the mill (see Figs. 144a and 144b for data on the present relative water levels and depth of the millpond, which would have been greater originally).

The Headrace and Bypass Channel

The headrace and bypass channels were cut into the exposed bedrock but have been badly disturbed by later quarrying activity. Each channel has been filled at many points with quarrying debris, and the subsequent formation of pools along their length is clearly a residual feature of the later infilling, rather than being for any milling purpose.

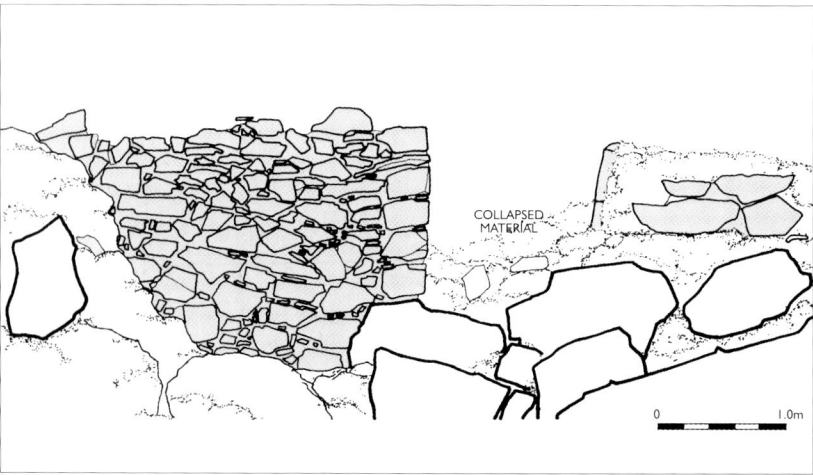

(a) (b)

The topography of the site appears to have completely governed the layout of these channels. The bypass channel's relatively abrupt exit over the adjacent cliff face (see Fig. 144a) would have admirably suited the millwright's purpose, particularly during wet spells, although there would have been little leeway for the construction of the headrace, owing to the proximity of the millpond to the cove and, of course, the millhouse perched upon its edge. In consequence, the fall from the inlet from the millpond to the undercroft or lower portion of the millhouse housing the waterwheel was quite sharp (Fig. 144). Other examples of early medieval Irish horizontal-wheeled mills maximise the fall from the millpond to the mill itself, wherever possible. This latter purpose, however, might normally be effected over a longer distance to minimise erosion of the sides of the mill channel. In the case of the High Island mill, however, the effects of erosion would have been negligible, as the channels had been excavated into exposed bedrock. Silting would have been a problem, but not a serious one given the relatively short length of the headrace, which not would have required much effort to clean out when required.

Figure 145

Plan and elevation of the mill building on High Island, Co. Galway. Drawings by G.D. Rourke.

The Mill Building and the Mill Mechanism

The remains of the mill building would suggest that this was originally a rubblestone, rectilinear structure, approximately 6.50m (N-S) x 3m (E-W), with an off-centre opening (c.1.60m wide at the west) along its short axis to accommodate the waterwheel assembly (Fig. 145). The short tailrace channel (Figs. 142a and 144a), which discharged the outfall into the deep cove (*Cuan a' Mhuilin*) over a vertical cliff face, was excavated into the bedrock.

At the vast majority of the other known horizontal-wheeled mill sites of the period in Ireland, the superstructure of the building is likely to have been of either slotted planks or wattle. But at High Island the mill building was probably built entirely

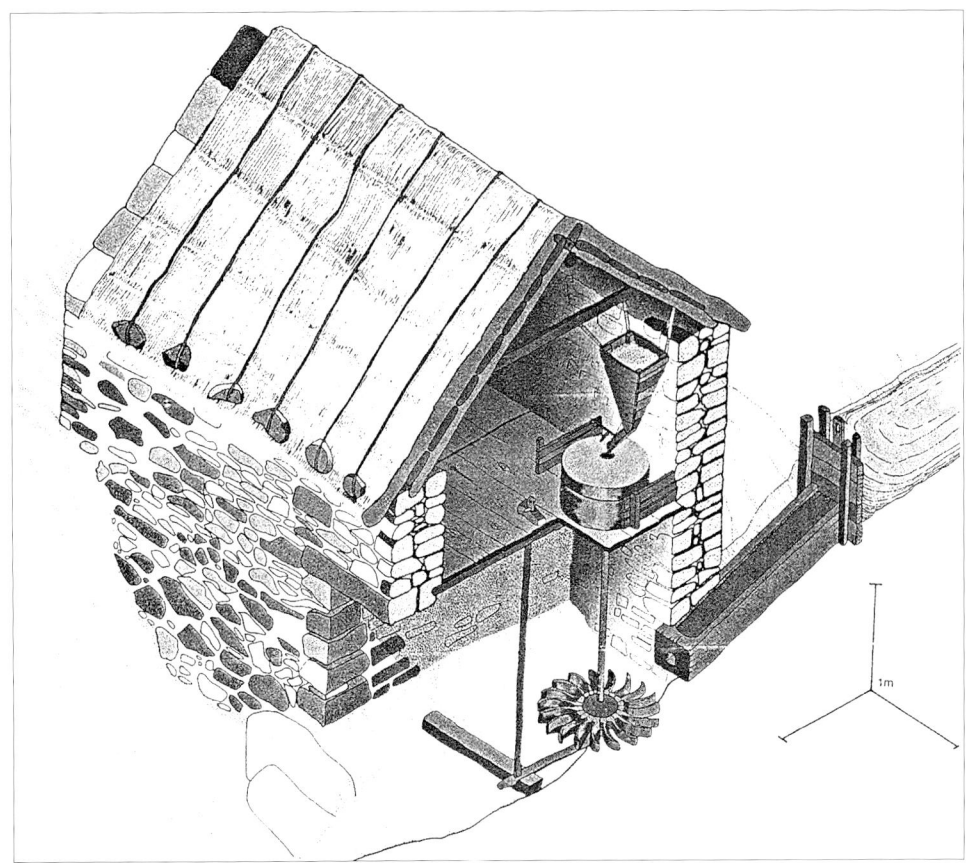

Fig 146

Conjectural reconstruction of the mill building on High Island, Co. Galway. Drawing by C. Rynne.

of rubblestone, with gables at its northern and southern ends, the structural use of timber being restricted to roofing components, flooring and to the mill's machinery. Again, at other contemporary sites large structural timbers were used both for the foundations and the superstructure of the millhouse. However, the monks at Iona in the seventh century took it upon themselves to tow large trees from the mainland using skiffs and currachs for constructing buildings (Hughes and Hamlin 1977, 45). Yet while the abundance of building stone on the High Island may have generally made this unnecessary for important buildings, the mill flume would have required a sizeable balk of timber from a mature tree (see Fig. 146).

At the eastern end of the mill, a wooden flume or penstock would have directed incoming water onto the vanes of the millwheel. This was in essence a wooden channel, the internal area of which was hollowed and splayed inwards from its rear end towards the perforated hole at its fore end (Fig. 146). Water pressure would have been built up in the headrace channel immediately in front of the penstock, the difference in height between the level of the impounded water and the tailrace channel forming an effective or operational head (Rynne 1992a, 57–59).

The entire waterwheel assembly would have been housed in the undercroft of the mill, and would have consisted of a horizontal waterwheel with nineteen dished paddles set into a central hub which, with the axle or driveshaft, would have been made out of a single balk of oak. The drive to the upper millstone was direct (no gearing would have been involved), with every revolution of the waterwheel producing a corresponding revolution of the upper millstone. As milling was normally a two-stage process, which required that the millstones be finely adjusted, the mill would have been equipped with a simple lever mechanism. An upward movement of the vertical arm of this lever caused a corresponding movement of the entire waterwheel assembly and, as the driveshaft was directly connected to the upper millstone, it was possible to lift or lower the latter as required. Grain feed to the millstones, via a hopper, is likely to have been automatic (Rynne 1990, 24–26). The millstones would probably have been about 1m in diameter and have been fashioned out of sandstone (see Fig. 146)

The Water Supply of Early Irish Watermills

The remains of an early monastic watermill and its millponds and feeder channels on High Island provide a truly unique insight into the arrangement of the water supply of early Irish horizontal-wheeled mills and also those of similar mills in the northern islands of Britain. The available data on the type of milldams and millponds used to supply early Irish watermills is quite meagre, compared with what is currently known about the actual mill buildings and plant. This is generally the result of the circumstances in which these mills normally come to light. Earlier field clearance activities have usually obliterated any surface features of dams or millponds. The first indications of the existence of an early watermill in the vicinity, therefore, frequently appear when drainage and dredging operations disturb structural parts of a mill building. The vast majority of early mill sites in Ireland, therefore, have been chance finds related to the mill building and plant. The High Island remains are thus a valuable addition to our knowledge of milldams and millponds, not only in Ireland but also for future discoveries elsewhere.

Milldams, Millponds and Millraces in the Early Medieval Period

Thus far the only excavated example of a milldam associated with an Irish horizontal-wheeled mill was investigated at Mashanaglass, County Cork, which, although originally thought to be of seventeenth-century date, is clearly an early medieval structure (Rynne 1990, 25). The Mashanaglass milldam consisted of two earthen banks, which survived to a maximum height of 3 feet 9 inches (1.14m), each revetted with stone and divided by a narrow central channel (Fig. 141). One arm of the dam extended across an adjacent stream. The flow of the stream was interrupted and incoming water was encouraged to settle in a basin-like area immediately behind artificial embankments. The remains of three substantial stakes were examined *in situ* outside the revetment walls on both the eastern and western faces of the dam's southern arm (Fahy 1956, 15–16). A sluice gate controlling the admission of water into the mill's headrace channel is likely to have been positioned within the central channel dividing the arms of the dam. Dams of tamped clay have been noted in association with other Irish horizontal-wheeled mill sites at Milverton, County Dublin (O'Donovan 1858–9, 252) and at an early ninth-century site at Crushyriree, County Cork.

In a late sixth-early seventh-century law tract on *distraint* (the seizure of chattels to make a person pay rent etc. or meet an obligation, or to obtain satisfaction by their sale), *De Ceithri Slichtaib Athgabála*, the term *topur* is used for the natural source of the mill's water supply and forms the first part of the 'eight parts of the mill'. Now the proper meaning of *topur* is 'well', but the original explains that a well or spring need not be the only source of water impounded for the use of a mill (MacEoin 1982, 15). Where more recent interpretations of these terms are concerned there is a certain degree of confusion as to the means by which water comes to rest in the *tir linde* or 'the land of the pond'. If one considers that a dam would provide an artificial boundary for the area in which the water is collected, there should be no need for confusion, the 'land of the pond' being the area flooded by it. In addition, in at least one manuscript of the tract on *athgabála* or distraint, there is an explanatory note which states that 'The water which is drawn from the source comes to rest in the land of the pond'.

Further confusion has arisen in relation to the term *tuididen*, which Prof. Binchy (1955, 57, n.2) translated as an 'act of leading water'. Prof. MacEoin (op. cit. 15) proposes that *tuidin* ('millstream'), which is used in another manuscript of *De Ceithri Slichtaib Athgabála*, should be retained in relation to the means by which water was drawn from the source, and that the form *tuidnid(h)e* be viewed as a corruption of *tuiden*. Two different conclusions may be drawn from this: firstly, that it was common practice to cut a channel from the water source to the millpond, as is implied by MacEoin, or secondly, that *tuididen*[210] (obstructing the natural flow of a stream by building a dam across it) and *tuidnid(h)e* do in fact designate an act of leading water to a millpond other than by connecting source and pond by an artificial channel. In view of the High Island evidence there can no be little doubt that water could be led to 'the land of the pond', although the island setting would be largely atypical of early Irish mill sites. The likelihood that the upper storage reservoir feeding the main pond was formed by the construction of a low dam across the stream, and that an opening in this dam controlled the flow of water down the hillside, also throws light on the term *brigat na linne*, or 'neck of the pond'. This has been incorrectly interpreted by both Todd (1848, 200, 5) and MacEoin (1982, 16) as the rear end of the mill flume, but can only be the opening in the dam which allowed water into the headrace channel or the sluice gate posited for the control of water from the High Island upper millpond into the main, lower millpond.

Early documentary and archaeological evidence for the use of millponds outside Ireland is quite rare. Dams were of course widely used in classical antiquity for irrigation purposes, and the large water-storage reservoirs formed by the construction of large gravity dams at Mérida in western Spain and at Homs in Syria are amongst the greatest civil engineering achievements of the ancient world (White 1984, 102–03). The earliest known dams for water power, dating from the Roman period, appear to have been diversion dams, built across small rivers or streams, where the function of the dam was to raise the level of a natural watercourse and divert it into a feeder or headrace channel for a mill. The overflow dam or weir for the third-century AD Roman vertical watermill at Haltwhistle Burn Head, on Hadrian's Wall, consisted of a barrage of granite blocks thrown across an adjacent stream (Simpson 1976). In the immediate post-Roman period the construction of mill weirs is described in early hagiographical literature. Around the turn of the sixth century AD, Gregory of Tours described the construction of a mill dam for the monastery of Loche: 'When he had driven poles across the river and brought together heaps of huge stones, he built a weir and collected water into the channel, by the force of which he made the wheel of the mill rotate at great speed' (*Vitae Patrum* XVII 2, Horn 1975, 229; Rahtz and Bullough 1977, 20; Wikander 1985, 151). The Salic laws of the late sixth century AD even prescribe a fine for the destruction of milldams (Koehne 1904, 34–5; Wikander op. cit. 152). At least one Saxon site, Wharram Percy, has produced evidence for a milldam, along with evidence for internal revetting (Young et. al 1983, 209), a practice that is well documented in later medieval accounts (Rynne 1988, I, 148ff).

The formation of millponds, however, is less well documented in early medieval European sources. Millponds are referred to in the sixth-century Visigothic law code and in *c.* AD 740 there is a reference to a *stagnum fluminus* at Tauberischafscheim in Germany (Wikander op. cit. 152). From the early Irish law tract on distraint, *De Ceithri Slichtaib Athgabála*, it is clear that the term *lind* or *tir linde* was in use in sixth-century Ireland to denote millponds, the earliest known non-Latin term for this feature in post-Roman Europe. Occurrences of related terms in other vernacular languages are somewhat later. The earliest known use of the Old English compound *mylepul* ('millpond'), for example, occurs in an Anglo-Saxon charter of AD 833 (Rahtz and Bullough 1977, 23). There can be little doubt that by the later medieval period, millponds were common features of the landscape, the maintenance of which, along with related features such as a millraces and sluices, often proved to be a heavy financial burden on both monastic and manorial estates (Chadwick 1911, le Patourel 1956, Faull and Moorhouse 1981). It is also clear that they were very common in the early historic Irish landscape, so much so that early Irish jurists went to great lengths to provide a legal framework for the water rights pertaining to them. The law tract *Coibnes Uisci Thairidne*, which forms part of the *Senchas Már* collection of early Irish legal texts, compiled between the seventh and eighth centuries AD, deals with establishment of watercourses, including those used to supply watermills (Binchy 1955); from this it may be inferred that both millraces and millponds were a common feature of the Irish landscape by this period. *Coibnes Uisci Thairidne*, indeed, is the most comprehensive legal text dealing with such matters to have survived from the early medieval period in Europe.

The almost complete surviving sections of the rock-cut headrace/inlet channel and the bypass channels of High Island are unique in Europe. Bypass channels for early medieval watermills have hitherto not been recorded, although their existence at certain early sites would not be an unreasonable inference. From the Roman period onwards there is archaeological evidence for timber or stone-revetted headrace and tailrace channels (Rynne 1988, I, 150–152). Their function, in all cases, was to counteract the erosive action of water passing through these channels, but in instances where the bed of the channel was excavated into bedrock, this would have been unnecessary. When this did occur, as at the ninth-century mill at Cloontycarthy, County Cork, which had an elaborate rock-cut headrace and tailrace channels (Rynne 1988, I, 149), the bedrock was encountered only a short distance beneath the surface. On High Island the millwright would have had no alternative but to excavate the millrace and bypass channel into the bedrock, a particularly tedious process involving the cutting of ledges to ensure a gradual fall from the millpond to the millworks. The headrace channel at Mashanaglass, County Cork (Fahy 1956, 17), was 150 feet (*c*.45.75m) long from the remains of the millpond to the original millhouse and was around 2 feet 6 inches (*c*.0.76m) wide and around 2 feet 10 inches (0.86m) deep. The High Island channel appears to have been of similar proportions, although the adjacent cove would have ensured a completely free run-off of water from both the tailrace channel of the mill and the bypass channel.

St Moling is said to have dug his own millrace as a penance (Plummer 1968, 1, lxxxii, 193–94; MacEoin 1982, 15), whilst in another legend, St Féchín of Fore is alleged to have cast his crozier into a lake, whereupon 'the crozier went through the mountain and the water came in rivers on the track of the crozier and drowned the (mill) wright who was asleep in the place of the millpond' (Stokes 1891, 344–45; Plummer 1968, 2, 8, xiv; Wikander 1985, 151, n.21). Both of these saints' Lives are much later than the period and events they purport to describe. Nonetheless, in the seventh-century legal tract *De Ceithri Slichtaib Athgabála*, the millrace is termed the *tuidin*, and in *Coibnes Uisci Thairidne* a provision is made to compensate those whose land is traversed by a millrace. Indeed, in early Irish law, it was not possible to prevent one's neighbour from leading a millrace across one's land, although individuals were compensated (at least in theory) by being allowed to use the mill within a complex system of rotation (Binchy 1955).

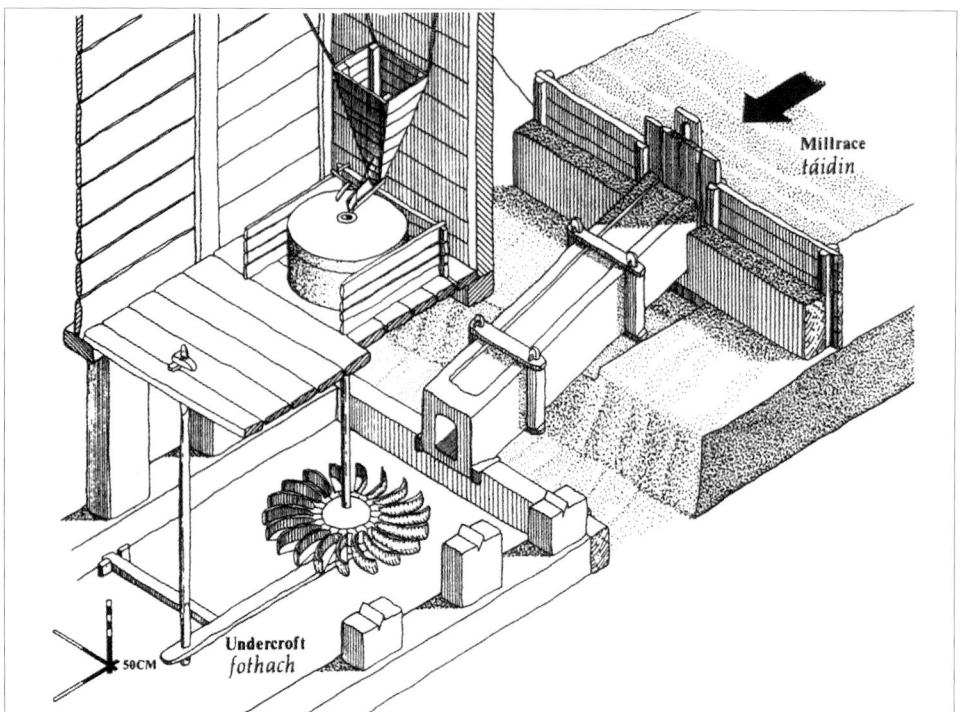

Figure 147

Reconstruction of an ninth-century horizontal mill, based on an excavation at Cloontycarthy, Co. Cork. Drawing by C. Rynne.

The Cultural Affinities of the High Island Mill

Most Irish horizontal-wheeled mill sites, dated to the period between the seventh and the eleventh centuries, bear similarities to those of Mediterranean Europe (Rynne 1992b). Those of the High Island mill, however, would appear rather to have been influenced by the mill-building traditions of the northern islands of Britain. The traditional horizontal-wheeled mills of the Orkney and Shetland Islands share close stylistic similarities with those of Scandinavia and, by extension, with those of Central and Eastern Europe, the Alpine regions, and vast tracts of South Western and Eastern Asia. Those of mainland Scotland, however, and its western islands, appear to have been influenced by early Irish millwrighting practices. Irish influences are suggested not only by close stylistic similarities between the Irish mills and those recorded on mainland Scotland but also by linguistic survivals. The Scots-Gaelic term used to denote the distinctive dished or scooped design of these paddles, *sgiathian*, would appear to be derived from Old Irish *sciatha*, a term used in the eleventh-century saga *Togail Bruidne Da Derga* for the vanes of a waterwheel (Knott 1936, 794; Curwen 1944, 141; MacEoin 1982, 18).[211] The convergence of vernacular terms for horizontal waterwheel paddles in early medieval Ireland and nineteenth-century Scotland is hardly coincidental. Indeed, the only known vernacular Irish phrase used for horizontal-wheeled mills in the west of Ireland, *muileann ton le talamh* (Deering 1857, 91–92; Lucas 1953, 6), is mirrored exactly in the Scots-Gallic phrase for similar mills in Scotland, *muileann-stáir-ri-láir* (Cheape 1984, 25).

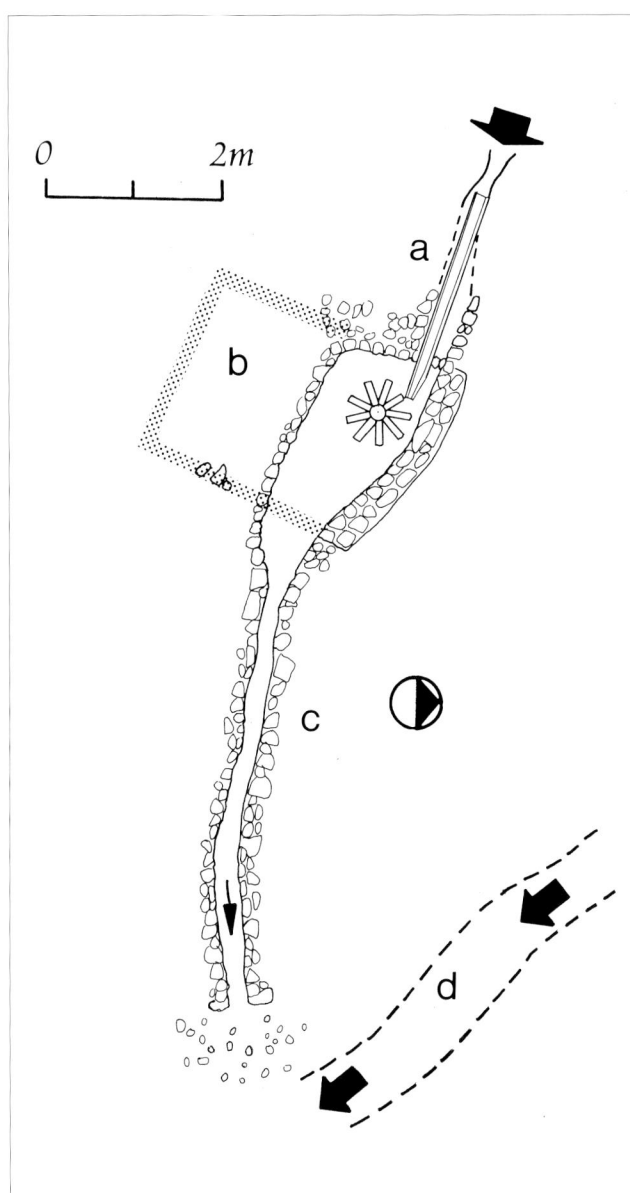

Figure 148
The excavated mill remains at Earl's Bu, Orkney (Batey, 1992, 303).

The vast majority of Irish horizontal-wheeled mills were housed in solid timber-framed structures (Rynne 1988, I, 54–58) (Fig. 147). Certain mainland Scottish mills with similar timber foundations have been recorded in Sutherlandshire during the late nineteenth century (Goudie 1886, 283), but unlike the traditional horizontal-wheeled mills of the Orkney, Shetland and Scandinavia, they share the distinctive Mediterranean-type waterwheel design.

The High Island mill differs principally from the more typical Irish horizontal-wheeled mills of the period in the way in which it straddles its feeder channel and in being provided with a bypass channel. Stone walling is, of course, by no means rare in early medieval Irish horizontal-wheeled mills, but when it is present it is nearly always provided to revet the sides of the earth-cut excavation made to accommodate the mill undercroft.

The oaken sole plates of these mills are clearly intended to support timber-framed buildings, and even though some sections of these walls are built directly on top of the foundation beams, it is clear that their presence is to prevent loose material from the sides of the construction trench falling into the undercroft. Indeed, at the ninth-century Cloontycarthy mill in County Cork (Fig. 147), a revetment wall appears to have extended up as far as the floor of the grinding room and may possibly even have positioned flooring joists. Moreover, the early medieval mill at Mashanaglass, County Cork, was clearly a stone building on three sides (Fahy 1956, Rynne 1990, 25); the layout of its undercroft (which is typically floored with wooden planks) is similar to many other Irish sites. The undercroft of the High Island mill, in sharp contrast, is not. It is, in direct contrast, much narrower, and was clearly intended to straddle the millstream in such a way as to create minimal interference to it, other than was necessary to accommodate the penstock or flume. In all of the other recorded examples of early Irish horizontal-wheeled mill sites, the creation of the mill undercroft did involve a substantial widening of the millstream, to accommodate the excavation in which foundations of the mill were laid. And, while the setting of the undercroft (well beneath ground level as in case of the early Irish examples) was clearly intended to maximise the fall from the rear end of the penstock to the floor of the undercroft, the undercroft was deliberately widened.

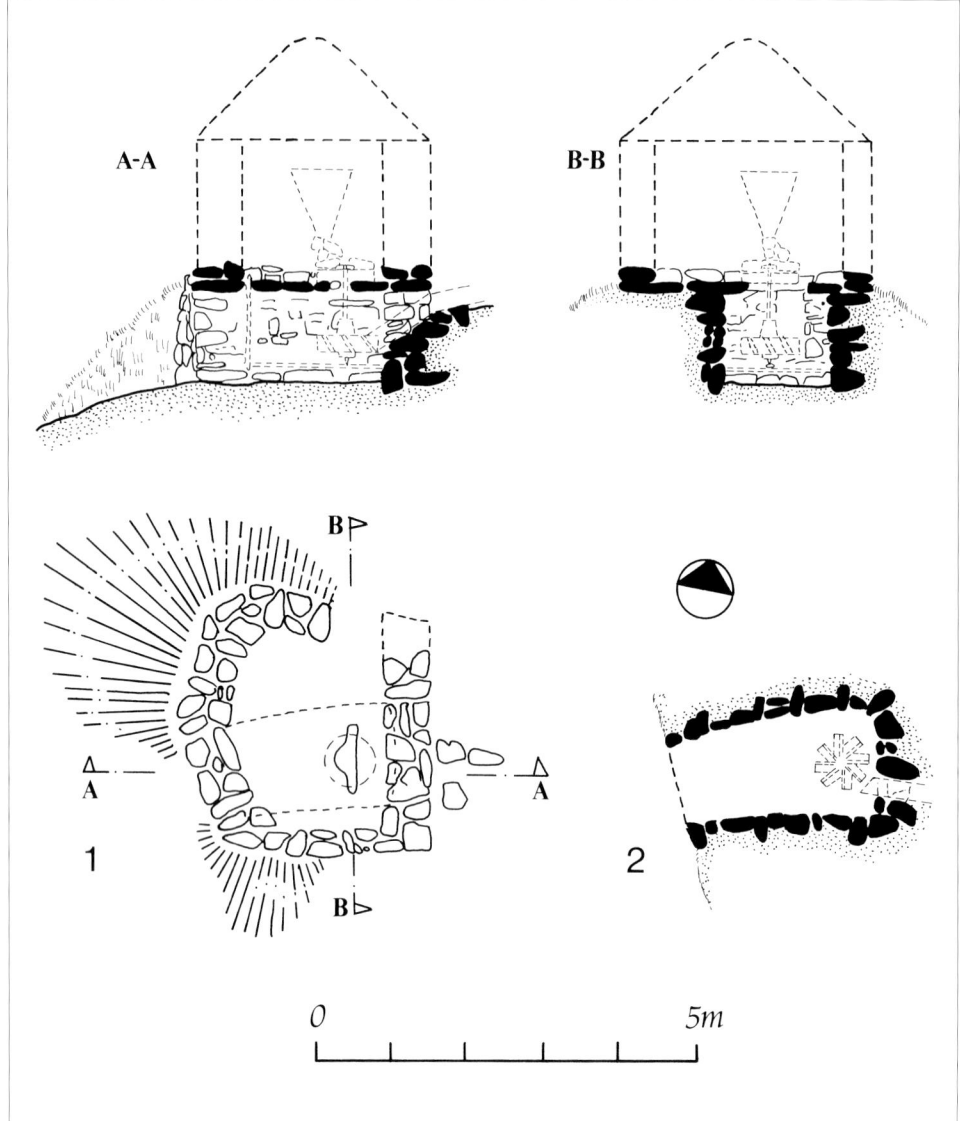

Figure 149
The eighteenth-century stone mill at Balmaciver, Kintyre peninsula, Scotland, which bears a close resemblance to the High Island, Co. Galway, mill (RCAHMS 1971, fig. 183). Courtesy RCAHMS.

The closest external chronological parallel for the Irish mills, a ninth-century Saxon example, at Tamworth, Staffordshire, has an undercroft similar to many Irish examples and, like the latter, was a timber-framed structure (Rahtz 1992). In certain mainland Scottish mills and in the Orkney and Shetland examples, however, the small stone mill buildings effectively straddle the *lade* or millstream, without making provision for a wide undercroft, as was demonstrably the case in all of the recorded Irish examples, the sole exception being the High Island mill. Furthermore, the High Island mill was also provided with a bypass channel, a feature typical of north British mills.

The surviving remains of the High Island mill bear close stylistic similarities to the Shetland-type mills of northern Britain. A similar structure has recently been excavated at a Viking period site at Earl's Bu, Orkney, the earliest clear-cut case for the existence of such a mill in either northern Britain or Scandinavia.[212] (Fig. 148). The closest parallel, however, for the High Island mill is an eighteenth-century horizontal-wheeled mill building at Balmacivar on the Kintyre peninsula (Fig. 149). The High Island mill is the first of its type to have been investigated in Ireland, although its occurrence should not come as a surprise, given the monastic contacts between Ireland and north Britain during the early medieval period. The spread of similar mills throughout Scandinavia and the islands of north Britain has traditionally been associated with Norse colonisation, leading to the term 'Norse mill' being applied to these and similar mills. The term is a misnomer, as these mills are clearly a pre-Viking development, although the claim for a late prehistoric horizontal-wheeled mill at Bølle in Jutland cannot be sustained (Steensburg 1952 and 1978, Rynne 1988, II, 194–95).

Notwithstanding the obvious stylistic similarities between the mills of Scotland, Orkney, Shetland, the Faeroes and those of Scandinavia, the terminology of watermills in the northern isles of Britain, as Alexander Fenton has demonstrated (1978, 410), 'show links with Scandinavia only in relation to those parts that are the same as in hand mills'. For mainland Scotland there are strong indications for an early Irish influence on horizontal watermill design, based on the type of waterwheel employed and on linguistic evidence. Is the High Island mill-type the precursor of the Scottish mills? The problem with the Irish evidence is that it has too few chronological parallels, not only from northern Britain, but from all of continental Europe. Nonetheless, on present evidence there is every possibility that Irish developments were the main influence on similar developments in northern Britain.

Early Monastic Watermills in Ireland and Europe

The Rule of St Benedict of *c*. AD 530 provides the earliest indication of the importance of self-sufficiency in water supply, both for domestic needs and for hydro-power in the early European monastery (McCann 1952, Ch. 66, Bond 1989, 84). Sophisticated water-management systems — the backbone of civilisation in the ancient world — were of course a legacy of Roman civilisation. Without irrigation, agriculture could not be sustained in many parts of the Roman Empire, and in many areas of southwestern Asia and north Africa, watermills effectively shared water with irrigation networks. Episodes in early ecclesiastical literature also indicate the growing importance of water-powered mills to monastic communities (Horn 1975, Wikander 1985).

However, the earliest recorded instance of water power being an important factor of location for any European monastery is that at Liessies, which Count Wibertus and Countess Ada built for their daughter Hiltud (d. AD 790) during the reign of King Pepin (Horn 1975, 229). This latter monastery, and others like Corbie from at least the tenth century onwards, were the precursors in terms of water management of the twelfth-century Cistercian monasteries. The vast majority of the pre-tenth-century Irish watermill sites have no ecclesiastical associations and appear to have been a response to the introduction of improved agricultural techniques, greater crop yields and increasing rural population during the early historic period. Furthermore, ownership or part ownership of mills and grain-drying kilns was clearly widespread amongst all ranks in early Irish society.

The skills of the *saer muilin*, or millwright, were widely available throughout Ireland before the provision of watermills was considered to be a priority for the larger Irish monastic communities. From early hagiography it is clear that in early communities grain was processed with rotary querns, hand mills that were suitable for small communities but became increasingly impracticable as and when the community increased. According to Gregory of Tours, before the construction of the mill at the monastery of Loche by Abbot Ursus 'the brothers ground the wheat required for their sustenance by turning the millstones by hand (*molam mann vertentes*)' (Horn 1975, 229). Similar episodes are described in later Irish hagiography, most notably in the *vitae* of St Finnian of Clonard and St Ciaran (Plummer 1968, vol.1).

However, the earliest record of an Irish monastery investing in a watermill is at Kildare in the late seventh century, described in an episode in Cogitosus' *Vita* of St Brigid. This *Vita*, along with Adomnán's *Vita Columbae* (see below), is one of three surviving seventh-century Irish hagiographical tracts (Sharpe 1982) and provides a detailed account of the cutting and fitting of a millstone to the monastery's watermill (Thomas 1971, 210–11; Connolly 1987, 24–25). There is also a curious reference in the *Vita Columbae*, compiled in the 690s by Adomnán, the ninth abbot of Iona (Anderson and Anderson 1961, 109–12; Sharpe 1995, 43–53), to a *crux molari infixa lapidii* (*Vita Columbae*, III, xxiii, Sharpe 1995, 227), or a 'cross fixed in a millstone', which Joyce (1903, 334) saw as an explicit reference to a water-powered millstone. The inference drawn by Joyce was by no means unreasonable, even though the cross involved is likely to have been wooden, as a rotary quernstone could not have provided a solid base. Furthermore, Adomnán also refers to the use of a grain-drying kiln, a facility that by the early medieval period is clearly associated with the use of water-powered milling in Ireland (Rynne 1988, I, 133). Very recently the curious use of a millstone at Iona, referred to by Adomnán, was actually recorded at Clonmacnoise, where the base of the north cross (*c*. AD 800), during its removal, was found to be set in the bedstone of a horizontal-wheeled mill (Manning 1992, 8–9). Indeed, recent excavations beside a shallow stream on Iona called *Sruth a' Mhuilinn* ('the mill stream'), although far from conclusive in terms of the remains of any recognisable mill structure, would also suggest that a water-powered mill was used here during the early medieval period (O'Sullivan 1994).[213]

Cogitosus refers to late seventh-century Kildare as 'a vast metropolitan city' (Connolly 1987, 6) which, while doubtless an exaggeration, is perhaps some indication that the monastery and nunnery at Kildare supported what was, by contemporary standards, a large population. Water power in early Irish monastic contexts, as has been shown above, must date to no later than the latter part of the seventh century. The *Cáin Domnaig* or 'Law of Sunday', one of the four main *cána* or laws, is a late eighth or early ninth-century law tract which deals with Sunday observance (O'Keefe 1905, 17, 263; Hamlin 1982, 11). In one section of the text the Church sought to outlaw 'grinding in mill or quern' on the Sabbath by imposing fines, which were higher on Church-owned mills than on those controlled by the laity; clearly because the Church was expected to show an example in the area of Sunday observance (Hamlin op. cit. 11). Thus by the late eighth century, Church-owned mills must surely have been sufficiently common to feature in legal texts.

The Agrarian Economy of an Early Irish Island Monastic Community

More recent summary accounts of the development of agriculture in early medieval Ireland (e.g. Mytum 1992, Patterson 1994) have focused on the evidence that has, for whatever reason, rarely come to light — the sickles, the grain-drying kilns, the ploughs — rather than on the widespread evidence for water-powered grain mills, from which we can safely infer the widespread existence of the former. All of these implements form part of a series of often elaborate crop-processing techniques for cereals, of which milling is the penultimate stage before consumption, but only the existence of water-powered mills can provide any firm indications as to the scale of operations involved.

The use of water power in agriculture and industry in the Roman and succeeding early medieval periods provides a solid index of the extent of agrarian and technological development in any given area. There can be little doubt that the widespread use of water-powered grain mills in early medieval Ireland reflects a large-scale increase in the cultivation of cereal crops. Despite an extraordinary recent claim that farmers in early medieval Ireland were 'technologically conservative' (Patterson 1994, 68), the very existence of the watermill in early Irish society must surely be a firm indication of what must have been, in relative terms, the advanced state of early Irish agriculture. Nonetheless, we have also been assured that 'mills spread only very slowly between the fifth and tenth centuries in northern Europe and archaeology does not suggest that Ireland was any exception to this trend' (Patterson 1994, 68). In fact there are more scientifically dated early medieval watermill sites in the Irish province of Munster alone than there are in the rest of Europe and, if we add up the existing corpus of early medieval Irish sites dated by either dendrochronology or radiocarbon dating, the total exceeds that of both medieval Europe and Asia.

Indeed, these same 'technologically conservative' early Irish farmers also built the most remarkable milling complex yet to come to light from early medieval Europe, on Little Island in Cork Harbour. Of all the regions in medieval Europe where water power is known to have played an important role in agricultural development, only in Ireland has it been possible to point to the evolution of regional millwrighting styles in the early medieval period. Moreover, the earliest indications that a specialised trade of millwrighting existed anywhere in early medieval Europe (apart from the vast corpus of Irish archaeological evidence) is the Old Irish term *saer mulinn*, or millwright. On present evidence, therefore, there can be little doubt that where the use of water-powered mills was concerned, early medieval Ireland certainly did not lag behind contemporary Europe, and if the archaeological record can be taken as index of its development, it was, if anything, more advanced in this regard than either Anglo-Saxon England or Merovingian Gaul.

The inescapable fact which the existence of the enormous corpus of early medieval Irish mill sites lead us to is that Ireland, in the early medieval period, was not a technological backwater. Its agricultural development was advanced enough to enable the widespread use of water-powered grain mills amongst all levels of early Irish society. Indeed, it is difficult to explain the existence of so many mills in early Irish society (relative to other areas of contemporary Europe in which more advanced ploughs were used) without the introduction of advanced tillage techniques. All of the more recent commentators would tend to agree that improved methods of food production facilitated population growth in Ireland during the same period (Ryan 2000). However, the reasoning behind this is rather specious, insofar as some have argued that this productivity was brought about without the use of coulter ploughs. These latter were one of the principal means by which agricultural productivity was increased in Europe from perhaps the late Roman period onwards. Yet in Ireland, which has the largest concentration of early medieval watermill sites in Europe, we are asked to believe that the coulter plough was unknown.

Incredibly, the most recent archaeological and documentary studies of the early Irish plough base their claims regarding the non-use of such ploughs entirely on negative evidence (Brady 1992; Kelly 1997). By following the same line of reasoning the vertical-wheeled watermill and the tide mill, before attested archaeological discoveries, could not have existed in Ireland before the Anglo-Norman period and the sixteenth century respectively. Archaeologically, both of the latter were early sixth-century developments in Ireland (Rynne 1989). The advanced state of mechanised milling in early medieval Ireland — which has no equal in either Europe or South-Western Asia — is by itself the surest indication, in the absence of archaeological discoveries, that advanced ploughs were used in Ireland in the same period.

In the context of the agricultural regime of High Island or in the wider sphere of tillage in early medieval Ireland, the existence of a watermill implies the existence of larger crops which cannot be satisfactorily processed by hand mills, and of a community with sufficient resources to build and maintain it and large enough in terms of overall numbers to make the investment worthwhile. The correlation between population densities and the use of water-powered mills can be demonstrated from the Roman period onwards, and it is inconceivable that watermills in early medieval Ireland would have been built without sufficient levels of population to make their existence worthwhile. 'Even the most simple water-mill', as Wikander (1984, 26) has pointed out, 'has the capacity which far exceeds the needs of a single family. Under normal conditions, it is not likely to be used unless a considerably larger population has to be supplied, preferably a hundred individuals or more'. The existence of a watermill on High Island, therefore, points to a larger monastic community than has previously been thought possible.

In the early medieval period any variety of watermill would have represented a sizeable investment, even for a large community. As we have already seen, the High Island community went to great lengths to establish a watermill on their island, an installation that made ingenious use of the limited water resources available to it. The likelihood is that the watermill was built to service the needs of a self-sufficient monastic community, with sufficient numbers not only to justify its construction but also to ensure that its cereal crops, grown on the island and imported onto it, could be processed without relying on the use of mills established on the mainland. However, it has recently been suggested that 'the siting of the mill near the hermitage' indicates that 'the working of the mill was a duty of the community to be performed in solitude' (Herity 1990, 96). Furthermore, as 'there are no other traces of cultivation now discernible on the island', cereals processed were 'probably imported to the island, implying a fairly significant traffic in pilgrims' (Herity, op. cit. 97). What is implied here is that pilgrims journeying to the island brought their own grain with them, which the monks were obliged to grind. However, there is no evidence in contemporary literary sources that monastic communities milled cereals as a 'service' for anyone. In point of fact, early monastic mills were built to service the needs of the monastic community: secular communities may well have used monastic mills by agreement, but there are no indications that monasteries were ever obliged to accommodate them.

The second suggestion, that grain was imported onto the island for a 'fairly significant traffic of pilgrims', is also unacceptable. Although monasteries were obliged to provide hospitality, it would make much more sense if prospective pilgrims brought their own processed provisions, rather than the monastery going to seemingly great lengths, on a small island, to provide a processing facility for the needs of visitors, which could be much more conveniently met on the mainland. If pilgrims could ship oats or wheaten grains to the island, why could they not bring oaten flour or meal? In any case, the island's relative inaccessibility during the winter months would have meant that the mill would have found little use in the very period when its water supply would have been at its most plentiful, assuming, that is, that the greater portion of the island's population was a transient one. Moreover, if pilgrims were expected to bring their own grain with them, either for their own needs or, indeed, as a gift to the monastery, was this grain kiln-dried on the island using imported fuel or was this undertaken on the mainland? Either way, it makes little sense to undertake the less-specialised tasks such as threshing, winnowing and perhaps drying (see below) on the mainland and to locate the most expensive and technically demanding installation on an island out at sea.

With regard to evidence for cultivation on High Island, if the vast majority of settlement sites of the period have produced little surface evidence for cultivation, then we should hardly be surprised if there were none on High Island. This does not, however, rule out the likelihood that cereal crops were grown within the environs of, for example, raths or early monasteries. By the same token, we cannot discount the possibility that cereals were grown on High Island, purely on the basis that there are no obvious surface indications of such activity. As has been seen, there are some indications from crop marks that the upper pond was used to irrigate a small area of what is likely to have been cultivated land.

Nonetheless, it is almost impossible to gauge the extent to which tillage was practised on the island in the early medieval period, or the relative levels of imported and 'home-produced' cereals consumed there. What is clear, however, is that large amounts of cereals were processed there, in quantities that clearly justified the construction of a watermill. There can be little doubt that the mill was built to service the needs of a community of monks and their tenants, who lived on the island the whole year round. The mill effectively rendered the island more or less self-sufficient in all of the requisite needs for processing cereal crops, enabling the island's community to produce fresh flour and meal during the winter months, when access to the mainland would have been restricted.

Cereal Crop Processing in Early Medieval Ireland

The existence of the High Island mill raises many questions in relation to the way in which the cereal crops ground in it were processed before milling. As has been seen earlier, it seems very unlikely that the less technically demanding pre-milling procedures, such as threshing and winnowing, were all undertaken on the mainland, with bulk, kiln-dried grain being shipped out to the island for milling. Indeed, even if this were the case, large quantities of grain would have to be brought to the island, which, at the very least, would have required a kiln house and a barn for storage. As will be seen below, the existence of these associated structures, which may be inferred from that of the mill itself, would suggest that more elementary crop processing was also conducted on the island.

Harvesting

Regardless of the consumption preferences for cereal crops in early medieval Ireland, some form of rudimentary processing would have been necessary. At harvest time the ears could either be cut high in the stalk or lower down to form sheaves. Harvesting the ears separately from the stalk was practised throughout early medieval Europe, a practice which, while much slower than harvesting the grain with the stalks, allowed the ears of grain to be collected with little mixture of weed seeds. Transportation was greatly simplified, while the amount of grain normally lost during the removal of the grain from the field to the threshing barn or kiln house was considerably reduced. The amount of time needed to thresh the grain was also reduced, whilst the storage of the ears was much easier than bulk grain, which tended to spoil more rapidly, or sheaves, which necessitated more storage space (Hillman 1985, 6; Sigaut 1988, 19). The practice is obliquely referred to in the eleventh-century *Togail Bruidne Da Derga*, in which the hair of Conaill Chernaig is said to have been as big as a *cliab buana* ('reaping basket', Stokes 1901, 198–9; Joyce 1903, 273). Other documentary sources, however, suggest that sheaves were also harvested and stored in ricks or stacks (Plummer 1968, 127). Indeed, sheaves could also have been stored in barns which, as contemporary sources indicate, must have been at least as common as grain-drying kilns and mills (see below).

Threshing

In the early medieval period flail threshing was introduced into Ireland, eventually replacing more primitive techniques that could only accommodate small-scale domestic production (O Danachair 1955, Rynne 1988, I, 119–21). In the early law tracts the flail (O. Ir. susta, Mod. Ir. *suiste*) is mentioned as part of the 'equipment' of the grain-drying kiln (Gailey 1970, 65), and a passage in the *Bretha Étgid* ('judgements of inadvertence') deals with compensation arising from injury from a flail during threshing (O Danachair op. cit. 13, Gailey loc. cit.).[214] The O. Ir. term *susta* is an early borrowing from the Latin *fustis* (literally 'rod', 'stick'), which probably came into Irish in the second half of the fifth century AD (Jackson 1953, 143). The use of the *fustis* or single-piece flail in Roman farming practice is described by Columella in *De Re Rustica* (II.10.14, White 1970, 185). However, the context in which *susta* is referred to in the *Bretha Étgid*, which deals with accidents resulting from the use of a flail at a drying kiln, strongly suggests that a two-piece flail was involved (C.I.H. 273.29, O Danachair op. cit. 13; Kelly 1988, 149). Indeed, it has even been suggested that *susta* originally designated a single-piece flail and was later applied to the two-piece flail upon its adoption (Duignan 1944, 140–141).

In early medieval Ireland threshing appears to have been carried out in the kiln house, which probably contained both a grain-drying kiln and some form of threshing floor. The *Críth Gablach* lists a share in a drying kiln, a barn and a mill amongst the property qualifications for the status of *Ócaire* (Duignan 1944, 131). What the early

Irish sources actually mean by a 'barn' is by no means clear. It may well have been a storehouse situated near a kiln house. In Adomnán's *Vita* of Columcille (liber I, cap. xxxv) the monastic community at Iona is said to have had a *canaba* (nominally a barn or a storehouse), which clearly refers to the use of a grain-drying kiln (Whitaker 1957; Gailey op. cit. 64). Indeed, the *familia* of St Cainnech were obliged to thresh in the open air simply because they did not have a *canaba* for the drying and threshing of their cereal crops, whilst in the *Vita* of St Ciaran there is an unequivocal reference to a kiln in a *canaba* (Scott 1951, 204). The *Gerefa*, which deals with the duties of the Anglo-Saxon reeve, also suggests that both the kiln and the threshing floor were housed within a single building in Anglo-Saxon England (Monk 1977, 259). Where early Irish practice was concerned, it would appear that either the ears or the sheaves may actually have been dried before threshing, the converse being the case in more recent times (Gailey op. cit. 68). On the other hand it may well have been that the kiln house was sufficiently large to accommodate the storage of grain in the ear, along with a kiln and a threshing area, and that the grain was dried almost immediately after threshing. In more recent times, the practice of drying sheaves before threshing was generally confined to the Baltic regions (Sigaut 1988, 7).

Winnowing

After threshing, all forms of free-threshing cereals such as breadwheat (*T. aestivum*), all the ryes (*Secale cereale agg*), oats (various *Avena* spp.) and barley (various *Hordeum* spp.), in which the grains immediately fall free during threshing (Hillman 1981, 1985), were traditionally separated from the debris detached with them in a two-stage cleaning process involving winnowing and sieving. In its essentials the winnowing process involves blowing air over the debris, which carries off the light chaff along with the lighter fragments of rachis. In early Irish society both threshing and winnowing were considered to be work for slaves. St Cainnech's monks appear to have winnowed by hand on flagstones in an open field, although it is also possible that the function of the *seiche*, or 'hide', which is listed amongst the equipment of the kiln house in the early sources (Gailey op. cit. 65), may well have been that of a winnowing sheet.

In more recent times women got rid of the chaff (*cáith*) by winnowing through the fingers, using a special winnowing sheet called a *caetig or cáiteach* (Joyce 1903, 275). Alternatively, the grain could be poured from a *dallán* (blind sieve) or a *bodhrán* (a skin tray also used as a drum) on a moderately breezy day (Lucas 1951, 146–7); a practice often conducted on high windy places known colloquially as 'shilling' (i.e. shelling) hills (Estyn Evans 1976, 213). Again, in more recent times, the grain was cleaned before winnowing by being passed through woven ash riddles (Lucas op. cit. 158, Bell and Watson 1981, 221). Although 'barns' are referred to in the early law tracts (see below), thus far there are no indications that these were specialist structures like those that have been excavated on Anglo-Saxon period sites (e.g. Chalton, Hampshire, see Addyman et al. 1972; 1973), with opposing doors to facilitate both threshing and winnowing.

Sieving

Flail-threshed crops require much additional cleaning preparatory to either milling or storage as seed (White 1970, 186, 486 n.62). In Roman farming, the use of sieves (*capisterium*) is described by Columella (*De Re Rustica* II.9.II, White op. cit. 187) and in the immediate post-Roman period by Boethius, who refers to *melu* or grain that has passed through a sieve (Grube 1934, 147). In the Anglo-Saxon *Gerefa* it is stated that 'One must have sieves, coarse sieves, hair sieves and poles for supporting the sieve' (Monk 1977, 257). And as two varieties of sieve appear to have been involved, one can reasonably infer that at least two sievings were necessary, the first with a coarse riddle (to eliminate weed heads, rachis fragments and all contaminants coarser than the grain); and a second with a finer sieve, to remove awn segments (part of the grain, detached through threshing), small weed seeds and small stones (Hillman 1985, 9). The use of the sieve (Old Irish *criathar*) for dressing flour is referred to in the laws of fosterage, which stipulate that its use be taught to fostered girls, whilst the *criathar* is one of three items of domestic utensils associated with the *cumal* or bondmaiden in *Bretha Étgid* (Rynne 1990, 27). In Ireland up until recent times, a rudimentary sieve called a *criathar* was used for crop cleaning and sorting, which had mesh sizes appropriate to the crop being cleaned (Joyce 1903, 343; Lucas 1951, 146–155).

Storage

After the cereal grains were cleaned and sorted it seems likely that they were temporarily stored before kilning. The contemporary Irish documentary sources indicate that threshing was conducted either within the vicinity of the kiln or a structure housing it, and one might expect that both the cleaning and sorting of the grain would have been carried out in the same place. There can be little doubt from these sources that the watermill, the kiln and the barn in early Irish society were functionally related (Mytum 1992, 195). All three structures must surely have occurred with the same frequency in the early Irish landscape, but thus far only the watermill has featured prominently in the archaeological record; the others have all but eluded archaeological investigation. In more recent times in County Cork, grain with chaff has been stored near drying kilns in straw-rope granaries (Mod. Ir. *fhóir*), a practice that has also been recorded in northern Scotland (Lucas 1958; 1959; Fenton 1978). It may well have been that similar structures were widely employed in early medieval Ireland, which would go a long way in explaining the absence of more permanent grain-storage facilities in the archaeological record.

However, while such granaries may have sufficed for small volumes, and it is clear that grain was also stored in boxes and chests (O'Corráin 1972, 52), the scale of grain production that may be inferred from references to barns and watermills, must surely have involved larger structures. Malt production, for example, may well have involved a reasonably large covered area or a barn-like structure to enable the barley to germinate. Nonetheless, an entry in the *Annals of Ulster* for AD 787 refers to a fire in the monastery of Clonard, during which half of the grain in storage was destroyed. The text adds that grain was stored *in ballerio* (a 'bath' or 'bathing place'), which presumably refers to a storage pit. However, while there is no native Old Irish word for a barn, the word *saball*, from Latin *sabellum*, is used in the laws from at least the seventh century (O'Cróinín 1995, 94).

Kiln Drying

It may well have been the case in early medieval Ireland that either the ears of grain or the sheaves were dried before threshing. However, while this may not have been always necessary, some form of elementary parching or kilning was necessary to facilitate milling (Monk 1982, Rynne 1990). In *Críth Gablach* ownership of a 'drying kiln (*áith*), a barn, a mill (his share in the latter so it grinds for him)' are deemed to be some of the property qualifications for the status of independent farmer (Binchy 1941; Duignan 1944, 140). The same tract also itemises the kiln equipment as a broom (*scuab*), a hide (*seiche*) and a flail (*suste*) and, from the available references to kilns in the laws, there can be little doubt that these were substantial structures (Gailey 1970, 65). Furthermore, the term *áith* 'for linguistic reasons must be older in Ireland than the fifth century AD' (Gailey op. cit. 69). Kiln houses similar to those implied by the contemporary sources are thus far absent from the archaeological record. Similar period structures have not turned up elsewhere in Europe, although a likely candidate is indicated on the ninth-century plan of St Gall. On the latter, one of the buildings positioned next to the watermills is identified as *locus ad torrendas annonas* ('the place in which the grain is parched'), on one side of which a square kiln platform is indicated (Horn 1975, 223).

The Early Medieval Population of High Island

All of the available indications strongly suggest that the construction of the High Island mill was an act of self-sufficiency rather than of self-indulgence. Contemporary sources, which include the earliest Irish and European hagiography, make it abundantly clear that watermills were only built by monastic communities whose numbers were sufficiently large to justify the investment. Early medieval monasteries in Ireland were also, of course, centres of population, but when the decision to construct a watermill was made, for whatever reason, it is likely that the nearest suitable site within the environs of the community would have been chosen.

From perhaps the eighth century onwards, water-powered machinery was becoming an integral part of the precincts of continental monasteries, although there is no evidence of this trend in Ireland until the advent of the Cistercians in the late twelfth century. However, as the *Cáin Domnaig* clearly indicates, monastic watermills must surely have been a common feature of Irish monastic estates by the end of the eighth century. In such circumstances the watermill is likely to have been constructed on a suitable site, as near to the monastic enclosure as circumstances would allow. But within the confines of an island of some 33 hectares (80 acres) the idea of constructing a mill as an afterthought for a 'hermitage', a term which, if applicable in the present context, presumably implies a small number of people, would appear to defy rational explanation.

However, the uniqueness of the High Island mill may lead us into the danger of viewing it in isolation; its monastic association is only evident because of the confines of the island. A similar mill on the mainland could well be situated near a monastic settlement, but not near enough to make the association an unambiguous one. Similar circumstances, indeed, could also arise in the case of secular settlements where there may well be a seemingly clear-cut spatial relationship between a mill and a ringfort but no certainty that this relationship was ever a chronological one. But in both cases there could be little doubt that the existence of the mill indicates a need to cater for the requirements of sizeable communities.

As in the case of more recent water-powered grain mills, early mills were built as close to the eventual consumer as possible, to minimise transportation difficulties and because the use of millstones simply impaired the keeping quality of the flour and meal. In the more recent roller mills, the germ is removed from the rest of the grain, but when millstones are used, the germ is ground up with the rest of the grain, giving it a sour taste and increasing the risk of attack by insects. The flour produced in this manner was also more susceptible to changes in humidity. Its keeping qualities were therefore limited, and while grain could evidently be stored for relatively long periods of time, flour and meal could not, and had to be consumed within a much shorter period of time, up until the introduction of roller milling into these islands in the 1870s (Perren 1990, 422–23). Flour and meal in the early medieval period, therefore, were milled at regular intervals in either rotary querns or watermills to ensure fresh supplies.

As has been demonstrated above, if one views the High Island religious community simply as a hermitage it is very difficult to see the necessity of building a watermill to accommodate pilgrims. It would have been much easier for visitors to bring processed flour and meal to the island, assuming that is, that pilgrims did not stay on the island for a number of weeks. Even if this were the case (and this seems highly unlikely), then the mill would be virtually redundant over the winter months, when access to the island would have been restricted.

That considerable effort was expended on the construction of the watermill cannot be disputed. In normal circumstances such a mill would be almost continually in use to produce fresh supplies of flour or meal from stored grain, save for short periods in the summer months when water levels were low. At the very least the mill would also require a storage facility such as a barn, along with a kiln to dry the grain preparatory to milling. Threshing floors would also be required to process grain either imported onto or grown on the island. Its water reservoirs and plant would also need regular maintenance. Indeed, in view of the ancillary processes required to prepare cereal crops for consumption outlined above, and of the rather basic necessity of ensuring that these processes and the structures associated with them be relatively close to each other, it is impossible to view the mill on High Island as an installation that could have existed by itself, without the existence of ancillary structures. Grain grown on the island, or imported onto it, would have been threshed, winnowed, sieved, dried and milled by the monks, their tenants and their families.

The mill alone could have met the needs of up to one hundred individuals, although it is likely that the island could only have sustained considerably less than this, perhaps fifty to seventy people. Up until recent times this well-watered island could still provide ample grazing for sheep, and it is likely that early medieval inhabitants kept their own flocks and also, perhaps, a small dairy herd. A diet further supplemented by vegetables and fresh seafood could also have sustained a small island community, but while it is unlikely that the island could have produced enough cereals to sustain its inhabitants, the watermill would have freed them from a reliance on mainland watermills during the winter months.

The horizontal-wheeled mill and its feeder reservoirs clearly dominate the early medieval landscape of High Island, and it would appear that more effort was expended on these features than on any structures within the small monastic enclosure. In view of this, can the mill be realistically viewed as an afterthought? If the original island settlement did in fact begin as a hermitage, accommodating a handful of monks, then the High Island setting could be viewed as ideal for an embryonic religious community. However, it seems barely credible that a hermitage would immediately equip itself with a watermill. The rotary quern is an extremely common feature of artefact assemblages recovered from early medieval Irish settlement sites, and there can be little doubt that on many of these sites small-scale domestic grinding operations were a common undertaking. One can only presume that on the Atlantic islands off the Galway coast, where other religious communities were established, the absence of suitable hydraulic heads for water-powered mills compelled the monks to use rotary querns. One would expect that a similar *modus operandi* would have obtained on High Island, if a small group of monks had already settled there before the watermill was constructed.

Notes

[210] *tairidin* in *Coibnes Uisci Thairidne*.

[211] Dished horizontal waterwheel paddles of unknown date have been found at Dalswinton in Dumfriesshire and at Gutcher in Shetland. The Dalswinton example is apparently similar to an as yet unpublished Irish example from Horseleap, Co. Meath (Maxwell 1955, 186 and 1956, 132). In the central highlands of Scotland the term *muilinn dubh* was used, which in the Hebrides normally refers to the horizontal-wheeled variety. The term *laddle miln*, which is used in the Montgomery Manuscript of *c*.1698 to describe traditional mills in Ulster in which 'the axel tree stood upright and ye small stones or querns [such as are turned with hands] on ye top thereof; the waterwheel fixed at ye lower end of ye axel tree, and did run horizontally among ye water; a small force driving it' (MacAdam 1850, 13), was also used in mainland Scotland. A *ladill myll* was in operation on the Banff estate in Aberdeenshire in 1534, whilst *laidle miln* is mentioned in 1684 at Glenprosen Angus (Shaw 1984, 8–9). In an Ulster context the term *laddle miln* may indicate a Scots-Irish influence, albeit as a Scots label for a pre-existing Irish milling practice. There can be little doubt that horizontal waterwheels with dished paddles were still quite common in the western provinces of Ireland in the sixteenth and seventeenth centuries, and that mills of this type were probably still in use in Ulster before the plantation period (Rynne 1988, I, 228–30).

[212] On present evidence, the earliest clear-cut case for the existence of such mills in either northern Britain or in Scandinavia, during the early medieval period, is at Earl's Bu, Orkney (see Fig. 148). There are also claims for an early medieval horizontal-wheeled mill at Ljørring (Steensburg 1959 and 1978) in Denmark, dated by radiocarbon dating to AD 910. However, it seems more likely that the Ljørring mill, along with a further Danish site at Omgård (Nielsen 1977 and 1986) dated by dendrochronology to AD 840–41, was a vertically wheeled mill.

[213] The suggestion by Anderson and Anderson in their translation of the life of Columba, 1961, 115, and by Richard Sharpe in the most recent edition of the saint's life, 1995, 373, n.406, that the millstone involved was a rotary quernstone, can no longer be accepted. The existence of the grain-drying kiln on Iona during Columba's time would also suggest that a water-powered mill was in existence on the island in the early medieval period. The discovery of a water-powered millstone dating from the later medieval period during excavations on the island, which appears to have been re-used as the base for a wooden cross, would suggest that the practice noted by Adomnán and recorded at Clonmacnoise survived into the later medieval period; see Barber 1981, 308.

[214] In *Ancient Laws of Ireland* the *Bretha Étgid* or 'judgements of inadvertence' is translated under the incorrect title of *Lebar Aicle* or 'The Book of Aicill', see Kelly 1988, 272.

Chapter Eleven

High Island Over the Centuries

Round the wrecked laura
Needles flicker
Tacking air, quicker and quicker
To rock, sea and star.

Richard Murphy, *High Island*.

Small groups of people would naturally have come over the centuries to live on High Island, at least on a seasonal or short-term basis, attracted by good grazing, a ready supply of fresh water, colonies of sea birds and abundant marine life. We have, fortunately, found a few traces of their presence here.

The most impressive evidence for earlier occupation of the island comes from pollen core samples taken in the summer of 1999 by Molloy, Fuller and Conaghan, botanists from the National University of Ireland, Galway. The samples, taken from the hill 100m east of the millpond, reflect vegetation development and landscape change over the last 4000 years. They noted that generally pollen collected in such a relatively small, peaty basin like this could be expected to originate from local plants growing within 50m of the sampling site (see graphs and report in Appendix Two for more details).[215]

The presence of barley (*Hordeum*) in the sample for Zone 1 (*c.* 2240–540 BC) suggests arable activity on this hillside and, hence, human occupation of the island as early as the late Bronze Age. During this same period some woodland cover of predominantly pine and hazel with small amounts of elm, alder, oak and birch existed on the island. The botanists note, however, that these woodlands probably consisted of patches of low scrub set in a generally open landscape, rather than the canopy woodland found on the mainland during this period.

The following period, Zone 2 (*c.* 540 BC–AD 640), which roughly corresponds to the Iron Age, shows a marked decrease in pollen for pine, hazel and elm, with an increase in grass and ribwort plantain, possibly a sign of increased human activity. Evidence for arable activity is minimal, with only one record of rye pollen from this period. The ashy material found in the church — pig bones, fish and bird bones — further indicates the presence of Iron Age people on the island. We can not, as yet, be certain that the evidence from pollen and ash indicates contemporary occupation. They might instead be signs of short-term occupancy of two different groups of people.

Specific inferences and conclusions must, of necessity, be cautious until more pollen core studies are run, particularly in view of the difficulties of precise dating and the possibilities of skewed distributions in pollen samples. The results, nevertheless, appear to justify earlier arguments that the island was settled before the early medieval period and further strengthen our belief that crops were raised on this hill both before and after the monks.

Structural evidence for pre-monastic occupation of the island is less certain and difficult to place chronologically. At present, the earliest visible structure that is pre-monastic is probably the large stone enclosure wall, later to become the monastic enclosure wall. A few of the other structures on High Island may also belong to a pre-monastic period, such as the long field wall running the length of the valley and some of the structures scattered through the monastic valley itself. If the large enclosure were to be considered one of the western stone forts, a number of reasons often proposed for their construction may be eliminated here. Its topographical position, in a shallow valley, does not appear to be defensive, nor is it a reasonable location for a ceremonial site. The purpose of this enclosure was almost certainly pure habitation and it was most likely just a secular cashel. The time of its construction remains unknown, aside from predating the monastery.

The most substantial and long-term occupation of the island appears to be that of the early medieval monks. Remains of their settlement, still clearly visible in stone structures and in the landscape, testify to their strong presence here for centuries. Molloy, Fuller and Conaghan found a strong upsurge in arable activity during this period (Zone 3) with identified grains of rye (*Secale*), barley (*Hordeum*) and wheat (*Triticum*). This marked increase of arable crops in the early medieval period accords well with the establishment of a monastery and a mill. The increase in arable crops was also accompanied by a further decline in arboreal pollens, a normal decline in areas where people are living. The presence of wheat is surprising in the windy, marine environment. Oats might have been expected to be the most practical cereal grain for the acid soil, exposed location and damp Atlantic climate, particularly the bristle-pointed oat (*Avena strigosa*).

It is clear that more studies are needed to explore all the agricultural questions and possibilities raised by the mill and its transformed landscape in the early medieval period as well as in the earlier occupation of the island. Many questions remain to be answered. It is certain that the large quantities cited for wheat in the Butser Ancient Farm Project Trust (Reynolds 1978, 1979, 1981) are in no way comparable for High Island. At present, however, the extent of arable acreage is unknown, as is the yield capacity of the land. The exciting preliminary results of Molloy, Fuller and Conaghan clearly demonstrate the value of continuing investigations.

Seventh to Eleventh Centuries

Legend attributes the foundation of the monastery to St Féchín in the seventh century, but neither the elusive solitary reference to its foundation by St Féchín nor anything found in the course of our examination dates conclusively to the seventh century. It is, nevertheless, possible that the legend is correct or that monks from Omey, in the name of a monastic familia devoted to Féchín, founded the site in the late seventh to early eighth century. Continuing excavation may yet be able to establish the earliest period for the existence of the monastery.

What then can be recognised with assurance as dating roughly to these centuries? No structure outside the monastic enclosure may as yet be dated, although the 'guesthouse' and the long wall that ends in the millpond predate the horizontal watermill, based on their structural relationships to it. The guesthouse almost certainly belongs to this period, probably dating to somewhere in the ninth century or early tenth century. It is unlikely, because of its rectangular shape, to be earlier than the ninth century (see above, ch. 4, for discussion about the use of rectangular secular buildings); and because of its relationship with the watermill, it is unlikely to be much later.

Construction of the horizontal watermill, with the accompanying enlargement of the natural pond into a millpond and the transformation of the hills to the east to form both a gravity dam and a water reservoir, was a major event. This is the sign of a dramatic change in the life of the monastery. A small ascetic community would have no need for such extravagant projects; querns and handmills had continued to be used by small groups of people for many centuries. Watermills were expensive and time-consuming to build and to maintain and, as Rynne has stated, were rewarding and productive only for a minimum population of fifty to a hundred people. The High

Island population must have substantially increased with the use of the watermill, most probably in the numbers of monastic tenants. The intensification of cereals necessary to feed so many extra people is currently one of several questions being addressed in the research pollen study of environmental change over the centuries in the monastic area by the Department of Botany, National University of Ireland, Galway.

It would be difficult to over-emphasise the economic significance of milling and the consequent increase in productivity for all levels of society. Mills freed many hands for other tasks and, moreover, opened up a new source of revenue for the owners. Secular and ecclesiastical owners both charged fees, often in the form of a percentage of the cereal to be ground. An idea of the profitability of mills may be seen in the remaining fragment of an early ninth-century inventory of the royal Carolingian estate at Annapes, which relates that as much grain was brought to the manor as fees for use of the mill and breweries as the estate grew on its own (Duby [1962] 1963, 363–364). Once in common use, mills remained profitable for hundreds of years, indeed, the decided advantage of owning a local monopoly on milling shows in a fifteenth-century document from the north of England. In 1438 the Reeve's account for the Manor and Borough of Leeds in northern England shows that the rent from the farm of two watermills, £14 13s. 4d., far surpassed the next most profitable source of revenue, the £9 from the farm of the town there, including £4 13s. 4d. 'from the rents of the burgesses of the town of Leeds, including the toll of the markets and fairs there and the fines for baking and brewing and the amercements of the court of the burgesses…'[216]

Construction of the mill can only be dated relative to other structures, at present. It was built after the guesthouse and before a last building phase of the monastery. It is possible that the dates fall somewhere between the ninth to mid tenth centuries, after construction of the rectangular guesthouse, but still close to the period of the greatest production of horizontal watermills, AD 770–850, when dendrochronological dates on the timber from watermills indicate 56 per cent of them were built (Baillie 1998).

Any attempt to date the mill's origins must also weigh other factors, such as its difference in style from the ones dated by Baillie, a style whose chronological framework is not well known (see Rynne above) and the long survival of horizontal mills on Ireland's western coast. The mill must have been in existence if the monks were grinding up island stone for mortar aggregate for the lower paving stones in a church which was possibly built in the second quarter of the eleventh century.

There are reasons for believing that the mill closed before another building phase of the monastery (the last phase?). The mill stream itself was blocked at some time by what appears to be remnants of quarrying on the south bank. The stone here is distinctive, a wavy schist with minor quartz veining, identical to some of the stone used in the church, particularly that on the western façade. Much of the mill building itself, moreover, indeed its entire eastern end, is missing. There is no trace of collapsed stone on the ground, so a possible conclusion is that the building was taken down and the stone used elsewhere by the monks. In addition, little structural evidence remains of tenant structures, which may also have been dismantled and reused elsewhere.

The closure of the mill suggests that the experiment of turning High Island into a larger monastery had proved undesirable or unsuccessful. Perhaps they suffered adverse environmental conditions, a series of drought years or extremely wet years, creating stressful living conditions for a population of fifty to seventy people. An eighty-acre island is a small catchment area for such a large population, even one that includes rich sea resources. The enterprise may have been overly ambitious for such a small island.[217]

The transformation of the landscape on High Island for the mill reveals a profound understanding and skilful use of water engineering on a small monastic island in the Atlantic. From its unlikely presence here, several general observations may be made about the benefits of milling and the transfer of knowledge about it that may help to place the High Island mill in a larger context and underscore the importance of its contribution to knowledge.

Monastic interest in water management is recorded by the late fifth century to early sixth century, when Gregory of Tours recorded the construction of two mills and St Benedict included mills in his rules for monks.[218] By the twelfth and thirteenth centuries Cistercians, Carthusians and Augustinians were building aqueducts, sophisticated fish ponds, and elaborate internal water-supply systems that led water through pipes from outside sources, directed it around an internal distribution system, and flushed the waste water out of the monastery again. By this time water was also powering fulling mills for the manufacture of wool.

Outside of Ireland, however, little is known from archaeology or documentation about milling technology between the sixth and the ninth centuries in Western Europe.[219] The richness and abundance of the Irish material, in which linguistic, documentary, dendrochronological and archaeological evidence converge to show substantial milling activity in Ireland by the late sixth to mid seventh century, is invaluable because it is over one hundred years earlier than evidence for other areas. This is particularly startling in view of persuasive arguments that milling technology spread from the Mediterranean (see Rynne 1998b). Regional adaptations doubtless differed, but such a large geographical and chronological disparity in the adoption of a practical technology between Ireland and the Continent is not likely under these circumstances. Trade towns were developing during these centuries in Ireland, Britain and on the Continent, along with agricultural and population expansion; the advantages of mills would have been clear. The Irish evidence for horizontal mills is, therefore, of great importance to all early medieval scholars, as old chronological and development models are undergoing a necessary revision. It also supports the new approaches of scholars towards understanding the origins, levels and social-economic effects of technology on individual cultures, as well as its dissemination, adoption and modification throughout a broader region of interacting cultures.[220]

In the initial centuries of the early medieval period, Irish culture began to change in fundamental ways. These changes are most easily marked in the adoption of a foreign religion, Christianity, and a foreign written language, Latin, as well as water-engineering skills and other technologies originating outside of the country. The cultural transformation, however, was not forced by external agents but self-driven. Such swift voluntary changes argue for an internally dynamic culture in active contact with other regional cultures, with exchanges of information and ideas going in both directions.

In the absence of a unifying governing force for Western Europe, one of the most efficient mechanisms for information flow must have been through Christianity and its network of monasteries. The monasteries, including a number of Irish foundations on the Continent, were economic and cultural powers, natural gathering places for the exchange of goods, information and knowledge. In the predominantly agricultural land-based economy, monasteries had all the assets — manpower and wealth — to use new technology as readily as any of the great secular lords. They had, in addition, an educated population fluent in Latin, the universal language for all schooled Christians, as well as the same communal religious life. Across Europe the monasteries and great ecclesiastical sites formed a natural and easy communication network, one that was also connected to ruling families in each region. Messages and visitors constantly travelled between monasteries and kingdoms throughout Europe and beyond. The sophisticated mill technology on High Island, the transformation of the landscape to accomplish its purposes, were actions taken by people who were accustomed to working with the technology.

It is evident that if there were a ninth or early tenth-century guesthouse and horizontal watermill, there were also other structures, a church, living cells, etc. from the same period. Little, however, that is now visible within the monastic enclosure could belong to this early period. Two sides of the church enclosure wall, some of the burials, the cross in its northeastern corner, and a few of the other cross stones may be all that is left of the seventh through tenth-century monastery here. None of the other visible structures, neither the church nor the two cells, probably belong to this period. As excavations continue, evidence of earlier structures will likely be revealed; however, much of the building stone of these structures was probably reused in later ones.

It is logical that few elements within the monastic enclosure date to an early period, because structures need constant repair and are often replaced or improved. Stone for building was readily available nearby and also in the walls of the earlier

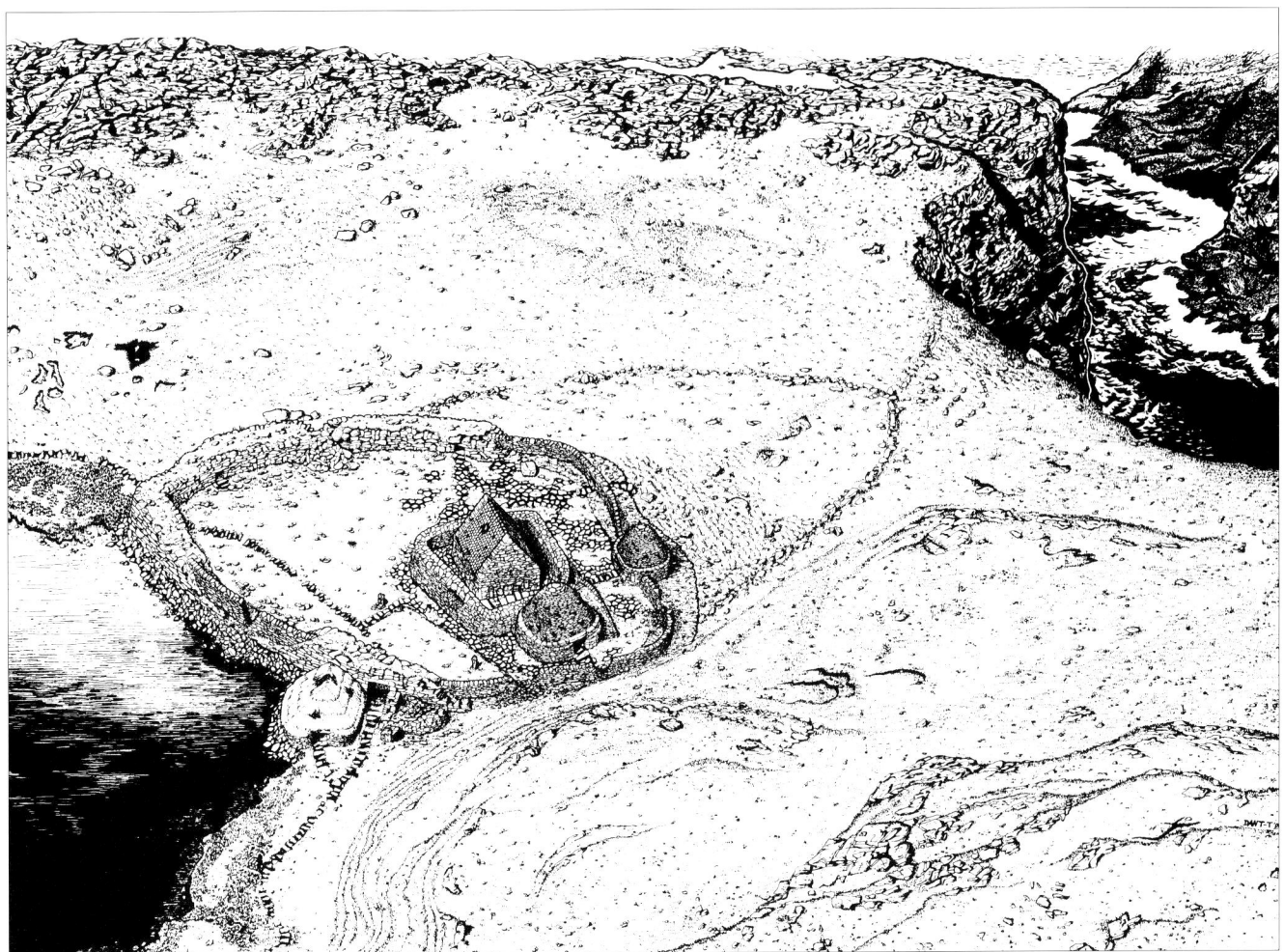

Figure 150
Reconstruction drawing of the monastery of High Island, Co. Galway, as it might have looked shortly after the departure of the monks, when the buildings were beginning to decay. Reconstruction based on knowledge of structures as of the end of excavation in 1997. Reconstruction drawing by D. Tietzsch-Tyler.

cashel. A small colony of monks arriving to occupy a stone cashel, and wishing to establish a church and cells quickly before the onset of winter, would almost certainly use such a convenient 'quarry'; it has already been suggested that it was the monks who removed stones from the enclosure wall in order to position Cell A, and to facilitate movement around Cell B. The first material evidence that the monks used stone from the enclosure wall showed up in 1997 in the excavation of a trench running from the large wall chamber in the monastic enclosure wall to the church enclosure wall. The height of the monastic enclosure wall in this area is low, right at the level of the large wall chamber's lintel stones. It was surprising, therefore, to find that there was little large stone collapse from the enclosure wall in this area.[221] Instead, under the upper sod and soil layers there was a sizeable area of small stone chippings, a few metres long and several centimetres deep, of sharply faceted mica-schist pieces; clearly detritus from stone-working. The monks themselves must have been taking and reworking stones from the monastic enclosure wall. The stone-working evidence constituted the first trace of monastic activity under the naturally accumulated soil and sod; it is reasonable, therefore, to assume that this activity took place during a late stage in the monastery.

There is nothing unusual or unique in the dismantling of the wall by the High Island monks. One of humankind's oldest traditions is the reuse of any material that is close at hand, such as the foundation of Thomas of Bayeux's eleventh-century Norman cathedral in York, which used both Roman stone and the occasional Anglo-Saxon sculpture (Senior 1989, 226). It would have been natural for the early monastic colonists to reduce the height of the cashel wall considerably in order to construct the walls of their first church and their cells, and to continue to use the stone as suited their needs.

Late Tenth to Thirteenth Century

We have no idea what the original structures inside the monastic enclosure looked like. Most of the church complex that is still visible, the church and the two cells, represents the last period of active occupation of the monastery from the late tenth to sometime in the twelfth century. This last period is, not surprisingly, also the one richest in both documentary and visible archaeological evidence. That this was an active, dynamic period for the monastery is shown in the number of building phases of the present church. We have traced remnants of the last three or four churches that existed from roughly the ninth century to sometime in the twelfth century, a period of perhaps 300 years; it is likely, moreover, that a number of earlier churches also existed here or close by.

Cells A and B were probably built contemporaneously because they are identical in plan and similar in style of masonry and building technique, but no precise date can be established for their construction. It is, however, clear that Cell B is built against and, therefore, later than the church enclosure wall and probably belongs sometime between the tenth and twelfth centuries. We do not know, however, how or whether they relate to any of the construction phases of the church. The opening in the enclosure wall and the blocked passageway were also made after the enclosure wall was built, but that only demonstrates a relative time-frame for the opening and the passageway itself.

St Gormgal

The most extensive amount of documentary information about the monastery dates from the eleventh century and consists of material concerning St Gormgal. In either 1017 or 1018 four monastic annals, *The Annals of Ulster*, *The Annals of Inisfallen*, *The Chronicum Scotorum* and *The Annals of the Four Masters*, record the death of St Gormgal. Gormgal, moreover, was included in two martyrologies, books written to record the feast or death day of important saints, both Irish and foreign. John Colgan and Michael O'Clery, two of the great seventeenth-century Irish scholars connected to the

Franciscan centre at Louvain, stated that the *Martyrology of Cashel*, now lost, listed Gormgal as a saint to be commemorated and designated 5 August as his memorial day.[222] The twelfth-century *Martyrology of Gorman*, written by Marianus Gorman, abbot of Cnoc na nApstol, contains a verse for Gormgal on 5 August testifying to the reverence still felt for the High Island saint at that time:

> *Gormgal [who is] with his good King,*
> *a sacred thing I shall declare him to the world.*[223]

John Colgan had more information about Gormgal in the seventeenth century, because he stated that he possessed an old and clearly divinely inspired poem, a most elegant and pious little work concerning his relics and virtues written by a distinguished cleric of the same period, St Corcrán, who sent it to the brothers on High Island. Colgan elsewhere refers to Gormgal as a man of famous sanctity, whose anchoritic and strict life made the island famous.[224] Corcrán also recorded the names of other saintly hermits who were buried on the island with St Gormgal. Among the names listed are: Maelsuthunius, Celecharius, Dubthacus, Dunadach, Cellachus, Tressachus, Ultanus, Maelmartinus, Coromachus, and Conmachus also mentioned in the same poem.[225] Corcrán's poem no longer exists, unfortunately, but we know that he himself was a famous anchorite and scholar, who died in 1040 at Lismore in Waterford, as noted in the *Annals of Inisfallen*: 'Corcrán Clérech, head of the piety of Ireland, rested in Christ in Les Mór Mo-Chutu'.[226] Although it is wonderful and rare to know the names of the monks at High Island, the names themselves are fairly common in the genealogies and are, therefore, difficult to link to regional families. Moreover, while it is likely that some of these men were contemporaries associated with Gormgal, this is not certain from Colgan's language: '...and the other saintly hermits who, with Saint Gormgal, rest there on the same island...' (Colgan [1645] 1948, 715, n.13).[227] The elaborate burials behind the church strongly suggest that High Island revered a number of their members as saintly both before the time of Gormgal and after his death, and their names would certainly have still been known.

High Island is in an area of Connacht that was relatively obscure in the tenth and eleventh centuries. No powerful political dynasties or monasteries developed there or were directly involved in the major events of the time. It is unlikely that any of the annals or martyrologies, all written in prominent mainland monasteries, would have had a particular interest in recording the names of ecclesiastics in this area except under exceptional circumstances. It is, therefore, an impressive tribute to the fame of Gormgal as a saintly anchorite that he received so much notice from leading ecclesiastics of his day. When Colgan says that Corcrán's work concerns Gormgal's virtues and relics, it is evident that High Island had already become a pilgrimage destination and may even have been one before Gormgal's death. The skeletons in both grave no. 5 and grave no. 6 date to 980–1023, dates that neatly encompass Gormgal's death in 1017 or 1018. One of these graves is probably that of Gormgal, but it is not really possible to determine which one, in view of the special care given to both these graves. Grave no. 6 may be the grave that impressed George Petrie in 1820, although with the absence of the recumbent stone and footstones of grave no. 5 we cannot be certain of that either. It is wise to be cautious here, since the treatment of all the graves behind the church indicates that several men, probably distinguished abbots, were particularly cherished by their monks.

There is no mention of the monastery after the death of Gormgal in the monastic annals, but the dates of the later burials and the later construction of a new church and its remodelling clearly show that a flourishing monastery continued for another century or more. There are three dates that support the conviction that the monastery was no longer in active use by about AD 1200. The first two are the last known dates for monastic activity, both of them before the end of the twelfth century: the last burial behind the church and the radiocarbon date for the mortar of the western gable (Chapter 6). A church, of course, usually continued to be used for some time after its last period of construction and, in addition, a single radiocarbon date from the charcoal fraction found in mortar would not usually be adequate support for such a conclusion. The combination of the last monastic dates, however, in conjunction with the burial of a secular young man inside the church between AD 1163 and 1230, present converging lines of evidence for this belief, thereby considerably strengthening the case that the monastery ceased to exist by the end of the twelfth or beginning of the thirteenth century.

It appears that sometime around the end of the twelfth century the High Island monks left the island, or at least gave up the struggle of full-time occupation. The reasons remain unknown. Was it the reforms and changes in the Irish Church in the twelfth century that caused young monks to lose their enthusiasm for island monasticism, and the monastery gradually faded away as the older residents died? Had the weather begun its medieval deterioration, making the troublesome landing on the island still more difficult? All the nearby still-inhabited islands such as Inishbofin and Inishturk offer easier access with more protected harbours or sand beaches. Difficulty of access in centuries of deteriorating climate must have discouraged settlement on the island.

We know little about the island in the centuries after the burial of the young man in the church. It is next mentioned in written documents in the late eighteenth century as being owned by the Martin family, one of the fourteen great families known as the Tribes of Galway. The Land Registry Office records not a purchase, but a 1794 lease between Richard Martin, the owner, and John Bodkin, the tenant who leased Friar and High Islands.[228]

Nor has archaeology offered much evidence of post-monastic habitation. Excavation so far only shows short-term occupation of the island, perhaps only a few people who occasionally used monastic structures for shelter. Except for the brief nineteenth-century occupation of the copper miners, no one has lived on the island long enough to make noticeable changes to the early medieval structures or landscape. The land was still considered valuable in the nineteenth century as grazing land, because an 1837 survey of the estates of Thomas Martin pointed out: 'Omey and High Islands are reclaimable and at present produce excellent feed for all kinds of stock'.[229] A large island offering excellent grazing must surely have been owned. Why wasn't it occupied? The apparent lack of settlement in the intervening centuries begins to make sense if you believe that the owners didn't want it to be occupied. If a succession of large landowners controlled the island they might well have preferred to keep the island reserved exclusively for its best use, grazing, and only occasionally send people out for a few days to check on and shear the flock, etc.

In the little that is known about the history of land ownership in Connemara in the later medieval period there are hints that such a scenario was possible. The Omey Island monastery continued to exist for a few centuries after High Island had ceased to function, and it may have retained ownership and supervision of it until it, too, stopped operating. The next possible owner of the island might well have been the powerful O'Flaherty clan. The O'Flahertys, pushed west of Lough Corrib after the thirteenth century by the English, had become the great Catholic landlords of the region during this time, owning, among other tracts of land, a great part of Connemara. When the O'Flahertys developed serious cash shortages, Nimble Dick Martin, the late seventeenth-century patriarch of the Martin family, loaned them considerable sums against their land holdings. When the debt could not be paid back, Martin acquired practically all the land of this ancient clan. Although the details of this land exchange are unknown, it is plausible that High Island came into Martin hands as part of this transaction.[230]

Today and for unknown centuries past, the only inhabitants of the monastery have been the little storm petrels seeking refuge and safe nesting under its tumbled stones from the predatory great black-back gulls who nest nearby. The sense of quiet isolation makes it difficult to imagine now that the island was ever anything other than a seabird sanctuary. And yet the results of intensive field examination and a limited amount of archaeological exploration have revealed fragmentary glimpses of dynamic human activity on the island, activity whose nature changed and evolved for hundreds of years. Our knowledge about the island has increased substantially, even dramatically, in areas such as the horizontal watermill, but it is oddly unbalanced. The monks of High Island have left clear evidence for a number of sophisticated techniques that are surprising for a medium-sized island monastery. In their use of water-powered technology and irrigation, in the making of special mortar for bedding surfaces and in a number of other ways they have shown themselves as more advanced than their general culture was thought to be. The logical conclusion is that one of the wonderful advantages about undisturbed sites is that they demonstrate how much there still is to learn about medieval life. And yet many fundamental questions remain unanswered. For all periods of occupation our data about daily life are sadly lacking; we know little about the types of fuel used or where it came from, where the cooking and midden areas were, or what types of craftworking went on here, what they were eating, etc. The untroubled condition of the remains on High Island, however, offers consolation in the hope for solutions to these problems in future explorations.

The entire island, not a single structure or two, not just the monastery itself or the horizontal mill, offers a microcosm of early medieval monastic life; an opportunity to explore the evolution and change of medieval life over the centuries, perhaps unparalleled elsewhere. One of the most prestigious early medieval monastic sites in Galway, and its landscape, have been preserved as a gift and a legacy from the past to the people of Ireland, and to all medieval scholars.

Notes

[215] This basin was unlikely to have been influenced by pollen blowing from the mainland to the east.

[216] *The Manor and Borough of Leeds, 1425–1662*, ed. Kirby 1983, 4.

[217] On optimum and critical carrying capacities, see Hassan 1981, ch. 9. Populations rarely get to maximum, but adverse events, social and environmental, can cause people to move.

[218] See Rynne above in Chapter 9. For more details, see Horn 1979, 2:229; Gregorii Episcop Turonensis, ed. Bruno Krusch in *Mon. Germ. Hist., Scriptores rerum merovingicarum* 1885, I: 734–735; *The History of the Franks* by Gregory of Tours, ed. Dalton 1927, II:103. McCann 1952, ch. 66.

[219] In Carolingian times the sources are almost exclusively documentary, such as the inventories of large Carolingian monasteries recorded in the ninth century. In 1996 Champion published his detailed research into the polyptyques, inventories or lists of possession of important ninth-century abbeys located between the Loire and the Rhine. He estimates that over two hundred mills had been active at these abbeys in the ninth century and concluded that mills were an important part of monastic and royal life in that century and were probably important earlier. More archaeological evidence is present in Anglo-Saxon England, most notably from the sophisticated eighth-century mill building at Tamworth, Staffordshire, and the ninth-century mill with three parallel vertical wheels on the royal estate at Old Windsor (Rahtz and Bullough 1971–2, 15–38; Williams, Shaw and Denham 1985, 21–26, 36–37).

220 A new attitude towards the evidence, which probably began with the Swedish scholar Wikander around 1980.

221 This trench was 2m wide and excavation went not much lower than the detritus by the end of the 1997 season. We do not know, therefore, the full extent of this area.

222 Colgan [1645] 1948, 5; 141, note 13 and O'Cleary, MS, Bibliotheque Royal, Brussels, 5100–4, f. 229a, as reprinted in Stokes, 1895, xvii.

223 *Félire húi Gormáin* was written in a monastery of the Canons Regular of Saint Augustine near the town of Louth sometime between 1166 and 1174. Kenney [1929] 1993, 482–483; text and trans. of O'Cleary's transcript of 1630 in Bibliotheque Royale, Brussels, 5100–4 in *Martyrology of Gorman*, ed. Stokes 1895. We owe the reference to the *Martyrology of Gorman* to a letter written by John V. Kelleher to Richard Murphy in 1971, who kindly shared it with us. Kelleher noted that the Irish is somewhat convoluted and that Stokes' English translation could be improved, and we have corrected in accordance with his suggestion: 'Gormgal minn nosmolab do domhan 'ga degrigh' in Stokes 1895, xviii. There is a marginal note in the MS to the same effect in Latin: 'Sacramentum quod praedico coram mundo suoque optimo Rege'.

224 'Habeo pervetustum, e plane divinum huius Corcrani ad fratres Monasterii de Ardoilen in Connacia opusculum de reliquiis et virtutibus S. Gormgalii ...' ASH, ed. Colgan [1645] 1948, 206, n.3. And 'post S. Fechinum sua anachoresi, et arctissima vita plurimum nobilitavit S. Gormgalius, vir celebratae sanctitatis...' Ibid., 141, n.13.

225 ASH, ed. Colgan [1645] 1948, 715, n.13. See also Kenny [1929] 1993, 459.

226 'Corcrán Clerech, cenn crabuid na Herend, quieuit in Christo I Liss Mór Mo-Chutu', *Annals of Inisfallen*, ed. Mac Airt [1951] 1977, 204–205. See also 1040 in the *Annals of Ulster* and the *Annals of the Four Masters*. Further legends attached to Corcrán are recorded in Mac Airt [1951] 1977, 576–577, n. 8 and O'Donovan 1851, 804–805. Professor Ní Chatháin, who helped us immensely with this research, also pointed out that Corcrán is mentioned in the *Life of Anmchad*. When Anmchad exceeded orders on the amount of drink to serve visiting brethren, Corcrán sent him off into exile and he died as a recluse in Fulda in 1043.

227 '...alisque Sanctis Eremitis eiusdem insula, quod cum S. Gormgalis ibi quiescant Sancti...' (Colgan [1645] 1948, 715, n.13). Several annals (AU, AI, and AFM) list the deaths of two Máel Suthains in the eleventh century. A Máel Suthain is also connected with a number of legends, among them that he was the *anmchara* of Brian Boroimhe (see O'Curry Ms. Mat. 1861), but nothing connects these men with the one who was buried on High Island. In his letter of 9 April, 1971, John Kelleher noted that 'except for Máel-Suthain, Ultán and Máel-Martain all the names including Gormgal occur in the Dál Cais geneologies. To be sure, they occur in other genealogies too, but the concentration is significant'. Ní Chatháin, however, feels that this part of Galway was out of O'Brien territory and the names too common to make this assertion.

228 Land Registry Office, Dublin, Land name book 49, p. 448, no. 319813. John's wife, Mary, was still alive in 1837 and still a tenant of High Island.

229 Public Records Office records, National Archives, Dublin. M2429–2433. Particulars, Valuation and Report of the Estates of T. B. Martin, Esq. by Tristan and Hardy, Solicitors London, 1837.

230 Nimble Jack Martin well deserved his nickname. After a series of adroit manoeuvres after the defeat of James II he succeeded in 1698 in being pardoned for backing the wrong side and even received confirmation of his title to the Galway lands. Public Records Office records, National Archives, Dublin. Deed 20, 511–550.

Appendix One

List of Secular and Ecclesiastical Sites Studied in County Kerry and County Galway

Site Number	Townland	Dimension (maximum)	Type of Site

Iveragh Peninsula, County Kerry

Site Number	Townland	Dimension (maximum)	Type of Site
556	Ballynakilly	3.00m	secular
557	Baslickane	3.50m	secular
558	Baslickane	2.30m	secular
559	Beenbane	2.90m	secular
560	Caherbarnagh	2.60m	secular
561	Caherbarnagh	2.30m	secular
562	Caherdaniel	3.60m	secular
563	Caherdaniel	2.60m	secular
564	Cahereighterrush	3.60m	secular
565	Caherlehillan	3.60m	secular
566	Cahernageeha	2.90m	secular
567	Cahersavane	3.60m	secular
568	Cahersavane	1.50m	secular
569	Cashlagh	2.00m	secular
573	Darrynane Beg	3.50m	secular
574	Darrynane	1.20m	secular
575	Darrynane More	3.80m	secular
576	Derrineden	1.50m	secular

Site Number	Townland	Dimension (maximum)	Type of Site
577	Derrineden	2.30m	secular
579	Derrineden	1.45m	secular
581	Doory	2.30m	secular
584	Farraniaragh	1.30m	secular
587	Garreiny	2.80m	secular
588	Garreiny	2.50m	secular
589	Garrough	2.95m	secular
591	Gearha	2.10m	secular
594	Inchee East	2.80m	secular
595	Inchee West	2.30m	secular
596	Keeas	3.80m	secular
598	Killagurteen	2.30m	secular with 1 wall chamber
602	Kimego West	3.30m	secular with 2 wall chambers
603	Kimego West	5.50m	secular
605	Lislonane	3.00m	secular
606	Liss	2.70m	secular
607	Liss	2.30m	secular
608	Loher	3.10m	secular
609	Loher	4.00m	secular
612	Maghygreenane	3.20m	secular
613	Moneyflugh	3.00m	secular
614	Rinneen	3.00m	secular
615	Shanacashel	1.40m	secular
616	Shanaknock	3.00m	secular
619	Spunkane	2.70m	secular
620	Staigue	4.10m	secular with 2 wall chambers
621	Staigue	2.15m	secular
622	Teernahila	2.20m	secular
623	Teernahila	4.50m	secular
624	Teeromoyle	2.40m	secular
625	Tubbrid	2.00m	secular
927	Ballycarbery West	2.00m	ecclesiastical
931	Beenbane	2.40m	ecclesiastical
934	Caherlehillan	1.80m	ecclesiastical
948	Great Skellig	1.20m	ecclesiastical
951	Kildreelig	2.50m	ecclesiastical
963	Loher	2.30m	ecclesiastical
964	Port Magee	1.60m	ecclesiastical

Appendix One

Site Number	Townland	Dimension (maximum)	Type of Site

Dingle Peninsula, County Kerry

Site Number	Townland	Dimension (maximum)	Type of Site
536	Aghacarrible	3.00m	secular
537	Ballinknockane	1.50m	secular
538	Ballinknocknane	1.80m	secular
539	Ballintlea	2.10m	secular with 2 wall chambers
540	Ballybower South	2.10m	secular
547	Ballynavenooragh	3.60m	secular with 1 wall chamber
548	Ballyquin	4.40m	secular
549	Ballywiheen	1.75m	secular
551	Caherdorgan North	3.90m	secular
554	Carrigaha	2.50m	secular
556	Coumbowler	1.80m	secular
561	Doonties Commons	2.20m	secular
566	Foilatrisnig	1.30m	secular
568	Glanfahan	3.00m	secular with 1 wall chamber
570	Glanfahan	3.50m	secular with 1 wall chamber
571	Glanfahan	3.30m	secular with 3 wall chambers
577	Kilballylahiff	2.00m	secular
584	Lack	2.50m	secular
589	Smerwick	2.40m	secular
814	Ballinacolla	2.40m	ecclesiastical
815	Ballinacolla	2.20m	ecclesiastical
826	Ballynahow	0.95m	ecclesiastical
827	Ballywiheen*	2.40m	ecclesiastical
829	Caheracruttera	2.50m	ecclesiastical
832	Currauly	1.75m	ecclesiastical
834	Duagh	0.78m	ecclesiastical
843	Illauntanning	5.50m	ecclesiastical with 1 wall chamber
874	Reask	2.20m	ecclesiastical

West County Galway

Site Number	Townland	Dimension (maximum)	Type of Site
157	Carrownmoreknock	3.00m	secular
158	Carrownlisheen	3.26m	secular
160	Carrowntemple (bivallate)	3.50m and 5.00m	secular
177	Illauncarbry (bivallate; inner wall)	2.40m	secular
179	Inisheer	2.50m	secular
183	Killymongaun	1.00m	secular

Site Number	Townland	Dimension (maximum)	Type of Site
185	Lettergesh East	2.30m	secular
186	Lettergesh East	1.80m	secular
190	Oghil	3.30m	secular
192	Oghil (bivallate)	2.60m and 3.46m	secular
194	Rusheeny	1.70m	secular
193	Onaght	3.45m	secular
611	Roscam*	2.30m	ecclesiastical
546	High Island	3.20m	ecclesiastical
–	Caheradrine	2.00m	ecclesiastical[1]
–	Temple Kilmona	1.60m	ecclesiastical[1]

[1] Sites compiled in 1996. We included Caheradrine and Temple Kilmona supplied to us by Jim Higgins although they were not part of the West Galway survey.

These two sites were remeasured by Rourke and Marshall. At Roscam an editing mistake had caused the archaeologist's notes for the width of the entry into the monastery (4.5m) to be mistaken for the width of the walls. Ballywiheen had been incorrectly measured.

Note: Site numbers refer to *The Iveragh Penninsula Archaeological Survey, Dingle Penninsula Archaeological Survey* and *Archaeological Inventory of Co. Galway, Vol. 1, West Galway.*

Appendix Two

Vegetation and Land-use History on High Island: the results of preliminary investigations

Karen Molloy, Janice L. Fuller and John Conaghan[1]

Palaeoenvironmental Research Unit, Department of Botany,
National University of Ireland, Galway.
Enviroscope Environmental Consultancy, 52 Cluain Dara, Galway.[1]

High Island is a small isolated island situated 3.2km off the north-west coast of Connemara. The island measures approximately 1km long by 400m wide and attains a maximum altitude of 61m. The solid geology of the island is dominated by schist (Leake and Tanner 1994), which outcrops frequently and forms precipitous cliffs. At present the landscape is dominated by ungrazed maritime grassland, which has developed on a shallow peaty soil.

While there is some indication for Iron Age occupation on the island (Scally 1999), the archaeological evidence for human habitation relates primarily to the early medieval period. This includes a monastic settlement and an associated horizontal, water-powered mill. Construction of a mill system (including reservoir, millpond, millraces and mill) would have represented a significant investment. Rynne (Chapter 10) therefore suggests that the island must have supported a sizeable community, in the region of fifty to seventy people.

In order to determine the environmental context for the archaeological remains, palaeoenvironmental investigations were initiated in September 1999. The primary aims of these investigations were to establish: 1) the nature of the vegetation and environmental conditions in prehistoric times, and whether evidence exists for prehistoric human activity; 2) the impact of human activity associated with monastic settlement on the landscape of High Island; 3) the presence or absence of evidence for cereal cultivation on the island.

Site-specific palaeoenvironmental studies, in particular pollen and charcoal analysis, are extremely powerful tools in so far as they allow for the reconstruction of past environments. The basis of pollen analysis is that pollen is produced in abundance by plants and preserves well in anaerobic and acidic environments, such as peat. Analysis of the pollen composition of sediments that have accumulated over time can provide a quantitative record of past vegetation and environments. Information can be gleaned on the nature of past vegetation composition, the role people have played in shaping the modern landscape, the timing, intensity and duration of human activity on the landscape, and finally the nature of farming activity (pastoral or arable farming).

To date several palaeoenvironmental studies have been carried out in north-west Connemara. These include studies at Connemara National Park (O'Connell et al. 1988), Lough Sheeauns (Molloy and O'Connell 1991) and at Derryinver on the Renvyle peninsula (Molloy and O'Connell 1993). Further studies have been carried out on the nearby island of Inishbofin, located approximately 7km to the north of High Island (Ní Ghráinne 1993; O'Connell and Ní Ghráinne 1994). These investigations have provided an insight into the history of vegetation change in north-west Connemara over the past 10,000 years. Although these provide a general picture of regional vegetation history, the records from the above sites are site-specific and are not of direct relevance to High Island. In order to examine fully the interaction between people and the landscape, it was imperative that palaeoecological investigations be carried out on High Island.

Modern Vegetation of High Island

At present the island is dominated by ungrazed maritime grassland vegetation. This vegetation is characterised by plant species such as red fescue (*Festuca rubra*), ribwort plantain (*Plantago lanceolata*), bird's-foot trefoil (*Lotus corniculatus*), wild angelica (*Angelica sylvestris*) and Yorkshire fog (*Holcus lanatus*). Close to rock outcrops, where the soil is shallower and better-drained, plant species such as sea pink (*Armeria maritima*), sea centuary (*Centaurium erythrea*), cat's ear (*Hypochaeris radicata*), English stonecrop (*Sedum anglicum*) and buck's-horn plantain (*Plantago coronopus*) are frequent. Towards the southwestern end of the island there are a number of extensive flushed channels and hollows dominated by black sedge (*Carex nigra*) and marsh pennywort (*Hydrocotyle vulgaris*), with prominent wild angelica (*Angelica sylvestris*), creeping bent grass (*Agrostis stolonifera*) and tormentil (*Potentilla erecta*). This vegetation has developed on peat soils, which in some instances can exceed 1m in depth. One of the most striking features of the island's vegetation is the scarcity of woody shrubs. Shrub species abundant on the Connemara mainland, such as ling (*Calluna vulgaris*) and crowberry (*Empetrum nigrum*), are very rare and appear to be largely confined to the northeastern end of the island. The only tree species recorded from the island is creeping willow (*Salix repens*), which, as its name suggests, is a diminutive, low-growing species. Plant species associated with human disturbance/habitation, such as greater plantain (*Plantago major*), nettle (*Urtica dioica*) and alexanders (*Smyrnium olusatrum*), appear to be absent from the island.

Description of Coring Site

Field investigations concentrated in a gently sloping peaty basin (*c.* 20m x 30m) immediately below the site of the reservoir, which is thought to have supplied additional water to the millpond (Fig. 143), and about 100m upslope from the millpond. Although aerial photos suggest that cultivation ridges/drainage channels are present in this area, no variation in topography could be detected on the ground. This area is dominated by wetland vegetation in which black sedge (*Carex nigra*) and marsh pennywort (*Hydrocotyle vulgaris*) are prominent. Stratigraphical investigations carried out along a transect across the basin indicated a maximum peat depth of 1m in the centre. The sediment in this area consisted of uniform, well-humified sedge-peat.

Methods

In September 1999, duplicate cores (A and B), 50cm apart, were taken from the coring site (Fig. 143). The coring point was located 14m from the reservoir basal wall and about 100m from the edge of the millpond. The cores measured 82cm and 80cm, respectively. All investigations reported on here were carried out on Core A. Core B was wrapped in plastic and stored at 4°C. In total, twenty samples, each 1cm thick and 2cm^3 volume, were taken over the interval 8–80cm. Pollen sample preparation followed standard procedures as implemented at the Palaeoenvironmental Research Unit, NUI, Galway (see Molloy and O'Connell 1991). Pollen identification and counting was carried out using a Leitz microscope. A magnification of x400 was used in routine counting and x1000 oil immersion for critical examination of certain pollen. Pollen identifications were made to the lowest taxonomic level using various keys, including Moore et al. (1991), Fægri and Iversen (1989) and Reille (1992, 1995). Details of size of all grass pollen that fell within the definition of cereal-pollen as given by Beug (1961) were noted and examined at high magnification (see Table 2). Cereal-type pollen are plotted separately to grass pollen. An average of 1000 pollen grains and spores were counted per sample. Only terrestrial pollen and spores are included in the pollen sum. Charcoal particles (≥ 37μm) were also counted. The results are presented in a percentage pollen diagram (Fig. 151).

In order to attach a chronology to the pollen profile, three peat samples were submitted to the radiocarbon laboratory at Groningen University for dating (see Table 1).

Results and Discussion

Chronology

The results of radiocarbon dating are presented in Table 1 and indicated on the pollen diagram (Fig. 151). Radiocarbon dating indicates that sediment accumulation was slow in this basin. Peat accumulation began about 3700 BP. The large error attached to this date (see Table 1) may reflect the slow growth of peat at the base of the profile. Based on the two lower dates and also the pollen profile (see below), the upper date 640 BP is rejected as being too young. This may be as a result of root penetration through the peat and the introduction of younger humic acids. The chronology for the upper part of the profile is based on features in the pollen diagram that have been dated in other pollen profiles. In many pollen records from the west of Ireland an upsurge in arable activity is seen to begin about AD 500, associated with the Early Christian period (Molloy and O'Connell 1995; Molloy 1997). On High Island monastic settlement is thought to date from the seventh to ninth centuries AD (J.W. Marshall, pers. comm.). A date of about AD 650 is therefore applied to the surge in arable activity and in particular, to the increase in rye pollen in Zone 3. However, it should be stressed that this date is tentative, and additional independent dates are required to secure the chronology of the monastic settlement.

Table 1. Radiocarbon Dates from High Island

Depth (cm)	Age (BP)	Age (cal. AD/BC§)	^{14}C Lab. no.
37–40	640 ± 70	1350 ± 50	GrN-25385*
57–60	2150 ± 70	210 ± 150 BC	GrN–25384
77–80	3700 ± 110	2100 ± 180 BC	GrN–25182

§ ± value represents the calibrated age range (end points of 68% (1σ) confidence level) divided by 2

* date rejected, see text

General Considerations Relevant to Interpretation of the Pollen Data

Apart from the many considerations involved in interpreting standard pollen profiles from bogs and lakes, the interpretation of data from a small basin such as this requires an appreciation of the pollen source area being sampled. In general, the smaller the basin size the more local the resultant vegetation picture. In the present situation the pollen source area is very local so that much of the pollen can be expected to arise from plants growing within a radius of about 50m of the sampling point. As can be seen in Figure 151, much of the pollen profile is dominated by herbaceous vegetation representative of a variety of open habitats, including pasture, arable and wet areas. Many important herbaceous taxa, e.g. dandelion-type, clover and some cereal, only produce small quantities of pollen and so their presence even in low quantities in a pollen record is significant. In general, pollen dispersal of herbaceous taxa is much more limited than arboreal taxa because of proximity to ground level. This poor dispersal can result in the over-representation of local plants so that a very good insight into local vegetation can be obtained. However, it can also 'swamp' the pollen record so that regional vegetation, i.e. woodland composition, at a greater distance from the site can be poorly reflected in the pollen spectra. It should also be noted that in the percentage pollen diagram, some of the curves plotted include several species or even a complete family, which may include plants from different habitats. Details outlining some important species that may be contributing to the pollen taxa are now considered briefly:

a) Dandelion-type (Liguliflorae): includes plants such as dandelion, hawkweed and cat's ear that occur in a wide range of open habitats, including pasture and meadow but also arable and fallow ground. This curve is generally considered to reflect anthropogenic activity (Behre 1981).

b) Umbellifers (Apiaceae): includes a wide range of umbelliferous plants, including wild celery, cow-parsley, wild angelica (common on the island today), wild carrot and hogweed, to name but a few. Marsh pennywort is also a member of this family but its pollen is easily identified and is plotted separately. Members of the Apiaceae occupy a wide variety of habitats, including hedgerows, damp meadows, waste places, pastures and salt marshes. There is also the possibility that this group includes pollen of alexanders (*Smyrnium olusatrum*), an introduced winter green often associated with monastic settlements, although this plant was not observed growing on the island at present.

Vegetation and Land-use History

Based on major changes in the percentage pollen representation, the pollen diagram (Fig. 151) has been subdivided, for ease of description, into three zones as follows. Only the main taxa are plotted.

Zone 1 (spectra 80–64cm; *c*. 3860–2460 BP; *c*. 2240–540 cal BC)

This zone opens during the Bronze Age at about 2100 BC and extends into the Iron Age. While substantial levels of arboreal pollen (*c*.14–25 per cent) are recorded (predominantly pine and hazel, with lesser amounts of elm, alder, oak and birch), the landscape near the sampling site appears to have been largely open during this period. The pollen assemblage is dominated by non-arboreal pollen types, including grass (*c*.35 per cent) and sedge (15–20 per cent), in addition to other grassland herbs, such as ribwort plantain, dandelion, umbellifers, buttercup and, at the top of the zone, clover, meadowsweet and sorrel. Fire may have played a role in maintaining this open landscape (see curve for charcoal). An interesting feature of the zone is the substantial representation of the fern, adder's tongue. This is a small fern, less than 15cm tall, generally found in pasture, meadows and rocky ground. It is not often recorded with such high values in pollen diagrams and probably grew close to the sampling site. Whilst it was not recorded during the visit to the island, suitable habitat for the species is present and future visits at an earlier time of year may result in its detection.

The overall impression of the landscape at this time is of open rough grassland with a relatively high species diversity. Many of the herbs recorded are indicative of open/disturbed ground and are often associated with anthropogenic activity (see Behre 1981). The record for cereal-type pollen at 72cm, identified as barley (*Hordeum*), suggests that some limited arable farming may have been practised on the island towards the end of the Bronze Age. However, considering the exposed location of the island, it is not possible to say whether the open nature of the vegetation is the result of human activity or reflects the natural vegetation on the island.

While the landscape was predominantly open, it was not without a woody element. In an island situation such as this it is difficult to say with certainty whether the low level of arboreal pollen recorded represents pollen transported from the mainland or reflects the actual presence of trees on the island. Pollen analysis on Inishbofin indicates that the island had substantial woodland cover consisting of pine, oak, birch, hazel and lesser amounts of elm and alder until about 4000 BP, when human activity on the landscape led to woodland clearance (O'Connell and Ní Ghráinne 1994). In Connemara substantial woodland cover existed into the Bronze Age and pine remained an important woodland component until about 3500 BP. Based on these findings and the prevailing westerly wind direction, it is probable that High Island supported some tree cover in the prehistoric period. It must be pointed out, however, that this tree cover was more likely to have consisted of patches of low scrub with occasional taller trees, rather than a tall canopy woodland such as developed in Connemara.

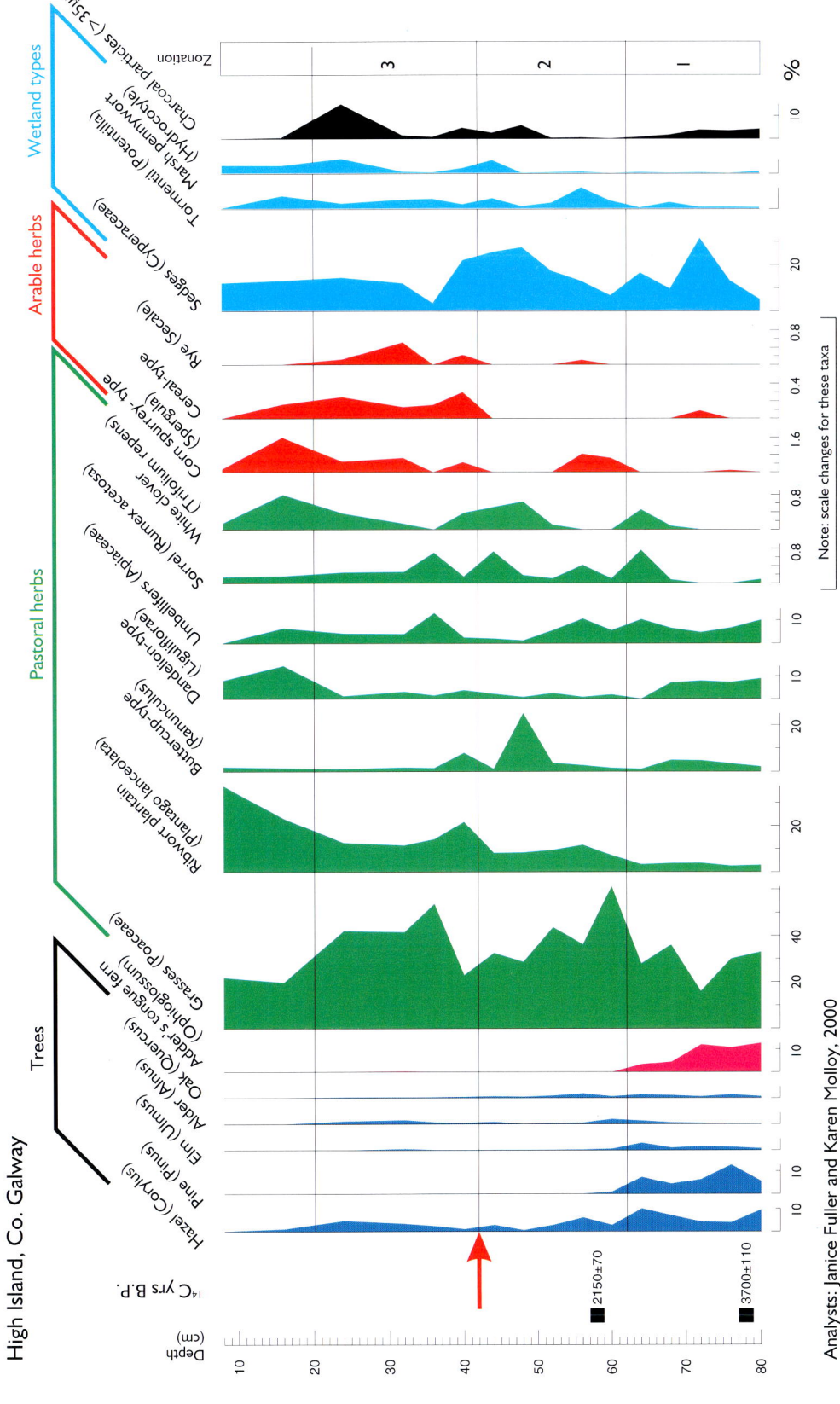

Figure 151
Percentage pollen diagram from a peat core taken on High Island. The coring site lies east of the millpond and downslope of the reservoir. A red arrow denotes the rise in arable activity thought to be associated with Early Christian settlement.

Zone 2 (spectra 60–44cm; *c.* 2460–1330 BP; *c.* 540 cal BC–AD 640)

In this zone arboreal pollen representation falls to less than 10 per cent, accounted for by sharp declines in pine, hazel and elm. This coincides with a marked increase in grass and also ribwort plantain, a plant strongly associated with anthropogenic disturbance on the landscape. Tormentil, which favours heaths and wet pastures, also appears to have increased sharply. These changes are interpreted as representing the further opening up of the landscape in the Iron Age, possibly as a result of human activity. Renewed woodland clearance and expansion of area under pasture centred on 2400 BP is also seen from profiles in Connemara (Lough Sheeauns, Molloy and O'Connell 1991; Derryinver Hill, Molloy and O'Connell 1993). It is probable that as the basin infilled with peat, the sampling area decreased in size, so that the vegetation reflected in this zone is predominantly influenced by local herb species.

Most pollen diagrams from western Ireland record an event known as the Late Iron Age Lull, centred on AD 50–400, which is thought to represent the regeneration of woody taxa in response to a cessation or decline in farming intensity in the landscape. Such an event does not register in this profile; however, it is likely that farming activity on the island was already minimal. It is also possible that the exposed climatic conditions contributed to the failure of woody species to re-establish on the island.

Zone 3 (spectra 40–8cm; *c.* 1330 BP; AD 640 to recent)

An open landscape, dominated by grass, ribwort plantain and a suite of other herbs indicative of rough grassland or pasture, again prevails in this zone. A significant feature of this zone is the record for cereal-type pollen. A total of seventeen cereal-type pollen grains were recorded in Zone 3 (see Table 2), eight of which were identified as rye (*Secale*). Five grains are assigned to non-determined (broken, corroded, folded) category. It is likely that these include grains of wheat and barley rather than rye, which is a particularly distinctive pollen type. While archaeobotanical remains of rye have been reported from Carrowmore, County Sligo, from a late Bronze Age context, it is more frequently associated with Early Christian sites (Monk 1986, Kelly 1997). In many pollen diagrams from the west of Ireland, the rise in cereal pollen, including rye, signifies the onset of the Early Christian period, *c.* AD 500 (Weir 1995, 1993; O'Connell et al., in press; Fuller 1999). Interestingly at Church Lough on Inishbofin, the site of the monastery of St Colman (founded AD 665), while occasional rye pollen grains were recorded, wheat appears to have been the main crop cultivated (Ní Ghráinne 1993). Here on High Island rye appears to have been the main crop, with some evidence for wheat and barley. This increase in arable activity is presumably associated with the monastic settlement, the dating of which remains uncertain.

Appendix Two

Table 2. Details, including size statistics, of cereal-type pollen recorded in the High Island profile. P+A and P refer to the mean diameter of the pore, plus annulus and pore, respectively.

Zone	No. of grains	Mean (μm)	Max. (μm)	Min. (μm)	P+A (μm)	P (μm)	T	H	S	N-det.
3	17	43.97	50.7	41.0	9.75	3.6	2	2	8	5
2	1	50.7	50.7	—	—	—	—	—	1	—
1	1	>39.4*	>39.4*	—	9.0	3.6	—	1	—	—

H, *Hordeum*-type; T, cf. *Triticum*-type; S, *Secale*-type; N-det., Non-determined

Measurements relate to axis of greatest length; *grain folded

Cereals, in particular *Triticum* and *Hordeum* which are self-pollinating plants, generally produce relatively low amounts of pollen, which is poorly dispersed (Hall 1989; Vurola 1973). Low amounts of cereal pollen in the fossil pollen records can, therefore, be highly significant. Rye, however, is wind-pollinated and known to disperse pollen more freely (Hall 1988). In general, cereal pollen dispersal is considered to take place mainly during harvesting (Vurola 1973), although Hall (1988) suggests that effective dispersal of cereal pollen only occurs if vigorous harvesting techniques are employed. However, given that pollen studies beneath a modern oat crop yielded relatively low levels of cereal-type pollen (O'Connell 1990), the cereal curves in the High Island profile can be regarded as significant and can possibly be interpreted as reflecting cereal cultivation near the sampling site.

While the presence of edible plants such as alexanders and wild carrot on the island cannot be ruled out, it is more likely that the abundance of umbellifer pollen in the earlier part of this zone reflects the growth of wild angelica, which is frequent on the island today.

Another interesting feature of his zone is the curve for corn-spurrey-type, which includes the pollen of corn-spurrey (*Spergula arvensis*) and sea-spurries (*Spergularia* spp.). Whilst it is possible that the pollen in the profile is that of corn-spurrey, a common weed associated with cultivation, it is more likely that sea-spurrey, present on the island today, is represented.

The upper part of the zone is defined by the decline in the representation of rye and cereal-type pollen. Other herbaceous plants indicative of rough pasture increase in importance; these include ribwort plantain, dandelion-type and clover. The increase in tormentil and marsh-pennywort may reflect a change to wetter conditions at the coring site. It is assumed that arable activities associated with the monastic settlement had ceased and the landscape had taken on its modern appearance. The increase in levels of microscopic charcoal in the upper part of the profile reflects an increase in burning within the landscape, perhaps as a method of promoting grass growth, although this requires more detailed analysis.

Conclusions

While the results of palaeoenvironmental investigations reported here are preliminary, they do provide a valuable insight into the changing landscape on High Island, both in later prehistory and the early historic period. Some of the more important features to emerge include the evidence for limited woodland cover, which was subsequently removed as the area under grassland expanded during the Iron Age. The expansion of herbs and rise in cereal pollen in the upper part of the profile are interpreted as reflecting an increase in agricultural activity, thought to be associated with the monastic settlement. Presumably the emphasis was on pastoral activities but with a significant arable component. The thin soil cover, rocky terrain and lack of shelter from wind and salt spay would have provided less than optimal condition for cereal cultivation on High Island. However, the pollen evidence suggests that rye, wheat and barley were cultivated, although it is unlikely that the area under cultivation was extensive. Importation of cereals to the island may, therefore, have been necessary, in addition to the local crop, for use in the mill. Analysis of pollen profiles from other locations on the island will help clarify the land-use history of High Island.

References

Behre, K.E. 1981. The interpretation of anthropogenic indicators in pollen diagrams. *Pollen et Spores* 23, 225–245.

Beug, H.-J. 1961. *Leitfaden der Pollenbestimmung für Mitteleuropa und angrenzende Gebiete. Lieferung 1*. Gustav Fischer, Stuttgart.

Fægri, K. and Iversen, J. 1989. *Textbook of Pollen Analysis* (4th ed.), by Fægri K., Kaland P.E., Krzywinski K. Wiley, New York.

Fuller, J.L. 1999. Long-term vegetation dynamics and land-use history at Mayo Abbey, Co. Mayo. Forbairt Report.

Hall, V.A. 1988. The role of harvesting techniques in the dispersal of pollen grains of Cerealia. *Pollen et Spores*, 30, 267–270.

Hall, V.A. 1989. A study of the modern pollen rain from a reconstructed 19th century farm. *Irish Naturalists' Journal*, 23, 82–92.

Kelly, F. 1997. *Early Irish Farming*. Dublin Institute for Advanced Studies, Dundalgan Press, Dundalk.

Leake, B.E. and Tanner, P.W.G. 1994. *The Geology of the Dalradian and Associated Rocks of Connemara, Western Ireland*. Royal Irish Academy, Dublin.

Molloy, K. 1997. Prehistoric farming at Mooghaun: a new pollen diagram from Mooghaun Lough. *Archaeology Ireland*, 11 (3), 22–26.

Molloy, K. and O'Connell, M. 1991. Palaeoecological investigations towards the reconstruction of woodland and land-use history at Lough Sheeauns, Connemara, western Ireland. *Review of Palaeobotany and Palynology*, 67, 75–113.

Molloy, K. and O'Connell, M. 1993. Early land use and vegetation history at Derryinver Hill, Renvyle Peninsula, Co. Galway, Ireland. In: Chambers, F.M. (Ed.). *Climate Change and Human Impact on the Landscape*. Chapman and Hall, London, pp. 185–199.

Molloy, K. and O'Connell, M. 1995. Palaeoecological investigations towards the reconstruction of environment and land-use changes during prehistory at Céide Fields, western Ireland. *Probleme der Küstenforschung im südlichen Nordseegebiet*, 23, 187–225.

Monk, M.A. 1986. Evidence from macroscopic plant remains for crop husbandry in prehistoric and early historic Ireland: a review. *Journal of Irish Archaeology*, 3, 31–36.

Moore, P.D., Webb, J.A. and Collinson, M.E. 1991. *Pollen Analysis* (2nd ed). Blackwell, London.

Ní Ghráinne, E. 1993. *Palaeoecological Studies Towards the Reconstruction and Land-use History of Inishbofin, Western Ireland*. Unpublished Ph.D. Thesis, University College Galway.

O'Connell, M. 1990. Early land use in north-east County Mayo — the palaeoecological evidence. *Proceedings of the Royal Irish Academy*, 90C: 259–279.

O'Connell, M., Molloy, K. and Bowler, M. 1988. Post-glacial landscape evolution in Connemara, western Ireland with particular reference to woodland history. In: Birks, H.H., Birks, H.J.B., Kaland, P.E. and Moe, D. (Eds.). *The Cultural Landscape — Past, Present and Future*. Cambridge University Press, Cambridge, pp. 487–514.

O'Connell, M. and Ní Ghráinne, E. 1994. Palaeoecology [of Inishbofin]. In: Coxon, P. and O'Connell, M. (Eds.). *Clare Island and Inishbofin Field Guide No. 17*. Irish Quaternary Research Association, Dublin, pp. 60–103.

O'Connell, M., Molloy, K., Holmes, J.A., Jones, R., Saarinen, T., Roberts, M., McDermott, F., Hawkesworth, C.J., Barton, K., Leuenberger, M., Eicher, U., Chambers, F.M., Hunt, J.B., van der Plicht, J., van Geel, B., Schettler, G., Dalton, C., Battarbee, R.W., Dörfler, W., Usinger, H. and Haas, J.N. 2000. Timing and Mechanisms of Holocene Climate Change in NW Europe (TIMECHS): Multidisciplinary Investigations of Calcareous, Lake Sediments from Inis Oírr, Aran Islands, W. Ireland. In: *Proceedings of European Climate Science Conference, Vienna* (19–23, October 1998). EU Commission, Brussels (CD ROM).

Reille, M. 1992. *Pollen et Spores d'Europe et d'Afrique du Nord*. Laboratoire de Botanique Historique et Palynologie, Faculté, des Sciences et Techniques Saint-Jérôme, Marseille.

Reille, M. 1995. *Pollen et Spores d'Europe et d'Afrique du Nord*. Supplement 1. Laboratoire de Botanique Historique et Palynologie, Faculté, des Sciences et Techniques Saint-Jérôme, Marseille.

Scally, G. 1999. The early monastery of High Island. *Archaeology Ireland*, 13 (1), 24–28.

Weir, D.A. 1993. Dark Ages and the pollen record. *Emania*, 11, 21–30.

Weir, D.A. 1995. A palynological study of landscape and agricultural development in County Louth from the second millennium BC to the first millennium AD. *Discovery Programme Reports* 2, 77–126.

Vuorela, I., 1973. Relative pollen rain around cultivated fields. *Acta Botanica Fennica*, 102, 1–27.

Bibliography

Acta Sanctorum veteris et maioris Scotiae seu Hiberniae, sanctorum insulae. Edited by John Colgan. Louvain, 1645. Reprint. Dublin: Dublin Stationery Office, 1948.

Addyman, P.V., D. Leigh, and M.J. Hughes. 'Anglo-Saxon Houses at Chalton, Hampshire.' *Medieval Archaeology* 16 (1972): 2–12.

Addyman, P.V., D. Leigh, and M.J. Hughes. 'Anglo-Saxon village at Chalton, Hampshire, 2nd interim report.' *Medieval Archaeology* 17 (1973): 1–25.

Adomnán. *Vita Columbae. The Life of St Columba, Founder of Hy: written by Adomnán*. Edited and translated by William Reeves. Dublin: Irish Archaeological and Celtic Society, 1857.

Adomnán's Life of Columba. Edited and translated by A.O. and M.O. Anderson. London, 1961. Revised by M. Anderson. Oxford: University of Oxford Press, 1991.

Alan, J. Romilly and Joseph Anderson (with introduction by Isabel Henderson). *The Early Christian Monuments of Scotland*, 2 vols. Society of Antiquaries of Scotland, 1903. Reprint. The Pinkfoot Press: Bulgavies arguis, 1993.

The Anglo-Saxon Chronicle. Edited by G.N. Garmsway. London: Everyman's Library, 1953.

The Annals of Inisfallen. Edited and translated by Séan Mac Airt. Dublin, 1951. Reprint. Dublin: Dublin Institute for Advanced Studies, 1977.

Annála Rioghachta Éireann. Annals of the Kingdom of Ireland by the Four Masters: from the earliest period to the year 1616. Edited and translated by John O'Donovan, 7 vols. Dublin: Hodges and Smith, 1848–1851.

Annála Uladh: annals of Ulster. Edited and translated by William M. Hennessy and B. MacCarthy, 4 vols. Dublin: HMSO, 1887–1901.

Archaeological Inventory of County Galway. Vol I, West Galway. Compiled by Paul Gosling. Dublin: The Stationery Office, 1993.

Argyll: an inventory of the monuments. Vol. 4, Iona. Royal Commission on the Ancient and Historical Monuments for Scotland. Edinburgh: HMSO, 1982.

Athanasius, Saint. 'Life of Antony: a Greek text and Latin translation by Evagrius.' In *Patrologiae cursus completus, Series Latina*, edited by J.P. Migne, vol. 26, cols. 835–976. Paris, 1887.

Athanasius, Saint. *The Life of Antony and the Letter to Marcellinus*. Translated and with introduction by Robert C. Gregg. Classics of Western Spirituality. New York: Paulist Press, 1980.

Augustine, Saint. *The Confessions of St Augustine, Book VIII*. Edited and translated by C.S.C. Williams. Oxford: Blackwell, 1953.

Augustine, Saint. *De moribus ecclesiae catholica et de moribus Manichaeorum*. Edited and translated by Donald A. Gallagher and Idella J. Gallagher. Fathers of the Church, vol. 56. Washington, D.C.: Catholic University of America Press, 1966.

Baillie, M.G.L. *Tree-ring Dating and Archaeology*. Chicago: University of Chicago, 1982.

Baillie M.G.L. 'Dendrochronology: the prospects for dating throughout Ireland'. In *Irish Antiquity: essays and studies presented to Prof. M.J. O'Kelly*. Cork: Tower Books, 1981.

Bailey, R.N. 'St Cuthbert's Relics: some neglected evidence.' In *St Cuthbert His Cult and His Community to AD 1200,* edited by G. Bonner, D. Rollason and C. Stancliffe, 231–246. Woodbridge, Suffolk and Wolfesboro, N.H.: Boydell and Boydell and Breney, 1989.

Barber, J.W. 'Excavations on Iona 1979.' *Proceedings of the Antiquaries of Scotland* 3 (1981): 282–380.

Barber, J.W. 'The Horizontal Watermill: a contribution to its early history.' *Prace I Materialy Muzeum Archaeolicznego I Ethnogrficznego W. Lodzi. Seria Archaeologicnza* 25 (1978): 345–356.

Barry, T.B. 'Archaeological Excavation at Dunbeg Promontory Fort, Co. Kerry, 1977.' *Proceedings of the Royal Irish Academy* 81C (1981): 295–329.

Batey, C. 'Earl's Bu: the excavation of a Norse horizontal mill.' *Current Archaeology* 152 (1992): 303–304.

Batey, C. 'A Norse Horizontal Mill in Orkney.' *Review of Scottish Culture* 8 (1993): 20–28.

Bede, the Venerable. *Historiam ecclesiasticam gentis Anglorum historiam abbatum, Epistolam ad Ecgbertum, una cum Historia abbatum auctore anonymo. Ad fidem codicum manuscriptorum denuo recognovit, commentario tam critico quam historico instruxit.* Edited by Carolus Plummer, 2 vols. Oxford: Clarendon Press, 1896.

Bede, the Venerable. *Bede's Ecclesiastical History of the English People*. Edited and translated by Bertram Colgrave and R.A.B. Mynors. Oxford Medieval Texts. Oxford: Oxford University Press, 1969 and 1979.

Bede, the Venerable. *A History of the English Church and People*. Edited and translated by Leo Sherley Price. Penguin, 1953. Revised by R.E. Latham. London: Penguin, 1983.

Bell, J. and M. Watson. *Irish Farming Implements and Techniques: 1750–1900*. Edinburgh: J. Donald, 1986.

Benedict, Saint. *The Rule of St Benedict*. Edited and translated by Abbot J. McCann. London, 1952.

Benoit, P., M-Ch. Bailly-Maître et al. 'Les Meules Rotatives Médiévales pour le Broyage des Minerais.' In *Techniques et Économie Antiques et Médiévales: le temps de l'innovation. Colloque international (C.N.R.S.) Aix-En-Provence 21–23 Mai 1996. Paris*', edited by Dimitri Meeks and Dominique Garcia, 62–68. Paris: Editions Errance, 1997.

Berger, R. 'Radiocarbon Dating of Early Medieval Irish Monuments.' *Proceedings of the Royal Irish Academy* 95C (1995): 159–174.

Bethada Náem nÉrennn: lives of Irish saints. Edited and translated by Charles Plummer, 2 vols. Oxford: Oxford University Press, 1922 and 1997.

Biddle, M. 'Excavations at Winchester 1971: tenth and final interim report.' *Antiquity Journal* 55 (1975): 295–327.

Biddle, M. 'Archaeology, Architecture, and the Cult of Saints in Anglo-Saxon England.' In *The Anglo-Saxon: papers on history, architecture and archaeology in honour of Dr. H.M. Taylor,* edited by L.A.S. Butler and R.K. Morris, 1–31. Council of British Archaeology 60, 1986.

Binchy, D.A. *Críth Gablach*. Medieval and Modern Irish Series, 11. Dublin: Dublin Institute for Advanced Studies, 1941. Reprint. Oxford: University of Oxford Press, 1979.

Binchy, D.A. (ed.) 'Irish Law Tracts Re-edited.' *Coibnes Uisce Thairidne, Eriu* 17 (1955):52–84.

Binchy, D.A. 'Bretha Déin Chécht.' *Eriu* 20 (1966): 1–66.

Binchy, D.A. 'Brewing in Eighth-Century Ireland.' In *Studies on Early Ireland: essays in honour of M.V. Duignan,* edited by B.G. Scott. Belfast: Association of Young Irish Archaeologists, 1982.

Bitel, L.M. *Isle of the Saints: monastic settlement and Christian community in early Ireland*. Cornell University, 1990. Reprint. Cork: Cork University Press, 1993.

Boddington, Andy. 'Models of Burial, Settlement and Worship, The Final Phase Reviewed.' In *Anglo-Saxon Cemeteries: a reappraisal. Proceedings of a conference held at Liverpool Museum, 1986,* edited by Edmund Southworth, ch. 10. The National Museums and Galleries on Merseyside, 1990.

Boddington, Andy et al. *Raunds Furnells: the Anglo-Saxon church and churchyard*. Raunds Area Project English Heritage Archaeological Report 7, 1996.

Bond, C.J. 'Church and Parish in Norman Worcestershire.' In *Minsters and Parish Churches: the local church in transition 950–1130,* edited by John Blair. Oxford University Committee for Archaeology 17. Oxford: Oxford University Press, 1988.

Bond, C.J. 'Water Management in the Rural Monastery.' In *The Archaeology of Rural Monasteries*, edited by Roberta Gilchrist and Harold Mytum, 83–111. British Archaeological Reports, British Series 203. Oxford, 1989.

Bond, Francis. *The Chancel of English Churches*. Oxford: Oxford University Press, 1916.

Bonnet, Charles. *Les Fouilles de l'Ancien Groupe Épiscopal de Genève (1976–1003)*. Genève: Fondation des Clefs de Saint-Pierre, Service cantonal d'archéologie, 1993.

The Book of Kells: reproductions from the manuscript in Trinity College Dublin. With a study of the manuscript by Françoise Henry. New York: Alfred A. Knopf, 1974.

Bouton, J. de la Croix and J. B. Van Damme. *Les Plus Anciens Textes de Citeaux: sources, textes et notes historiques*. Citeaux Commentarii Cisterciennes: Studia et documenta, vol. 2. Achel: Abbaye Cistercienne, 1974.

Brady, N. 'Reconstructing a Medieval Irish Plough.' *Jornadas Internacionales sobre Technologia Agraria Tradicional* (Madrid) 1 (1992): 31–44.

Braun, J. *Der Christliche Altar in seiner geschichtlichen Entwicklung,* 2 vols. Munich: Alte Meister Guenther Koch, 1924 and 1932.

Brown, Peter. *The Cult of the Saints: its rise and function in Latin Christianity*. The Haskell Lectures on History of Religions; New Series, No. 2. University of Chicago Press, 1981. Reprint. Phoenix, 1982.

Buckley, V.M. and P.D. Sweetman. *Archaeological Survey of County Louth*. Dublin, 1991.

Bullough, Donald. 'Burial, Community and Belief in the Early Medieval West.' In *Ideal and Reality in Frankish and Anglo-Saxon Society: studies presented to J.M. Wallace-Hadill*, edited by P. Wormald, D. Bullough and R. Collins, 173–201. Oxford: B. Blackwell, 1983.

Butler, Lawrence. 'The Church in Eastern England, AD 900–1100: some lines of development.' In *Anglo-Saxon Cemeteries 1979*, edited by P. Rahtz, T. Dickinson and L. Watts, 383–389. British Archaeological Research, British Series 82, 1980.

Byrne, F.J. *Irish Kings and High-Kings*. London: Batsford, 1973.

Carrig Conservation Engineering. *Reports on the Composition of Bedding Mortar and Plaster Samples from High Island, Co. Galway to the National Monuments Service*. October 1995 and November 1997.

Carwood, Caroline. 'The Wooden Artefacts from Loch Glashan Crannog.' *Proceedings of the Society for Scottish Antiquaries* 120 (1990): 79–94.

Chadwick, S.J. 'Account Rolls of Dewsbury Rectory, 1348–1560.' *Yorkshire Archaeological Journal* 21 (1911): 352–392.

Cheape, H. *Kirtomy Mill and Kiln*. Scottish Vernacular Buildings Working Group, 1984.

Chapelot, J. and R. Fossier. *The Village and House in the Middle Ages*. London: B.T. Batsford 1980 and 1985.

Cherry, B. 'Ecclesiastical Architecture.' In *The Archaeology of Anglo-Saxon England*, edited by David M. Wilson, 151–200. Cambridge: University of Cambridge Press, 1976 and 1986.

Chronicon Monasterii de Abingdon. Edited by J. Steveson. Vol. 2. London: Rolls Series, 1853.

Chronicum Scotorum: a chronicle of Irish affairs, from the earliest times to AD 1135, with a supplement containing the events from 1141–1150. Rerum britannicarum medii aevii scriptores, 46. Edited and translated by W.M. Hennessy. London, 1866. Reprinted and revised by D. MacFirbis. Wiesbaden: Krau Reprint, 1964.

Columbanus, Saint. *Sancti Columbani Opera*. Edited and translated by G.S.M. Walker. Scriptores Latini Hibernaie 2. Dublin: Dublin Institute for Advanced Studies, 1957.

Connant, K.J. *Carolingian and Romanesque Architecture 800–1200*. The Pelican History of Art 20, edited by Nikolaus Pevsner. London: Penguin, 1959 and 1966.

Connolly, S. 'Cogitosus's Life of St. Brigit: content and value.' *Journal of the Royal Society of Antiquaries of Ireland* 117 (1987): 5–27.

Corpus Iuris Hibernici, 4 vols. Edited by D. Binchy. Dublin: Institiúid Ard-Léinn, 1978.

Cotter, Claire. 'Western Stone Fort Project: interim report.' In *Discovery Programme Reports: 1 project results 1992*. Dublin: Royal Irish Academy, 1993.

Cotter, Claire. 'Western Stone Fort Project: interim report.' In *Discovery Programme Reports: 2 project results 1993*. Dublin: Royal Irish Academy, 1995.

Cotter, Claire. 'Archaeological Excavations at Skeam West.' *Mizen Journal*: Mizen Archaeological and Historical Society 3 (1995): 71–78.

Cowman, Des. 'Life and Work in an Irish Mining Camp c. 1840: Knockmahon copper mines, Co. Waterford.' *Decies: Journal of the Old Waterford Society* 14, (1980): 29–42.

Cowman, Des. 'Life and Labour in Three Irish Mining Communities circa 1840.' *Journal of the Irish Labor History Society* 9 (1983): 10–19.

Cox, J.C. *The English Parish Church*. London and New York: B.T. Batsford and Scribner, 1914.

Cramp, R. 'Jarrow Church.' *Archaeology Journal* 133 (1976a): 220–228.

Cramp, R. 'Monkwearmouth Church.' *Archaeology Journal* 133 (1976b): 230–237.

Crawford, H.S. 'A Descriptive List of Early Irish Crosses.' *Journal of the Royal Society of Antiquaries of Ireland* 37 (1907): 256.

Crowe, C. 'A Note on White Quartz Pebbles Found in Early Christian Contexts on the Isle of Man.' *Natural Historical Antiquarian Society* 7.4 (1982): 413–415.

Curwen, E.C. 'The Problem of Early Watermills.' *Antiquity* 17 (1944): 130–136.

Dalland, Magnar. 'The Excavation of a Group of Long Cists at Avonmill Road, Linlithgow, West Lothian.' *Proceedings of the Society of Antiquaries of Scotland* (1993): 377–444.

Deering, M. 'Correspondence.' In *Ulster Journal of Archaeology* 5 (1857): 91–92.

Deetz, J. and E. Dethlefsen. 'The Doppler Effect and Archaeology: a consideration of the spatial aspects of seriation.' *Southwestern Journal of Anthropology* 21 (1965): 196–206.

Deetz, James. *In Small Things Forgotten*. New York: Anchor Books, 1977.

Dicuil. *De Mensura Orbis Terraae*. Edited and translated by A. Letronne. Paris: S. Mathiot, 1814.

Doherty, C. 'Exchange and Trade in Early Medieval Ireland.' *Journal of the Royal Society of Antiquaries* 110 (1980): 67–89.

Doherty, C. 'The Use of Relics in Early Ireland.' *Irelund und Europa, Die Kirche in Frumittelalter*, edited by P. Ní Chatháin and M. Richter, 89–104. Stuttgart: Klett-Cotta, 1984.

Doherty, C. 'Monastic Towns in Early Medieval Ireland.' In *The Comparative History of Urban Origins in Non-Roman Europe*, edited by H.B. Clarke and A. Simms, 45–75. BAR International Series, 255, 1985.

Doherty, C. 'The Basilica in Early Ireland.' In *Peritia* 3 (1984): 303–315.

Domergue, C. et al. 'Les Moulins Rotatifs dans les Mines et les Centres Métalluriques Antiques.' In *Techniques et Économie Antiques et Médiévales: le temps de l'innovation. Colloque international (C.N.R.S.) Aix-En-Provence 21–23 Mai 1996. Paris*', edited by Dimitri Meeks and Dominique Garcia, 48–61. Editions Errance, 1997.

Duby, G. *L'Économie Rural et la Vie des Campagnes dans l'Occident Médiéval*. France: Aubiers, Editions Montaigne, 1963. Translated by C. Postan in *Rural Economy and Country Life in the Medieval West*. Columbia, South Carolina: University of South Carolina Press and Edwards Arnold Ltd, 1968.

Duignan, Michael. 'Irish Agriculture in Early Historic Times.' *Journal of the Royal Society of Antiquaries of Ireland* 74 (1944): 124–145.

Duignan, Michael. 'Early Monastic Site: Kiltiernan East Townland, Co. Galway.' *Journal of the Royal Society of Antiquaries of Ireland* 81, Part I (1951): 73–75.

Dumville, David et al. *St. Patrick, AD 493–1993*. Studies in Celtic History 13. Woodbridge, Suffolk: The Boydell Press, 1993.

Eddius Stephanus. *The Life of Bishop Wilfrid*. Edited and translated by B. Colgrave. Cambridge: University of Cambridge Press, 1927.

Edwards, Nancy. *The Archaeology of Early Medieval Ireland*. London: B.T. Batsford, 1990.

Edwards, Nancy. 'A Group of Shafts and Related Sculpture from Clonmacnoise and its Environs.' In *Clonmacnoise Studies: vol. 1, seminar papers 1994*, edited by H.A. King, 101–118. Ireland: Dúchas, The Heritage Service, 1998.

Evans, E. *Irish Folkways*. London, 1957. Reprint. Great Britain: Routledge and Kegan Paul Ltd, 1976.

Fahy, E.M. 'A Horizontal Mill at Mashanaglass, Co. Cork.' *Journal of Cork Historical and Archaeological Society* 61 (1956): 13–57.

Fanning, T. 'Excavation of an Early Christian Cemetery and Settlement at Reask, Co. Kerry.' *Proceedings of the Royal Irish Academy* 81C (1981): 3–172.

Farr, Carol A. *Lection and Interpretation: the liturgical and exegetical background of the illustrations in the Book of Kells*. Unpublished Ph.D dissertation. University of Texas at Austin, 1989.

Farr, Carol A. *The Book of Kells: its function and audience*. The British Library Studies in Medieval Culture. London and Toronto: The British Library and University of Toronto Press, 1997.

Faull, M. and S.A. Moorhouse (eds.) *West Yorkshire: an archaeological Survey to AD 1500*. West Yorkshire Metropolitan County Council, 1981.

Féchín, Saint. *Vita S.Fechini: alia vita seu supplementa ex Mss Hibernicus*. Compiled and translated from Irish into Latin by John Colgan. In *Acta sanctorum Hiberniae*, edited by John Colgan, 133–139. Louvain, 1645. Reprint. Dublin: Ordnance Survey Office, 1948.

Féchín, Saint. 'Life of St. Féchín of Fore', edited and translated by W. Stokes from MS. 9194 – Philips Library, Cheltenam. In *Revue Celtique* 12 (1891): 344–47.

Félire húi Gormáin: the martyrology of Gorman. Edited and translated by Whitley Stokes. Henry Bradshaw Society 9. London: Harrison and Sons, 1895.

Félire Óengusso Céli Dé: the martyrology of Oengus the Culdee. Edited by Whitley Stokes. Henry Bradshaw Society 29. London, 1905. Reprint. Dublin: Dublin Institute for Advanced Studies, 1984.

Fenton, A. *The Northern Isles, Orkney and Shetland*. Edinburgh: Small, 1978.

Ferguson, George. *Signs and Symbols in Christian Art*. Oxford: Oxford University Press, 1954 and 1972.

Fergusson, Peter. 'Porta Patens Esto: notes on early Cistercian gatehouses in the north of England.' In *Medieval Architecture and its Intellectual Context: studies in honour of Peter Kidson*, edited by Eric Fernie and Paul Crossley, 49–59. London and Roncerverte: The Hambledon Press, 1990.

Findlay, William M. *Oats: their cultivation and use from ancient times to the present day*. Aberdeen University Studies 137. Edinburgh and London: University of Aberdeen, 1956.

Gailey, A. 'Irish Corn Drying Kilns.' *Ulster Folklife* 15/16 (1970): 52–71.

Garitte, Gérard. 'Un Témoin Important du Texte de la Vie de S. Antoine par S. Athanase: la version inédite des archives du Chapitre de S.Pierre à Rome.' *Études de Philologie, d'Archéolgie et d'Histoire Anciennes*. Brussels: L'Institut Historique Belge de Rome, 1939.

Geake, Helen. *Use of Grave-Goods in Conversion Period England, c.600–850*. British Archaeological Research, British Series, 261, 1997.

Gibbings, R. *Lovely is the Lee*. Great Britain: J.M. Dent and Sons, Ltd, 1945.

Goudie, G. 'On the Horizontal Water-mills of Shetland.' *Proceedings of the Society of Antiquaries of Scotland* 20 (1970): 257–297.

Grabar, André. *Martyrium: recherches sur le culte des reliques et l'art chrétien antique*, 2 vols. Paris: Collège de France, 1943–1946.

Graves, Rev. C. 'On the Similar Forms of the Christian Cross found on Ancient Monuments of Egypt and Ireland.' *Journal of the Royal Society of Antiquaries of Ireland* 1 (1891): 346–349.

Gregory, Bishop of Tours. *Liber Vitae Patrum*. In *Monumenta Germaniae Historica: scriptores rerum Merovingicarum*. Edited by Bruno Krusch, vol.1, 734–735. Hannover: Imperial Library of Hannover, 1885.

Gregory, Bishop of Tours. *The History of the Franks by Gregory of Tours*. Translated by O.M. Dalton, 2 vols. Oxford: The Clarendon Press, 1927. Reprint. Farmborough, England: Gregg Press, 1967.

Gregory, the Great, Saint and Pope. *Gregorii I papae Registaurm epistolarum*. Edited by P. Ewald and L.M. Hartmann. In *Monumenta Germanica historica inde ab anno Christi quingentesimo usque ad annum millesimum et quingetesimum. Epistolae: v.1–2*. Berlin: Weidmann, 1887–1899. Reprint. Munich: Monumenta Germanica Historica, 1978.

Grube, F.W. 'Cereal Foods of the Anglo-Saxons.' *Philological Quarterly* 13 (1934): 140–158.

Halsall, G. *Settlement and Societal Organization in the Merovingian Region of Metz*. Cambridge and New York: Cambridge University Press, 1995.

Hamlin, Ann. 'Using Mills on Sunday.' In *Studies on Early Ireland: essays in honour of M.V. Duignan,* edited by B.G. Scott. Belfast, 1982.

Hamlin, Ann. 'The Study of Early Irish Churches.' In *Irelund und Europa, die Kirche in Frühmittelalter,* edited by P. Ní Chatháin and M. Richter, 117–126. Stuttgart: Klett-Cotta, 1984.

Hamlin, Ann. 'The Archaeology of the Irish Church in the Eighth Century.' *Peritia* 4 (1985): 279–299.

Harbison, Peter. 'Early Irish Churches'. In *Die Iren und Europa in Früheren Mittelalter*, edited by H. Lowe, vol. 2, 618–629. Stuttgart: Klett-Cotta, 1982.

Hassan, Fekir A. *Demographic Archaeology*. New York and London: Academic Press, 1981.

Hayden, Alan. *Report on the Excavation of a Number of Early Medieval Buildings at Bray Head, Valencia Island, Co. Kerry, 1997* to Dúchas, The Heritage Service. September, 1997.

Healy, J. 'An Island Shrine in the West.' *Irish Ecclesiastical Record* Series 3, 11 (1890): 673–686.

Henderson, George. *From Durrow to Kells: the insular gospel-books 650–800*. New York: Thames and Hudson, 1987.

Henderson, Isabel. 'The Shape and Decoration of the Cross on Pictish Cross-Slabs Carved in Relief.' In *The Age of Migrating Ideas: early medieval art in northern Britain and Ireland*, edited by R.M. Spearman and J. Higgitt, 209–218. UK and USA: National Museums of Scotland and Alan Sutton Publishing, 1993.

Henderson, Isabel and Elizabeth Okasha. 'The Early Christian Inscribed and Carved Stones of Tullylease, Co. Cork.' *Cambridge Medieval Celtic Studies* 24 (Winter 1992): 1–36.

Henry, Françoise. 'The Antiquities of Caher Island, Co. Mayo.' *Journal of the Royal Society of Antiquaries of Ireland* 77 (1947): 23–38.

Henry, Françoise. *L'Art Irlandaise*. 3 vols. Zodiac, 1963.

Herbert, Máire. *Iona, Kells and Derry: the history and hagiography of the monastic familia of Columba*. Oxford: Clarendon Press, 1988.

Herity, Michael. 'The Forms of the Tomb-Shrine of the Founder Saint in Ireland.' In *The Age of Migrating Ideas: early medieval art in northern Britain and Ireland*, edited by R.M. Spearman and J. Higgitt, 188–195. UK and USA: National Museums of Scotland and Alan Sutton Publishing, 1993.

Herity, Michael. 'The High Island Hermitage.' *Irish University Review* 7 (1977): 52–69.

Herity, Michael. 'The Layout of Irish Early Christian Monasteries.' In *Ireland und Europa, die Kirche in Frühmittelalter*, edited by P. Ní Chatháin and M. Richter, 105–116. Stuttgart: Klett-Cotta, 1984.

Herity, Michael. 'The Ornamented Tomb of the Saint at Ardoileán, Co. Galway.' In *Ireland and Insular Art, AD 500–1200*, proceedings of a conference at University College Cork, 31 October–3 November 1985, edited by M. Ryan, 141–142. Dublin: Royal Irish Academy, 1987.

Herity, Michael. 'The Hermitage on Ardoileán, County Galway.' *Journal of the Royal Society of Antiquaries of Ireland* 20 (1990): 65–101.

Higgins, J.G. *The Early Christian Cross Slabs, Pillar Stones and Related Monuments of County Galway*, 2 vols. British Archaeological Research, International Series S375. Oxford, 1987.

Hillman, G. 'Reconstructing Crop Husbandry Practices and Charred Remains of Crops.' In R. Mercer (ed.) *Farming Practice in British Prehistory*. Edinburgh: University of Edinburgh Press, 1981.

Hillman, G. 'Traditional Husbandry and Processing of Archaic Cereals in Recent Times: the operations, products and equipment that might feature in Sumerian texts. Part II: the free threshing cereals.' *Bulletin on Sumerian Agriculture* 2 (1985): 1–31.

A History of the Ordnance Survey. Edited by W.A. Seymour. Folkstone: Dawson, 1980.

Hoare, F.R. *The Western Fathers*. Spiritual Masters. London: Sheed and Ward, 1954.

Hope, W. H. St. J. *English Altars from Illuminated Manuscripts*. Alcuin Club Collections 1. London and New York: Longmans Green and Co., 1899.

Hopper, V.F. *Medieval Number Symbolism: its sources, meaning, and influence on thought and expression*. Columbia University Studies in English and Comparative Literature 132. New York: Cooper Square Publishers, 1969.

Horn, Walter. 'On the Origins of the Medieval Cloister.' *Gesta* 12 (1973): 14–52.

Horn, Walter. 'Waterpower and the Plan of St. Gall.' *Journal of Medieval History* 1 (1975): 219–58.

Horn, Walter. 'The Medieval Monastery as a Setting for the Production of Manuscripts.' *The Journal of the Walters Art Gallery* 44 (1986): 16–47.

Horn, Walter and Ernest Born. *The Plan of St. Gall: a study of the architecture and economy of, and life in a paradigmatic Carolingian monastery*, 3 vols. Berkeley, Los Angeles and London: University of California Press, 1979.

Horn, W., J.W. Marshall, G.D. Rourke et al. *The Forgotten Hermitage of Skellig Michael*. Oxford, England, Berkley and Los Angeles: University of California Press, 1990.

Howells, W.W. 'The Early Christian Irish: the skeletons at Gallen Priory.' *Proceedings of the Royal Irish Academy* 46C (1941): 103–219.

Hubert, J., J. Porcher and W.F. Volbach. *Europe of the Invasions: the arts of mankind*. New York: G. Braziller, 1969.

Hughes, Kathleen. 'The Distribution of Irish Scriptoria and Centres of Learning from 730 to 1111.' In *Studies in the Early British Church*, edited by Nora Chadwick, 243–272. Cambridge: Cambridge University Press, 1958.

Hughes, Kathleen. *Early Christian Ireland: introduction to the sources*. The Sources of History: studies in the use of historical evidence. London: Hodder and Stoughton, 1972.

Hurley, Vincent. 'The Early Church in the South-West of Ireland: settlement and organisation.' In *The Early Church in Western Britain and Ireland*, edited by S. Pearce, 297–332. British Archaeological Research, British Series, 102. Oxford, 1982.

The Irish Penitentials. Edited by Ludwig Bieler. Scriptores Latini Hiberniae V. Dublin: Dublin Institute of Advanced Studies, 1963. Reprint. Oxford University Press, 1975.

Ivens, R.J. 'Dunmisk Fork, Carrickmore, Co. Tyrone: excavations 1984–1986.' *Ulster Journal of Archaeology* 52 (1989): 17–110.

Jackson, K.H. *Language and History in Early Britain*. Edinburgh: University of Edinburgh Press, 1953.

Jerome, Saint. *De viribus illustribus sive scriptorinus ecclesiasticus cum Gennadio de iisdem*. Edited by William Herding. Leipzig: B.G. Teubneis, 1879.

Jope, E.M. et al. *An Archaeological Survey of County Down*. Belfast: Her Majesty's Survey Office, 1966.

Joyce, P. *The Social History of Ancient Ireland*. Vol. 2. London, 1903.

Kelly, Fergus. *Early Irish Farming: a study based mainly on the law-texts of the 7th and 8th centuries AD*. School of Celtic Studies, Dublin Institute for Advanced Studies. Dundalk: Dundalgan Press Ltd and Dublin Institute for Advanced Studies, 1998.

Kelly, Fergus. *A Guide to Early Irish Law*. Dublin: Dublin Institute for Advanced Studies, 1988.

Kenny, James F. *Sources for the Early History of Ireland. Vol I: ecclesiastical*. New York: Columbia University Press, 1929. Reprint. Dublin: Four Courts Press, 1993.

Kinahan, G.H. 'The Ruins on Ardillaun, Co. Galway.' *Proceedings of the Royal Irish Academy* 10C (1866–1869): 551–555.

Kinahan, G.H., J. Nolan, H. Leonard and R.J. Cruise. *Memoirs of the Geological Survey: explanatory memoir of the geological survey of Ireland, illustrating the geological structure of the district around Clifden, Connemara*. Dublin, London and Edinburgh: Her Majesty's Stationery Office, 1878.

Knox, H.T. 'Notes on Gig-mills and Drying Kilns near Ballyhaunis, Co. Mayo.' *Proceedings of the Royal Irish Academy* 26C (1906–7): 263–273.

Koehne, C. *Das Recht der Mühlen bis zum Ende Karolingerzeit. Ein Beiträge zür geschichte des Deutschen Gewerberechts*. Breslau: M. and M. Marcus, 1904.

Krautheimer, Richard. *Studies in Early Christian, Medieval and Renaissance Art*. New York University Press and University of London Press, 1969.

Lacy, B. et al. *Archaeological Survey of County Donegal*. Lifford: Donegal County Council, 1983.

Ladner, Gerhart B. *God, Cosmos and Humankind: the world of early Christian symbolism*. Berkeley: University of California Press, 1995.

Land Registry Office, Dublin. Land Name Book 49, p.448, no. 319813. *Lease made August 2nd, 1794 by Richard Martin to John Bodkin of Martin land on Omey, Friar and High Islands*.

Leabhar Breac: the speckled book (otherwise styled *Leabhar Mór Dúna Doighe*). Edited by Joseph O'Longan. Dublin: Royal Irish Academy, 1872–1876.

Leabhar Breathnach Nennius' Historium Britonium. Edited by J.H. Todd. Dublin: Irish Archaeological Society, 1848.

Leask, H.G. 'Further Notes on the Church.' *Journal of the Royal Society of Antiquaries of Ireland* 59 (1929): 26–28.

Leask, H.G. 'The Church of St. Lua, or Molua, Friar's Island, Co. Tipperary, near Killaloe.' *Journal of the Royal Society of Antiquaries of Ireland* 60 (1930): 130–136.

Leask, H.G. *Irish Churches and Monastic buildings. Vol. 1: the first phases and the romanesque*. Dundalk: Dundalgan Press, 1955 and 1977.

Lehmann, E. 'Saalraum und Basikika.' *Kunstchronik* 11 (1958): 291–292.

Liber Pontificalis. Edited by L. Duschesne, 3 vols. Paris: E. Thorin, 1886–1892. Reprint. Paris: E. de Boccard, 1955.

Life of St. Declan of Ardmore. Edited and translated y Rev. P. Power. Irish Texts Society 20. London: Irish Texts Society and David Nutt, 1914.

Lionard, P. 'Early Irish Grave-slabs.' *Proceedings of the Royal Irish Academy* 61C (1961): 53–169.

Lives of the Saints from the Book of Lismore. Edited and translated by Whitley Stokes. Anecdota Oxoniensia, Mediaeval and Modern Series 5. Oxford: The Clarendon Press, 1890. Reprint. New York: AMS Press, 1989.

Lowrie, Walter. *Art in the Early Church*. New York: Pantheon Books, 1947.

Lynam, Shevawn. *Humanity Dick Martin, King of Connemara 1754–1834*. London, 1975. Reprint. Dublin: Lilliput Press, 1989.

Lynn, C.J. 'Early Christian Period Domestic Structures: a change from round to rectangular.' *Irish Archaeological Research Forum* 5 (1978a): 29–45.

Lynn, C.J. 'The Excavation of Rathmullan: a raised rath and motte in Co. Down.' *Ulster Journal of Archaeology* 44–45 (1981–1982): 65–171.

Lynn, C.J. 'Houses in Rural Ireland.' *Ulster Journal of Archaeology* 57 (1994): 81–94.

Lucas, A.T. 'Making Wooden Sieves.' *Journal of the Royal Society of Antiquaries of Ireland* 81 (1952): 146–7.

Lucas, A.T. 'The Horizontal Mill in Ireland.' *Journal of the Royal Society of Antiquaries of Ireland* 82 (1953): 1–36.

Lucas, A.T. 'An Fhóir: a straw rope granary.' *Gwerin* 1 (1958): 1–20.

Lucas, A.T. 'An Fhóir: a straw rope granary, further notes.' *Gwerin* 2 (1959): 1–10.

MacAdam, R. 'Ancient Water Mills.' *Ulster Journal of Archaeology* 4 (1856): 6–15.

McCormac, F.G. and M.G.L. Baillie. 'Radiocarbon to Calendar Date Conversion: calendrical bandwidths as a function of radiocarbon precision.' *Radiocarbon* 35 (1993): 311–316.

McCormac, F.G. Report on mortar analysis, August 1995, of High Island samples.

McCormick, F. 'Excavations at Iona, 1988.' *Ulster Journal of Archaeology* 56 (1993): 78–107.

McCormick, F. 'Cows, Ringforts and the Origins of Early Christian Ireland.' *Emania* 13 (1995): 33–38.

McCormick, F. 'Iona: the archaeology of the early monastery.' In *Studies in the Cult of Saint Columba,* edited by Cormac Bourke, 45–68. Dublin and Portland: Four Courts Press, 1997.

MacEoin, G. 'The Early Irish Vocabulary of Mills and Milling.' In *Studies on Early Ireland: essays in honour of M.V. Duignan,* edited by B.G. Scott. Belfast: Association of Young Irish Archaeologists, 1982.

McGuire, R. and M.B. Schiffer. 'A Theory of Architectural Design.' *Journal of Anthropological Archaeology* 2 (1983): 277–303.

Macalister, R.A.S. 'The Antiquities of Ardilaun, County Galway.' *Journal of the Royal Society of Antiquaries of Ireland* 26 (1896): 197–210. (Also published in the RSAI Guide 1905, 47–53).

Macalister, R.A.S. 'On Some Excavations Recently Conducted on Friar's Island, Killaloe.' *Journal of the Royal Society of Antiquaries* 59 (1929): 16–25.

Macalister, R.A.S. 'The History and Antiquities of Inishcealtra.' *Proceedings of the Royal Irish Academy* 33C (1916): 93–174.

Magraidin, Augustin. *Vita S. Fechinii, Abb. Fovarensis.* In *Acta sanctorum Hiberniae etc.*, edited by John Colgan. Louvain, 1645, 130–133. Reprint. Dublin: Stationery Office, 1948.

Manning, Conleth. 'Excavation at Moyne Graveyard.' *Proceedings of the Royal Irish Academy* 84C (1984): 237–268.

Manning, Conleth. 'Archaeological Excavations of a Succession of Enclosures at Millockstown, Co. Louth.' *Proceedings of the Royal Irish Academy* 86C (1986): 35–81.

Manning, Conleth. 'The Base of the North Cross at Clonmacnoise.' *Archaeology Ireland* 2.2 (summer 1992): 8–9.

Manning, Conleth. 'Clonmacnoise Cathedral — the oldest church in Ireland?' *Archaeology Ireland* 34 (winter 1995): 30–33.

Manning, Conleth. 'Clonmacnoise Cathedral.' In *Clonmacnoise Studies I*, edited by H. King, 57–86. Ireland: Dúchas The Heritage Service, 1998.

The Manor and Borough of Leeds, 1425–1662: an edition of documents. Edited by Joan W. Kirby. Publications of the Thoresby Society LVII. Leeds: Thoresby Society Publications, 1983.

Marshall, J.W. and Claire Walsh. 'Illaunloughan: life and death on a small early monastic site.' *Archaeology Ireland* 8 (winter 1994): 24–28.

Marshall, J.W. and Claire Walsh. *Illaunloughan Excavations 1992–1995* (forthcoming).

The Martyrology of Tallaght. From the *Book of Leinster* and MS 5100–4 found in the Royal Library Brussels. Edited by R.I. Best and H.J. Lawlor. Henry Bradshaw Society LXVIII. London: Harrison and Sons, 1931.

Herrmann-Mascard, Nicole. *Les Reliques des Saints: formation coutumière d'un droit.* Société d'historie d'un droit. Collection d'histoire institutionnelle et sociale 6. Paris: Klinchsieck, 1975.

Maxwell, S. 'A Horizontal Mill Paddle from Dalswinton.' *Transactions of the Dumfriesshire Galloway Natural Historical Antiquary Society* 33 (1954–55): 185–196.

Maxwell, S. 'Paddles from Horizontal Mills.' *Proceedings of the Society of Antiquaries Scotland* 88 (1954–56): 231–32.

Michaels, Joseph W. *Dating Methods in Archaeology*. New York and London: Seminar Press, 1973.

Mitchell, Frank and Michael Ryan. *Reading the Irish Landscape*. Dublin: Town House and Country House, 1997.

Mohr, Michael, Ph.D. Candidate, Department of Statistics, University of California, Berkeley. Report to J.W. Marshall on the statistical validity of Lionard's work (1961, 95–169) 1989.

Monk, M. *The Plant Economy and Agriculture of the Anglo-Saxons in Britain: with particular reference to the 'Mart' settlements at Southampton and Winchester.* Unpublished M.Phil. dissertation, University of Southampton, 1977.

Monk, M. 'Post-Roman Drying Kilns and the Problem of Function: a preliminary statement.' In D. O Corráin (ed.) *Irish Antiquity: essays and studies presented to Prof. M.J. O'Kelly*. Cork: Tower Books, 1981.

Monk, M. 'Evidence from Macroscopic Plant Remains for Crop Husbandry in Prehistoric and Early Ireland: a review.' *Journal of Irish Archaeology* 3 (1985–6): 31–35.

Monk, M. 'The Archaeobotanical Evidence for Field Crop Plants in Early Historic Ireland.' In *New Light on Early Farming*, edited by Jane M. Renfrew, 315–324. Edinburgh: Edinburgh University Press, 1991.

Monk, M., J. Tierney and M. Hannon. 'Archaeobotanical Studies and Early Medieval Munster.' In *Early Medieval Munster: archaeology, history and society,* edited by M. Monk and J. Sheehan, 65–75. Cork: Cork University Press, 1998.

Moore, M.J. *Archaeological Inventory of County Meath*. Dublin: Stationery Office, 1987.

Morris, C.D. and N. Ernery. 'The Chapel and Enclosure on Brough of Deerness, Orkney: survey and excavations, 1975–1977.' *Proceedings of the Society of Antiquaries of Scotland* 116 (1986): 301–374.

Morris, J.H., C.B. Long, B. McConnell and J.B. Archer et al. *Geology of Connemara: an introduction to the physical structure, ancient environments and modern landscapes of parts of Northwest Galway and Southwest Mayo to accompany the bedrock geology 1:100,000 scale map series, sheet 10, Connemara*. Edited by J.H. Morris and E.V. Macdermot. Dublin: Geological Survey of Ireland, 1995.

Morris, Richard. *The Church in British Archaeology*. The Council for British Archaeology, Research Report 47, 1983.

Morris, Richard. 'Churches in York and its Hinterland.' In *Minsters and Parish Churches: the local church in transition 950–1200*, edited by John Blair, 191–200. Oxford University Committee for Archaeology 17, 1988.

Murphy, Richard. *New Selected Poems*. First published as *The Price of Stone* by Wake Forest University Press, 1983. Reprint. Great Britain: Faber and Faber Ltd, 1989.

Murray, H. 'Documentary Evidence for Domestic Buildings in Ireland c.400–1200 in the Light of Archaeology.' *Medieval Archaeology* 23 (1979): 81–97.

Mytum, Harold C. *The Origins of Early Christian Ireland*. London and New York: Routledge, 1992.

Nash-Williams, V.E. *The Early Christian Monuments of Wales*. Cardiff: University of Wales Press, 1950.

Nielsen, L.C. 'Omgård-en vestjysk landsby fra vikingetid. En redegørelse forfortsatte undersøgelser 1976.' *Hardsyssel Arbog* (1977): 59–74

Nielsen, L.C. 'Omgård. The Viking Age Water-mill Complex: a provisional report on the 1986 excavations.' *Acta Archaeologica* 57 (1986): 177–210.

Oat Science and Technology. Edited by H.G. Marshall and M.E. Sorrells. Agronomy 33. Madison, Wisconsin: American Society of Agronomy and Crop Science Society of America, 1992.

O'Brien, E. 'Pagan and Christian Burial in Ireland during the First Millennium AD: continuity and change.' In *The Early Church in Wales and the West: recent work in early Christian archaeology, history and place-names,* edited by N. Edwards and A. Lane, 130–137. Oxbow Monograph 16, 1992.

O'Brien, E. 'Post-Roman Britain to Anglo-Saxon England: the burial evidence reviewed.' BAR forthcoming.

O'Brien, E. and Roberts, C. 'Archaeological Study of Church Cemeteries: past, present and future.' In *Church Archaeology: research direction for the future,* edited by J. Blair and C. Pyrah, 159–181. Council for British Archaeology Research Report 104, 1996.

O'Connell, J.W. 'St. Enda of Aran: tracing an early Irish saint.' In *The Book of Aran*, edited by J. Waddell, J.W. O'Connell and A. Korff, 136–147. Kinvara, Co. Galway: Newtownlynch, 1994.

Ó'Corráin, Donnchadh. 'The Early Irish Churches: some aspects of organisation.' In *Irish Antiquity: essays and studies presented to Professor M.J. O'Kelly*, edited by D. Ó'Corráin, 327–341. Cork: Tower Books, 1981.

Ó'Corráin, Donnchadh. 'Some Legal References to Fences and Fencing in Early Historic Ireland.' In *Landscape Archaeology in Ireland*, edited by T. Reeves-Smyth, 247–251. British Archaeological Reports, British Series 116. Oxford, 1983.

Ó Cróinín, D. *Early Medieval Ireland 400–1200*. Harlow: Longman, 1995.

Ó Danachair, C. 'The Flail and other Threshing Methods.' *Journal of the Cork Historical and Archaeological Society* 60 (1955): 6–14.

O'Donovan, W.J. Note on Milverton, Co. Dublin in *Journal of the Royal Society of Antiquaries of Ireland* (1858–9): 252.

O'Donovan, W.J. Report to the Ordnance Survey. *Ordnance Survey Letters, Galway. Vol III* (1839): 80–7.

O'Donovan, W.J. Letter of February 26, 1841 in *Ordnance Survey Memoranda. Vol. I,* (1841): 384–385.

O'Flaherty, B. 'Loher Cashel.' In *Excavations 1985: summary accounts of archaeological excavation in Ireland*, edited by Claire Cotter, 26–27. Dublin, 1986.

O'Flaherty, Roderic. *A Choro-graphical Description of West or H-Iar Connaught*. 1641. Reprinted and edited by James Hardiman from a MS. in the Library in Trinity College: Irish Archaeological Society, 1684. (See also new facsimile edition; Galway: Kenny's Books and Art Galleries, 1978).

O'Flanagan, M. *Letters containing information relative to the antiquities of the County of Galway collected during the progress of the Ordnance Survey in 1838*. Bray, 1927.

Ó Floinn, Ragnall. 'Clonmacnoise: art and patronage in the early medieval period.' In *From the Isles of the North: early medieval art in Ireland and Britain. Proceedings of the Third International Conference on Insular Art, Belfast, April 1994*, edited by Cormac Bourke, 252–259. Belfast: HMSO, 1994.

Ó Floinn, Ragnall. 'Insignia Columbae I.' In *Studies in the Cult of Saint Columba*, edited by Cormac Bourke, 136–161. Dublin: Four Courts Press, 1997.

O'Keefe, J.G. 'Cain Dommaig.' *Eriu* 2 (1905): 189–214.

O'Keefe, Tadhg. Lecture on the excavation at Omey Island, Co. Galway, IAPA Conference, 1994.

O'Kelly, M.J. 'Church Island near Valencia, Co. Kerry.' *Proceedings of the Royal Irish Academy* 59C (1958): 57–136.

O'Kelly, M.J. *Archaeological Survey and Excavation of St. Vogue's Church, Enclosure and Other Monuments at Carnsore, Co. Wexford*. Dublin: Electricity Supply Board, 1975.

On the Life and Labours of John O'Donovan, LL.D. Dublin Review 102. Reprint. London: Thomas Richardson and Son, 1862.

Ordnance Survey in Ireland: an illustrated record. Dublin: Ordnance Survey Office of Ireland, 1991.

Ordnance Survey Letters, Galway. Vol. 3. Dublin: Dublin Ordnance Survey Office of Ireland, 1839.

Ordnance Survey Memoranda, Galway. Vols. 1 and 2. Dublin: Ordnance Survey Office of Ireland, 1839.

Ordnance Survey Namebook, Omey Parish, Galway. Dublin: Ordnance Survey Office of Ireland, 1839.

O'Reilly, Jennifer. 'The Book of Kells, Folio 114r: a mystery revealed yet concealed.' In *The Age of Migrating Ideas: early medieval art in northern Britain and Ireland*, edited by R.M. Spearman and J. Higgitt, 106–114. UK and USA: National Museums of Scotland and Alan Sutton Publishing, 1993.

Ó Ríordáin, S.P. *Antiquities of the Irish Countryside.* Cork University Press, 1942. Revision by R. de Valera and 5th reprint. London and New York, 1978.

Ó Ríordáin, S.P. and J.B. Foy. 'The Excavation of Leacanabuaile Stone Fort, near Caherciveen, Co. Kerry.' *Journal of the Cork Historical and Archaeological Society* 46 (1941): 85–99.

O'Sullivan, Ann and John Sheehan. *The Iveragh Peninsula: an archaeological survey of South Kerry.* Cork: Cork University Press, 1996.

O'Sullivan, J. 'Excavations beside Sruth a' Mhuilinn ('the Mill Stream'), Iona.' *Proceedings of the Society of Antiquaries of Scotland* 124 (1994a): 491–508.

O'Sullivan, J. 'Excavation of an Early Church and a Women's Cemetery at St. Ronan's Medieval Parish Church, Iona.' *Proceedings of the Society of Antiquaries of Scotland* 124 (1994b): 327–365.

O'Sullivan, Jerry and Heather James et al. *Excavation of an Early Medieval Altar at Trahan O Riain, Inishmurray, Co. Sligo.* An excavation for the National Monuments and Historic Properties Service, Ireland. Glasgow: Glasgow University Archaeological Research Division, 1998.

O'Sullivan, Michael. Report to National Monuments Service on the geology of High Island based on trips to the island in 1992 and 1996.

Parsons, David. 'Sacraium: ablution drains in the early medieval church.' In *The Anglo-Saxon Church*, edited by L.A.S. Butler and R.K. Morris, 105–121. Council of British Archaeology, Research Report 60, 1986.

le Patourel, J. (ed.) 'Documents Relating to the Manor and Borough of Leeds 1066–1400.' *Publications of the Thoresby Society*, 45, no. 104, 1956.

Patrick, Saint. *St. Patrick: his writings and Muirchu's life.* Edited and translated by A.B.E. Hood. History from the Sources. London and New Jersey: Phillimore and Rowman and Littlefield, 1978.

The Patrician Texts in the Book of Armagh. Edited and translated by L. Bierler. Scriptores Latini Hiberniae 10. Dublin: Dublin Institute for Advanced Studies, 1979.

Patrologia cursus completus. Series Latina. Edited by J.P. Migne. 222 vols. Paris, 1844–1859.

Patrologia Greca. Series Greca. Edited by J.P. Migne. Vols. 80–84. Paris, 1857–1866.

Patterson, Nerys. *Cattle Lords or Clansmen: the social structure of early Ireland.* Notre Dame: University of Notre Dame Press, 1994.

Peña, I., P. Castellana and R. Fernandez. *Les Stylites Syriens.* Studium Biblicum Franciscanum Collectio minor 28. Milan: Franciscan Printing Press, 1983.

Peña, I., P. Castellana and R. Fernandez. *Inventaire du Jébel Baricha: recherches archéologiques dans la région des villes mortes de la Syrie du Nord.* Studium Biblicum Franciscanum Collectio minor 33. Jerusalem: Franciscan Printing Press, 1987.

Perren, Richard. 'Structural Change and Market Growth in the Food Industry: flour and milling in Britain, Europe, and America, 1850–1914.' *Economic History Review* 3 (1990): 420–437.

Petrie, George. *The Ecclesiastical Architecture of Ireland*, 2 vols. Dublin: Hodges and Smith, 1845.

Petrie, George. 'Comments on a talk by Mr. Bergin to the Royal Irish Academy.' *Proceedings of the Royal Irish Academy* 4 (1847–1850): 273–274.

Picard, Jean-Charles. 'Presentation du Thème du Colloque'. In *L'Inhumation Privilègiée du IV au VIII siècle en Occident: actes du colloque tenu á Créteil les 16–18 mars, 1984*, edited by Y. Duval and J. Ch. Picard, 9–12. Paris: L'Université de Paris, 1986.

Pietri, Luce. 'Les Sépultures Privilègiées en Gaule d'après les Sources Litteraires.' In *L'Inhumation Privilègiée du IV au VIII siècle en Occident: actes du colloque tenu á Créteil les 16–18 mars, 1984*, edited by Y. Duval and J. Ch. Picard, 133–142. Paris: L'Université de Paris, 1986.

Pocknee, Cyril E. *The Christian Altar: in history and today.* London: Canterbury Press, 1963.

Public Records Office. Irish National Archives, Dublin. Deed 20, 511–550. *Copy of the letters patent granted to Captain Richard Martin of several thousands of acres of coarse mountain land in the remotest parts of the County of Galway.* July 5, 1698. Detailed itemisation of land granted lost.

Public Records Office. Irish National Archives, Dublin. M2429–2433. *Particulars valuation and report of the estates of T.B. Martin, Esquire by Tristan and Hardey Solicitors.* London, 1837.

Public Records Office. Irish National Archives, Dublin. Deed M3438a. *Petition of Henrietta Jane Emma Beaumont and Richard Beaumont, executors of the estate of R.T. Wentworth for sale of incumbered estates in Ireland of Thomas Barnwell Martin, d. 1847.* Dublin, 1848.

Radford, C.A.R. 'St. Ninian's Case.' *Transactions of the Dumfrieeshire Galloway Natural Historical Antiquary Society* 28 (1950): 85–126.

Rahtz, P. and D. Bullough. 'The Parts of the Anglo Saxon Mill.' *Anglo Saxon England* 6 (1977): 15–39.

Rahtz, P. and R. Meesom. *An Anglo-Saxon Watermill at Tamworth: excavations in the Boleridge Street area of Tamworth, Staffordshire in 1971 and 1978*. CBA Research Report no. 83, London, 1992.

Rahtz, P. and K. Sheridan. 'A Saxon Watermill in Bolebridge Street, Tamworth.' *Transactions of the South Staffordshire Archaeological and Historical Society* 13 (1971–72): 9–16.

Rahtz, Philip. 'Grave Orientation.' *Archaeology Journal* 135 (1978): 1–14.

Rappoport, Amos. 'Vernacular Architecture and the Cultural determinants of form.' In *Buildings and Society: essays on the social development of the built environment*, edited by Antony D. King, 283–301. London, Boston, Melbourne: Henley, 1969.

Reeves-Smyth, T. 'Landscapes in Paper: cartographic sources for Irish archaeology.' In *Landscape Archaeology in Ireland*, edited by T. Reeves-Smyth and F. Hammond, 119–178. British Archaeological Research, British Series 116, 1983.

Reynolds, Peter. 'Archaeology by Experiment: a research tool for tomorrow.' In *New Approaches to our Past: an archaeological forum, 1978*, edited by Reynolds, 39–55. Southampton University Press, 1978.

Reynolds, Peter. *Iron Age Farm: the Butser experiment*. London: British Museum Publications, 1979.

Reynolds, Peter. 'Deadstock and Livestock.' In *Farming Practice in British Prehistory*, edited by Roger Mercer, 97–121. Edinburgh: Edinburgh University Press, 1981.

RIA MS 12T9, Royal Irish Academy, Dublin. A Petrie collection of drawings that contains two drawings made by W.F. Wakeman.

RIA MS 12T16, Royal Irish Academy, Dublin. W.F. Wakeman drawings.

Richardson, Hilary. 'Number and Symbol in Early Christian Irish Art.' *Journal of the Royal Society of Antiquaries of Ireland* 114 (1984): 28–47.

Robinson, P. 'Vernacular housing in Ulster in the seventeeth century.' *Ulster Folklife* 25 (1979): 1–28.

Rodwell, W. 'The Archaeological Investigation of Hadstock Church, Essex: an interim report.' *Antiquity Journal* 56 (1976): 55–57.

Rodwell, W. and K. Rodwell. 'Excavations at Rivenhall Church, Essex: an interim report.' *Antiquity Journal* 53 (1973): 219–231.

Ryan, M. 'Furrows and Browse: some archaeological thoughts on agriculture and population in early medieval Ireland.' In A.P. Smyth (ed.) *Seanchas: studies in early medieval Irish archaeology, history and literature in honour of Francis J. Byrne,* 30–36. Dublin: Four Courts Press, 2000.

Rynne, Colin. 'The Introduction of the Vertical Watermill into Ireland: some recent archaeological evidence.' *Medieval Archaeology* 33 (1933): 21–31.

Rynne, Colin. *The Archaeology and Technology of the Horizontal-Wheeled Watermill, with Special Reference to Ireland*. Unpublished Ph.D. thesis, University College Cork, 1988.

Rynne, Colin. 'Some Observations on the Production of Flour and Meal in the Early Historic Period.' *Journal of the Cork Historical and Archaeological Society* 95 (1990): 20–29.

Rynne, Colin. 'The Early Irish Watermill and its Continental Affinities.' In *Medieval Europe Vol. 3*, Technology and Innovation, 21–25. University of York Press, 1992.

Rynne, Colin. 'Early Medieval Horizontal-Wheeled Mill Penstocks from Co. Cork.' *Journal of the Cork Historical and Archaeological Society* 97 (1992): 54–68.

Rynne, Colin. 'Milling in the 7th-Century: Europe's earliest tide mills. *Archaeology Ireland* 6, no. 2 (summer 1992): 22–24.

Rynne, Colin. 'The Craft of the Millwright in Early Medieval Munster.' In *Early Medieval Munster: archaeology, history and society*, edited by Michael A. Monk and John Sheehan, 87–101. Cork: Cork University Press, 1998.

Rynne, Colin. *Technological Change in Anglo-Norman Munster*. Barryscourt Lectures III. Barryscourt Trust, Cork County Council and Gandon Editions: Kinsale, 1998.

Sacrorum conciliorum nova et amplissima collectio. Councils of the Catholic Church. Edited by G. Mansi, et al. Florence and Venice: A. Zetta, 1757–1798. Reprint. v.1–31 facsimile of original Mansi. Paris: H. Welter, 1901.

Sader, Youhanna. *Croix et Symboles dans L'Art Maronite Antique*. Collection Héritage Patrimoine, 2. Beyrouth: Sader, 1993.

Salin, E. *La Civilisation Mérovingienne d'après les Sépultures, les Textes et le Laboratoire,* 2 vols. Paris: Picard, [1952] 1973.

Scott, B.G. (ed.) *Studies on Early Ireland: essays in honour of M.V. Duignan*. Belfast: Association of Young Irish Archaeologists, 1982.

Scott, L. 'Corn Drying Kilns.' *Antiquity* 25 (1951): 196–208.

Senior, John R. 'The Selection of Dimensional and Ornamental Stone Types used in some Northern Monasteries: the exploitation and distribution of a natural resource.' In *The Archaeology of Rural Monasteries*, edited by Roberta Gilchrist and Harold Mytum, 223–239. British Archaeological Research, British Series 203, 1989.

Sexton, R. 'Porridges, Gruels and Breads: the cereal foodstuffs of early medieval Ireland.' In *Early Medieval Munster: archaeology, history and society*, edited by M. Monk and J. Sheehan, 76–86. Ireland: Cork University Press, 1998.

Sharpe, R. 'Vitae S. Brigidae: the oldest texts.' *Peritia* (1882): 81–106.

Shaw, J. *Water Power in Scotland 1550–1870*. Edinburgh and New Jersey: Humanitas Press, 1984.

Sigaut, F. 'A Method for Indentifying Grain Storage Techniques and its Application for European Agricultural History.' *Tools and Tillage* vol. 6, 1 (1988): 3–32.

Simms, Katherine. 'Guesting and Feasting in Gaelic Ireland.' *Journal of the Royal Society of Antiquaries of Ireland* 108 (1978): 67–100.

Simpson, G. (ed.) *Watermills and Military works on Hadrian's Wall: Excavations in Northumberland 1907–1913.* Kendal: T. Wilson, 1976.

Sirat, J., M. Vieillard-Troiekouroff and E. Chatel. *Recueil Général des Monuments Sculptés en France Pendant le Haut Moyen Age (IX–XV siècles). Tome III: Val-D'Oise et Yvelines.* Comité des Travaux Historiques et Scientifiques: Mémoires de la section d'archéologie, II, 1984.

Small, A., C. Thomas and D.M. Wilson. *St. Ninian's Isle and its Treasure.* Aberdeen University Studies series 152, 2 vols. London: Oxford University Press, 1973.

Steensburg, A. *Bondehöse og Vandmoller i Denmark gennen 2000 aar.* Copenhagen, 1952.

Steensburg, A. 'En Skvatmølle i Ljørring.' *Kuml* (1959): 130–135.

Steensburg, A. 'The Horizontal Watermill: a contribution to its early history.' *Prace i Materialy Muzeum Archaeolicznego i Ethnograficznego W. Lodzi. Seria Archaeologicnza* 25 (1978): 345–356.

Stokes, W. *The Life and Labours in Art and Archaeology of George Petrie, LL.D., M.R.I.A.* London, 1868.

Stokes, W. 'The Destruction of Da Derga's Hostel.' *Revue Celtique* 17 (1901): 165–215.

Stout, Matthew. *The Irish Ringfort.* Irish Settlement Studies, 5. Dublin and Portland, Oregon: Four Courts Press and the Group for the Study of Irish Historic Settlement, 1997.

Strabo, Walahfrid. *Vita S. Galli*. In *Monumenta Germaniae Historica: scriptores rerum merovingicarum*, vol. 4, edited by Krusch, 280–337. Hannover and Leipzig: K.W. Hiersemann, 1902.

Stuiver, M. and G.W. Pearson. 'High-precision Calibration of the Radiocarbon Time Scale, AD1950–5000BC.' *Radiocarbon* 28 (1986): 805–838.

Swan, Leo. 'Enclosed Ecclesiastical Sites and their Relevance to Settlement Patterns of the First Millenium AD.' In *Landscape Archaeology in Ireland*, edited by T. Reeves-Symth and F. Hammond, 269–294. British Archaeological Research 116.

Swan, Leo. 'Monastic Proto-towns in Early Medieval Ireland: the evidence of aerial photography, plan analysis and survey.' In *The Comparative History of Urban Origins in non-Roman Europe*, edited by H.B. Clarke and M. Simms, 77–103, 2 vols. British Archaeological Research S255I, 1985.

Sweetman, David. 'Souterrain and Burials at Boolies Little, Co. Meath.' *Ríocht na Mídhe* 7 (1982–1983): 42–57.

Taylor, H.M. 'The Position of the Altar in Early Anglo-Saxon Churches.' *Antiquity Journal* 53 (1973): 52–58.

Taylor, H.M. *Anglo-Saxon Architecture*. Vol. 3. Cambridge: Cambridge University Press, 1978 and 1984.

Testa, E. *Il Simbolismo dei Giudeo-Cristiani*. Publicazione dello Studium biblicum Franciscarum, 14. Jerusalem: Franciscan Press, 1962.

Thesaurus Palaeohibernicus: a collection of old-Irish glosses, scholia, prose, and verse. Edited and translated by W. Stokes and John Strachan. 2 vols. Oxford University Press, 1901–1903. Reprint. Dublin, 1975.

Thomas, Charles. *The Early Christian Archaeology of North Britain*. The Hunter Marshall Lectures delivered at the University of Glasgow in January and February, 1968. London and New York: Oxford University Press, 1971.

Thomas, Charles. *A Provisional List of Imported Pottery in Post-Roman Western Britain and Ireland*. Institute of Cornish Studies, Special Reports 7. Redruth, 1981.

Togail Bruidne Da Derga. Edited by E. Knott. Dublin: Stationery Office, 1936.

Treffort, C. *L'Église Carolingienne et la Mort: christianisme, rites funéraires et pratiques commémortives*. Centre Interuniversitaire D'Histoire et D'Archéologiques Médiévales and Presses Universitaires de Lyon, 1996.

'Vita St. Fursei'. In *Monumenta Germanica Historica: scriptores rerum Merovingaricum*, edited by Krusch, 423–429. Hannover and Leipaig, 1902.

Vitae Sanctorum Hiberniae, Partim Hactenus Ineditae ad Fidem Codicum Manuscriptorum Recognavit Prolegominis Notis Indicibus Instruxit. Edited by Charles Plummer, 2 vols. Oxford: Clarendon Press, 1910 and 1968.

Waddell, John. 'The Archaeology of the Aran Islands.' In *The Book of Aran*, edited by J. Waddell, J.W. O'Connell and A. Korff, 75–136. Newtownlandlynch, Kinvara, Co. Galway: Tír Eolas, 1994.

Wakeman, W.F. 'An Uninhabited Island.' *Hibernian Magazine* 4 (July to December, 1863): 213–224.

Wakeman, W.F. 'Aird Illawn, or High Island, Connemara.' *Dublin Saturday Magazine*, vol. 2, 83 (1867): 367–368.

Wallace, P.F. *The Viking Age Buildings of Dublin*, 2 vols. Dublin: Royal Irish Academy, 1992.

Wasserschleben, Hermann. *Die Irische Kanonensammlung*. 2nd edition. Leipzig: B. Tauchnityz, 1885.

Waterman, D.M. 'The Excavation of a House and Souterrain at White Fort, Drumaroad, Co. Down.' *Ulster Journal of Archaeology* 19 (1956): 73–86.

Waterman, D.M. 'A Marshland Habitation Site near Larne, Co. Antrim.' *Ulster Journal of Archaeology* 34 (1971): 65–78.

Wessel, Klaus. *Coptic Art*. Translated from German by J. Carroll and S. Hatton. London: Thames and Hudson, 1965.

Westropp, T.J. *Illustrated Guide to the Northern Western and Southern Islands and Coast of Ireland*. Dublin: Royal Society of Antiquaries of Ireland Handbook, Series VI, 1905.

Whitaker, I. 'Two Hebridean Corn Kilns.' *Gwerin* 1 (1956–7): 161–70.

White, K.D. *Roman Farming*. London: Thames and Hudson, 1970.

White, K.D. *Greek and Roman Technology*. New York: Cornell University Press, 1984.

Whithorn and St. Ninian: the excavation of a monastic town 1984–91. Edited by Peter Hill. United Kingdom: The Whithorn Trust and Sutton Publishing Ltd, 1997.

Whittow, J.B. *Geology and Scenery in Ireland*. Pelican Geography and Environmental Studies, edited by Peter Hall. London: Penguin, 1975 and 1978.

Wikander, Ö. *Exploitation of Water-Power or Technological Stagnation? a reappraisal of productive forces in the Roman Empire*. Scriptorum Minora. Regiae Societatis Humaniorum Litteratum Lundensis, vol. 3. Lund: CWK Gleerup, 1983–1984.

Wikander, Ö. 'Mill-channels, Weirs and Ponds: the environment of ancient watermills.' *Opuscula Romana* 13, 7 (1985): 149–154.

Williams, J., M. Shaw and V. Denham. *Middle Saxon Palaces at Northampton*. Archaeological monograph 4. Northampton: Northampton Development Corporation, 1985.

Wilson, D.M. 'The Vikings' Relationship with Christianity in Northern England.' *Journal of British Archaeology* 3, 30 (1967): 37–46.

Winchester in the Early Middle Ages. Edited by Martin Biddle. Winchester Studies I. Oxford, 1976.

Young, Bailey K. *Quatre Cimetières Mérovingiens de L'Est de la France: Lavoye, Dieue-sur-Meuse, Mézières-Manchester et Mazerny. Études Quantitative et Qualitative des Pratiques Funéraires*. British Archaeological Reports, International Series 208, 1984.

Young, S.M., J. Clarke and T.B. Barry. 'Medieval Britain in 1982.' *Medieval Archaeology* 27 (1983): 209.

Index

A
Abbot's Cell. *see* Cell A
Acta Sanctorum Hiberniae, 11
Adomnán, St, 3, 111, 120, 202, 208
agrarian economy, 203–6
altars, 70–1
   and relics, 119
Anglo-Saxon Chronicle, The, 182
Anglo-Saxon culture, 3
   barns, 208–9
   churches, 72, 78, 82, 85, 88, 89–90, 106
   burials, 105
   kilns, 208
   watermills, 196, 200, 204
'animal corral,' 62
Annals of Inisfallen, 222, 223
Annals of the Four Masters, 11, 120, 222
Annals of Ulster, 9, 210, 222
anthropomorphic stone, 159
Antony, St, 1–2, 5
Aran Islands, County Galway, 4, 5, 151, 174, 180
Ardfert, County Kerry, 91
Ardmore, County Waterford, 175
Ardoilean. *see* High Island

Athanasius, Patriarch of Alexandria, 1–2
Augustine, St, 2, 164
Augustinian order, 219
aumbry, 79–82

B
Baillie, Michael, 54–5, 218
Ballyshannon, County Donegal, 105
Balmaciver, Scotland, *200*, 201
Barnack church, Northamptonshire, 79
Bede, the Venerable, 4–5, 92
Benedict, St, 46, 219
Bertwald, archbishop, 92
Betha Mochuda, 175
Binchy, D.A., 195
Boddington, 88
Bodkin, John, 224
Boethius, 164, 209
Book of Imaidh, 11
Book of Kells, 149–50, 165, 167
Book of Lindisfarne, 167
Bordesley Abbey, 90
Bray Head, County Kerry, 54
Brendan, St, 182
Bretha Comaithchesa, 39
Bretha Etgid, 207, 209

Brian Boru's Well, *29*, 30–2, 39
   cross stone, 142, 160, 164
Brigit, St, 92, 202
Bronze Age, 174, 181, 216
Brough of Deerness, Orkney, *122*
burials, 140, 223–4
   alignments, 122–4
   within Church, 91–3
   Church enclosure wall, 102–24
   conclusions, 121–4
   grave goods, 92–3
   Grave no. 1, 107, 154, 165–6
   Grave no. 2, 107, 154
   Grave no. 3, 107–8, 154, 164–5
   Grave no. 4, 108, *109*, 152–3, 155, 165–6
   Grave no. 5, 109–12, 152, 164–5, 165–6, 224
   Grave no. 6, 112–16, 149–52, 165–6, 224
   Grave no. 7, 116–18, 147–8, *148*, 165–6
   Grave no. 8, *117*, 118–19, 147
   Petrie's special tomb, 115–16
   seen as saints, 106

   tombs, 104–7
Butser Ancient Farm Project Trust, 217

C
Caher Island, County Mayo, *122*, 128, 160, 164
Cahergal, County Kerry, 77, 180
Cain Domnaig, 203, 211
Cainnech, St, 208
Canones Hibernenses, 51
Canterbury, 49, 70
Carnsore, County Wexford, 82, 84–5, 87, 91
Carolingians, 182, 218
Carrownaseer, County Galway, *122*, 127
Carthusian order, 219
Cashel, County Tipperary, 176
cashels, 180–1
Cathach of Saint Columba, 163
Cathal MacAodha, King, 175
Cell A, 58, 59–60, 88, 90, 130–2, 181, 221, 222
   passage to, 127–30
Cell B, 90, 101, 132–6, 158, 221, *222*
   cross stone, 144–5
   lintel-cross, 146

cells, 16, 33, 130
Cemetery, 139–40
cereal crops, 205–6
  processing, 206–10
Chad, St, 92
Chorographical Description (O'Flaherty), 191
Christ Church, Canterbury, 49
Chronicum Scotorum, 222
Church, 70–93
  alignment, 122–4
  altar, 83–5
  aumbry, 79–82
  burial in, 91–3
  burials behind, 102–19
  entry to, 76–7
  floor, 86–90
  foundations, 90–1
  masonry styles, 73–6
  plaster, 85–6
  walls, 77–83
  conclusions, 121–4
Church enclosure wall, 83, 99–102
  burials, 102–24
  cross stone, 146
  conclusions, 121–4
Church Island, County Kerry, 51, *52*, 54, 101
churches, 69–70
  burial of saints, 119–21
Ciarán, St, 4, 120, 202, 208
circular structure, 38–9
Cistercian order, 49, 90, 201, 211, 219
Clonard, County Meath, 202, 210
Clonfert, County Galway, 166, 168
Clonmacnoise, County Offaly, 4, 92, 120, 152, 202
  cathedral, 86
  crosses, 167–9
Cloontycarthy, County Cork, 197, 199
Cogitosus, 92, 202–3
Coibnes Uisci Thairidne, 196–7
Colgan, John, 11, 59, 222–3
Colman, Bishop of Lindisfarne, 4–5
Columba, St, 3, 51, 111, 120, 175, 208
Columbanus, St, 2, 3, 46
Columella, 207, 209

Conall mac Comgaill, King, 175
Conamaicne Mara, 183
Cong, County Mayo, 9
Conlaed, Bishop, 92
Conwall, County Donegal, 157
copper miners, 11–13, 49, 225
Coptic church, 163
Corbie monastery, 201
Corcran, St, 223
Corcranus, blessed, 11
Cork, County, 210
Cotter, Claire, 181
Crith Gablach, 46, 207, 210
cross stones, 16, 41, 50, 115–16, 139–40
  altar, 85
  Brian Boru's Well, 31–2
  Cell B, 134–5
  Church enclosure wall, *100*, 101–2
  dating of, 169
  discussion of styles, 162–9
  individual descriptions, 141–61
  reused, 106, 155
Crushyriree, County Cork, 195
cupboards, 79–82
currachs, 183
Cuthbert, St, 46, 92, 163

D
De Ceithri Slichtaib Athgabala, 195, 196, 197
De Mesura Orbis Terrae (Dicuil), 182
De Re Rustica (Columella), 207, 209
Declan, St, 175, 183
Deetz, J. and Dethlefsen, E., 169
dendrochronology, 54–5, 218
Dicuil, 182
Dingle Peninsula Survey, 178
Discovery Programme, 181
distraint, law of, 195, 197
Du Noyer, G.V., 14
Dún Aengus, Inis Mór, 174
Dún Fearbhai, Inis Meain, 180
Durham, Rites of, 82

E
Eadbert, Bishop, 92
Earl's Bu, Orkney, 199, 200–1
Eddius Stephanus, 71
Egypt, 1–2, 3, 164

Elcock, C., 160
enclosure walls, 176–82
  secular v. ecclesiastic, 179–80
  wall chambers, 180
Enda, St, 4, 5
evangelist symbols, 165
exile, 2–3

F
Faroe Islands, 3, 201
Fanning, Thomas, 59
Farr, 149–50
Fechín, St, 5, 8–9, 11, 183, 197, 217–22
Fenton, Alexander, 201
Fermanagh, County, 165
field system, 38
Finnian, St, 202
flagged pathway, 40
Fore, County Westmeath, 5, 8–9, 197
Friar Island, 224
Fursa, St, 92

G
Gall, St, 92
Gallarus, County Kerry, 127
Gallen Priory, 106
Galway, County, 4–5, 164, 168, 178
gatehouses, 49–50
geology, 12–13
Gerefa, 208, 209
Gibbings, Robert, 101, 133
Gibbons, M., 159–60
Glastonbury, 90
Glendalough, County Wicklow, 32, 105, 157
Gormgal, St, 11, 13, 18, 59, 222–4
  and Brian Ború, 30
Gospel Book of Saint Gauzelin, 165
Grabar, Andre, 119
granite sphere, 161
Greenland, 3
Gregory of Tours, 196, 202, 219
Gregory the Great, Pope, 120
guesthouse, 50–1, *52*, 217, 218

H
Haltwhistle Burn Head, Hadrian's Wall, 196
hand cross, 157
Hankin, Professor David, 180

Hartlepool abbey, 167
harvesting, 207
Hayden and Walsh, 54
Healy, 191
Hebrides, 182
Herity, Michael, 18, 121, 159
  enclosure wall, 62
  entrances, 49, 60
  millpond, 191
Hexham, 71
Higgins, J., 157, 160, 162
High Island. *see also* Monastery
  aerial views, *9*, *24*
  contour map, *10*
  early medieval population, 210–12
  history, 8–13, 173–7, 215–26
    Iron Age, 87–8
    prehistory, 215–17, 225
    seventh to eleventh centuries, 217–22
    tenth to thirteenth centuries, 222–6
  landing areas, 23–4, 26
  location map, *4*
  physical description, 7–8
  plans, *25*, *36–7*
    Ordnance Survey, 1841, *15*, 16
    Ornance Survey, 1839, *12*, 13, 24, *36*, 41
Historiam Ecclesiasticam Gentis Anglorum, 4–5
Hopperstad, Norway, 85
horizontal watermill, 40–1, 54–5, 89, 185–212, 217–18
  building and mechanism, 192–4
  closure of, 218–19
  contour plan, *188*
  cultural affinities, 198–201, 220
  headrace and bypass channel, 191–2
  millpond, 191
  water supply, 186–91
Hua Suanaig, judgment of, 2
Hypogeum of the Dunes, Poitiers, 85

I
Iceland, 182
Illaunloughan, County Kerry, 62, 101, 105, 140

Illauntannig, County Kerry, 57, 85
   enclosure wall, 176, *177*, 178–9, 180–1
Immrama, 182
Inchagoill, County Galway, 157, 166, 168
Inis Meain, Aran Islands, 180
Inis Mór, Aran Islands, 4, 5, 161, 167, 174, 180
Inishbofin, County Galway, 5, 224
Inishcealtra, County Clare, 105, 157
Inishglora, County Mayo, 71, 91
Inishmurray, County Sligo, 52, 71, 161, 175, 177, *178*, 179
Inishturk, 224
Iona, 3, 157, 161, 163, 164, 175, 193, 202
   enclosure wall, 176
   kiln, 208
Iron Age, 87–8, 181, 216
island monasticism, 182–3
Italy, 3
Iveragh Survey, 178

J
Jarlath, St, 4
Jarrow, 85
John Scottus Eriugena, 164
Joyce, 202
Jutland, 201

K
Kelly, Fergus, 39
Kildare monastery, 92, 202–3
Kill Cemetery, 159–60
Killaloe, County Clare, 79, 82, 85–6, 91
kiln drying, 210
Kiltieran East, County Galway, 127
Kiltiernan, County Galway, 123
Kinahan, George, 17, 18, 24, 26, 30, 35, 104
   Cell A, 129, 130, 131–2
   Cell B, 132
   Church, 71, 79
   cross stones, 31, 41, 141, 142, 143
   enclosure wall, 61, 62
   field wall, 38
   guesthouse, 50
   'Pound,' 63
   wall chambers, 56, 58–9, 59
kitchen garden, 62

L
landing cross, 24, *26*
landing places, 8, *34*, 34–5
Larcom, Captain, 14
Larne, County Antrim, 53
Leabhar Breac, 111
Leacanabuaile, County Kerry, 53–4, 180
leachta, 28, 29, 31, 36–7, 49, 99–100, 159
   near entrance, 41, 50
Leask, 85
Leeds borough account, 218
Lichfield Gospels, 165
Liessies monastery, 201
limestone, 112–13, 115, 151
Lindisfarne abbey, 4–5, 163, 167
lintel-cist graves, 105
Lionard, Pádraig, 105, 163
   cross typology, 166–9
Lismore, County Waterford, 175, 223
Little Island, Cork Harbour, 204
Loche monastery, 196, 202
Loher, County Kerry, 53–4
Lynn, C.J., 53, 54

M
Macalister, R.A.S., 17–18, 24, 26, 30–1, 85, 157
   Cell A, 129
   Cell B, 133
   Church, 76, 79, 83
   cross stones, 31, 141, 142, 144, 167
   enclosure wall, 62
   field wall, 38
   wall chambers, 56, 57
McCormick, Finbar, 176
Macdurnan Gospels, 165
MacEoin, Gearoid, 195
Mangan, James Clarence, 14
Manning, Conleth, 86
Marianus Gorman, abbot, 223
Maronite church, 163
Martin, Colonel Richard ('Humanity Dick'), 11–12, 13
Martin, Richard, 224
Martin, Richard, 'Nimble Dick,' 225
Martin, Thomas, 225
Martin, Thomas Barnwell, 13
Martin family, 17, *224*
martyrdom, 3
Martyrology of Cashel, 223
Martyrology of Gorman, 223
Mashanaglass, County Cork, *187*, 194–5, 197, 199
Mayo, County, 185
Mellebaude, Abbot, 85
Merovingians, 3, 164, 167, 204
milldams, 194–5
millpond, 39, 40–1, 50, 100, 186, 191
   enlarged, 54
millponds, use of, 196–7
millraces, 197
millstones, 202
millwrights, 202, 204
Milverton, County Dublin, 195
miners' cottages, 8, 24, 26–8
mine-shaft, 26
Mochoemog, St, 175
Mochuda, St, 175
Moling, St, 197
Molloy, K., Fuller, J.L. and Conaghan, J., 215–17
Monastery. *see also* Church; Monastic enclosure wall
   aerial views, *32*, *33*, 63
   agrarian economy, 203–6
   approach from southwest landing, 34–41
   cereal processing, 206–10
   description of, 32–4
   foundation of, 8–9, 11
   guesthouse, 50–1
   history
      seventh to eleventh centuries, 217–22
      tenth to thirteenth centuries, 222–6
   mainland contacts, 182–3
   plans, *17*, *47*
   scholarly studies of, 13–18
   site of, 8
   site sections, *48*
   structures north of, 60–4
Monastic enclosure wall, 45–64, 175–83
   Cell A, 59–60
   date of, 175–7
   eastern side, 60
   as 'quarry,' 221–2
   south, 55
   southeastern entrance, 49
   southwestern entrance, 55–6
   structure, 177
   structures attached, 49–50
   wall chambers, 56–8, 180
monasticism, 1–5
   agrarian economy, 203–6
   architecture, 45–6
   cultural affinities, 219–20
   guesthouses, 51
   island monasticism, 182–3
   land endowments, 174–5
   watermills, 201–3, 219–20
Monkwearmouth, 70, 85
mortar, 88–90
   bedding material, 131
   samples, 74
mudrock, 160
Muirchu, 175
Murphy, Richard, 8, 13, 27, 31, 83

N
Nantes, Council of, 92
Nash-Williams, 163
National University of Ireland, Galway, 215, 218
Nendrum, County Down, 175
Neolithic period, 174
Nicaea, Council of, 120
Nivelles, 72
Northumbria, 163

O
O Corráin, Donnchadh, 39
O Riordáin, Sean, 53–4
O'Brian, King Muirchertach, 176
occupation, 216–17
   evidence of, 173–7
   pre-monastic, 225
O'Clery, Michael, 222–3
O'Curry, Eugene, 14
O'Donovan, John, 30, 41, 102
   Cell A, 129, 130, 131–2
   Cell B, 132
   Church, 71, 79
   enclosure wall, 48
   entrances, 60
   High Island survey, 14–16
   'Pound,' 63
   stations, 28–9

wall chambers, 57, 58, 59
O'Flaherty, Roderic, 13, 30, 53–4
    watermill, 185, 191
O'Flaherty clan, 225
O'Floinn, Dr Raghnall, 166
O'Keefe, Patrick, 14
O'Kelly, Michael, 51, 54, 82
Old Minster, Winchester, 85
Omey Island, 9, 11, 13, 74, 111, 183, 217, 225
    missing cross, 160
    orans figures, 149–50
Ordnance Survey, 14–16
    Fair Plan, 1839, *12*, 13, 24, 36, 41
    plan, 1841, *15*, 16
    stations, 28–9
Orkney Islands, 3, 174, 198, 199, 200–1
Ormesby church, 106
O'Sullivan, Michael, 35, 160

P

Patrick, St, 3, 175
paving, 100–1, *103*, 124
pebble stones, 161
Pepin, King, 201
Peregrinatio, 3
Peronne, 92
Petrie, George, 8, 13–14, 15, 17, 18, 30, 41, 133, 158, 185
    burials, 102, 104, 121
    Cell A, 128–9, 130
    Church, 71, 76, 79, 83, 85
    cross stones, 37, 157
    enclosure wall, 47–8
    guesthouse, 50
    leachta, 36
    millpond, 191
    pathway, 40
    pebble stones, 161
    rectangular structure, 35
    'special tomb,' 115–16, 224
    stations, 29
    structures attached to entrance, 49
wall chambers, 56, 58, 59
pilgrimage stations, 28–9, 31, 36, 39
pilgrimages, 28, 120, 223–4
plaster, use of, 85–6
ploughs, 204
pollen analysis, 215–17, 233–42
ponds, 39, 50, 55
population size, 210–12
'Pound,' the, 63–4
Power, Rev., 182

R

rabbits, 27
Rathmullan, County Sligo, 53
Raunds Furnell chapel, 72, 78, 88, 90–1
Reask, County Kerry, 59, 105, 127, *128*
rectangular structures, 35, 49–50
    in medieval Ireland, 51–5
Reculver, 90
relics, cult of, 119–20
Repton, 85
reservoir, 40–1
ringforts, 45–6
Roscam, 179
Roscommon, County, 185
round dwellings, 51–5
Royal Society of Antiquaries of Ireland, 17–18, 57
Rule of Patrick, 46

S

sacred area, 127–8
St Augustine's abbey, 90
Saint Gall monastery, 45, 92, 210
St MacDara's Island, County Galway, 164
St Molua's church, Killaloe, 79, 82
    removal of, 85–6, 91
St Vogue's church, Carnsore, 82, 84–5, 87, 91
Saint-Denis monastery, 72
saints
    burial of, 119–21
    land endowments, 175
Scandinavian watermills, 198–201
Scotland, 105, 164, 196, 210
    watermills, 198–9, 200–1
Sheep Island, 175
Shetland Islands, 3, 182, 198, 199, 200, 201
sieving, 209
Simeon the Stylite, St, 163
Skeam West, County Cork, 93
Skellig Michael, County Kerry, 71, 79, 101, 135, 136, 162
socket stones, 157
Soiscéal Molaise shrine, 165
Spain, 196
Staigue Fort, 180
storage (cereals), 209–10
Sunday observance, 203
Sutherlandshire, Scotland, 199
Swan, Leo, 177
Swithin, St, 119
Syria, 163, 164, 196

T

Tamworth mill, Staffordshire, 200
Tauberischafscheim, Germany, 196
Temple Breccan, Inis Mor, 161
Theodore, archbishop, 92
Theodoret, 1
Thomas of Bayeux, 222
threshing, 207–8
Togail Bruidne Da Derga, 198, 207
Trier Gospels, 165, 167
Tuam, County Galway, 4

U

Uraiccecht Becc, 46

V

Vikings, 53, 93, 167, 201
Visigoths, 196
Vita Columbae (Adomnan), 202
Vita S. Brigidae (Cogitosus), 92, 202–3
Vita S. Patricii (Muirchu), 175
Vitae Sanctorum Hiberniae, 51

W

Wakeman, W.F., 14, 16, 28, 83, 85, 99, 121
    burials, 102, 104, 109, 110
    Cell B, 132, *133*
    cross stones, 31, 101–2, 116, 140, 142–4, 146, 157–60, 162
    stations, 24
Wales, 163
wall chambers
    large, 56–7
    small, 57–9
walls, 38–40. *see also* Church enclosure wall; Monastic enclosure wall
water reservoir, 40–1
water rights, 196–7
watermill. see horizontal watermill
watermills, 185–6, 211, 218–20
    cultural affinities, 198–201
    early monastic, 201–3
    importance of, 203–6
    milldams, millponds and millraces, 194–7
    water supply of, 194
wedge tombs, 174
Western Stone Fort Project, 180–1
Wharram Percy, 196
Whitby, Synod of, 4–5
white quartz, 111–12, 113, 114
Whithorn, 85
Wibert, Prior, 49
Wikander, 205
Wilfrid, Bishop, 71
Winchester, 119
winnowing, 208–9